AF796532

Full Circles

A Carpenter and Philly Novel

(Fourth in a Series)

Ken Behar

Full Circles
(Fourth in a Series)

Copyright © 2018 by Ken Behar
All Rights Reserved.

This is a work of fiction. Names, characters, businesses, organizations, places and incidents are products of the author's imagination or are used fictitiously and are not to be construed as real. Any resemblance to actual events or locales or persons, living or dead is entirely coincidental.

978-0-9961462-4-1 (paperback)
978-0-9961462-5-8 (eBook)

Library of Congress Control Number: 2018914483

Published by: Ken Behar
Lexington, Massachusetts

Cover design by Angela Valenti

To Rose and Bea

Also by the author:

Ghosts Can Only Go Straight
(Turn of the Century Tales)

Not Too Shabby
(Barrister Tales from Ed's Breakfast Emporium)

HOOPS

Carpenter and Philly Novels:
Turn The Page
No Right Answers
Coin Flips
Full Circles

January

Philly's Untitled Playlist

The Wall

Pink Floyd

1

Philomena Piper scanned the overcrowded courtroom and was reminded why she disliked criminal law. The scores of seemingly lost souls waiting for and probably dreading the moment when cases would be called were beyond depressing. But here she was starting out 2010 seated in a Middlesex Superior Court criminal session because nothing was going to keep her from getting her first look at Colin Feeney, the seventeen-year-old motherfucker who, while driving drunk, had killed her fiancé, leaving his mountain bike a twisted wreck and Philip Sizemore with no measurable brain activity.

Paul Sullivan, the first Cambridge police detective to arrive at Philip's accident scene, was conversing with the assistant district attorney assigned to Feeney's case. He towered over Heidi Greenbaum, a short, trim woman with black hair that curled up at her shoulders. Greenbaum's counsel table was covered with file folders. Philip's case was probably a run-of-the-mill matter in a caseload that could choke a horse.

As Paul Sullivan headed to where she was seated, Philly was struck again by how handsome he was: tall and trim and dark complexioned with intense, brooding dark eyes. He couldn't be more than a few years older than she was.

"How are you doing?" Sullivan asked as he took a seat beside her.

Philly hated that question no matter how well-intentioned. If she answered truthfully that she felt like shit, the questioner would resent the truth. Whoever asked the question only wanted to hear the lie that she was doing okay. "I feel like shit."

"I told you not to come," Sullivan came back, not put off by her bitter tone.

"I know. But I need to see the bastard who killed Philip."

"You don't," Sullivan countered. "But I understand."

"All rise!" a court clerk intoned.

The woman assuming the judge's bench had long straight brown hair and sported round, gold, wire rimmed glasses perched on the end of her nose.

"Judge Irene Caffrey," Sullivan whispered.

"Good morning, everyone," the judge greeted those in attendance. "Please be seated. The clerk will call the list and we'll try to move things along. I'm going to apologize in advance for the delays we typically experience."

"This could be a wait," Sullivan said. "We're toward the end of the list."

Great, Philly thought. But it was not as if she had urgent work demanding attention. If she wasn't waiting for Colin Feeney's case to be called for a pretrial conference, she'd be sitting in her office twiddling her thumbs. Even Carpenter, the over-sixty lawyer who shared her office suite and whose referrals were largely responsible for her civil litigation practice getting off the ground, was out of work.

The clerk called the first case and Philly closed her eyes.

Philly started at the nudge to her ribs. Sullivan pointed to the front of the courtroom and she wondered whether she had drifted off. She didn't think she'd slept; the sounds of the court doing business had continued to register after she closed her eyes.

"The Commonwealth versus Colin Feeney," the clerk announced.

Greenbaum reached for a file folder on the prosecutor's table while a young, athletic-looking man, dapperly dressed in a gray pinstriped suit, advanced to the table reserved for defendants' lawyers. "Evan Blake for the defendant." Blake turned and motioned toward the back of the courtroom. A rangy, sandy-haired teen got to his feet with his head lowered. "Please come forward, Colin," Blake instructed.

The youth advancing toward the defendants' counsel table had hazel eyes and angry red acne blotches on the cheek facing her. He was slouched over and Philly couldn't tell whether his posture had a hint of attitude or reflected fear. He was wearing worn jeans and a blue hoodie and carried an army jacket.

"We're here to set a trial date for your case, Mr. Feeney," the judge said. "Currently you are on bail and in the custody of your father. If there's anything you don't understand, make sure that Mr. Blake explains it to you. Do you understand?"

"Yes."

The word came out so softly that Philly realized that Feeney was terrified. Good, she thought. Fuck the kid.

"Has there been any discussion between counsel as to when this case can be tried?"

"No, Your Honor," Greenbaum responded.

"Is the first week of March agreeable?" the judge inquired as she leaned over the bench to better view the calendar showing on her clerk's computer screen.

"That's agreeable," Blake and Greenbaum said together.

"How long do you expect this trial to take?"

"One to two days," Greenbaum said.

"That sounds about right," Blake chimed in.

"Any other business?" the judge inquired. "No? Then we'll proceed to trial the first week in March. Next case."

Philly sipped black tea in the courthouse cafeteria conscious of Paul Sullivan staring at her as his coffee cooled. "What?' she challenged.

"I was wondering what your next move is now that you got your look at Feeney."

"I haven't thought that far ahead. The only thing I want is for that miserable piece of shit to pay for what he did."

Sullivan sighed, blew on his coffee, didn't say anything.

"What's the evidence going to be?"

"I'd prefer you heard that from Ms. Greenbaum," Sullivan said.

"Cut the shit!" Philly snapped. "I'm asking *you*. What's the big deal? You've never given me details."

Sullivan continued to regard her evenly. "I can tell you that when I arrived on the accident scene, Feeney had liquor on his breath. He refused to take a breathalyzer test. I tried to question him but that didn't go particularly well. For the most part he didn't respond. He might have been in shock. The few words he got out were somewhat slurred."

"What else?" Philly demanded when Sullivan didn't offer any further details.

"There were two witnesses. They pretty much confirmed what the department's accident reconstruction expert concluded. Feeney ran a stop sign and caught Mr. Sizemore's bike broadside. Each witness gave a statement that Feeney was going pretty fast. Mr. Sizemore was wearing one of those yellow Day-Glo vests, so he should have been easy to see. It was a clear day."

Philip had been a careful biker; Philly couldn't imagine him doing anything risky.

"Does the kid have a record?"

"No."

"I didn't see the kid's parents in court."

"His mother died three years ago. His father works construction and probably had a job to go to."

"Is Blake a public defender?"

"I don't think so."

They sipped their beverages in silence, Sullivan looking at her as if trying to divine what was inside her head. "Why do you keep staring at me like that?"

Sullivan set down his coffee mug. "I'm just going to say this to you. You've got a lot of anger in you and I understand why. He killed your fiancé and completely altered your life. I get it. But somehow, you're going to have to get by that. It can't be good for the baby you're carrying, and I can tell you from experience that over time, it's not going to be good for you."

"So I'm just supposed to forget about everything?" Philly raised her voice.

"I didn't say that. I said you're going to have to get by your anger."

"There's not a fucking chance in hell that's going to happen."

Sullivan resumed sipping at his coffee, plainly disappointed in her answer. Tough shit, Philly thought.

"So, what *are* you going to do?" Sullivan asked.

The answer was simple; she should have thought of it before. "I'm going to do what lawyers do best. I'm going to sue the fucking little prick."

Sullivan showed no reaction to her heated statement. "Say you sue this kid. What are you going to get out of it? You're not going to see a dime. Feeney's just a kid."

"Revenge," Philly said with conviction. "I want to make that little prick's life a living hell. And he's not just any kid. He killed someone I loved."

Sullivan broke off eye contact and glanced at his watch. Philly had been uncomfortable under his gaze.

"I've got to get going," Sullivan said. "Before you make any final decision, talk to me."

"What's that going to accomplish?"

Sullivan shook his head ruefully. "Not a lot from what I can tell. But do it anyway. Humor me."

"I'll think about it," Philly said, just to end the conversation thinking she'd seen the last of Sullivan until Feeney's trial.

Carpenter glowered at the photograph mounted across from his desk, and the black man in the photograph did what he did best, glowered back. The photograph had been a gift from Philly and last year Carpenter had engaged the man in dialogue frequently enough to call into question his sanity. There had been those embarrassing moments when he had let loose with a loud, torrent of abuse at the photograph and Philly had entered his office to find him alone. She probably thought he was losing it.

At the moment, Carpenter was obsessing over one of his ongoing worries, the lack of billable hours in his litigation practice. As the economy continued to stall, he was completely out of new work. Philly was in the same predicament. But if he was looking for sympathy from the photograph, Carpenter knew that he was looking in the wrong place. The man's unforgiving stare rarely provided comfort.

A sharp knock on his door preceded Philly's entrance. She moved sluggishly toward his visitor chair, her expression sullen. There had been a time when that was her typical expression. But then Philip Sizemore had come into her life and she had mellowed, become less tightly wound. Since Philip's death, Philly was reverting to her angry, belligerent, former self.

"What's with you, Miss Sunshine?"

"Very funny. I stopped off to see the pretrial conference for the miserable little prick who ran down Philip. The trial's set for early March."

For the next two months, Carpenter foresaw Philly thinking about the kid who had killed Philip, obsessed with payback. She probably wouldn't be able to concentrate on work even if there was work to do. "What's the kid like?"

Philly shrugged. "I don't know. Your basic sullen teenager. I have a favor to ask you."

Carpenter didn't want to hear her request. With no work in the pipeline, Philly's favor had to be personal. "What?"

"I want you to represent me. I want to sue the little shit who ran Philip down."

Carpenter tried to keep his expression blank. Philly was seething, no doubt worked up from seeing the kid who had brought a mountain of misery into her life.

"You're supposed to say it would be your pleasure," Philly said.

Carpenter tried to measure the depth of Philly's anger. She was in dress down mode today, wearing jeans, a dress white shirt that was not tucked in, and running shoes. She wasn't showing but she'd only been pregnant what . . . eight weeks give or take? "How much thought have you given this lawsuit idea?" he asked.

"It just came to me today."

Last month Philly had told him not to go easy on her because of her pregnancy. Carpenter had agreed, knowing that she wanted their office suite to be a place where business was as usual and they could talk frankly to each other. He had his own reason for wanting their work environment to be a place where nothing was held back. Getting into it with Philly would take his mind off his recent cancer diagnosis—chronic lymphocytic leukemia or CLL. "What's your legal theory?" he challenged her.

"I haven't gotten that far. I figured you'd be full of ideas."

"Did you?" Carpenter snapped, not bothering to hide his irritation. "You never married Philip, right? So where do you get off to sue because he died. The last I heard, a girlfriend didn't have standing to sue someone who injured her boyfriend. Do you know something I don't know? Maybe your kid can sue once it's born. Maybe Philip's parents can sue."

"We were engaged and I'm carrying his kid for Christ's sake!" Philly exploded. "Doesn't that count for anything?"

"I don't think so," Carpenter said. He pointed at Philly's left hand. "Where's your engagement ring?"

Philly's look turned sheepish. "We never got around to buying one. Philip gave me this shell shaped like a ring as a stand-in for a real ring. After he proposed and I said yes, he found it on a beach when we were on the Cape last August. It fit perfectly on my ring finger. I've got it back at the apartment."

"A shell?" Carpenter said, deliberately exaggerating his amazement.

"We just never got around to buying a ring. What's the big deal?"

Carpenter decided to lighten up. Having been dealt a vicious blow, Philly had an excuse for not thinking things through clearly. "Are you looking for money from this kid?" he asked, trying to keep his voice even.

"He probably doesn't have any money," Philly said.

"Then you're just looking to make his life miserable, is that it?"

"Yeah, pretty much."

Philly was staring at him defiantly, daring him to turn her down. Well, if she wanted honesty, she was going to get it. "I don't think I should represent you. I also don't think you should be thinking about a lawsuit right now. At least wait until the criminal matter is over."

"This is not what I wanted to hear," Philly said with undisguised bitterness.

"Well, that's tough," Carpenter said. "I'm your friend. I'm supposed to tell you what you don't want to hear."

Philly stood. "I've got to go."

"Sit down," Carpenter said in a sharp tone meant to get her attention. "We're not done."

"I think we are."

"You remember the last day of '09 when we went out to lunch?" Carpenter asked, ignoring Philly's last comment. "During the meal, you took a slug of my beer. What the hell was that about? It's been bugging me. You shouldn't be drinking anything, and you know it."

Philly colored, lowered her head, and avoided his gaze. "You need to answer me," Carpenter insisted. "What you did has me worried."

The crimson flush left Philly's face and her bone white coloring returned. Against her mop of black curls and dark eyes, her white skin was vivid. "I just wanted to do something that was bad for me," Philly said in a soft voice. "I'd had it with everything and I mean everything. It was my way of spitting in the world's eye. I don't expect you to understand."

"You're right, I don't understand. There are some things that are just plain dumb and that was one of them. I want to hear you say that you're not going to do that again."

Philly shook her head. "I'm not going to make any promises I might not keep."

Carpenter sighed. When it came to their offices, business was not going to be as usual. Not even close.

Carpenter was packing up to go home when his phone rang. He'd been thinking about the useless day that had passed. The woman in his life, Maxine French, was off visiting one of her kids so he wouldn't be able to unload his miseries on her. Worse, he was going to have to cook tonight, a task he hated.

"Carpenter."

"This is Anna Finn. You probably remember me as Anna Penn."

"What a pleasant surprise," Carpenter said, meaning it. "The last time I spoke to Robert he said you two were engaged. I take it you got married."

"We did. It was a spur of the moment thing. We basically eloped."

"Congratulations. You sound great." There had been a time when Carpenter doubted he would ever be saying those words to his former client. She had been sued, had fought through a brutal bout of depression with professional help and hospitalization, and had dealt with divorcing a cheating husband. But now she was married to Robert Finn, one of his major referral sources who had referred Anna Finn's case.

"I am great. I feel reborn actually. I'm not sure I ever properly thanked you for helping me several years back. I was going through a bad time as you know, and proper manners was one of the things that got away from me."

"Don't mention it."

"I gave your name to a couple who lives near me in Stonington. Their son is a special needs student and Stonington has refused to pay for a program for the boy in a private school. We were talking, and they think they need a lawyer. I immediately thought of you."

"That's very kind. I'm grateful." Carpenter knew next to nothing about special needs students' legal rights, but he wasn't about to tell Finn that. He still entertained the fantasy that he could master any new subject matter if given enough time.

"I'm the one who's grateful to you," Finn said. "Robert sends his regards by the way."

"I'm delighted to hear you sound so upbeat."

"I have Virginia Morse and Jenny Mize to thank for that."

"Really?" Virginia Morse had sued Finn, claiming that a car accident that had left her paralyzed below the waist had been Finn's fault because of champagne Finn had served at a party for teens. But after admitting at her deposition that alcohol played no role in the car accident, the girl had withdrawn her suit. Jenny Mize had been Virginia Morse's best friend but had also befriended Finn during the lawsuit and its aftermath.

"Even after she went away to college, Jenny stayed in touch with me. She visited me several times after I was hospitalized. One day, well after I was discharged and without giving me any warning, Jenny brought Virginia to visit me. When I opened the door and saw Virginia in her wheelchair, I could have killed Jenny. But Jenny knew what she was doing. The three of us talked for hours. At the end, I felt as if a weight had been lifted off me. Virginia asked me to forgive her for the suit she brought against me and I did. I think that meeting has been largely responsible for my getting over my depression. I don't think I would have been able to marry Robert if that meeting hadn't taken place."

"You're full of good news," Carpenter observed.

"It's about time," Finn replied.

A Special Needs Student

2

Philly sat at her desk and stared at her computer screen. The possibility of Carpenter bringing in a new client should have energized her. If it were last year, she would be searching the Internet to learn about special needs students to appear informed at the meeting with the potential client. Instead she felt lethargic and listless. She jumped when her intercom sounded. "A Mr. Ramirez is on the line for you," the part-time receptionist announced.

"Shit!" Philly muttered. "Tell him I'll be right with him."

Raul was the last person she wanted to hear from. A former lover, Raul was insufferably upbeat. Philly preferred to wallow in her funk. Still, she owed it to Raul to be civil. He and his girlfriend, Isabella, had graciously included her in their recent New Year's Eve plans. She had enjoyed herself and was grateful not to have spent the night alone. Raul and Isabella had gone out of their way to make her feel included, even conspiring to plant simultaneous kisses on her cheeks at the stroke of midnight.

"Hey, Raul," Philly said, after picking up the phone.

"Isabella and I have been thinking, my esteemed Philly," Raul began without small talk. "We have considered the pros and cons of your most excellent idea. The truth is, we have talked of little else since the New Year has begun."

Philly couldn't recall coming up with any recent idea let alone an excellent one.

"We would like to join you in your venture," Raul said. "We hope you will consider us as possible partners. You know that I have investments which can be part of the down payment. I have a steady job. Isabella has a steady job. And a major benefit for you is that Isabella and I will be available to help you with the new baby."

"What the hell are you talking about?" Philly managed to get in when Raul paused for breath.

"The house you want to buy. Isabella and I wish to join you in the purchase."

Oh, that! Philly dimly remembered mentioning to Raul and Isabella in the course of their New Year's Eve party, her off-the-wall plan to buy a house using Philip's trust fund money that his family insisted she take. The truth was, she couldn't bear living in the apartment that constantly reminded her of her brief time with Philip, and had been toying in a half-assed way with the idea of buying a house that could accommodate tenants. Maybe having people around would translate into help when the baby came and would provide a stimulating environment for the kid. She probably had her head up her ass but Carpenter, for one, had not shot the idea down. How much detail had she provided to Raul and Isabella? She hadn't been drinking during the New Year's Eve celebration, but she couldn't recall just what she'd said to Raul and Isabella about her half-baked idea.

"I don't know, Raul," Philly wavered, although she did know. Raul had an uncanny ability to drive her nuts. He was kind and considerate and honest. But the way he talked coupled with his effervescence would send her around the bend in short order.

"I have sprung this on you unexpectedly," Raul said. "You will need to think about this. But I want you to listen to me, dearest Philly. Please do not let stubbornness or pride control your thinking. Being a single mother cannot be easy. In your heart, you know that Isabella and I will treat your baby as if it were our own. It would be our privilege to help you. Plus, I am very handy. I am capable of fixing many things. I will be an asset as your co-home owner. It is also my hope that you and Isabella will become close friends. There are many advantages to joining together on this."

Raul had a way of making telling points in his odd style of speaking. "I don't know," Philly repeated.

"I am not expecting any immediate answer from you, Philly. But I will tell you this. There is a place in Brighton that may be perfect for what you have in mind. Isabella and I have looked at the property. It is a three-story house. Some rooms could be rented. I would encourage you to see the house."

"Jesus, Raul! I feel like you're steamrolling me. Enough!"

"I am sorry, Philly. My enthusiasm sometimes gets the best of me as you know. I will not push the matter any further. But there is one more thing. Last year, you helped Isabella's uncle, Santiago. Remember?"

Philly had filed an unsuccessful lawsuit to keep Isabella's uncle in a Massachusetts hospital when the hospital threatened him with discharge to his homeland. Losing that case had been a low point in 2009. Even though Santiago was now doing well in Guatemala, she felt that she had let Isabella and Raul down. "I remember that I lost the case."

"You never forwarded us a bill for your services. We have asked you many times."

"Forget it," Philly said. She had never been able to bring herself to bill Isabella and Raul, and mentally had written the work off as a pro bono effort.

"That is what we thought you would say," Raul replied. "We will not forget it. You will find that we have taken matters into our own hands."

"What the hell are you talking about?"

"You will find out soon enough."

"Don't do anything stupid, Raul."

"The same applies to you my dear Philly."

"And I'm not your dear Philly, for Christ's sake!"

"But you are, Philly. You will always be dear to me. I must go now and leave you to your thoughts. I will call you soon. We have much to discuss."

Philly slammed her phone down when the line went dead. Raul had pretty much talked himself out of their going in together on a house. He would be insufferable to be around. But though he infuriated her, he had a way of making valid points and she couldn't quite close the door on the joint venture he had proposed. At least she knew Raul, trusted him. Raul might drive her to homicide, but he truly was generous and kind. Maybe the devil you knew was a better option than a stranger.

Philly silently fumed. She didn't feel comfortable talking to Carpenter about Raul's proposition. But Maxine was another story. Maxine was going to rue the day she had told Philly to call her any time with a problem.

"Anna Finn speaks very highly of you," Max Lawson said.

Philly judged the Lawsons to be in their late thirties. Max Lawson had thick black hair, a rugged looking face, and a solid build; if it weren't for the troubled look in his brown eyes, he probably would have come across as a hard-nosed, tough guy. Sylvia Lawson's stress showed, too. Each time she swept her reddish-brown hair away from her face, Philly was struck by the woman's gaunt features and the anxious look in her brown eyes as she glanced about the office suite's conference room.

"It's all true," Carpenter said, and Philly took his light tone as evidence he had picked up on the Lawsons' unease.

"Are you familiar with special education programs?" Max Lawson followed up.

"I've never had a case involving that program, but I know something about it," Carpenter said. "A school system has to determine whether a student has special needs. If that's the case, the school system has to meet the needs. This involves coming up with an Individualized Education Program called an IEP.

The program has to be appropriate to the student's needs, and if the school district can't fulfill that plan, then it has to place to student somewhere that can."

Philly felt herself reddening when she caught Carpenter's quick, rebuking glance. Carpenter had done the initial research she hadn't done. He must have concluded that he couldn't count on her to pitch in.

"That's right," Max Lawson confirmed. "There's no question our son, Jack, has special needs. He has concentration and socialization issues."

"Can you be a little more specific about that?" Carpenter followed up. "What is the IEP supposed to address?"

"Well," Max went on, "before he had the IEP, he couldn't stay focused on his work, would jump up and run around the classroom, butt in on what other people were doing, that kind of thing. And he doesn't, you know, 'play well with others.' He'd get angry about stuff and wouldn't wait his turn. There were times when he'd get into a tantrum and start hitting out. That kind of stuff."

"Is he on medication?" Carpenter asked.

"That's a main issue," Sylvia Lawson said. "Jack is nine and in the fourth grade. So far, Max and I have accepted the individualized education program that the Stonington school district has come up with for Jack. But this year we didn't. The IEP is designed to mainstream Jack as much as possible, and we have no problem with that. We want him in a regular classroom. It also calls for special tutoring and weekly meetings with a psychologist who covers all the schools in the Stonington school district, and we're okay with that too. But we're no longer okay with the part of the IEP that requires Jack to take medication. The medication calms him down but also makes him lethargic and kind of loopy. We want the medication cutback dramatically until hopefully the medication can be discontinued. The school district won't agree. We found a private school called The Wilton Center for Creative Learning, not far from Stonington. It's a very progressive school and has come up with an IEP that agrees with our approach on medication. But the Stonington school district won't approve their plan for use in Jack's school and has refused to pay to transfer Jack to Wilton. We've asked for a hearing on that decision. Max and I know that we need a lawyer."

Carpenter's jaw muscles were working overtime, the giveaway that he was focusing fully on the Lawsons' problems and considering approaches. Philly wouldn't be able to contribute anything substantive to this meeting; she really had let him down.

"Do you think the school district's position is motivated by money?" Carpenter asked.

"I think that's a part of this," Max Lawson responded. "The Wilton Center has yearly tuition of thirty thousand. But in fairness to Stonington, I think it believes its own plan for Jack is appropriate."

Carpenter nodded. "I'm sure you realize that you may have a problem if the school district's plan *is* appropriate. I've given the law a quick look and the way I understand it is that if a school system's plan is appropriate, the town would have discharged its legal obligations even if another plan may be more appropriate."

"That's what Jack's school principal told us," Max Lawson replied. "But we don't think keeping Jack on drugs is appropriate. Jack's being moved through the school system but it's like he's in a trance from the medication."

"How's your son doing?" Carpenter asked.

"He's below grade level in reading and writing, but he's above grade level in math."

"Has Jack ever become violent while in the Stonington schools?"

"Twice in first grade he had to be restrained," Sylvia Lawson said. "He hurt several students and that led to the start of medication."

"If the Stonington IEP is upheld, will you send Jack to the Wilton Center anyway?" Carpenter asked.

"Financially, that would be challenging," Max Lawson said. "But we haven't ruled anything out."

"What kind of medication is your son on?" Carpenter inquired.

Sylvia Lawson rummaged in her purse and extracted a piece of paper. "We thought it would be easier if we made a list," she said, passing the paper across the conference room table to Carpenter.

Carpenter studied the list but didn't position it so that she could also get a look which told Philly how steamed at her he was.

"You're going to need an expert witness," Carpenter said.

Max Lawson nodded. "The Wilton Center may be able to provide someone."

Carpenter frowned. "If the expert is from the Wilton Center, there would be a financial motive for the expert to provide you with helpful testimony."

"We thought of that," Sylvia Lawson said. "But we think they have someone with pretty good credentials who could be helpful."

Carpenter wrote on his notepad.

"What do you charge for your services?" Max Lawson asked.

Carpenter provided his $350 hourly rate. "If Ms. Piper joins me in handling this matter, her hourly rate is substantially below mine."

Philly picked up on Carpenter's conditional statement.

"I'm interested in your case," Carpenter said. "If you hire me, I'll need you to sign an engagement letter. I'd like to email you a copy of the engagement letter so you understand what our arrangement would be. You need to think about this and get back to me with any questions before you make a final decision. I know this can't be easy for you."

The Lawsons exchanged a glance that Philly couldn't read. What if her own kid had special needs or some God-awful mysterious disease that ensured a lifetime of parental anguish? There were some things you just had to put out of your mind.

Carpenter returned to the conference room after showing the Lawsons out. When he started to gather his papers, Philly realized that he wasn't going to say anything to her.

"I'm sorry I didn't contribute much," Philly offered.

Carpenter mumbled something she didn't catch and headed for the door.

"Look, can we talk for a minute," Philly said.

Carpenter resumed his seat. "So, talk," he said.

"I'm sorry I didn't do any research on special needs programs," Philly said.

When Carpenter didn't respond her irritation rose. "I just said I was sorry, for Christ's sake!"

"Sorry doesn't cut it," Carpenter said. "I'm not minimizing what you've been through. But I've got my own miseries to deal with as you know. If people are foolish enough to pay me money to help them, then I'm goddamn well going to help them and not go about it in a half-assed way because I've got my own problems."

Carpenter was right. But Philly wasn't certain that she could put her problems to the side. "I'm just feeling a little overwhelmed right now . . ."

"That doesn't cut it either," Carpenter came back. "If we're going to make a go of it this year and work together like last year, you need to suck it up and get your shit together. If I can't count on you, I won't. Can I be any clearer?"

"All right. You've made your fucking point."

"Can I count on you? I need to hear it from you."

"Yeah, you can count on me," Philly said, telling the geezer what he wanted to hear but having no clue whether it was the truth.

"All right," Carpenter said. "Glad to hear it. Let's hope the Lawsons sign on. No harm in starting out a year with a tough case. You know what they say when the going gets tough?"

Philly nodded, didn't say anything. Carpenter's aphorisms were wearing thin.

3

Philly was breathing hard as she followed Isabella up the stairs to the third floor of the Brighton house, a reminder that her recent lethargy was eating away at her fitness. The number of things that she should be doing but failed to do was increasing exponentially. She unbuttoned her parka and loosened her scarf.

The third floor had its own entrance and stairway. There were two large bedrooms off a narrow hallway plus a bathroom and a recessed area that currently housed a refrigerator. There was no kitchen area on the third floor, so any cooking would have to be done on hotplates.

"These are the bedrooms that could be rented out," Isabella said, as she opened one of the bedroom doors.

Philly stepped inside. The room was spacious now but with a bed, bureau, and desk would be confining. The tenants' lack of access to the first and second floors was a plus and a negative. Her idea of tenants being at the ready to help with her baby would be out, but there would be more privacy for everyone. "How come it's vacant now?" she asked.

"The owner thinks it will be easier to sell the house if there are no tenants," Isabella explained. "When we go inside to see the other floors, you'll see that all furniture has been removed.

"How long has the place been on the market?"

"Seven months."

"Has the price dropped in that time?"

"No."

The owner's asking price was $535,000. To buy the house alone, Philly would have to get a mortgage even if all of Philip's trust fund money was put toward the purchase price. "Let's see the other two floors," she said.

Isabella led the way down the stairs and outside and then in through the front door. The broker had had another engagement but had trusted Isabella to pick up the keys and return them.

Immediately off the front entry hall was a spacious living room. "Raul and I thought this could be a common living room," Isabella said. "It's also big enough for a dining room table."

Philly silently agreed; the room was spacious enough to serve a dual function. There was a small kitchen on the first floor as well as a full bath with a tub. In addition, there were two bedrooms, one almost as big as the third-floor bedroom she had viewed, and a second bedroom maybe two thirds the size of the first. If she took the first floor, her baby's room would be next to hers.

The second floor also had a full bath but no tub. Two bedrooms were at one end of the hall and a third bedroom at the opposite end. The rooms were good sized. Conceivably the third bedroom could also be rented out.

In the unfinished basement, storage shelves had been anchored along some of the walls above a concrete slab floor.

"You and Raul must have come up with some idea of how you want to do this," Philly said when they had returned to the first-floor living room.

"Let me make a suggestion," Isabella said, smiling. "Let's return the keys to the broker and have lunch. We can talk then."

"Sounds like a plan," Philly said, zipping up her parka again.

Isabella opted for a Taco Bell and when their enchiladas were served, Isabella applied hot sauce liberally. Philly was at a stage of pregnancy where nausea was no longer a problem, but she decided not to push her luck and laid off the hot sauce. Lately she was ravenous all the time. She hadn't begun to show and couldn't figure out where the massive amounts of food she was ingesting went. She had only gained a pound.

They ate for a time in silence and Philly took the opportunity to study Isabella. She was a beauty: tall, slender, dark complexioned, with her most distinctive feature soulful, luminous eyes that were almost black.

"Is this awkward for you?" Isabella asked.

"A little," Philly admitted.

"I would like to clear the air about several things," Isabella said, her expression solemn. "I know that you and Raul were in an intimate relationship. That is not a problem for me. But if it's a problem for you, you need to tell me. I promise you I'll put a stop to this house talk before Raul gets up more of a head of steam. Please be honest with me."

During the time she was trying to keep Isabella's uncle in Massachusetts, Philly had viewed his niece as an overwrought, high strung woman overwhelmed by her uncle's ordeal. Now she was seeing a calm, deliberative, no-nonsense side to her.

"The truth is," Philly said, "I do find going in together on a house awkward. And it's not because Raul and I were together. We would never have worked out as a couple. It sort of has more to do with Raul. I think we aggravate each other."

Isabella smiled. "Yes, I can understand that. Raul gets something in his head that excites him and he can't think of anything else. He can't understand why anyone won't share his enthusiasm. This is one of the things that I love about Raul. But I appreciate that this quality may not be attractive to everyone."

"That's why we would never have made it as a couple," Philly said, deciding to reciprocate Isabella's candor. "Raul has a way of driving me nuts."

Isabella's smile faded. "So maybe this house idea is a bad idea."

"I'm still thinking about it," Philly said in what she hoped was a friendly tone. "I recognize Raul's good points. He's caring, kind, and honest. His enthusiasm can be endearing; it's not always a turnoff. Frankly, I can't make up my mind."

Isabella shook her head. "You have a doubt. I think now is the time to nip this in the bud before Raul becomes even more taken with the idea."

"Has Raul done something I don't know about?"

Isabella shrugged. "He's already making plans. He's getting carried away."

"What kind of plans?"

Isabella sighed. "He's figuring out down payments and rental charges and the cost of having the house inspected. He's getting ahead of himself obviously, but I have learned that telling him to slow down often has no effect. For the moment, I've stopped urging him to move slowly."

"Unbelievable!" Philly exclaimed softly. "So how does he see this working?"

"Do you really want to know?"

"Sure. Why not?"

Philly knew that she was sporting a dazed expression as Isabella rattled off facts and figures. In Raul's plan, he and Isabella would own fifty percent of the property jointly, and Philly would own the other fifty percent. Philly and her baby would occupy the bedrooms on the first floor—less worry about stairs when the baby started to become mobile. Raul and Isabella would take over the two bedrooms at one end of the second-floor hallway and use one for a shared home office. The bedroom at the opposite end of the second floor would be a home office for Philly unless they needed to rent that room out. Each bedroom on the third floor would be rented out at $650 a month. Raul had even estimated a twenty percent down payment.

"You asked," Isabella said when she had concluded her account.

Philly was convinced that Isabella had spared her innumerable details that Raul had come up with. "Are you still a social worker?" she asked.

"Yes. I'm still at Brigham and Women's Hospital."

"What about you and Raul and marriage?" Philly asked next. It seemed forward, in a way, but a house was a long-term commitment, and she'd be foolish not to think about what could make it unstable.

"We plan on getting married. If we were to go through with the house purchase, that might accelerate our marriage plans."

Philly resisted the urge to tell Isabella to move forward on marriage. Philip had wanted to get married in the worst way and she had deprived him of that joy. She had put Philip off for reasons that were trivial and now it meant that she probably had no standing to sue the little shit who had run him down.

Philly thought about her options. Raul could certainly be annoying, but when she had described Raul's good points and irritating points to Maxine, Maxine had replied that, "Generosity, kindness, and honesty can't be overrated." It was that comment that had convinced Philly to see the property.

"You're right," Philly said. "I do have a reservation about us teaming up. But I haven't ruled anything out."

"It's very important to me that you be completely comfortable with this," Isabella said earnestly.

"I don't suppose there's any way to tone Raul down," Philly said.

Isabella laughed. "You already know the answer to that."

"Well, this is a treat," Howie Silver said to Carpenter after a waitress had taken their orders and departed.

Carpenter had chosen a small, family run Italian restaurant he liked. They were in a booth that afforded privacy. He guessed it had been a year since he and Howie had gotten together. They had litigated against each other on a number of occasions and had become something more than acquaintances but not exactly close friends. *Wise* was not a word Carpenter threw around when it came to other lawyers, but he would have been hard pressed to come up with the name of another lawyer who was sager than Howie.

"You're right, it is a treat to have lunch with you," Carpenter said. "But as is usually the case when I seek you out, I have a selfish agenda."

Howie laughed. "Whenever you try to pick my brain on a case that's troubling you, I have to remind you that the pickings are slim."

"It's not about a case," Carpenter clarified. "I wish it were. It's about me." He took a breath and plunged on. "I'd like this to stay between us. I found out last month that I have cancer. It's a chronic form of leukemia."

Howie's usually upbeat demeanor turned serious. He was slight and trim. In court, he was a fighter.

"Crap! I'm sorry to hear this. It's a shock."

"I appreciate that," Carpenter said, noting Howie's genuine concern. "Right now, I don't have any symptoms and until I do, no treatment is called for. It has to do with my white blood cell count being elevated. A lot of the time, people have this and don't know it, and sometimes they live out their lives and die from natural causes or some ailment that has nothing to do with their cancer. So here I have this incurable disease that doesn't require any treatment at the moment. My problem is that I can't stop thinking about it. I'm trying to get ideas on how to live with this damn thing. I'm talking mentally."

"Crap!" Howie said again, this time more softly.

The waitress set down their orders and left. They ate for a time in silence, but Carpenter never doubted that Howie was thinking about his problem.

"It's very hard to put yourself in someone else's position," Howie broke the silence. "I was trying to think through what I would do if a doctor told me I had your condition. Of course, you can't really say what you would do until you're faced with a situation. But I think I would continue to go about my business. I would try not to think about what was going on inside my body. None of this is very insightful and falls under the easier said than done category. But that's what I've come up with off the top of my head."

Howie hadn't suggested anything new, but at least had spared him the platitude to live each day as if it were his last.

"I'm going to talk about this with Rabbi Feldman," Howie said. "The rabbi may have a way of viewing your situation that hasn't occurred to me. Of course, you could visit him yourself. There's no question that he would make time for you."

Rabbi Feldman was actually a former client of Carpenter's, and when it came to wisdom, Rabbi Feldman also had it in abundance. Carpenter was convinced that Howie came up with some of his creative solutions to legal problems by talking them through with the rabbi. Howie, of course, had never acknowledged any such collaboration.

"Let me think about talking with the rabbi," Carpenter said, not totally comfortable with the idea of doing so.

"What have *you* come up with?" Howie asked. "How are you dealing with this so far?"

"I'm pretty much trying to do what you suggested. I've decided to keep on trucking. My doctors say I shouldn't make any major life-changing decisions based on the diagnosis. But somehow that doesn't sound right to me."

Howie picked at his salad. "It doesn't sound right to me either, but what the hell do I know? It doesn't seem to me that there's any such thing as business as usual after you hear the word leukemia."

Carpenter nodded. "That's what I said to my doctors, but they've stuck by their advice. They say there's a reasonable chance nothing will come of this. I'm having trouble believing them. How the hell do you put something like this out of your mind?"

"You don't," Howie said with conviction. "That's putting your head in the sand. I guess one thing I would do in your situation is try to do things that I liked, things that made me happy. I don't see how you could go wrong doing what you enjoy."

"That's what Maxine, the current lady in my life, keeps telling me. You've met Connie, but I don't think you've met Maxine. She wants us to travel. But what I really want to do is keep practicing law and bitching and moaning about it."

Howie laughed. "Then do it," he advised. "You don't need anyone's permission."

It's not that easy, Carpenter thought, but maybe he was missing a trick and it was as easy as Howie made it seem.

"You working on anything exciting?" Howie asked.

Carpenter shook his head. "The truth is business is down. Last year was a good year, but so far this year promises to suck."

"There you go," Howie said with a mischievous grin.

"What?"

"You're doing what you like to do, bitching and moaning. Stop complaining."

Two Computer Repairpersons

4

Sometimes you did a good job for a client, but the client ended up dissatisfied because he didn't get everything he wanted. Marty Fine was one of those clients. Were Carpenter to list former clients who would never refer a case to him, Marty Fine's name would be high on the list. Yet Herbert Stanton and Millie Lane were sitting in the office suite conference room facing him and Philly, because Marty Fine had provided Stanton with his name.

Neither potential client appeared outgoing. The two worked as computer repairpersons and troubleshooters. Stanton was of average height, thin, probably about forty years of age. He had sandy hair and close set, blue eyes. Lane looked to be Stanton's age. She had black curls that were not nearly as impressive as Philly's and a round face that Carpenter thought bland. Both were casually but neatly dressed in jeans and sweaters, winter boots and parkas.

"How do you know Marty Fine?" Carpenter began.

"I'd been checking the computers at the company he works for, and I'd given him my home phone number for emergencies," Stanton said. "He called me at home early one morning, and I had to tell him I had just been fired. I filled him in and I said I thought I needed a lawyer. He gave me your name. He said you had helped him out in a sticky situation a while back."

Philly was taking notes, at least for the moment having put her own problems to the side.

"Why don't you go over what happened. You mentioned that the company you worked for is called Wise Computer Consultants."

"Right," Stanton said. "The company has service contracts with a lot of businesses in Boston and the surrounding suburbs. They have about ten people who do what we do. We get paid on an hourly basis and at the end of each day, for each client, we e-mail in the hours we worked and our travel time."

"Sounds straightforward," Carpenter said.

"It is. But we got fired because there were times during the work week when . . . we would get together."

Stanton had avoided the word, but Carpenter saw no reason to. "So you were having an affair," he said, trying not to sound judgmental.

Stanton and Lane colored slightly. "Yes," Stanton said weakly.

"Is that why you were fired?" Philly asked.

Lane nodded. "Bruce Bolton called us into his office. He owns the company and he said that he didn't need a reason to fire us but, if we wanted one, it was because we were seeing each other at motels during the normal work week. Then he told us to clear out our desks."

"Did the company have a policy against employees dating?" Carpenter asked.

"No," Stanton and Lane answered in unison.

"Then what was the problem?" Philly joined the discussion.

"That's what I wanted to know," Stanton said. "We thought we'd been very discreet. We only get paid for the actual time we spend with a client and for travel time. We'd only get together if neither of us had a work assignment. We never thought that we were doing something on company time."

Stanton made quotation marks in the air with his fingers when he said *company time.* Carpenter wrote the words on his notepad.

"Bolton asked us to hand in our cell phones, the ones that the company had given us," Stanton continued. "When we did that, Bolton said something like we were the reason the company had put GPS trackers in the phones."

Carpenter fought the urge to curse modern technology. Here he'd been thinking that this possible case was some garden variety employment mess, when the case was likely to turn on some goddamned, modern technology he knew nothing about.

"Did you know about the GPS before?" Philly asked.

"No," Stanton and Lane again replied as one.

"Did you meet at your homes?" Philly asked.

"Sometimes," Stanton said. "We liked going somewhere else."

"Do you want your jobs back?" Carpenter asked.

Lane nodded. "We've both been with the company for about three years. We're good workers. In this economy, we think it will be difficult to find comparable work."

"And I don't like it that the company was spying on us," Stanton chimed in.

"Did you have written employment contracts with the company?" Carpenter asked.

"No," Stanton replied.

"In that case, this Mr. Bolton was probably correct that you were employees at will and that he could let you go for no reason. It may be difficult to get your jobs back."

"What about our privacy rights?" Stanton asked.

Carpenter nodded toward Philly. She had recently researched privacy rights in a number of cases they had worked on together.

"You both have a right to privacy," Philly explained. "Massachusetts actually has a statute that grants you that right. You may have a case that your privacy rights were violated. We'd need to do further research on that. But it remains to be seen what monetary damages you could recover if you proved that the company violated your privacy rights."

"They probably kept track of our whereabouts on weekends," Lane said. While the woman had initially struck him as bland, her expression left Carpenter with no doubt as to her anger at being spied on.

"How much would it cost to sue the company?" Stanton asked.

Lane seemed to be suffering from sticker shock at the $350 and $200 hourly rates that he and Philly charged. Carpenter wondered what Stanton and Lane were paid per hour but believed it wasn't prudent to ask.

"What about a contingency arrangement?" Stanton followed up.

Carpenter decided to be frank with the couple. "Ms. Piper and I often take cases on a contingency basis. We do that when we believe there's a reasonable chance to recover substantial monetary damages. I'm not inclined to go the contingency fee route in your case because your damages may be minimal. Let's say the company violated your right to privacy. That doesn't mean that you will get back pay for the time you were out of work because the company could have fired you without having any reason to do so."

Stanton and Lane looked crestfallen. Carpenter considered what a jury might decide on the facts the couple had related. A jury might be pissed off at the company's Big Brother spying tactics and stick the company for a sizable punitive damage award. But there was no way to predict the likelihood of that happening. The couple's case might consume hours that would never be paid for.

"What if we gave you a retainer?" Stanton pursued. "Would you work on a contingency if we did that?"

"What amount did you have in mind?" Carpenter asked. "We've done fee arrangements of that kind in the past."

When Stanton and Lane exchanged a glance, Carpenter sensed that the couple had already worked through responses to the various potential decisions that might have to be made at this meeting.

"Five thousand dollars," Stanton said.

Carpenter knew that if he were busy, he would reject the amount. But with time on his hands and Philly with free time, it was tempting to take on the case albeit for the wrong reason. The Lawsons had signed an engagement letter but that special needs case was the only billable hour case he currently had going. Carpenter decided to temporize.

"Ms. Piper and I will consider your proposal and get back to you. Whatever we decide, my advice is that you make a serious effort to find new jobs."

Philly was doodling on her notepad when Carpenter returned to the conference room after showing Stanton and Lane out. She seemed abstracted. "What do you think?" he asked as he sat down.

"I don't see this as a big damage case unless there's a punitive damage award," Philly said. "The retainer could be the only money we see in this case."

Carpenter didn't like Philly's apathetic body language but was relieved that she had been paying attention and thinking clearly about taking on the case. "If we were busy," he said, "I'd probably say no to them. But we're not busy so I'm thinking we say yes."

"If the case goes to trial, we'll lose our shirt," Philly pointed out.

"There's that."

"I don't like it that this company could have fired them for the hell of it," Philly added.

"Yeah, but it didn't. It fired them for a reason. I'm thinking it might be okay to use this GPS stuff on employees so long as you tell the employees first." Carpenter thought that a jury comprised largely of working stiffs might stick it to an employer that didn't respect employees' privacy on their own time. "I'm going by instinct—more like playing a hunch—but I'm going to take the case. If you're on board, we'll split the retainer. I'm thinking that you take first shot at the court complaint."

"Sure," Philly said, her listlessness still apparent.

"Perk the hell up!" Carpenter barked.

Philly shrugged. "I've been kicking around the idea of buying a house along with Raul and his girlfriend, Isabella. I keep going back and forth on it. It's been driving me crazy."

"You and Raul?" Carpenter asked in amazement.

"Yeah. I was stupid enough to mention to him what I was thinking, and now he's all hot to trot."

"Maybe *you* can picture a scenario in which you don't strangle Raul."

"I can't believe I'm leaning toward going in with them," Philly said. "Talk about playing a goddamn hunch!"

5

Philly decided to take an afternoon spinning class at Pedal Pusher Galleries to clear her head. She had felt guilty deliberately leaving her office at a time Carpenter wouldn't likely observe her departure, because two of his cases required work on her part. Nevertheless, with the house decision hanging over her, work was the last thing she wanted to think about.

"We're going to warm up for about six minutes," Kris, one of her favorite instructors, announced. "We need to get warm and get our heart rates up."

Philly settled on a moderately fast pace with little resistance. She was counting on Kris' usual mellowness to permit her mind to drift to the house issue. As she pedaled, she thought of the fetus growing inside her. Didn't one of the baby books say that the fetus now was about the size of a finger? Philly wasn't sure; baby book information left her consciousness moments after she read it. However big the fetus was it was big enough to cause her to show. Looking in the mirror this morning, Philly was convinced that there was a thickening about her middle that hadn't been there before.

"Time to stretch," Kris announced.

After going over Raul's e-mailed calculations, Philly had to admit that his numbers made sense. He had priced out a mortgage for eighty percent of the purchase price at different rates of interest and had come up with a budget that figured in rental income, taxes, insurance, and mortgage payments. Philly had been unable to find fault with the figures. By making only a modest down payment, she would be able to keep most of Philip's trust fund in reserve.

"Time for our first working song. We're going to take it out of the saddle for some brief accelerations. On my count. One, two, three. Second position and pick up the pace."

Philly considered that if she wasn't spinning so hard, she'd probably have a visceral reaction against taking anything Raul did at face value. So perhaps the demanding exercise was responsible for her feeling of relief at someone else taking over the grunt work of running numbers.

"We're about to start our first hill. Turn your resistance knobs one full circle to the right. You should feel this."

Philly leaned over the handlebars, her hamstrings straining. Without warning, her face became coated with sweat.

"Another half turn to the right. This should be hard."

Tom Petty's *Breakdown* was blaring from the speakers in the rear of the spinning room, and Philly focused on the music, trying to match her pace to the beat. She loved the opening bars to this song the way Petty mimicked some edgy loner with a don't-give-a-shit attitude.

"We're halfway up the hill. Everyone is looking good."

Halfway up the hill, Philly thought. Was that the same as being halfway up a creek without a paddle? As good a time and place as any to make a decision, she reflected. The idea of not being alone on this venture tipped the scales. The truth was, right now she didn't trust herself to go into a home purchase on her own. Okay, then: she'd join Raul and Isabella. They needed a side deal on what would happen if either wanted to sell out. But Philly didn't see that decision point in the near future.

"Now we're going to head back down the hill," Kris announced. "Ease up on the resistance by a half a turn to the left."

It's all downhill from here, Philly thought.

"I can't figure out what to do about Philly?" Carpenter complained to Maxine over the phone. He'd seen her come back to the office late afternoon with her gym bag and knew that she had gone to one of those spinning classes she liked. He hadn't said anything, but inside he'd been steamed at her blowing off work.

"She's going through a tough time," Maxine said. "I think you need to cut her some slack. If she doesn't get something done on time, that's another matter. Then you'd need to get on her case."

Carpenter didn't want to listen to Maxine talk sense. He was in his condo's tiny kitchen talking on a land line. He stared at the bare wall behind where the sofa had been placed in his living room. For a moment, he was struck by the starkness of his existence. When Maxine wasn't around, his few possessions underscored how alone he was.

"She's never going to view the workday the way you do," Maxine continued. "If you're going to keep working with her, get used to that."

"Christ!" Carpenter grumbled.

"Has she missed any deadline you've set for her?" Maxine asked.

"No."

"The defense rests."

"But I don't like it," Carpenter griped.

"As I said," Maxine came back, "get used to it or find someone else."

Carpenter didn't want to get used to anything. He wanted things to be the way they were last year when he and Philly were on the same page when working together. Of course, during that time, Philip had been alive.

"I suppose you're right," Carpenter said.

"I'm always right. Outside of Philly, how are you doing?"

"There's been a little uptick in business," Carpenter reported. "Nothing major."

"This weekend, I'd like to stay at your place," Maxine said. "I know how to cheer you up."

"You've got your work cut out for you."

A Lawyer

6

Maybe 2010 was going to be the year when former clients who hadn't been thrilled with his services sent business his way. First there was Marty Fine giving his name to Herbert Stanton. Now it was happening again. Last month he had tried and won a jury case for a client who was, nevertheless, disappointed to recover only half of what he was looking for. Yet for some reason he had recommended Carpenter to Marshall Hyde, who was now sitting in Carpenter's conference room.

Hyde practiced criminal law with two other lawyers in Cambridge. He looked to be in his early forties, a large, heavyset man with a craggy face and dark, hard eyes. Carpenter considered whether he was making a mistake by not having Philly sit in on this meeting. Probably. But sometimes, when you were pissed off at someone, there was something undeniably satisfying about letting your irritability govern your thinking. Besides, Philly had work she could be doing.

"How do you know Jeffrey Naylor?" Carpenter asked.

"We go to the same gym and we've struck up a friendship. I mentioned my situation and told him I was shopping for a lawyer. He gave me your name. He said you wouldn't let him push you around."

"You mentioned on the phone that this is a Board of Bar Overseers matter. What's going on?"

"You don't practice criminal law, do you?" Hyde asked.

"Right," Carpenter said, hoping that Hyde would leave it at that so he didn't have to explain his distaste for Hyde's specialty.

"There's this judge who from time to time runs the first superior court criminal session over in Woburn where they moved the Middlesex County courthouse. He splits time in that session with three other judges. The Honorable Samuel Porter has been driving the criminal bar nuts."

Carpenter tried for a sympathetic look. It came with the territory that judges drove litigators nuts, so a lawyer complaining about a judge didn't count for much in his view.

"You're probably aware that a criminal defendant has a right to a speedy trial. If a criminal case gets heard within three or four months, nobody gets bent out of shape. That time frame is a rule of thumb that prosecutors and defense lawyers pretty much accept. Of course, prosecutors and defense attorneys cut deals to put off a trial and that's also par for the course. But when you come before Judge Porter for an arraignment or some initial matter, he sets a case down for trial in two or three weeks."

Carpenter tried to match Hyde's indignant look. Two to three weeks seemed like a short time but maybe criminals wanted a day in court as soon as possible.

"Two or even three weeks is an impossible time frame to meet," Hyde continued. "Prosecutors typically accept the short time ordered by Judge Porter because they don't want to piss off the judge, and because usually all they have to do is get a police officer up to speed as a witness. But for a busy defense lawyer, it's impossible to get ready in that time; there's no chance to investigate a case or to file motions. What usually happens is that defense counsel ends up asking for a continuance and then the case goes to the end of the trial list and you're lucky if you get heard in eight months. Basically, Judge Porter is forcing criminal defendants to waive their right to a speedy trial."

Carpenter understood Hyde's point. If a criminal defendant requested that an unrealistic trial date be continued, the defendant would have difficulty later complaining that he was denied the right to a speedy trial. What he couldn't figure out was what the Board of Bar Overseers had to do with the situation Hyde was describing.

"I've got this blog I put out," Hyde resumed, "and I basically unloaded on Judge Porter for what he was doing. The blog got sent to the Board of Bar Overseers and now I'm facing a complaint for unprofessional conduct."

Carpenter's knowledge of blogs was vague. He couldn't recall looking at one. But this was hardly the thing to say to Hyde at this juncture.

"Here's what I wrote," Hyde said as he slid several sheets of paper across the conference room table.

Carpenter tried to keep his expression neutral as he read the document. He wasn't opposed to someone sounding off on whatever subject he fancied. But he couldn't imagine a clear-thinking lawyer ever referring to a judge as pigheaded, a tyrant, or a bully. To his way of thinking, judges were probably no different than any other discrete group: they looked out for their own and took umbrage at intemperate comments directed at one of their fraternity. Interestingly, Hyde must not have feared retaliation from other judges.

Hyde was staring at him. Carpenter supposed that one way to encourage Hyde to retain him was to tell the lawyer that his blog was great. Instead he said, "Do you have a copy of the complaint letter that the Board of Bar Overseers sent to you?"

Hyde rummaged in his briefcase and sent another document across the conference room table.

The gist of the Board's complaint was that a personal attack on a sitting judge was unprofessional and brought disrespect to the legal profession. With all the biting lawyer jokes making the rounds, Carpenter privately believed that a case could be made that the legal profession was already held in no respect. Still . . .

"Was there any other response to your blog?" Carpenter asked.

Hyde's severe expression softened. "I was blown away. I got over three hundred hits and they were all supportive. There were some lawyers who said they wished they had my guts because Judge Porter had been taking advantage of the criminal bar far too long."

Carpenter wondered whether his own career would be harmed if he took Hyde's case. Judges in civil cases might not look kindly on a lawyer who defended another lawyer's attack on a fellow criminal jurist. And that could be serious. A judge who had it in for you could find myriad ways to stick it to you in the course of a trial. Close calls on evidentiary issues could go against you, or a judge's body language could indicate to a jury that your client's case was weak or suspect. Well, screw it, Carpenter decided. He was damned if he was going to turn down a case because judges might take it out on him later.

"Do you think any of these lawyers who voiced support for you would testify on your behalf?" Carpenter inquired.

"Who the hell knows," Hyde said irritably. "I could be all alone on this when push comes to shove."

"I'm interested in your case," Carpenter said, after a pause. "You can try to get the Board's complaint thrown out using some first amendment arguments. But if you want my opinion, I don't think the complaint against you will be dismissed. Some of the language you used was decidedly personal and heated. Here's the way I see this playing out. You'd file an answer to the complaint giving your side of the story. Once the Board assigns a lawyer to the case, your lawyer will confer with the Board's lawyer. The lawyer for the Board will likely try to settle the case by getting you to agree to some kind of disciplinary sanction. If you don't accept what the Board lawyer has in mind, you have a right to a hearing. I believe that you're going to need a fair number of lawyers to back you in your criticism of Judge Porter in order to prevail at the hearing and get a favorable recommendation from a hearing officer. Even if you get witnesses to back you, I'm concerned that a hearing officer might say that your language was intemperate."

Hyde listened impassively. "Naylor was right when he said that you'd tell it like it is," he finally commented. "You've made fair points. I can't tell you how pissed off I was at Porter. I was representing a defendant in a series of breaking and entering cases and there were complicated eyewitness identification issues in the case. When Porter set the case down for trial in two weeks it sent me over the edge. I probably should have let my blog sit for a few days until I had cooled down. But I didn't."

"If you decide to hire me," Carpenter said, "I'm sure I could get an extension to reply to the Board's complaint."

"I'm leaning toward hiring you," Hyde said. "I can't complain about your hourly rate because mine's slightly higher. But let me sleep on it. That's probably what I should have done before unloading my blog."

7

Maxine was leading the way along a trail that snaked through forest land, the trees mostly bare, the ground frozen, the sky a pale blue that Carpenter associated with cold. And it was cold, especially with the steady wind coming at them head-on no matter which way they turned on the trail. If there was conservation land to be found, Maxine found it. Today she had them hiking in Great Brook Farm State Park in Carlisle. Carpenter had yielded to the weather and was wearing a wool stocking cap pulled down over his ears. He hated hats of any kind, and the one he had on itched. But he had to admit it made walking bearable. It probably was a first, he thought, that he wasn't thinking about work. Instead he had been worrying about his failure to get aroused last night when Maxine showed up at his condo intent on keeping her promise to cheer him up. He couldn't shake the notion that last night's dismal performance had something to do with his cancer, was some side effect of CLL that none of his doctors had told him about. If Maxine was disappointed, she'd hidden it well.

Maxine paused when the trail forked and studied her map. Carpenter drew up beside her, fretting about last night and wondering why he wasn't more upbeat because of the two new cases that had come in. The computer repair duo, Stanton and Lane, had signed a modified contingency fee agreement, and

Marshall Hyde had inked an engagement letter. Work on Hyde's case would be at an hourly rate. For a year that had started with no business prospects, the past week offered promise. Philly, God bless her, had even crunched out an excellent draft court complaint challenging Stanton's and Lane's firing.

"Let's go to the left," Maxine said decisively, and Carpenter found himself nodding. As was usually the case when they were on the move, he didn't really care which direction they took.

The left fork was wide and Carpenter drew abreast of Maxine. They walked for a time in silence. He scratched at his ears but the itching didn't go away.

"I'm thinking I should go see that rabbi I was telling you about." Carpenter had filled Maxine in on his lunch with Howie Silver. Howie's comment that the rabbi would make time for him had been nagging at him. He needed to set up a meeting so he couldn't be faulted for leaving a stone unturned.

"Sounds like a good idea."

"I can't imagine what the guy can say to me," Carpenter groused.

You'll never know unless you go see him."

Carpenter mumbled something unintelligible and picked up his pace to stay abreast of Maxine.

"You're out of sorts," Maxine said. "And it has nothing to do with last night."

Carpenter silently agreed. Out of sorts was the right term. Since the year had begun his life was out of sync. When he catalogued what was bugging him—business prospects for the upcoming year, fucking cancer, Philly turning into a head case that he couldn't get a handle on—the list was impressive. Now he could add not getting it up to the miseries besetting him.

Maxine looked at her watch. "Fifteen more minutes before we head back," she announced.

"Great," Carpenter said.

Raul was like a juggernaut, a wired Latino Energizer bunny that would never run down. He and Isabella were seated at the dining room table in Philly's apartment and she couldn't recall when she'd last had visitors who weren't members of Philip's family. The broker for the Brighton property they were interested in had provided Raul with architectural plans and he was now declaiming about measurements. Philly glanced at Isabella and received a grin in return.

"We need to review next steps," Isabella interrupted Raul. "Room size won't matter if we don't get the property."

Raul was brought up short by Isabella's practical suggestion. But he recovered quickly. "I have made a list," he declared and circulated copies.

Philly glanced at Raul's checklist. The first item read: *Make Formal Offer.*

"I don't think we should agree to their asking price," Philly said.

"I do not want to lose the property," Raul replied immediately. "Remember that the broker has said the seller will not move off the asking price."

"I want your permission to make an offer that is fifty thousand below the asking price." Philly had assimilated the Carpenter truism that every price was negotiable.

Raul looked shocked by that suggestion. "That is far too low."

"Raul, I negotiate for a living. Let me handle this."

"The broker said that the purchase price was not negotiable."

"I don't give a shit what the broker said. Let me handle this."

"Philly is right," Isabella chimed in. "This is one of her strengths. We should leave the negotiation to her."

Watching Raul's downcast expression, Philly wondered whether this partnership could be saved. This was their first real business meeting, and already she and Raul were at loggerheads.

"Raul!" Isabella said with some force.

"Okay," Raul said grudgingly.

The second item on Raul's list was *Home Inspection.* "Do you have a home inspector in mind?" Philly asked.

"There is one on Angie's List who comes highly recommended. That is my preference. His charges are in line with the charges of other inspectors."

"Okay," Philly said. "Once the offer is signed, call the guy up and introduce yourself."

Philly consulted Raul's list. *Mortgage* was the third item noted. "Let me throw something out to you about getting a mortgage. Philip's sister, Pamela, says that her family uses a bank in North Andover, and Philip's parents have some influence with the bank. If we can check off the first two items on your list, let me see what the North Andover bank can do for us." Philly had already resolved to keep Philip's trust fund monies with the North Andover bank if the institution provided the mortgage.

Isabella and Raul exchanged a glance and Raul shrugged. "I do not see how that can hurt," he said. "Okay."

"Let's say our business meeting is over," Philly said. The last thing she wanted to do was attack the other items on Raul's checklist.

Raul gave his to do list a lingering glance; he threw up his hands when Isabella said, "I second that motion."

"How is your pregnancy going?" Isabella asked.

"I've started to show. I guess it's for real."

"That's wonderful!" Isabella exclaimed. "When you get further on and start in with childbirth classes, I hope you will consider me for your coach. It would be an honor."

Philly didn't want to think about the delivery. But she was touched by Isabella's offer. "That's very generous of you. I'll probably take you up on that."

Raul was studying the architectural plans and Philly wondered whether he was feeling excluded. She needed to remember that buying a house was a major life decision for him. For a guy who had recycled cans for a decade to earn extra money, Raul was about to take a dramatic step up and become a home owner.

"Raul," Philly said, and she waited until he looked up. "You need to pace yourself. Let's not get ahead of ourselves. That often leads to disappointment."

"I am sorry but as you know, I cannot help myself from thinking ahead. I am nervous about this negotiation you want to have."

"Then welcome to my world. Nervousness and uncertainty are a way of life."

8

"I thought I made it clear to Mr. Ramirez," the broker said. "The selling price is five hundred thirty-five thousand. The seller is not prepared to go lower."

Philly held her phone away from her ear and took several deep breaths. "I'm aware of what you told Mr. Ramirez. Subject to the usual contingencies, we're making an offer of four hundred eighty-five thousand."

"I have no authority to accept that offer as I've tried to make clear."

Philly paused. If Raul were on the line, he'd probably be suffering cardiac arrest right now.

"Then I'm sorry to have taken up your time," Philly said. "Here's my office phone number if the seller ever has a change of heart." She gave out her number and asked the broker to repeat it.

"Do you have financing?" the broker asked.

"No, but financing is not a problem. I've come into a considerable sum of money and I don't anticipate any problems in obtaining a conventional mortgage." Philly paused a beat. "Even in today's lending environment," she added.

"It's a shame that you're not willing to meet the seller's price," the broker said.

"No," Philly said. "The shame is that the asking price is too high and the seller won't come down. Mr. Ramirez and I are in no rush. We have all the time in the world. Sorry we can't do business. Have a nice day."

Philly set down her phone and figured it was a tossup whether she had torpedoed the deal that Raul had his heart set on. Still, she had a hunch that she had played the negotiation correctly.

When her phone rang, Philly's first thought was, that was quick. "Philomena Piper."

"Ms. Piper. This is Daniel Spring. You probably don't remember me."

But Philly did. "I remember you very well, Mr. Spring. I have you to thank for a number of referrals you've sent my way." Spring was a teachers' union representative in the Boston school system who had sent her several cases.

"I've given your name to a couple who have gotten into a dispute with the Dixfield school district. Do you know where Dixfield is?"

"It's near Rowley."

"Right. The couple's name is Harrington. John and Naomi Harrington. I believe they're going to give you a call."

"Can you tell me what the case is about?"

"I'd rather you hear it from them. It's complicated."

What isn't complicated, Philly thought. "I just want you to know how much I appreciate your thinking of me when it comes to referrals like this. I'm very grateful."

"I think I told you this before," Spring said. "I believe I'm doing a favor for anyone I give your name to."

Sitting in Rabbi Feldman's study at his temple in Beverly, Carpenter found another reason to like his former client: the study was messy with papers and books cast about randomly on flat surfaces and the floor. Carpenter had in innate distrust of neat people; he couldn't dispel the notion that a neat freak lacked the imagination to come up with a creative solution to a complex problem. Organization had its place, but sometimes clutter brought on a breakthrough thought. Insights sometimes came to him as he hunted about his office searching for a file folder.

Feldman was unprepossessing, the kind of guy you wouldn't notice if you passed him on a street. He was middle aged, of medium height and build. For a religious leader with a large following, his voice, while not quite a monotone, was seldom inflected to drive home a point. Yet judging from a Friday night service he had attended several years ago, Carpenter knew that when the rabbi spoke, his congregation listened.

"It is very good to see you again," Feldman said. "Howie explained your situation to me and said you might call. I am very pleased that you did. Why don't you start by telling me why you wanted to meet."

"I want to hear what advice you have for me about my situation," Carpenter began. "I've got this incurable disease that for the moment requires no treatment. Yet I find myself obsessing about it. Right now, I'm a little less compulsive when it comes to thinking about it but, when I first got the diagnosis, I couldn't think of anything else. My doctors say I should go about my business and not make any major life changes because of this. But that doesn't sound right to me. I'm trying to figure out how to live my life with this killer lurking in my body. I haven't been doing well dealing with this mentally."

Feldman nodded and then became lost in thought, his expression serious. "Howie told me what he said to you," Feldman said. "He told you to do what you enjoy. That is sound advice in my opinion."

That's it? Carpenter thought. Did I just drive to Beverly so a rabbi could repeat the obvious advice of a friend?

"You could also follow your doctors' advice and go about your business," Feldman added.

"But it's not business as usual," Carpenter protested.

"No, it isn't," Feldman concurred.

"What would you do in my situation?" Carpenter asked.

"That is not relevant as you lawyers sometimes say."

"Then what is relevant?"

Rabbi Feldman became lost in thought again. Carpenter sensed that the rabbi would not be discomfited if the silence dragged out indefinitely.

"You say that you want to stop obsessing about your cancer," the rabbi said.

Carpenter flinched when Feldman said cancer. "Right."

"Why do you want to stop obsessing about your cancer?"

"Because it's driving me nuts!"

Feldman was regarding him with a faraway look as if his mind had drifted from the purpose of this meeting.

"A while back I read this detective novel," Feldman said, his gaze focused. "For some reason it has stayed with me. The detective was in his forties and had a brain tumor. He called the tumor Bob."

Did rabbis read detective novels? Carpenter had no idea what to make of the rabbi's statement, but Feldman was plainly waiting for him to pick up the conversational ball. "Bob?"

"Yes, Bob. The detective would carry on conversations with Bob."

"You're saying he would talk to his tumor?"

Feldman nodded.

"I don't have a tumor. I've got . . . my cancer is in my blood."

"You have leukemia," Feldman said. "If you were to give your leukemia a name, I wonder what you would call it."

"Give it a name?" Carpenter felt adrift the more he repeated in question form something the rabbi said.

"What name would you give your leukemia?" Feldman asked.

"Jesus, I don't know. What kind of a question is that?"

"I'm curious. What would you name your leukemia?"

The name Fred popped into Carpenter's head. He didn't know any Fred. "Fred," he said.

"What would you like to say to Fred?"

"I'd like to tell him to drop dead and get lost."

"So tell him."

Carpenter stared at Feldman, but the rabbi had retained his serious expression and seemed to be waiting for an audible response.

"Fred, please drop dead and get the fuck out of my life."

Feldman nodded.

"Sorry, rabbi. I didn't mean . . ."

"There is nothing to be sorry about. And you did mean to use the f-word. I've actually heard it more than once before. I, myself, don't use it as much as when I was a young man, but perhaps that's my loss. The word can be liberating."

Carpenter couldn't believe that he had loosed an f-bomb in front of a rabbi he had sought out for help. Truly this meeting would leave him more unhinged than he was before it took place.

Rabbi Feldman stood. "I'm sorry I have nothing brilliant to offer to ease your situation. But it was a pleasure to see you again. I'm always available to you."

Carpenter shook the rabbi's outstretched hand and realized that the meeting was at an end. He was being dismissed, not exactly a brush off but definitely a dismissal.

"Thank you for seeing me," Carpenter said, unable to see one helpful thing he could take away from this meeting.

Carpenter listened to Maxine's breathing on the phone. He had just finished telling her about his meeting with the rabbi and he wished that she were with him so he could see her reaction.

"Where did the name Fred come from?" Maxine asked.

"I don't know. I pulled it out of my ear. He was sort of pressuring me to come up with a name and Fred popped into my head."

"Did you really tell Fred to fuck off?"

"Yeah. That was not one of my shining moments. The rabbi didn't seem to mind."

"How did it feel to tell Fred to fuck off?"

Carpenter had been so irritated by the inconclusive nature of his meeting with the rabbi that he hadn't thought about any other feeling he'd experienced. He remembered the word that the rabbi had used. "It felt sort of liberating."

Maxine didn't say anything. Carpenter turned away from the sorry sight of his living room couch with nothing on the wall behind it. Why had he suddenly started to give a shit about his furnishings?

"I think the rabbi wants you to talk to Fred," Maxine said.

"You're kidding!"

"No, I think he wants you to try talking to Fred."

Carpenter contemplated that option. Besides telling Fred to fuck off, he had little to say to his disease. 2010 was clearly the year he in which he would be involuntarily committed. Babbling to an unresponsive photograph of a black man and cursing out an unseen killer lurking in his body had to be sufficient grounds for the men in white coats to cart him off. "That sounds crazy," he said.

"What else have you come up with?"

"Point taken."

"You sound good," Maxine said.

Carpenter harrumphed unintelligibly.

"Do you want to come to my place this weekend?"

"No. If you don't mind, I'd like you to come up here. Maybe we could do some shopping. I've been thinking of putting something up on my living room wall behind the couch."

"What? You hate shopping. You're actually thinking of decorating?"

"It's just something that's been bugging me recently."

"Forget what I said about you sounding good. Now I'm really worried about you."

A Mother and a Father

9

Philly had debated whether to have Carpenter sit in on her initial meeting with John and Naomi Harrington. She'd been pissed off when he'd told her he had met alone with a potential new client, a lawyer facing a disciplinary action by the Board of Bar Overseers. But she decided to have Carpenter join her and let his slight pass assuming it was a slight. Maybe he'd had a good reason for handling the initial lawyer interview alone. Besides, she didn't have the luxury of trading slights with Carpenter. If she was going to take on a case that couldn't be resolved before she delivered, she might need him to provide follow-through.

The Harringtons struck Philly as a quintessential yuppie couple in their mid to late thirties. John Harrington was a structural engineer and his wife an advertising company executive. Each was wearing a dark blue business suit and armed with a briefcase. John Harrington was dark complexioned; he wore his black hair long and Philly suspected that his rimless aviator glasses made him look younger than he was. Naomi Harrington was heavily made up; her dark red lipstick drew attention away from her long, angular face, made you focus on her mouth. This meeting had to do with their son Luke.

"Mr. Spring spoke very highly of you," John Harrington directed at Philly.

"He's very kind. But Daniel wouldn't tell me anything about your situation. He said it was best if I heard it directly from you."

"We want our son's complete school records," Naomi Harrington said.

"Have you asked for them?" Philly inquired.

"We have," Harrington said. "We were told by the superintendent of schools that certain records will not be turned over because the records are confidential."

Carpenter frowned. "I thought that parents had a right to see their kid's records," he said.

"That's what we thought," Naomi Harrington replied. "We asked the superintendent to answer us in writing. She opened her briefcase, extracted a copy of a letter, and slid the document across the conference room table.

Philly positioned the paper so that she and Carpenter could read it together. Superintendent William Burnside quoted a statute to support the Dixfield school district's position. Among other things, the statute shielded from disclosure any document dealing with a claim of child abuse. Philly's gut churned. She remembered Carpenter's misgivings representing a convicted sex offender. With her pregnancy, she didn't want anything to do with parents who abused their child.

"Do you have any idea why the school district pointed to a statute that refers to abuse?" Philly asked.

The Harringtons exchanged a glance. "Not really," John Harrington said. "A few weeks back, Luke came home from school acting somewhat withdrawn. It came out over dinner that his third-grade teacher, Ms. Larson, had asked him if everything was okay at home. Luke told us that he said everything was okay. Naomi confronted Ms. Larson and she was evasive to say the least. She mentioned that she had seen a document that gave her a concern and she wanted to follow up on it with Luke. Naomi asked for the document and Larson directed us to Superintendent Burnside."

"How's your son doing in school?" Carpenter asked.

"Academically he's doing fine," Naomi Harrington said. "Socially, he doesn't make friends easily and is somewhat withdrawn."

"Are you concerned about your son's socialization?" Carpenter followed up.

"Not really," Naomi Harrington said. "It's not like he doesn't have any friends. He plays at other boys' homes and friends come to our house to play."

Philly digested the information they'd been given. "I gather you want us to get you copies of the document your son's teacher referred to and any other records the school district plans to withhold from you."

John Harrington nodded. "We're concerned that school records about our son contain falsehoods about us. We think that's outrageous particularly if the source of false information was anonymous."

"Is there anything you haven't told us that might provide substance to an abuse accusation?" Philly asked.

The Harringtons shook their heads in unison.

"There are some things we just have to ask," Carpenter said. "I don't want you getting offended. Has your son ever received medical treatment for injuries?"

Naomi Harrington's jaw dropped in response to Carpenter's pointed question. Anger flashed briefly in her husband's eyes. "No," John Harrington said.

Carpenter nodded and signaled Philly to take charge and wrap up the meeting.

"We're interested in your case," Philly said. "If you retain me, the first step will be to contact the school superintendent. I suspect the superintendent will refer me to a lawyer and once I contact the lawyer, I believe I'll have a better idea of what's going on."

The Harringtons' expressions approached hostile. Philly wondered whether Carpenter's pointed question about medical injuries had permanently alienated them.

"I'll require an engagement letter," Philly continued. "I've asked Mr. Carpenter to sit in because we collaborate on cases. I need to tell you that I'm pregnant and if this matter should drag on for any reason, there may be occasion for Mr. Carpenter to fill in for me for a time."

Philly had expected the couple to offer congratulations on her pregnancy but no comment was forthcoming.

"If I could have your e-mail addresses I could forward a draft engagement letter for your consideration."

The Harringtons handed over business cards with home contact information added in pen.

"I believe we've gone as far as we can go for the moment," Philly wrapped up.

Philly returned to the conference room after seeing the Harringtons out and was confronted with Carpenter's customary scowl. She reflected that since the year began, they hadn't had the kind of sit down Carpenter liked when they reviewed cases and divided up work. True, the year had started out with little or no work. But recently, there had been a mild flurry of new business. If the Harringtons retained her, January would prove to be a decent month in terms of generating business.

"What did you think of them?" Philly preempted Carpenter by asking the question he typically fired at her following a meeting with a prospective client.

"I'm not sure," Carpenter said. "If I had to guess, I'd bet there's going to be a disturbing aspect to that document they're trying to get."

"I got an uneasy feeling when abuse came up. What if this couple did something bad to their son? I don't think I could take that."

Carpenter frowned in concentration, his jaw muscles working. "There's probably something in the document that raises an abuse question," he said. "I don't think the school superintendent would have hidden behind the statute he referred to if that weren't the case. But if the abuse issue is not true, the Harringtons have every right to be pissed."

"Do you think they'll hire me?" Philly asked.

"Yeah, I do."

"Then I better get to work on the engagement letter."

Philly started to rise but Carpenter gestured for her to keep seated, his expression pained.

"I want to clear the air about something," Carpenter said. "I should have had you present when I sat down with that lawyer, Marshall Hyde. I didn't have you sit in because I was sensing your attention was elsewhere and it bothered me. I'm trying to cut you some slack because of all you've been through. But lately I have the feeling that your head isn't into practicing law. If I'm off base here, you need to set me straight."

Carpenter's speech reminded Philly of one of the reasons she genuinely liked him. If something was bugging him, he got it out in the open so it didn't fester. With his cancer diagnosis, she knew that she should be cutting him the same slack he was giving her.

"I've got a lot going on and none of it's easy," Philly said. "I'm going forward with buying a house with Raul and Isabella. And I'm playing hard ball with the seller's broker so Raul is on my case for putting the deal at risk. I know you're not happy with me and some of that is deserved. I was pissed that you didn't have me sit in when you met with that lawyer. In fact, I was so pissed that I seriously thought about meeting with the Harringtons alone."

Carpenter scowled.

"I've started to show," Philly decided to add. "I look at myself in the mirror and I picture myself turning into a fat cow before too long."

"I don't want to hear the details of your pregnancy," Carpenter said. "Talk to Maxine about that stuff. But we've got to pay attention to business. You're literally going to be out of action this summer. So we need to focus on the cases that have come in."

"You're right," Philly nodded.

"We've got the special education hearing for the Lawsons coming up next month and I haven't done squat with the case. I'm thinking that you do the research and I deal with the witnesses."

"Sounds like a plan."

"I've marked up the complaint you did for the computer people, Stanton and Lane," Carpenter shifted gears. "Put it in final form and get it out to the clients. You did a good job on that."

"Thanks."

"This lawyer I was telling you about said some unflattering things about a sitting judge on a blog he has. I'll put a copy of the offending blog on your desk. I'm thinking you handle the first amendment research since the lawyer will be claiming he's got a right to free speech. Last year you did a fair amount of first amendment research. Are you okay with that?"

"Sure," Philly said, not sounding to herself as confident as she needed to be.

"Is this too much for you?" Carpenter asked.

"I don't know," Philly said dispiritedly.

"Well if it is, you need to let me know sooner than later. If this stretches you too thin, I've got some thoughts on how to deal with that."

"What thoughts?"

"That's a discussion for another day. By the way, when it comes to the Harringtons, you can tell them if I work on their case it will be at your hourly rate."

Philly knew that was a big concession on Carpenter's part. "Thanks," she said.

"Don't mention it. Now what the hell's going on with this broker you're fighting with?"

10

Raul's e-mails had increased from one a day to three and Philly had finally had it. She fired off an angry response, telling him to stop bugging her and then lying, telling him that she knew what she was doing when, in truth, she didn't have a clue.

Carpenter had been supportive of her approach with the broker, reminding her that the seller was incurring costs every day the property was unoccupied. His theory was that the seller would do a cost benefit analysis and, unless the seller was plain nuts, come down on the price.

Philly took some deep breaths to calm down and tried to get her head back into special education law. Her preliminary legal research had confirmed Carpenter's initial take-aways. It wouldn't be enough to show that the Stonington school system's IEP was inferior to the private school placement the Lawsons desired for their son; rather, the Lawsons basically had to prove that the school system's plan was deficient and didn't work. Making that case would be a tall order.

Philly started when her intercom sounded. "A Ms. Adams for you," the part-time receptionist announced.

"Tell her I'll be with her in a moment," Philly instructed, clearing her head of special education law to focus on the broker. Feign indifference, she counseled herself.

"Philomena Piper."

"This is Sheila Adams, Ms. Piper. The seller is prepared to drop his price ten thousand dollars. Are you and Mr. Ramirez still interested?"

Philly took her time considering her options. She knew what Raul's vote would be. Still, money was money. Philly decided to follow Carpenter's approach and try to get directly to a figure somewhere in the middle of the original offer and counteroffer. Not because she thought it would be more effective, but mainly to get the damn negotiation done. She was sick to death of Raul bugging her and didn't want a protracted back and forth with the broker.

"You sound like a no-nonsense woman," Philly said. "Mr. Ramirez and I appreciate the seller getting back to us. I mean that. We have a price in mind and rather than come back with a counteroffer lower than that price, I'm going to tell you what we're willing to pay. Do we understand each other?"

"Yes, we do," Adams said.

Philly had no idea whether the broker was sincere. "Good. If there's a deal to be made, five hundred ten thousand will get this done."

Adams didn't respond immediately. "If you go up another five thousand, I have authority to bind the seller. Otherwise I will have to go back to him."

Philly hesitated only an instant. She thought that Adams was bluffing but there came a point at which it made no sense to argue. "Okay," she said. "We have a deal as to price."

"Excellent," Adams said. "I'll e-mail you the offer form. I'm very pleased."

"Mr. Ramirez and I have a lawyer," Philly said. "You'll need to send the offer to him as well." Philly rattled off their lawyer's contact information. Carpenter had prevailed on her to have Morton, one of his Sunday morning breakfast companions known as the Barristers, handle the legal work, and Morton had agreed to do so at a reduced hourly rate. And Philly was relieved to have that off her plate; she and Raul and Isabella would be better served by having a real estate expert protect their interests.

"Excellent," Adams repeated.

Carpenter had been putting off talking with Fred. His current justification for procrastination involved his thinking about why things had returned to normal with Maxine in the bedroom. By a process of elimination, he decided Philly was responsible for the change. The notion that she was flipping out and wouldn't be there for him must have bothered him more than he had realized. Her return to a semblance of their former working relationship had plainly come as a welcome relief.

Carpenter felt ridiculous. Rabbi Feldman hadn't specifically suggested that he establish a dialogue with Fred; but that was the spin Maxine had put on his meeting with the rabbi, and he had promised her that he would give it a try. In a bizarre way he didn't understand, the photograph of the black man made the foolishness he was about to undertake easier to face.

"I'd like you to meet Fred," Carpenter addressed the photograph. "Fred's the miserable motherfucker who's trying to kill me. If it weren't for that, I'm sure Fred would be a great guy to pal around with."

The man's unforgiving stare ratcheted up a notch.

"Work with me here," Carpenter entreated the photograph. "I can't stop thinking about the fact that while I'm going about my business or at least trying to, Fred here is multiplying out of control and trying to kill me. I've told Fred to fuck off and leave me alone but that hasn't solved my problem."

Carpenter thought he had done an evenhanded job of explaining his dilemma; however, the man's expression didn't change.

"Jump in any time, Fred, if I'm not being fair to you."

Carpenter studied the photograph. The man was paying attention.

"I'll make a deal with you, Fred," Carpenter said, watching the photograph for any change in the man's expression. "You keep things exactly the way they are for ten years and then do whatever you're going to do. What do you say?"

Carpenter blinked twice to make sure he wasn't imagining anything. No, there was no question that the man was flat out angry, his glare as harsh as Carpenter had ever seen it and there had been times over the last couple of years when his look had been merciless.

Carpenter closed his eyes. The man in the photograph had been trying to tell him something. There was a reason that the guy had become pissed off, and Carpenter believed he had figured it out. The guy had been trying to tell him that you don't negotiate with terrorists and whatever the hell Fred might be or might not be, it was damn near certain that Fred was a fucking terrorist.

Carpenter opened his eyes. The man's expression was severe but no longer angry.

"Forget what I said, Fred. There's no deal to be made. I had it right the first time. Fuck off!"

11

The Wilton Center for Creative Learning occupied a campus in a wooded, isolated section of the town that was about three quarters of a mile from a main road. When the access road ended and the school came suddenly into view, Philly took in snow covered grounds and widely-spaced, red brick buildings. Carpenter was driving; he followed the arrow that pointed to the administration building. Philly felt as if she'd been transported to a movie set for the type of tony prep school featured in *Outside Providence.* No wonder a year's costs ran tens of thousands of dollars.

Maryanne Fairmount appeared immediately after they announced themselves to a secretary. The school's Director of Educational Programming was blond and blue eyed with a relaxed demeanor that Philly warmed to. She directed them to a small conference room with a square, metal folding table and four folding chairs. Philly had expected a better-appointed room given the sprawling campus.

Fairmount listened attentively as Carpenter explained the purpose of their visit. She had brought a file folder and a notebook to the meeting and made several notations in the notebook as he spoke.

"Here at Wilton we don't usually involve ourselves in IEP hearings," Fairmount said. "I understand that you would like someone at the school to provide you with an expert opinion that Stonington's IEP won't work. That someone would probably be me. I have a Ph. D in early childhood education. But from the basic facts that you recounted, I have doubts about whether I can offer the opinion you're looking for."

"Has your school evaluated Jack?" Carpenter asked.

"Yes." Fairmount opened her file folder and removed a sheet of paper. "Based on the tests we've run, and what the Lawsons have told us, Jack has two conditions, Attention Deficit Hyperactivity Disorder and Intermittent Explosive Disorder, that combine to cause the biggest difficulties."

"The Lawsons complain that Jack's drugged out," Carpenter said. "They claim that the medications he's on make him sluggish."

"Our evaluation of Jack confirmed his sluggishness. But there are two sides to the coin. Since he went on the medications, Jack hasn't been nearly as aggressive or suddenly lost his temper with his classmates, and he isn't as disruptive in the classroom."

"The Lawsons say that your school has come up with a plan that would help Jack get off the medications he's on. We need to understand your approach."

"It's not complicated," Fairmount said. "We have resources here so we can provide students with a lot of one-on-one attention and monitoring. That gives us a chance to get out in front of things before they happen, and also to coach students on social and coping skills in real-time. We're prepared to do that for Jack. The-one-on one attention and monitoring should help deal with any safety issues should Jack act aggressively toward anyone as his meds are being cut back."

Carpenter frowned, lost in thought.

"I need to tell you that the IEP we've come up with might not work," Fairmont continued. "We've explained that to the Lawsons. Generally, our philosophy is to avoid medication that is making a child sluggish and lethargic. We're prepared to try an IEP that seeks to minimize medication. But there's no guaranty our plan will work."

"Why won't Stonington go with a plan like yours?" Carpenter asked.

"It's costly. The one-on-one monitoring is labor intensive. And my guess is that Stonington believes its plan is working. Keep in mind that Jack is doing reasonably well academically in comparison to the other students in his class. It's understandable for parents not to want their kid to be drugged out in any way. But it may turn out that Jack doesn't function as well without the levels of medication that he's on."

"Ms. Piper and I have discussed this," Carpenter said. "We see the drug issue as our best chance to get your school's IEP in place."

Fairmont regarded Carpenter evenly, but her expression didn't offer hope in Philly's estimation.

"Can Jack attend his school in Stonington without taking his meds?" Carpenter asked.

"No," Fairmont said. "Jack's IEP calls for medications at their current levels. Stonington probably wouldn't mainstream Jack to the extent it has if Jack went off or reduced his meds, and he'd be taken out of the regular classroom setting a lot more. The school district would likely say there would be a safety issue."

"Which comes back to Stonington's not wanting to foot the bill for one-on-one supervision for Jack," Carpenter said.

The Catch-22 situation was bugging Philly: Jack couldn't prove that a medication-tapering plan would work for him unless he tried it; but trying the plan was impossible in Stonington because one-on-one supervision was too expensive. "Could Jack attend Wilton for a month on a trial basis to see how your plan would work out?" she asked.

"If the Lawsons were willing to pay for a month of schooling, I suppose what you suggest is possible," Fairmont said. "But this would have to go to Wilton's board. If I had to guess, I would say that the board would reject such a proposal."

"See what you can find out about a one-month trial period here," Carpenter requested. "I think we've gone about as far as we can go for today."

Fairmont nodded and rose to shake hands.

"What do you think?" Carpenter asked once he had gotten has car on the main road.

"While we were talking, the idea of sending Jack to Stonington without his meds popped into my head. A really bad idea, I know. If Jack went nuts and hurt someone, the liability exposure would be enormous."

"I had the same wicked thought," Carpenter said. "I wonder whether Jack takes his meds on weekends. I'm guessing that's part of Stonington's plan for him."

"Probably," Philly concurred. "What if the kid got sick for a couple of weeks and went off his meds?"

Carpenter shook his head. "Obviously, we need to make an effort not to do something really stupid."

Philly sat back in her seat and watched the countryside fly by. The Wilton Center was out in the sticks. Some of the houses they drove by had no neighbors. So far, no business area or even a strip mall abutted the road they were on.

"Damn!" Carpenter suddenly exclaimed. "We've been looking at this the wrong way."

"What are you talking about?"

"This one-on-one supervision that's hanging Stonington up. What if the Lawsons paid someone to provide the one-on-one supervision in Stonington while their kid's meds were cut back? If that worked, we could then argue that Stonington had to provide the one-on-one or send the kid to Wilton."

"The one-on-one in Stonington is sure to be cheaper than a month at the Wilton Center," Philly said.

"You would think," Carpenter said. "We need to kick this around some more. Time is running out."

"By the way, thank you," Philly said.

"For what?"

"For contacting your lawyer buddy, Morton. If the house inspection comes back okay, you're looking at a future homeowner."

"No shit!"

"And I reached out to the bank that Philip's family uses in North Andover. I've nearly got a mortgage lined up."

"No shit!" Carpenter repeated.

"The good year we had financially in 2009 helped a lot."

"It's 2010 I'm worried about," Carpenter came back.

12

Philly had pretty much concluded her research on Marshall Hyde's Board of Bar Overseers disciplinary case. That Hyde hadn't used profanity in referring to Judge Porter on his blog was in his favor. If he had called the judge an asshole, he'd be toast; vulgarities directed at judges had earned lawyers disciplinary sanctions ranging from a reprimand to a ninety-day suspension. And truth did not appear to be a defense. The Board's position was that a vulgarity directed at a jurist brought disrespect to the legal profession and amounted to conduct unbecoming a lawyer. Indeed, in the heat of a trial, the Board had even disciplined lawyers who had directed profanities at opposing counsel.

Philly considered the actual words used by Hyde in his blog to describe Judge Porter: pigheaded, tyrant, and bully. She had also examined the Code of Judicial Conduct and had found a canon which instructed judges to be courteous and respectful to counsel who appeared before them.

In briefing her about Hyde's case, Carpenter had mentioned asking Hyde whether other lawyers would testify about Judge Porter's unfair conduct. Based on her research to date, Philly believed that Hyde would be immensely helped by lawyers supporting his assessment that Porter was in fact pigheaded, a tyrant, and a bully.

But there was a similar approach that might benefit Hyde as effectively. Philly wrote down her idea as soon as it popped into her head. After reaching the mandatory retirement age of seventy, many judges began second careers as mediators or arbitrators. Others turned to consulting. Obtaining a retired judge as an expert witness might tip the scales in Hyde's favor if such a judge evaluated Judge Porter's conduct and gave the opinion that the jurist had been pigheaded and a tyrant and a bully. Coming from one of Judge Porter's peers, such an opinion would have particular force.

Carpenter liked a short, concise memo listing key points and identifying courses of action. Philly had done her homework this time, and it was only a matter of writing her memo. The research had taken her mind off the baby growing inside her. Not to mention how badly she wanted a beer.

Carpenter couldn't even begin a conversation with Fred unless it was in the presence of the photograph of the black man positioned on the wall across from his desk. Long ago, he had decided against coming up with a name for the black man, opting to keep the guy at a remove. He figured the more impersonal the guy was, the more the guy would give him hardnosed but necessary feedback.

Carpenter thought about why he was trying to talk to Fred. It had to do with Rabbi Feldman telling him about this detective novel he had read in which the detective had named his brain tumor Bob. Giving a name to a brain tumor made some crazy sense; a brain tumor could be seen by diagnostic medical equipment because it had mass and took up space. But CLL was running loose in his blood, hiding out in the liquid, and giving his CLL the name Fred seemed forced. Still, Carpenter felt he owed it to the rabbi to engage Fred in conversation. The alternative was to admit that the rabbi didn't know squat.

"How's it going, Fred? You behaving yourself?"

The man in the photograph regarded him neutrally.

"You need to keep yourself under control, Fred. Because if you don't, I don't think I can face the chemotherapy and all the other shit that I'd have to go through to bring you under control. You wouldn't like it either. So what do you say? In the words of Rodney King, why can't we just get along?"

Carpenter glanced at the photograph. The man's neutral expression remained in place.

"You see, Fred, we're in this together. If I have to go through shit, so will you. We're joined at the fucking hip so get used to it."

Carpenter paused. The man in the photograph had yet to turn ballistic. Did that mean the guy approved of what he was saying to Fred or was just plain bored? Rabbi Feldman might be on to something, Carpenter reflected, because there was something liberating about talking to Fred. Not that dialogue with his CLL would accomplish anything. Still, chalk one up for the rabbi.

A knock on his door startled Carpenter. "Come in."

Philly entered and moved to his visitor chair. Carpenter couldn't tell if she was showing; the long sleeve white shirt that she hadn't tucked into her jeans made an assessment impossible.

"I sent you an email memo about Marshall Hyde," Philly said, and then she proceeded to go over what she had concluded. Listening to her, Carpenter couldn't figure out if she was back to her old self.

"I like the idea of a retired judge as an expert witness," Carpenter said, wondering if he would have thought of that approach. "That was creative. Nice job."

Usually when he gave Philly a compliment she brightened, showed animation. On this occasion, Carpenter didn't notice any change in her demeanor or expression. "You okay?" he asked.

"You know I hate it when people ask me that," Philly said. "I'm not okay; I'm coping. I hope that this goddamn house deal goes through so I can get out of my apartment. I'm counting on a change of scenery helping me, but the change involves Raul so who the hell knows how that's going to go."

"Is your mortgage financing set?"

"Yeah. We're getting a courtesy rate because of Philip's family's relationship with a bank. That's made Raul happy because he'd been budgeting a higher rate. Also, the house inspection came back okay."

Carpenter nodded. Maybe Philly was coping. She was moving forward and that had to be a positive sign.

"Were you talking to someone before I came in here?"

Carpenter rolled his eyes. "You don't want to know."

"Are you okay?" Philly followed up.

Faced with the question, Carpenter understood why Philly hated it. "Tell you what. I won't ask if you're okay if you return the favor."

"Deal," Philly said, smiling for the first time since she entered the office.

A Stewardess

13

Carpenter sat in his office, a rare burst of January sun coming through his window, and considered his caseload. Michelle Smith was a part-time stewardess he was representing in a suit filed against her former lover of five years, Jerome Singer. At the end of 2009, he had sued Singer on Smith's behalf seeking to hold Singer to his promise to pay Smith's tuition to business school. Singer's answer to Smith's complaint denied that any promise had been made. Smith had some money saved up but, at a tuition rate of $40,000 a year, those savings would be taking immediate, sizable hits, so she was counting on the case moving forward.

According to Smith, Jerome Singer had confirmed his promise to pay for her business school tuition in the presence of another couple over dinner. But the husband, Brian Jenkins, worked for Singer and Smith believed he would place job security above the truth. If Brian Jenkins declined to outright lie, he would probably experience a memory lapse when it came to the dinner discussion. Smith had no idea whether the wife, Teresa Jenkins, would lie for her husband; she didn't really know the woman.

Carpenter needed to depose the couple. Neither deposition should exceed an hour. He'd depose Brian Jenkins early in the morning and his wife late morning.

As he set about drafting the deposition notices, he was interrupted by the part-time receptionist. "A Mr. Anderson is on the line."

Carpenter couldn't place the name. Since his late fifties, whenever a name eluded him, Carpenter saw the memory loss as a sign that his brain cells were being overrun by that plaque associated with Alzheimer's. If that came into his life, Carpenter was certain that he would be better off if Fred ran amok and did him in.

"Carpenter."

"This is Wayne Anderson. I represent Wise Computer Consultants. You represent Herbert Stanton and Millie Lane."

Carpenter breathed a sigh of relief. He had never run into Anderson before. "What can I do for you?" he asked, as he started to google his opponent.

"I want to see whether it's possible to settle this matter quickly."

"What did you have in mind?"

Anderson paused briefly. "My client was free to fire your clients at any time for no reason. But there is the cost of litigation to consider, and my client is prepared to offer three thousand dollars to make the case go away."

Anderson was saying exactly what he would be saying were their roles reversed. Anderson probably assumed that Stanton's and Lane's case was being handled on a contingency fee basis, and had made a lowball, money offer. Carpenter half smiled to himself. The lawyers Carpenter hung around with at Sunday breakfasts—the Barristers as they were called by the diner's owner—unanimously took the view that any initial offer divisible by three was designed to make the attorney receiving the offer envision putting a precise amount of money in his pocket based on a standard one third contingency percentage. Ergo, a thousand-dollar bill had just been dangled in front of Carpenter's nose.

Carpenter located Anderson on Google. The lawyer was a partner in a twenty-lawyer Boston firm that specialized in business litigation. Anderson was about fifteen years his junior. His photograph revealed an unsmiling man with thick, dark hair and dark eyes behind rimless glasses.

"No, that's not acceptable," Carpenter said.

"What do you see as your clients' damages?" Anderson replied immediately.

"It's hard to predict," Carpenter fired back. "But the privacy rights violations could trigger a six-figure award."

Anderson laughed. "If that's the way you've evaluated this case, I guess it was a mistake on my part to call."

"Not at all," Carpenter said. "I appreciate your trying to sort this out quickly."

"I'll either be filing an answer to your complaint or moving to dismiss the complaint."

When Anderson hung up, Carpenter addressed the photograph across from his desk. "This is the first opposing lawyer I've talked to this year. I'd forgotten how much fun it is to bang my head against a wall."

Philly studied her draft of a letter to the superintendent of schools on behalf of John and Naomi Harrington. She'd led off with the assertion that Luke Harrington had never been abused; therefore, Superintendent Burnside had no business refusing to turn over Luke's records to his parents by hiding behind a statute that referred to abuse. Second, if Luke had been abused or was suspected of being abused, his parents had a right to know the details of any such claim. Finally, if abuse suspicions were directed at Luke's parents, any interest in keeping the school records secret was trumped by the Harringtons' right to clear their name of false accusations, and for that, they needed the school records.

Philly was halfway through editing her draft when she heard Carpenter's knock on her door—three short raps. "Come in."

Carpenter entered and dropped onto her visitor chair. "I want to run something by you."

Philly nodded, noting Carpenter's excitement.

"What if we were to hire a student intern or a part time associate?" Carpenter said.

Philly hadn't seen that coming. True, there had been an uptick in business in January, but it wasn't as if they were rolling in work. "What are you thinking?" she asked neutrally.

"I'm thinking that in five months give or take, you're going to be bonding with a baby. I'm thinking about how I rely on you for legal research because I've lost patience with doing research on my own. I'm thinking that right now, with one exception—Michelle Smith's case—every case we've got going is a case we're working on together."

Well, Carpenter was right about that. Still . . . "I don't like the idea of taking on overhead," Philly said. "It's not like we have a lot of billable hour business."

"I've thought of that," Carpenter said. "Maybe we don't have to actually employ anyone. Back before we began to seriously work with each other, didn't you have lawyers throwing odd jobs at you?"

Philly nodded. That first year when she was on her own had been filled with anxiety as she had tried to make ends meet. She had picked up several minor tort cases and had done some brief writing for other lawyers on a contract basis. It had been a lousy, stressful first year.

"Maybe we can get someone lined up on a contract basis to take on that role," Carpenter elaborated. "That way, we only throw out work assignments when there's work to be done."

"What if someone wants a guaranty of a certain amount of hours a week?" Philly asked, thinking about her own experience.

"Then we negotiate. Remember, the economy is still in the crapper. There are lawyers out there sucking wind. I'm betting there are lawyers who would be grateful for anything thrown their way."

Philly knew that Carpenter was thinking ahead the way she should have been thinking. It was hard to fault his plan. "Do you have anyone in mind?"

"Actually I do," Carpenter said. "I've got two people in mind but I have no idea whether they're in Massachusetts let alone available. Do you remember that case we had last year about the law student?"

"The one who was threatened with expulsion because he didn't report an honor code violation?"

"Right. When we had the meeting before the Honor Code Committee, there were two graduated students on the committee who impressed me. I was thinking about digging out their names and trying to run them down."

"Okay," Philly said. She saw no downside to exploring what resources were available for when she was out of action.

"One more thing," Carpenter said. "You had a good idea about a retired judge. I've got a retired judge coming in here to talk to us about Marshall Hyde's case. She was a criminal lawyer before she went on the superior court bench and she presided over a lot of criminal and civil trials. You're going to love her. The Honorable Margaret Dorset is a piece of work."

Philly nodded, feeling anxious. If Carpenter threw one more thing at her, she suspected her circuits would overload. Too much was happening in her life too fast.

"We're closing on the house next week," Philly said. "Raul, Isabella, and I are good to go."

"That's great!" Carpenter said.

One can only hope, Philly thought.

14

Sylvia and Max Lawson looked fearful. Regarding the couple across the conference room table, Philly said a silent prayer that the baby inside her would never have to deal with special education.

"I wanted you to come in because we're at a crucial stage," Carpenter said, and he described their meeting with The Wilton Center's Maryanne Fairmont. The Lawsons had probably been hoping that Fairmont would guaranty that the Center's individualized education program would work miracles for their son, and that Stonington's IEP was woefully inadequate. Her more limited advocacy was a visible disappointment.

"Here's what we recommend," Carpenter said. "We think you should hire a special aide for Jack and send the aide to school with your son. At the same time, we propose that Jack begin to be weaned from his medications in a manner approved by the Wilton Center and the Center's consulting physician. The idea behind this is to have the aide serve as someone who will ensure safety at Stonington by intervening if Jack starts to act in a way that's dangerous to anyone else."

The Lawsons had that deer-in-the-headlights glazed expression that Philly had seen on the faces of some of her own clients when she had come up with a radical approach to their problems.

"Why don't we do this at the Wilton Center?" Sylvia Lawson asked.

"Because we don't have the time for Ms. Fairmont to get her school's board to approve the plan. Also, the Wilton Center doesn't typically admit a student mid-year so you may not be able to have Jack attend there."

"Won't we have to get the Stonington school district to agree?" Max Lawson questioned.

Carpenter handed a draft letter to each of the Lawsons. Philly had reviewed the letter before this meeting. As the Lawsons read the document, Philly observed Max Lawson nod his head and offer up a weak smile.

Carpenter waited until the Lawsons looked up. "If you go along with what we're suggesting, I want to deliver this letter to the superintendent tomorrow. It lays out exactly what we intend to do."

"What if Burnside says no," Sylvia Lawson asked.

"You'll note that this letter doesn't ask for the superintendent's permission," Carpenter came back. "But if Burnside writes back that Jack won't be permitted to attend school under the conditions set out in this letter, then we have two choices. We either go ahead without his approval, or try to get a court to allow the plan to go forward. I'd say we're probably locked into going to court."

Max Lawson's momentary upbeat expression disappeared. "Won't a court suit be expensive?" he asked.

"Yes. We're prepared to deal with the preliminary phase of the court suit for a flat rate of five thousand dollars. Our hourly charges would greatly exceed that amount."

"Sylvia Lawson's shoulders sagged. "This whole thing makes me want to cry."

"To win your hearing challenging Jack's current IEP," Carpenter said, "I believe we need something more than Ms. Fairmont testifying that the Wilton Center IEP *might* work. She can't guaranty that her school's IEP *will* work. In my opinion, we need some hard data that hopefully will show that one-on-one supervision addresses safety concerns and that getting Jack off his medicines makes him more alert and social."

"What if that causes him to lash out instead?" Max Lawson asked.

"Then it may be that taking him off his medications is a bad idea," Carpenter said. "If Jack becomes violent but you still think this is what you want for your son, then you may have to pay privately for a place like The Wilton Center which is willing to deal with the safety issue by providing a one-on-one monitor for Jack. But keep in mind that if Jack cannot be controlled without medication, I suspect that Wilton won't admit him."

"I don't know what to do," Sylvia Lawson said despairingly.

The familiar knot was back in Philly's stomach. How many times would she have to make decisions for the kid she was carrying in her belly, decisions that could blow up in her face? And decisions she'd have to make alone.

"I want your permission to deliver the letter I've drafted," Carpenter said forcefully. "There is no downside to delivering the letter. If the letter is rebuffed, it may help Jack's case at the hearing on the IEP."

Max Lawson nodded. "I think you're right." He glanced at his wife. "Send the letter and let us know what happens."

"You need to find someone to accompany Jack at school," Carpenter reminded the couple. "If Burnside goes along with what's in the letter, we need to be ready to follow through."

"Craig's List," Sylvia Lawson said. "It's a place to start."

Philly took in Carpenter's puzzlement. The geezer really did live in the past, she thought.

February

Philly's Untitled Playlist

The Old Apartment

Bare Naked Ladies

15

Philly had difficulty focusing as Carpenter and retired superior court judge Margaret Dorset exchanged greetings that segued into war stories. Carpenter had tried several cases before Dorset and was giving her grief over some of her evidentiary rulings which he seemed to remember as if they occurred yesterday. Dorset apparently also had encyclopedic recall of the cases she had presided over; she vigorously defended her rulings and chastised Carpenter for shoddy legal research. In ordinary circumstances, Philly would be hanging on their every word, anxious to soak up practical tips. But today she remained fixated on the fact that at this very moment she might be a homeowner.

Philly had thought that the purchase of a home would involve a degree of pomp and circumstance. Therefore, it was somewhat of a letdown to hear from their lawyer that because all the necessary documents had been signed in advance, the closing would be a "paper closing" conducted at the registry of deeds with neither buyer nor seller in attendance. A paralegal would see that the deed and mortgage were recorded, and then money would be wired to the seller from the lending bank in North Andover and from the clients' account which held the twenty percent down payment that she and Raul and Isabella were putting up. And that was that.

Philly tried to regain focus. The byplay between Carpenter and Dorset was good-natured. Dorset, who was well past the age-seventy, mandatory retirement age for judges, had white hair curled up at her shoulders, washed out pale blue eyes, saggy cheeks and an impressive double chin. The woman was heavy set and carried herself with authority. Philly imagined sparks flying when the former judge and Carpenter had squared off in a courtroom. After her retirement from the bench, Dorset had joined a company that offered mediation services and employed several other retired judges.

"So out of all the retired judges around, why me?" Dorset directed at Carpenter.

"Because you were always a pain in the ass and I think I need a pain in the ass for this case."

Dorset let loose with an impressive belly laugh. "I'm not as big a pain in the ass as I used to be," she confessed when her laughter subsided.

"Just so long as you haven't lost the knack, I'm okay with that."

"You always were a pisser, Carpenter. Okay, then. I need more detail."

Carpenter went over the background of Marshall Hyde's Board of Bar Overseers disciplinary case, providing Dorset with a copy of Hyde's blog as he did so. Then he nodded in Philly's direction and she filled the former judge in on her research on Board of Bar Overseers case law precedent.

Dorset considered the facts presented to her with a serious, unreadable expression. Philly assessed that she probably had the right temperament to be a judge. She took in everything and nothing seemed to faze her.

"Let's take the things your client said one at a time," Dorset said, "starting with pigheaded. Not an ideal choice of words from your client, but I've been called worse."

"Really!" Carpenter exclaimed.

"I remember a lawyer calling one of my rulings asinine, insane, insensitive, and a travesty of justice. My last year on the bench a woman lawyer called me an old fart."

Carpenter looked stunned. "What did you do?" he asked.

"Nothing," Dorset said. "In each case I said the same thing: 'I don't believe I heard you correctly, but my hearing might pick up if you say it again.'"

"An old fart . . ." Carpenter muttered.

"That probably crossed the line," Dorset said. "One of my failings as a judge may have been that I didn't take the trappings of the position as seriously as perhaps I should have. When I was on the bench, I always tried to remember what it was like to try cases. Some cases are bitterly contested and tempers flare. Lawyers get invested in their clients' position, and sometimes they get carried away. I know I did when I was practicing. So I tried to cut lawyers some slack when their emotions, passion, or rhetoric got away from them. Besides, I have a very thick skin."

Carpenter stared at her in astonishment. "You almost sound reasonable. What happened to the Judge Dorset I used to know? Who is this imposter?"

Judge Dorset shrugged. "Besides," she added, "I liked to mix it up with lawyers."

Philly wondered whether Carpenter would want Dorset to testify about being called an old fart; he probably would.

"I sometimes worked in the first criminal session where this Judge Porter sits. I can tell you that his scheduling criminal trials in two or three weeks is a form of bullying and he showed pigheadedness by not giving consideration to lawyers' difficulties with his deadlines. In my opinion, a busy criminal defense lawyer needs more time to file motions and interview witnesses not to mention prepare for trial. Bullying comes in because as your client points out in his blog, the judge was essentially forcing defendants to waive their right to a speedy trial by seeking to continue the unrealistic trial dates this judge was setting. Tyrant is a closer call, but a case could be made that Porter was using his position in the way a despot would govern."

Philly wrote down Dorset's last statement in detail.

"The board claims that our client brought disrespect upon the legal profession by using the words he did," Carpenter said. "Any thoughts?"

"It's not like your Mr. Hyde lost his temper in court and unloaded on the judge in front of a packed courtroom. I look at it more as an editorial or op ed piece. Suppose someone had observed Judge Porter in court and wrote a letter to the editor of a newspaper in which the letter writer called Porter exactly what your client called him. I think that would be fair editorial comment. I don't believe any lawyer gives up his first amendment rights to protest something when he becomes a member of the bar."

"You better want this job," Carpenter said.

"What if I don't?"

"Tough shit. You're hired anyway."

Philly stared at her phone willing it to ring and then her intercom sounded. "A Mr. Morton is on the line for you," the part-time receptionist said.

Philly grabbed her phone. "I hope you have good news for me."

"Congratulations," Morton said. "You are now a homeowner."

Philly was overcome with relief. She hoped to have her belongings and furniture transferred from her Somerville apartment to her new home in Brighton before the week was out.

"I really appreciate all you've done," Philly said.

"I didn't do anything," Morton disclaimed. "I turned everything over to a paralegal and stayed out of the way."

"You reviewed the closing documents and you came up with an agreement for us to sign if one of us died or wanted out. We're all very grateful."

"Don't mention it," Morton said, and Philly wondered whether all the Barristers used that phrase to deflect praise when they were paid a complement. "By the way, my paralegal tells me that this guy Raul you went in with can talk your ear off."

"You don't know the half of it," Philly said.

When Morton rang off, Philly decided to attend to some personal business. She took out her check book and paid the bills that should have been paid last month. Then she wrote out a $100 check to Fidelity Investments, an account that Raul had set up for her back when they were together.

On a whim, Philly went online to view her Fidelity account. With the economy inching up, the account balance had been improving of late but . . . that couldn't be right! The account history listed a deposit into her core cash account of $3,000 made last week. But she hadn't made the deposit. What the hell?

Philly thought of calling the Fidelity agent assigned to her, a man who also worked with Raul's account. Raul! Of course! Somehow he had arranged to deposit money into her account for the legal services Philly had provided to Isabella's uncle.

Philly considered her options. She could call Fidelity to undo the deposit. She could do nothing. She could use the money to buy something for their new house. Shit! Raul had this way of doing something for you that made you feel beholden to him.

Carpenter preached that when you didn't know what to do, do nothing. She decided to steer that course for the time being.

A Hedge Fund Data Analyst

16

"A Mr. Ramirez is on the line for you," the part-time receptionist announced shortly after Philly arrived at her office the following day.

Philly picked up her phone more anxious and irritated than pleased that Raul had called. This reaction boded poorly for their joint home ownership relationship.

"Hi Raul."

"My dearest Philly! Are you as excited about our new home as Isabella and I are?"

"Probably not," Philly said, and immediately wondered whether she had turned into a first-class bitch where Raul was concerned.

"You are always joking," Raul said. "Your sense of humor will be a major asset to our home owning experience."

Philly kept her mouth shut to avoid saying something that even Raul would take as non-humorous.

"I have recommended you to an acquaintance," Raul continued. "He is desperately in need of a lawyer and I immediately thought of you."

"I appreciate that," Philly said, meaning it. Funny how the thought of a new client could change your attitude toward someone who drove you nuts.

"His name is Frederick Chun and he worked for a hedge fund that I am familiar with. We became acquainted at an educational seminar on investment strategies and exchanged business cards. We have talked on the phone from time to time exchanging ideas. Frederick called me the other day to say he got fired."

"Do you know why he was fired?" Philly asked.

"He received an e-mail on his work computer with a link to what may be a pornographic website."

Philly's enthusiasm for the potential new case nosedived. "It's hard to blame the employer for firing your friend."

"You do not understand, dear Philly. The e-mail was sent to Frederick by a friend. Frederick never looked at the link and certainly never asked for it. He deleted the e-mail as soon as he read the subject line. He admonished his friend never to send him anything like that again. You do not know Frederick. He is a very upstanding individual of even temperament. He would never use his firm's computer for anything improper."

Perhaps, Philly thought, there was something to this case after all.

"Thanks Raul. I appreciate it. I'll wait to hear from your friend. When are you moving in?"

"Tomorrow. We are getting friends to help us. We briefly thought of hiring movers, but we find it necessary to pinch pennies."

Philly had opted for movers but decided to keep that fact to herself. Philip's trust fund money would pay for the move. "I'll be joining you two days later."

"Excellent. Then we will be a new extended family. Isabella and I can barely contain our excitement."

Try, Philly thought. But what she said was, "I'm excited too."

"There's a Craig Lannon calling for you," the part-time receptionist said over his intercom. "He said he represented the Town of Stonington."

"Carpenter."

"Craig Lannon. My firm represents the Town of Stonington. One of my partners is the town counsel. I'm getting back to you on the letter you wrote to Superintendent Burnside on behalf of the Lawsons."

That was quick, Carpenter thought. The school district must have come to an immediate decision on what it was going to do. "Thanks for calling."

"Well, you're not going to be happy with what I'm going to say. I'll provide you with a formal response, but I wanted to give you a courtesy call on my client's position. The school district considers Jack Lawson to be a threat to safety if he reduces his medications. That's the bottom line. His current IEP is appropriate and it's working fine. The school district doesn't want that to change."

"What do you mean a threat to safety?"

"I'm sure that you're familiar with the Lawson boy's file and history," Lannon said. "He was put on medications because of harmful behavior. Since he's been on the medications, the inappropriately aggressive behavior stopped."

"My client has dealt with the safety issue," Carpenter responded. "A competent individual will accompany Jack to school and watch him at all times. The medications he's on leaves him loopy and listless. That's not acceptable."

"I don't think that it's productive for us to debate this matter," Lannon said. "The two of us will not be able to work it out."

"Thanks for the heads up."

"You're welcome. Are you able to share with me your next move?"

"No," Carpenter said, and ended the call.

"A Mr. Chun is on the line for you," the receptionist announced to Philly.

"Philomena Piper."

"This is Frederick Chun. Raul gave me your name."

"Raul filled me in generally about why you're calling. How can I help you?"

"I want my goddamn job back!" Chun said immediately. "I can't stop my friends from sending me dumb shit. I don't even know what that asshole Alan sent to me. I deleted it as soon as I saw the words *Sexy Russian Vixens.* I can't let it get out that I was fired because of porn."

Raul had said Chun was even-tempered, but Chun sounded unglued. True, he had reason to be unhinged since, after all, he'd lost his job. Philly gathered her thoughts, took several deep breaths. "What's the name of the company you worked for?"

"Crowe Investment Strategies."

"What was the company's computer policy?"

"We weren't supposed to use the company's computer for personal use during work time."

"Did you give friends your office computer e-mail address?"

"Some had it. Before I would go home for the day, I'd send some personal messages on the office computer. Someone getting a personal message could reply directly to my office. But I figured I was on my own time. Besides all company employees do that."

Chun was right. It was simply more convenient to bang out some personal messages instead of going on the net to access your personal e-mail account. "Who's this guy Alan?"

"He's my brain-dead friend who sent me the porn. I swear to God I'd like to wring his fucking neck!"

"Are you sure he sent you porn?"

Chun didn't answer immediately. "Well, I never clicked on the link he sent. But knowing Alan, I'd guess it was porn."

"Are you able to send me your company's computer use policy by e-mail?"

"Yeah. I printed it out and I've got it somewhere."

Philly provided her contact information and received Chun's in exchange. They made an appointment to meet the following day.

17

They were in Carpenter's office, a gloomy February sky outside, and the Lawsons on his speaker phone.

"You're saying we should go to court," Max Lawson said after Carpenter had related his telephone discussion with the Stonington school district's lawyer and had advised the couple how he wanted to proceed.

"That's my recommendation," Carpenter confirmed. "But I want to be clear that it's a tossup whether a court will let Jack go to school with a monitor in place and his medications reduced."

"Why don't we wait to see whether the Wilton Center's board will permit Jack to go there for a month?" Sylvia Lawson asked.

"That's not an option," Carpenter said. "Maryanne Fairmont just received an answer from the school's president informally and he said no. They won't admit students for one-month periods."

"Go for it," Max Lawson said. "If I remember, the legal fees are capped at five thousand through the court hearing."

"That's right," Carpenter said. "There's a court filing fee of about three hundred dollars on top of that."

"Okay," Max Lawson said. "Are you all right with this, honey?"

"I guess so," Sylvia Lawson said without conviction.

Carpenter turned off his speaker phone, and immediately became lost in thought. "I hope you're okay with my low-balling the legal fees on this," he led off.

"I am," Philly said. Carpenter was convinced that ordinary people couldn't afford a lawyer and she concurred in his view. At least some cash would be coming in for their efforts. It promised to be a grinding year when it came to cash flow with no big payoff to ease the strain.

"Why don't I do the complaint and legal memorandum and you do the affidavits," Philly suggested, deciding to beat Carpenter to the punch and propose the usual way they divided up work on a lawsuit.

Carpenter nodded. "Remember, short and sweet."

"Got it, boss," Philly said, using a term that she knew irked Carpenter.

"You're trying to aggravate me, right?"

"That's part of my job," Philly said, grinning.

When Philly left his office, Carpenter began to list the points he wanted Maryanne Fairmont to make in an affidavit. Her testimony would likely determine whether the Lawsons got an injunction. As he wrote, he envisioned the Wilton Center bureaucracy objecting to the school's Director of Educational Programming getting involved in a lawsuit. No doubt some Wilton Center lawyer would scrutinize and pick apart any affidavit he prepared for Fairmont. Well, there were some things he could control and some he couldn't. Until the affidavit was done and presented to Fairmont, he wouldn't know which was which.

Frederick Chun was not what Philly expected. She had envisioned a nerdy, bespectacled, Asian guy sporting a cowlick and a pocket protector. She had suspected that Chun was a backroom grunt at Crowe Investment Strategies who ran numbers for the company. Instead, Chun turned out to be tall and rugged looking with a swimmer's build. He had a pencil thin moustache and a scraggly chin goatee. Once his ski parka was removed, Philly saw that he was dressed in black: black jeans, black turtle neck sweater, black sneakers and black socks. Carpenter was staring at Chun with the impassive look he bestowed on any potential client.

"Can you help me?" Chun asked as soon as he took a chair in the conference room.

"A qualified maybe," Philly said. "Let's start with your company's computer policy. It says and I quote: 'Use of any company computer for personal use during working hours is strictly prohibited. A violation of this policy could result in dismissal.'"

"I didn't use my computer for personal use," Chun protested. "All I did was hit delete."

"Did you hit delete during working hours?" Philly asked.

"Yes," Chun said, pulling on his goatee. "I saw the subject line of my friend's e-mail, and I permanently deleted the e-mail. That took about five seconds of precious work time."

"Do other employees send personal e-mails on the company's computers before or after or during work time?" Carpenter interjected.

Chun's look turned quizzical. "Do you really have to ask? Of course they do. We all do it. Where have you been?"

Philly suppressed a smile. Carpenter was clueless about standard operating procedure for any generation younger than his.

"How long had you worked there before you got fired?" Carpenter changed the subject.

"Two years, three months and thirteen days. But who's counting?"

"How were your employee evaluations?" Philly asked.

"Good. I got raises and bonuses. I was willing to do whatever they asked. I never complained."

"How big a company is Crowe?" Philly continued.

"There's about seventy employees."

"How many are . . . what is the politically correct term . . . Asian? Oriental?"

"There's a Korean woman and me. I don't care what term you use. I'm Chinese by the way."

"Has anyone else been fired because porn showed up on the person's computer?"

"I don't think so, but I have no way of knowing."

Philly paused and reviewed her notes. She glanced Carpenter's way and he nodded for her to proceed.

"Here's what we think," Philly said. "You were an employee at will. That means that you could be fired for any reason or no reason. Therefore, getting your job back is a long shot."

Chun frowned, visibly disappointed, and again reached for his goatee.

"You should immediately file for unemployment compensation. If the company opposes your application, it will give us an idea of where the company's head is at."

"I already filed," Chun said. "I didn't see a reason not to. Plus, I need the money."

"Good thinking," Philly said. "Next, if you hire me, I'll write a demand letter to the company asking the company to take you back. The gist of the letter will be that you didn't violate the company's computer policy and the reason for firing you was wrong."

Chun pondered the suggested approach. "What good's the letter going to do if they could have fired my ass for no reason?"

Philly noticed that Carpenter's hard stare was missing; he must have been impressed by Chun's good question.

"You raise a valid point," Philly said. "But we need to send the letter anyway for you to have any chance of getting your job back. The letter will also say that you are considering discrimination claims."

"Won't that piss them off?" Chun protested. "If they weren't going to fight me on unemployment compensation, wouldn't a letter that accused them of discrimination make them decide to fight me on everything?"

"That's a risk," Philly conceded, impressed with Chun's ability to analyze the pros and cons of the approach she had suggested. "Where we're going with all this is to try to get a lawyer involved on the other side. Neither Mr. Carpenter nor I believe that you did anything wrong. Maybe a lawyer reviewing the case will reach the same conclusion and advise your company accordingly."

"How much is all this going to cost?" Chun asked.

"My hourly rate is two hundred dollars," Philly said.

"Jesus! What about taking my case on a contingency?"

"We think it's a long shot that you'll recover any money," Philly said. "For us, a contingency doesn't seem like the way to go here."

"Shit!" Chun muttered. "I guess I better get my ass in gear and look for a new job."

"That would be prudent," Philly said.

"Can you find out whether porn showed up on the computer of any other employee?" Carpenter asked.

Chun reflected for a moment. "There's this guy in the company's IT department that I got to know pretty well. We went out drinking a few times. I'll call him on his cell, but I'm pretty sure he's not going to help me. Why the hell would he put his job at risk?"

"Make the call," Carpenter advised.

Chun nodded. "There's something else you should know. William Crowe, the guy who founded the company, is basically a prick."

As this bit of intelligence hung in the air, Philly tried to think through the legal fee issue that they needed to come back to. "Let me make a suggestion," she directed at Chun. "I'll charge you a flat rate of two hundred dollars to write the demand letter to the company. You'll approve it before it goes out. I'll let you know what response the letter gets, and then we'll talk. In the meantime, you call your IT buddy and send me an e-mail about what he has to say."

As Chun pondered her proposal, Philly wondered whether he was one of those guys who lived paycheck to paycheck regardless of whether he was being paid decent money.

"I'll send you an engagement letter spelling all this out. Right now, you're only on the hook for two hundred dollars. We'll talk about next steps when we get a little more information."

Chun nodded. "You're being more than fair. I appreciate it."

Philly returned to the conference room after showing Chun out. She sat back down and softly stroked her belly. Her showing was slight but plainly noticeable if you took the time to look. Fuck. Maternity clothes would soon be unavoidable. On top of that, lately she was feeling horny as hell. She'd read that this was a natural phase of pregnancy, but without Philip, what the hell was she supposed to do?

"What are you thinking about?" Carpenter asked.

"Maternity clothes. Feeling horny. Moving my shit into the house we just bought. The Lawson pleadings I need to pound out. Those are the main points."

"Sorry I asked. By the way, I think you handled Mr. Chun exactly right."

"Not much of a legal fee," Philly noted.

Carpenter shrugged. "I know. But you're trying to help the guy. He got screwed over. Let's turn over a few more cards before we decide to play or fold."

"Did I mention I get ravenously hungry out of the blue?"

Carpenter stood up. "I've heard more than I want to hear."

18

Philly put on her winter parka, opened the front door, and watched the moving van pull up. It was bitter cold outside with a slushy mix of snow and salt covering the streets and sidewalks. The move was going to cost her. She hadn't pre-packed much of anything and the movers had ended up doing the lion's share of the packing. She considered that money well spent. Before going to bed last night, she had knocked off a draft of the complaint to be filed on behalf of the Lawsons and had outlined the legal memorandum that needed to back up the complaint. If she'd had to pack, those tasks wouldn't have gotten done.

The two movers were built like pianos. They wore metal toed work boots and baggy, cut-short dungarees that reached slightly below their knees. Each sported a blond ponytail sticking out of a Boston Bruins cap. Their thick, pale legs were probably impervious to the cold. Frick and Frack Movers had come highly recommended.

Philly introduced herself. "Everything with a red sticker goes into the bedroom with a red piece of paper pasted on the door. Green stickers go in the room with a green sticker on the door. Everything else gets parked in the living room. From there a few items will go to the second floor."

"We'll be through before you know it," one of the movers said. Philly decided, arbitrarily, that the speaker was Frick and the other guy Frack.

Philly hadn't wanted to watch the parade of her possessions and Philip's possessions enter the house, so Raul had offered to man the front door and help the movers and she had taken him up on the offer. She hung out in the kitchen already cluttered with Raul's and Isabella's kitchenware. The kitchen window at the rear of the house faced the back of another house with a backyard as small as their own. A few snowflakes trickled past the window to the ground as if they had been squeezed out of the steel gray sky. Now that the move was actually happening, she fought a feeling of panic at having to deal with this new, major life change. Reflexively she rubbed her belly as she listened to the front door open and close, Raul giving directions, the sound of heavy items being set down on the living room floor. For a brief moment, she imagined Philip's arm around her, his blue eyes taking in the scene at the back of the house. But no. "It's you and me, baby," she whispered softly, watching the snow pick up as she continued to rub her belly.

"Philly, we could use your help," Raul called from the living room.

Frick and Frack were drinking Cokes that Raul had provided. They didn't appear winded and made short work of the drinks. Philly pointed to the items that needed to go to her second-floor office and, in short order, the living room began to clear.

Philly stood in the doorway of her bedroom to assess the situation. The bed wasn't quite where she wanted it to be. She would ask the movers to rearrange the bed and dresser.

The baby's room lacked any piece of furniture. For the moment it was a staging area filled with boxes that needed to get unpacked.

"How are you, Philly?"

Raul had come up beside her silently and, on this occasion, she didn't mind his question. "Nervous," she said.

"I understand. As our friends helped us move in, Isabella and I had butterflies in our stomachs. You will see. In a day, the butterflies will be gone."

"I hope this works," Philly said.

"Of course it will work," Raul exclaimed. "Do not be downcast, Philly. We are about to start an adventure together. You, me, Isabella, and your baby. I am looking forward to it."

Philly sighed. Maybe she should stop fighting Raul's enthusiasm and let it waft her forward. For there was no turning back now.

19

Philly logged into her work computer from her new home office and began to review an e-mail from Frederick Chun. She paused half way through and stared out the window, taking in the two-story house next to hers on the street where she now lived. The closeness of the neighboring building reminded her of Fall River where she'd grown up: houses nestled close together, no side yards to speak of, windows often providing a clear view of what was going on next door.

Her new office contained the two desks that she and Philip had used in their joint office in their Somerville apartment. Back there, even facing away from each other, Philip's close presence was a shared intimacy. But here she was alone.

At least the morning had gotten off to a good start. At nine, a knock on her bedroom door was followed by Isabella bringing her a cup of coffee, chiding her for being a sleepyhead. Philly couldn't remember when she had slept so late. Isabella had sat on her bed and chatted, all small talk, and Philly had let her housemate's words wash over her, not paying careful attention, but grateful for the company. It turned out that Raul had saved her some of the breakfast he'd made hours earlier.

Now she forced herself to read Chun's email slowly. Her client's IT friend refused to get involved and disclaimed any knowledge of any company employee receiving pornography. But the friend had told Chun that the company's server would show that a fair number of Crowe Investment employees received and sent dirty jokes in e-mails. Chun wanted to know whether this intelligence helped his case. In her e-mail back to Chun, Philly hedged her bets, saying only that it might.

She began a draft of a letter on Chun's behalf to Crowe Investment Strategies. Chun did not violate any company policy. He promptly deleted an inappropriate, unsolicited e-mail and never viewed the e-mail's link. His employer evaluations proved he was a good worker. A company culture was tolerated in which tasteless, off-color jokes were routinely received and sent by company employees on their work computers. The company should consider the consequences of terminating a member of a discrete ethnic minority in circumstances where the employee did nothing wrong. Philly concluded the letter by requesting a meeting on Chun's behalf to discuss the company's reversing the decision to terminate his employment.

She edited the draft and fired it off to Carpenter for his comments. Then she leaned back in her chair and let her mind drift as she looked out her window. When the baby came, this room would become her principal office. Carpenter was going to have to adjust to their interacting mostly by phone and e-mail. She might have to give up her Boston office to cut back on expenses. Carpenter would have a serious conniption fit if she even broached that idea. And then there was childcare. How old did a kid have to be before you could unload it into a daycare arrangement? Or would she ever want to trust strangers with her kid?

Philly left her computer on and went downstairs. The living room-dining room area had taken shape. The furniture from her apartment didn't clash too violently with a couch and chairs that belonged to Raul and Isabella and, of all things, the couple had come with a good-sized flat screen TV. They were all using the basement for storage. Raul had helped her bring her bicycles to the basement as well as the assorted boxes that contained items that didn't have to be unpacked immediately. Philly envisioned the boxes sitting unopened for years as life with a baby overwhelmed her.

Philly sat down in one of the easy chairs Raul and Isabella had brought to the move. The couple was out, and she felt restless in the house by herself. If Philip were around now he would be urging her to go on a bike ride with him. He had bought her a mountain bike and the light-weight warm clothing that made biking doable in winter. It seemed like an extraordinary effort to lug her bike up from the basement, fill the tires, and get into biking gear. She hadn't been on a bike outdoors since Philip had been killed. She knew what Philip would want her to do. "What the hell," she said and headed for the basement.

There were times when Carpenter enjoyed going to his office on a weekend. This wasn't one of them. Usually the absence of ringing phones and fellow human beings helped him to focus on the problem of the moment. But today, the goal of finalizing the court complaint that needed to be filed on behalf of Max and Sylvia Lawson eluded him. Thoughts of Philly had him distracted. Earlier she had sent him an e-mail with an attached draft letter she had written on behalf of Frederick Chun. Receiving the e-mail—he had yet to read it through—drove home that Philly would soon be unavailable and that they had made no firm plans on how to deal with her absence. She hadn't been overly receptive to his idea of lining up some backup contract labor. Knowing Philly, she probably hadn't thought through what was going to happen to her cases while she was dealing with a newborn. Maybe she had it in her head that he would simply step in and deal with her work.

Carpenter had tracked down the names and contact information of the two former Spenser New England School of Law students he was interested in talking to. Simon Jeffries and Rachel Boyle had stood up to an abrasive law school professor during a hearing before the law school's Honor Code Committee in which Carpenter had been involved the previous year. It had taken guts to stand up to the professor who fit Malcolm Hyde's choice of words very well: pigheaded, tyrant, bully.

Carpenter knew that he wouldn't be able to concentrate on the Lawsons' court complaint until he had tried to contact Jeffries and Boyle. He decided to start with Jeffries whom he vaguely recalled as a skinny, serious young man with slicked back dark hair. His telephone exchange was Boston.

"Jeffries."

Carpenter smiled. Here was another lawyer who led off with his last name.

"My name is Carpenter. I had a case before the Spenser School of Law Honor Code Committee representing a student who was accused of failing to report an alleged incident of cheating. You were a student representative on the Committee."

"I remember you and the case. What can I do for you?"

Carpenter laid out what he had in mind. Jeffries didn't interrupt.

"I'm interested," Jeffries said.

"What are you doing now?" Carpenter asked.

"Struggling," Jeffries came back immediately. "I'm working out of my apartment. I'm dealing with a few landlord tenant cases. I'm doing some volunteering for legal services. Plus, I wait tables."

"Have you looked for a law job?" Carpenter asked.

"That hasn't gone particularly well. I'm interested in working for a firm, but I graduated in the middle of my class. I was working during law school and couldn't put in the time it took to get good grades."

"I was told you had a reputation for taking on professors."

"What can I say. I like to argue."

"There was another student on the Honor Code Committee that I'm interested in. Rachel Boyle. Do you know what she's up to?"

Jeffries paused. Perhaps the young man didn't want anyone else to get a chance at the spillover legal work he was offering.

"Rachel's around," Jeffries said. "I actually bumped into her a few weeks back. She's working at a firm doing part time paralegal work. The firm won't take her on as a lawyer. Rachel doesn't have my problem with grades. She graduated near or at the top of our class."

Carpenter felt bad for the two recent law school grads. The down economy was putting a lot of dreams on hold.

"Rachel's great," Jeffries added. "She's smart as hell."

"I'm going to talk to her," Carpenter said. "Let me have your e-mail address, and I'll send you my contact information."

His telephone call with Rachel Boyle went well. Boyle expressed some understandable bitterness at being relegated to paralegal status. What Carpenter liked about each young lawyer was the refusal to beg or to come on as overeager; he knew that each wanted to be working on real cases and admired their restrained responses to his questions. He didn't envy them. They'd be competing for jobs with experienced lawyers who had been laid off and were probably willing to work for a lot less money than they had been making. At what point, he wondered, did a law school graduate come to the realization that his or her chosen profession wasn't going to pan out? What was the final straw that made you throw in the towel and kiss a three-year course of study goodbye?

Carpenter had tried to sound low key and matter-of-fact; he hadn't wanted to get the young lawyers' hopes up, yet he knew that they would now be obsessing over the remote opportunity he had dangled in front of them, praying it would pan out. Since none of the active cases he and Philly were handling involved big money, maybe it would turn out that he'd never follow up on the overtures he had made to Jeffries and Boyle.

With his outreach calls concluded, Carpenter made short work of the revisions to the Lawsons' complaint. The document would be filed Monday and he'd try to get a court hearing later in the week. His next task was to grind out affidavits for Sylvia Lawson and Maryanne Fairmont. Then he'd have to pay attention to what Philly proposed to do for Frederick Chun. Which meant that he wasn't going to be leaving his office any time soon to hook up with Maxine. There was work on his plate but not a lot of money to be made off any of it. It could be worse, he thought. He could have no work at all.

Philly struggled to get her mountain bike up the three steps to her front door and then had to balance the bike while she fished out her door key, opened the door, and maneuvered the bike into the front hallway. She glanced behind her at the street. The setting sun was a dull orange ball partially obscured by gray clouds. The few leafless trees on the street looked forlorn. Lights were on in neighboring houses, but no one was outside. It had been great to get outdoors and freeze her face off. Philly knew that she had scored a point with Philip.

"Let me help you!"

Raul took charge of her bike and closed the door behind her. "It is winter, Philly. What were you doing riding a bike in the freezing cold in your delicate condition?" Raul did look genuinely concerned.

Philly counted backwards from ten. It was too soon to kill Raul: they'd only been living in the same house for a few days; fairness entitled him to at least a week to live.

"I'm not a fucking invalid, for Christ's sake. When I can, I'm going to bike. It's something I love to do. And if I ever hear the words *delicate condition* leave your lips again, I'm going to have to hurt you."

Philly turned. Isabella was watching them from the doorway to the kitchen, smiling. "Raul wants to protect you. You know he means well."

"I know," Philly said, forcing the words out.

"Raul, take Philly's bike to the basement," Isabella directed. "I'm cooking tonight. We are mostly unpacked. It's a time to celebrate."

"Sounds good," Philly said. She didn't want cooking duties to fall exclusively on Raul and Isabella. Somehow, on top of everything else on her plate, she was going to have to learn to cook.

"Dinner is in an hour and fifteen minutes," Isabella said before retreating to the kitchen.

Raul hadn't moved; he was still holding Philly's bike. "We need to be nice to each other," he said, before rolling the bike toward the door to the basement.

Another thing easier said than done, Philly thought.

20

Across the conference room table, Carpenter was giving Philly his appraising gaze. "You're looking more settled. It's good to see that."

Philly shrugged and sipped at her coffee. It was eight thirty in the morning on a Monday and Carpenter wanted to review cases. "I got in some exercise on both days this weekend. I was out on my bike. I have to admit it makes me feel better."

Carpenter rolled his eyes, his reaction to her biking in February the same as Raul's. "You're a nut," he said, "but whatever rocks your boat. Let's start with Michelle Smith. I've scheduled the depositions of the couple that she claims heard Jerome Singer say he would pay for Smith's business school. I'm pretty sure Singer will retaliate and take Smith's deposition."

"Do you need any help?"

"No. The depositions aren't complicated. But thanks for asking. Did you see the edits I made to the letter you did for Chun?"

Philly nodded. Carpenter had only changed a few words and added a sentence. "I sent the revised letter to Chun and he's okay with it. It's going out today."

"Marshall Hyde," Carpenter said. "I've done a draft of Hyde's answer to the Board of Bar Overseers' complaint. I want you to review it before I send it to Hyde."

Philly nodded and made a note to herself to do some additional first amendment research.

"Wise Computer Consultants has moved to dismiss the suit we filed for Herbert Stanton and Millie Lane. Here's a copy of the dismissal pleadings. I'll do the opposition to the motion and you do the legal memorandum. Are you okay with that?"

"Sure," Philly said.

"What's going on with the Harringtons?" Carpenter went on. "Did the Dixfield school people answer your letter?"

"Not yet."

"Carpenter nodded. "The best for last," he said. "The Lawsons' complaint against the Stonington School District is going to be filed today. You did a nice job on that. I banged out affidavits for Maryanne Fairmont and Sylvia Lawson. Here are copies. I'm praying that Fairmont will help. If she doesn't, the Lawsons are probably screwed."

Philly reviewed her to do list. "We've got a lot going on but hardly any of it is billable hour work. We agreed to cap the legal fees on a lot of things."

"True, but we need to plug away. I don't know about you, but some of this stuff is interesting."

Carpenter had made a fair point. Still, last year they had interesting work that paid better.

"I contacted those two Spenser School of Law students I told you about," Carpenter said, and Philly's anxiety kicked in. He was probably doing the right thing; yet she felt both uneasy and threatened by other lawyers getting involved in their business.

"I know you're uncomfortable with this subject, but I wanted to find out whether they were available. I didn't promise them anything."

"Are they available?"

"Yeah, they are. They're both scraping along. It's not a great time for a lawyer to be looking for work. Simon Jeffries is waiting tables. Rachel Boyle is working as a paralegal."

Philly knew firsthand what it was like to eke out a living practicing law. This year, she and Carpenter might be in that situation.

"I liked them. I'd be willing to give them a shot if we need backup while you're dealing with your baby. I'm not going to do anything without talking it over with you. But I think it's good news they're available."

Although Carpenter's report was mostly good news, Philly fretted. His contingency planning emphasized how soon she would have to deal with a baby and childcare and God knew what else.

"We need to think about these things," Carpenter said, picking up on her ambivalence.

"I know," she said. "But I don't have to like it."

Carpenter sat back in his desk chair and confronted the photograph on the wall across from his desk. It had been a long but reasonably productive day, but the man's dour expression suggested that the past was the past, so what have you done for me lately? Fuck you, Carpenter thought as he met the man's gaze; he figured he had earned a little down time to rest on his laurels.

Sylvia Lawson's affidavit had been revised to her satisfaction. Hammering out an agreement with Maryanne Fairmont on her affidavit had turned into a three-hour negotiation but in the end, they had come up with a compromise version that would help the Lawsons and that Fairmont was confident the Wilton Center's board would approve. Drafts of deposition outlines were in decent shape for the couple who allegedly had heard Jerome Signer promise to pay for Michelle Smith's business school tuition. Even Philly had some good news: the morning mail had brought a letter from the Dixfield school system saying that it would release all Luke Harrington's records to his parents.

If Philly weren't pregnant, Carpenter would be heading for her office to ask her if she wanted a beer. Instead, here he was, staring at a photograph. "What are you up to, Fred?" he asked his CLL. "Long time no talk."

The look of the man in the photograph became more focused. Carpenter turned away from the photograph and tried to think of something he wanted to say to Fred. Today had been action packed and he hadn't given Fred a passing thought. Not thinking about Fred was a blessing. Yet Rabbi Feldman had sent him in the different, counterintuitive direction, of actively confronting Fred in conversation.

"I can't let you get the best of me, Fred," Carpenter said, addressing the photograph. "I'm not ready to pack it in or be diminished in any way, shape, or form. I want to be there for Maxine. I want and need to be there for Philly. I've got people counting on me, Fred, so continue to fuck off."

The expression of the man in the photograph gave away nothing.

21

"What are you going to entertain me with this morning?" Jeannie Smith said to Carpenter as she set up her stenographer equipment in the office suite's conference room.

Carpenter reflected that his stenographer of choice would never really change. She was in her seventies and maybe her hair would further whiten, her facial features further sag, or her pale skin would eventually look like it had never seen the light of day; but Smith's cranky feistiness, her defining characteristic, would remain unchanged.

"Routine," Carpenter said. "I'm hoping the witnesses remember a conversation in a way that will help my client."

"Good luck," Smith said dismissively. "People can't remember what they did yesterday."

"There's that," Carpenter said. Left unsaid was the worse prospect that people could have an incentive of their own to "remember" an event in a way that harmed your client.

The conference room door opened and two men entered. Even if he hadn't seen the man's picture on his firm's website, it would have taken Carpenter a millisecond to pick out the lawyer. Daniel Catching, counsel for the defendant, had the breezy, self-assured air of a litigator. He looked to be one of those guys in his late forties who would age gracefully. The gray at his temples added a touch of gravity to his unlined, angular face. His firm, WilsonCrane, was a large multi-state operation resulting from the merger of two already sizable New York and Philadelphia law practices. The new mega-firm now had a Boston presence with an office on State Street that handled the business work for Jerome Singer's loan company, was defending Singer in Michelle Smith's lawsuit, and had obviously agreed to provide legal representation to Brian and Teresa Jenkins.

The second man to enter the room, nervous and already perspiring, was Brian Jenkins. He was short and stocky and dabbed at his forehead with a handkerchief.

After introductions were made and the deposition ground rules agreed upon, Carpenter asked some background questions. Jenkins had worked for Jerome Singer's loan company for four years and held a vice-president title. As far as Carpenter could tell, his duties were to do whatever Singer told him to do. Jenkins current annual salary was $185,000 which Carpenter figured meant there were 185,000 reasons why Jenkins would testify favorably to his boss regardless of the truth.

"Last year, did you and your wife ever go out to dinner with Mr. Singer and Ms. Michelle Smith?" Carpenter asked his first important question.

"Yes."

"Do you remember when that occurred?"

"No. In the spring maybe but that would be just a guess."

"Was that the only time the two couples had dinner together last year?"

Jenkins paused and wiped his brow with a handkerchief. "I think so."

"Was there a reason the two couples went out to dinner?"

"No. It was just a social occasion. Jerome . . . Mr. Singer set it up. He asked me if Teresa and I would like to join him and Ms. Smith for dinner and I said yes."

"Do you remember anything that was discussed during that dinner?"

Jenkins colored and again wiped his brow, but his attorney was unperturbed by these signs of nervousness.

"Nothing specific," Jenkins said with a catch in his voice. "Just social talk as best as I can remember."

"Do you remember any specific matter that was discussed?" Carpenter pursued.

Jenkins glanced at Catching who was absorbed in writing on his legal notepad.

"I think we may have talked about how lousy the economy was and that the lending business was particularly hurting."

"Is there anything else that you recall being discussed?"

"Not really."

"Did the subject of Ms. Smith going to business school come up?" Carpenter asked.

Jenkins again glanced in Catching's direction, but his lawyer had his head lowered as he continued to take notes.

"It may have."

"What may have been said about Ms. Smith going to business school?"

Carpenter was surprised when Jenkins paused. Jenkins had to have expected the last question and should have had his story straight by now.

"I don't really recall. Ms. Smith may have said that she was going to business school, but I don't really remember if that came up."

"Was there any discussion of payment for Ms. Smith's business school tuition?"

Jenkins took a deep breath. "That's possible. I don't remember."

"You're being deposed this morning in a lawsuit brought by Ms. Smith against Mr. Singer. Do you know what the lawsuit is about?"

Jenkins nodded. "Ms. Smith wants Mr. Singer to pay for her business school tuition."

"During the dinner you've told us about, did Mr. Singer say anything that indicated he had agreed to pay for Ms. Smith's tuition?"

"I don't remember."

"Are you aware that your wife is going to be deposed after you?"

"Yes."

"To your knowledge is your wife aware of the subject matter of Ms. Smith's lawsuit?"

"Yes. I told her about it when we got the notices of the deposition and she asked me what they were about."

"Have you talked to your wife about the dinner I've previously asked you about?"

"Yes."

"Who brought up the dinner subject?"

"I did."

"Why did you mention the dinner to your wife?"

"Mr. Singer said we would likely be asked about it."

"Did he say why he thought you would be asked about that dinner?"

"He mentioned something about what Ms. Smith was alleging in her lawsuit."

"Did he say anything more specific?"

"No, not that I remember?"

"Did he say you might be asked whether the subject of Ms. Smith's tuition came up at the dinner?"

"He may have," Jenkins said, after a brief pause.

"You said that you talked to your wife after you both got deposition notices. Did that talk include the subject of Ms. Smith's tuition being discussed at that dinner?"

"Yes."

"What did your wife tell you about that subject?"

"Objection for the record," Catching said.

"You may answer my question, Mr. Jenkins," Carpenter directed.

"She remembered the subject coming up."

"Did she tell you anything more specific?"

Jenkins again dabbed at his brow with the handkerchief he had at the ready. "She remembered Jerome . . . Mr. Singer joking about it."

"Did she tell you in what way he was joking about it?"

"Something about another tuition bill. You'd have to ask her."

"How did you come to have Mr. Catching represent you at this deposition?"

"I told Mr. Singer that Teresa and I had been subpoenaed and he asked if we wanted to have a lawyer present. We both felt more comfortable with a lawyer present."

"Are you and your wife paying for Mr. Catching's representation."

"No, Mr. Singer is."

"Did Mr. Catching prepare you and your wife for the depositions today?"

"No."

"No further questions," Carpenter said.

"Then I believe this deposition is concluded," Catching responded. "Since that didn't take long, if Ms. Jenkins is in your waiting room, do you want to get her deposition underway?"

"Give me ten minutes," Carpenter said.

"That was one uncomfortable gentleman," Jeannie Smith said as soon as Catching had escorted Jenkins from the conference room. "What does business school tuition cost?"

"Forty thousand a year."

Smith's impressive white eyebrows rose a bit. "Is that all your client wants from this Mr. Singer?"

"That's all. They lived together for five years, but this is the only financial promise he made during that time. She wants to hold him to it."

"Good for her," Smith said.

Teresa Jenkins was short and stocky like her husband but strongly built. Carpenter pegged her for a woman who spent a fair amount of time in the gym. She was dark-complexioned with a round face and dark eyes set far apart. When introductions were made, the woman's grip was firm and cool.

Background questions established that Teresa Jenkins was a freelance editor whose clients were chiefly scientific publications. Jenkins had majored in biology in college and had kept up her interest in that subject after graduation. She and her husband had been married seven years and had no children. Teresa Jenkins looked Carpenter in the eye when she answered questions. Brian Jenkins could learn a few things about self-possession from his wife.

"At some time last year did you and your husband have dinner with Mr. Singer and Ms. Michelle Smith?" Carpenter asked.

"Yes."

"When was that?"

"The first Saturday in April."

"How can you be so sure of the date?"

"I wrote it down on my calendar. I looked it up in preparation for coming here."

"Was the first Saturday in April the only time last year that the four of you dined?"

"Yes."

"Do you remember anything that was said at the dinner."

"Yes," Jenkins said, nodding.

"What do you remember was said?"

"The men talked about the economy and how it had hurt the lending business. Frankly, I didn't pay much attention to their shop talk. I had met Ms. Smith before at company parties, but I had never gotten a chance to get to know her. We talked about her stewardess job and she brought up that she was thinking seriously about going to business school. She said that she became interested in business from talking with Mr. Singer about Mr. Singer's business."

"Do you remember anything else that was talked about during that dinner?"

"Yes," Jenkins said, and the way she was looking at him, Carpenter sensed she wanted him to get to the point of why she was being deposed.

"What else do you remember?"

"During the meal, the subject of Ms. Smith going to business school came up. I don't remember how it came up, but I remember that it did come up. Ms. Smith repeated what she had said to me, that she was thinking seriously about going to business school. I remember that Mr. Singer rolled his eyes and said in a joking tone that that was just what he needed, another person in his life with a tuition payment."

Carpenter took his time and wrote down Jenkins' answer. The woman's recollection fell short of an admission by Singer that he would pay for Michelle's tuition. Catching was watching him calmly. Carpenter strove to keep his expression neutral; the last thing he wanted was to give his opponent any hint that Jenkins' last answer had been a letdown.

"What did you make of Mr. Singer's comment?" Carpenter followed up, grasping at straws.

"Objection," Catching said.

"Are you able to answer my question?" Carpenter asked Jenkins.

"Yes," Jenkins said without hesitation, and Catching frowned.

"Then please do so even though Mr. Catching has objected to the question. Objections made at depositions sometimes get ruled on by judges."

"Even though Mr. Singer was talking in a joking tone, I took his comment to mean that he'd be dealing with Ms. Smith's tuition payments."

Carpenter's tension eased. "Why did you take his comment to mean that?"

"Because earlier on, when I was talking with Ms. Smith, she made the comment that Mr. Singer was totally supportive of her business school plans and very generous about her education. Mr. Singer's remark, although said jokingly, struck me as his owning up to help with Ms. Smith's tuition."

Carpenter asked Smith to read back Jenkins' answer and he wrote it down verbatim. On balance, Teresa Jenkins' recollection supported Smith's case. Catching would probably inform Singer that the loan company executive now had no chance of getting Smith's case dismissed. A trial was inevitable.

"No further questions," Carpenter said.

Catching was regarding Jenkins thoughtfully. Usually at a deposition, the lawyer defending the deposition rarely asked questions. Carpenter sensed that Catching was deliberating whether to depart from that general rule.

"Tell me, Ms. Jenkins," Catching said, "did you ever hear Mr. Singer say that he would pay for Ms. Smith's business school tuition?"

"No, not in those words. I've told you what I remember Mr. Singer saying."

Catching remained thoughtful for a long moment. "No further questions," he finally said.

"No further questions," Carpenter echoed. "Thank you, Ms. Jenkins."

As Jeannie Smith began to pack up her stenographer gear, Carpenter stayed silent knowing that she would offer her own assessment of the concluded deposition.

"What the hell is that woman doing married to a guy who's afraid of his shadow?" Smith let loose.

Carpenter shrugged.

"I'll tell you one thing," Smith continued. "That woman was trying to help your client. I think she admired her."

Carpenter offered another shrug.

"Cheer up, Carpenter," Smith said. "The woman helped your case. And if a jury ever gets a look at her husband, they'll never believe a word he says."

Carpenter grunted. Jeannie Smith's instincts were usually on the money. The depositions should have cheered him up. But what remained discouraging was that after the five-thousand-dollar retainer, the hours to be spent on the case would be significant. His client would be deposed, Jerome Singer would be deposed, and then there would be a bitter jury trial to follow. And in the end, the case would be what it always was, one of those he-said, she-said cases that could go in any direction.

22

The new building in Woburn that housed the Middlesex Superior Court had light and airy courtrooms that Philly was convinced Carpenter would soon start bitching about. He liked his courtrooms dark and gloomy and solemn with piss-poor acoustics so that you had to speak from your diaphragm to make sure you were heard.

Carpenter had exchanged papers with Craig Lannon, the attorney representing the Stonington school district, and after reviewing the affidavit of William Burnside, the Stonington superintendent of schools, had passed it off to her to do the same. But Philly couldn't stop staring at Lannon. The school attorney was tall and blond and blue eyed and had a willowy athlete's build. If Philip had lived to his mid-forties, he might have morphed into someone who looked like Lannon: touches of gray at the temples, barely noticeable crows' feet at the corners of the eyes, a waist that had probably gone up one belt size. Philly willed herself to look away. Philip would be frozen in her memory in his thirties; thinking of him at a later age would only be a painful reminder of what she would miss out on.

Burnside's affidavit held no surprises, and Philly whispered that conclusion to Carpenter. He handed her a second affidavit. Philly was impressed that the Stonington school district had come up with an expert on short notice. Florence Jefferson had a Ph. D in childhood education. She was a consultant to several school districts and had personally helped author dozens of individual education plans. She had reviewed Jack Lawson's files and his IEP and concluded that the IEP was doing its job and satisfied Stonington's legal obligations to Jack. After reviewing Lannon's legal memorandum, Philly concluded that Carpenter would be rowing upstream when it came to oral argument.

"Court!"

At the clerk's cry, everyone rose in the courtroom. The Honorable Richard O'Connell took his seat and gestured for those standing to be seated. Philly's research disclosed that the judge had been on the bench for five years.

"Max Lawson and Sylvia Lawson versus William Burnside, the superintendent of schools for the Town of Stonington," the clerk announced. "Counsel please identify yourselves."

After Carpenter and Lannon introduced themselves, the judge took his time reviewing papers in front of him. He was middle-aged, of slight build, and all business. Philly hoped that his purple bowtie augured a whimsical, creative, free-thinking streak because Carpenter was going to need a judge who was willing to think outside the box.

"Pardon me for taking up your time by further reviewing some of the papers," the judge began. "I've read everything and I believe I'm familiar with the facts. Let's start with you, Mr. Carpenter. The school district argues that I have no jurisdiction over this case because your clients, the Lawsons, have an administrative remedy available to them where they can challenge their son's IEP. What do you say to that argument?"

Carpenter stood and glanced briefly at the notes he had just made. "The Lawsons are in court precisely because the relief they are seeking in this case will make the administrative process meaningful. The Lawsons don't claim that the administrative process should be ignored. On the contrary, their position is that for the administrative hearing to be meaningful with respect to their son's IEP, it is important for their son to experience a time during which his medications are reduced. Stonington won't even consider that course of action; therefore, it has become necessary to go to court."

Judge O'Connell fiddled with his bowtie and regarded Carpenter solemnly. "The superintendent points out that Stonington's IEP is working. As long as it's working, the fact that a different IEP might work as well or better is beside the point. Isn't that the law, Mr. Carpenter?"

"That's what the majority of court decisions hold," Carpenter acknowledged. "But the fact is that the Stonington IEP isn't working. It is true that Jack Lawson is doing reasonably well academically as a fourth grader. But the evidence is also clear that it's almost as if he's in a daze. Another important goal of school is socialization, and the plan is not succeeding as to that objective. Jack doesn't socialize with classmates. His affect is sluggish and drowsy. His socialization skills and progress in that area have gone nowhere due to his medications. As Dr. Fairmont states in her affidavit, gradually taking Jack Lawson off his medications will permit an assessment of whether Jack's socialization skills and affect can improve. As long as he's on so many drugs, no one can tell."

"Would you agree, Mr. Lannon, that Jack's socialization is below average and that he exhibits lethargy and drowsiness?" the judge asked.

Lannon rose smoothly as Carpenter sat. "I would agree that Jack's socialization is below average and that he has been observed on occasion to appear somewhat lethargic. But I would underscore that since he has been on his medications, Jack has not acted in any way that would endanger others. The medications have kept his previous, dangerous behavior under control. Equally important is the fact that with medications in place, Jack has been largely mainstreamed. That is, the majority of his schooling is taking place in a regular classroom with the rest of the students his age. That's a tremendous accomplishment which I would ask the court not to lose sight of."

"But doesn't Mr. Carpenter have a point," the judge came back. "Isn't the school district putting the Lawsons in the position of being unable to prove that Jack could thrive in terms of socialization without medications or with reduced medications because the school district is unwilling to permit Jack to reduce his medications?"

"Respectfully, Your Honor, we need to keep in mind the legal principles that apply to IEPs. A school district's responsibility is to come up with an IEP that works for Jack in terms of mainstreaming him. Stonington has done that. Jack Lawson is mainstreamed. Stonington's plan doesn't have to be perfect, and Stonington isn't required to experiment by agreeing to tinker with an IEP that is working. There is nothing broken here that needs fixing."

O'Connell again fingered his bowtie. "I'm thinking for the moment as a parent. Suppose I'm a parent and I have a child who has special education needs. I see a plan in place for my child that meets some of those needs but not others. I consult an expert who tells me that there is a way to test whether the needs not being met can be met if the plan in place is altered in a certain way. Why not alter the plan?"

"Because, Your Honor, we are dealing with legal requirements that do not obligate a school system to change a plan that is working simply to meet a student's parents' desire for what they prefer or hope is perfect for their child. That's not the law nor should it be the law."

"Do you agree, Mr. Lannon, that the one-on-one monitor the Lawsons have agreed to provide at their expense will address the safety concerns if Jack starts to become aggressive?"

Lannon paused. "I don't know, Your Honor and, no one can know the answer to your question. Here's what the Stonington school district does know. Safety concerns have become a non-issue since Jack went on the medications he currently takes."

"Do you have anything you want to add, Mr. Lannon?"

"No, Your Honor. We've covered everything in the affidavits and legal memorandum."

"What about you, Mr. Carpenter? Do you have anything else to add?'

"Since Your Honor reminded us that you have read all the papers, I would simply emphasize the point that Doctor Fairmont has given her opinion that the one-on-one monitoring does address any safety concerns of Jack acting inappropriately in any way."

Judge O'Connell regarded counsel. "Since we're here in court, I suppose there is no chance that the parties can reach agreement on safety measures that would permit Jack to be weaned from medications for a brief period. Is my supposition correct?"

Lannon rose promptly. "That's correct." he said.

Philly expected the judge to say he would take the matter under advisement and issue a ruling shortly. Instead, the judge became lost in thought and Philly began to suspect that he would rule from the bench.

"We are all familiar with the legal standard for granting an injunction," Judge O'Connell said. "The party seeking an injunction has to show a likelihood of succeeding on the merits of his legal claims and has to show irreparable harm which, as the phrase suggests, is harm that cannot be repaired if an injunction is denied. The plaintiffs' legal claims are somewhat novel and it's a tossup in my opinion as to whether the plaintiffs will prevail on those claims. In my opinion, the question of harm tilts slightly in the plaintiffs' favor."

The judge paused and Philly tried to sit quietly and keep calm. There was now a distinct possibility that Carpenter had pulled off a near miracle.

"I'm going to allow the plaintiffs' motion for injunctive relief subject to the following. Instead of one monitor, the plaintiffs, at their expense, are to provide two monitors for Jack. I expect the chosen monitors to be on their toes. Second, the reduction in Jack's medications is to proceed at one half the pace that Doctor Fairmont proposes in her affidavit. Third, I want to see counsel in court one week from today to report on how Jack is doing. At that time, I will entertain a motion by Mr. Lannon to dissolve the injunction I have just ordered. Any questions?"

"No," Carpenter said rising.

Lannon rose. "Will Your Honor agree to stay your ruling for forty-eight hours so that Stonington may have an opportunity to appeal your ruling if it decides to do so?"

O'Connell took his time considering Lannon's request. "Will the parties agree to move back the hearing on the IEP for a week if I allow your request, Mr. Lannon?"

"That's agreeable," Lannon said.

"The plaintiffs are also agreeable," Carpenter said.

"Okay," the judge said. "The injunction will not go into effect for another forty-eight hours. The court will be in recess. The clerk will FAX you both a copy of my order before the day is out."

Philly felt that the Lawsons should be congratulating Carpenter effusively. Instead they were restrained, looked numb, and Philly reminded herself that lay people listening to a lot of legalese might not appreciate what their lawyer had accomplished. As Carpenter explained the judge's decision, Max Lawson frowned and his wife nodded reflexively.

"Do you think they'll appeal?" Max Lawson asked.

"I think there's a good chance they will," Carpenter acknowledged. "The Stonington school district thinks it's doing right by Jack and the judge's ruling is rather novel."

"The five thousand dollars we paid you doesn't cover the appeal, does it?" Lawson followed up.

"No," Carpenter said. "If an appeal is filed, I'll talk with you and discuss an arrangement on legal fees." Carpenter paused and studied the couple. "Will you be able to get a second monitor?"

"I think so," Sylvia Lawson said. "I've got someone in mind."

"We need to be clear about two things," Carpenter said. "First, if the judge's ruling goes into effect and Jack acts aggressively while his meds are being reduced, you're probably going to be stuck with Stonington's plan. Then your decision will be between going on with the Stonington IEP or enrolling Jack in a school like the Wilton Center, assuming that school is still on board with med reduction."

The Lawsons didn't respond to Carpenter's statement. Philly sensed that the high-risk nature of the judge's decision was starting to sink in.

"Secondly, you need to follow up with the monitors and give them a pep talk to be alert. The last thing anybody wants is for Jack to hurt anyone."

The Lawsons nodded their heads solemnly. "We get that," Max Lawson said, his expression downcast.

March

Philly's Untitled Playlist

Speechless

Lady Gaga

23

"Let's have a look," Dr. Amy Shumaker said.

Philly closed her eyes and tried to tune out what her OB-GYN was up to. If it weren't for a pathetic, drunken teenager, Philip would be holding her hand. She wouldn't be alone.

"Everything is progressing normally. I'm going to do an ultrasound. Are you going to want to know the sex of the baby?"

"Not right now." Maybe when she got closer to delivery she would have a change of heart, but she was okay with surprises, too. She and Philip had agreed on names, Benjamin if a boy, and Daisy of all things if a girl.

"This is going to feel cold," Dr. Shumaker said as she applied glop to Philly's abdomen.

Philly winced and Shumaker's lively green eyes sparkled with amusement. The red-haired physician's youthful appearance took getting used to. It was just plain weird to be treated by a female equivalent of Doogie Howser.

"Okay, look at the screen. The pulsing movement is the baby's heart beating."

Philly fought back tears. She had no one to share this moment with. Isabella had offered to come with her to this appointment and she had reflexively turned her housemate down. That had been a mistake, she now reflected.

"Are you okay?" Shumaker asked.

"Not really," Philly admitted.

"What can I do to help?"

"Bring Philip back."

Shumaker was regarding her with concern and Philly now regretted unloading on her doctor. "It's just a bitter sweet moment," she tried to explain.

Shumaker handed her a small stack of paper towels. "Get yourself cleaned up. I'll be back in a few minutes and then we'll talk."

Once Shumaker was back in the examining room, Philly steeled herself for the sound advice that she was about to receive.

"What are you doing for fun?" Shumaker asked.

Philly had been expecting a pointed question about her mental state. "I've gone biking. I try to fit in a spinning class when I can."

"Those are solo activities," Shumaker observed. "What about activities with friends?"

It felt like a trick question. Outside of Raul and Isabella and maybe Carpenter and Maxine, she had no friends. And perhaps it was a stretch to label that foursome as friends; she had no great desire to pal around with any of them. "I've got two people who joined me in buying a home," Philly said, and then she filled Shumaker in on Raul and Isabella.

"Besides talking with them over dinner, do you get out and do things with them?"

Philly shook her head.

"Have they offered?"

"Isabella offered to come here today."

"Why didn't you take her up on the offer?"

"Because I can be stubborn and dense."

Philly had to force herself to meet her doctor's appraising gaze.

"I'm giving you an assignment," Shumaker said. "I want you to do something with Raul and Isabella. And I don't mean taking them out to dinner."

Raul had said that they needed to be nice to each other, a thought that left Philly enervated. "I don't know," she temporized.

"Well, I do know," Shumaker said. "Or at least the MD after my name gives me the ability to claim I know what's best for you. I want you to do this and call me as to how it went."

Philly couldn't think of an activity that would be tolerable with Raul around. She must have looked ambivalent.

"That's an order," Shumaker said.

The Harringtons had called and were running late which gave Carpenter and Philly a few moments to discuss the latest developments in their active cases. Carpenter had been looking forward to this unexpected window for a discussion, but Philly looked decidedly out of sorts as if she had no patience for conversation. With her white shirt tucked into a dark blue skirt it was unmistakable that Philly had started to show. Was that what was bugging her?

"Lannon called me," Carpenter said. "Stonington's not going to appeal Judge O'Connell's order. I've called the Lawsons and they're thrilled. They've got the second monitor lined up."

Philly nodded desultorily but did contribute. "I got a response to the letter I wrote for Frederick Chun. His company doesn't want him back. Frederick's not a happy camper."

Carpenter reflected on how often a piece of good news was offset by a piece of bad news, as if there was only so much good karma to go around. "What's Chun going to do?"

"He's thinking about it. He really can't afford a lawyer. Plus, if he sued his company, I don't think he'd get his job back and recover back pay."

Carpenter silently agreed with Philly's assessment. It bugged him that a company could fire an at will employee without a reason and use that point to justify firing the employee for a trumped up or nonsensical reason. But taking Chun's case on a contingency basis made no business sense. If the case had to be tried, they'd never recover enough money damages to pay for the time that they'd put in. Unless, of course, a jury warmed to Chun and felt that he had acted appropriately in promptly deleting his friend's e-mail and decided to take it out on Chun's company.

"You're not thinking we should take on Chun's case, are you?" Philly asked.

Carpenter shrugged. "I'm keeping an open mind."

Philly rolled her eyes.

Carpenter moved on. "What the hell do the Harringtons want?"

"They wouldn't tell me on the phone."

"There must be something in the records they were sent that has gotten them in a snit."

"We'll find out soon enough," Philly said.

"What's gotten you in a snit?" Carpenter demanded, sick to death of Philly's put-upon attitude.

"My OB-GYN wants me to socialize with people. She wants me to do something with Raul and Isabella."

"What's the big deal?"

"I don't find it easy to be around Raul," Philly said. "Also, I've realized I don't have any friends."

"You've got Maxine and me."

"Do the two of you really want to hang out with me?"

Carpenter had long ago owned up to his reclusive streak; he didn't like hanging out with anyone. But he knew he should be supportive. "Yeah, we'd hang out with you. In moderation," he qualified so Philly wouldn't get the wrong idea.

"Thanks, but no thanks. You sounded like you'd do it as an obligation. I might take you up on it later, but I'm not desperate enough at the moment. I don't mean to sound ungrateful. I know the two of you are there for me, but we're not talking about that."

Carpenter said a silent thank you when there was a knock on the conference room door. John and Naomi Harrington entered, the living embodiment of a diversion that would permit him to put off dealing with Philly's personal problems. The Harringtons were again wearing dark blue suits and Carpenter wondered whether they coordinated wardrobes before leaving the house in the morning.

Carpenter moved to sit next to Philly. John Harrington took the seat he had vacated and his wife sat down next to him.

"How can we help you today?" Philly led off, all business, no preliminary chitchat.

Naomi Harrington glanced at her husband and cleared her throat. "This isn't easy for us to discuss," she said. "We went through the records that were sent to us. Luke must have said something to another student about being quieted and this other student must have told his or her parents. In any event, the school principal received an anonymous letter stating that Luke had been disciplined in a way that shocked the letter writer."

"What kind of discipline did the letter writer mention?" Philly asked, and Carpenter appreciated her not pussyfooting around.

Naomi Harrington colored but pushed on. "Luke standing in a very narrow, dark closet without room to sit down."

Philly blanched, for good reason, Carpenter thought. He wondered where people came up with harebrained ideas. Recently a college football coach had been fired for forcing a player to remain standing in a narrow enclosure and being ordered not to sit. Luke was a third grader. What the hell had the kid done to get saddled with that punishment?

"Is that a punishment you actually imposed on Luke?" Philly asked, evenly.

Carpenter realized there was a side benefit to Philly being cranky. She was going to ask the necessary, hard questions without batting an eye.

"We don't consider it a punishment," Naomi Harrington said, a little uneasily.

"But you're saying it happened," Philly followed up. "On how many occasions?"

"Not quite a dozen."

"What had Luke done?" Philly persisted.

"Mostly tantrums. For some, he needed to be restrained."

"Was this recommended by a doctor?" Philly asked.

"No."

"Where did you come up with this?"

"Sort of out of the blue," Naomi Harrington said sheepishly. "There was this one time when Luke was literally kicking and screaming. John was holding him, trying to get him to calm down, but Luke wriggled free and John must have pushed him into this closet off the front hall. John slammed the closet door shut and the screaming stopped instantaneously. We left Luke in the closet for about ten minutes. We listened at the closet door but didn't hear a sound. When we opened the door, Luke walked out as if nothing had happened."

"Has Luke ever had a tantrum at school?" Philly asked.

Naomi Harrington lowered her eyes. "No. He's never acted like that while in school."

"Have you seen a doctor about Luke's tantrums at home?"

"Yes," Naomi Harrington said. "Luke's been tested and they can't find anything wrong."

"Does a doctor know about the closet incident?"

"No."

"So you put Luke in the closet after the first time calmed him down?"

Naomi Harrington nodded.

"What happened?"

"Each time Luke calmed down."

"Was the closet ever locked?"

"No," Naomi Harrington answered.

Philly studied her clients for a long moment. "What is it you want us to do?"

"We want the school to permanently delete all the records that refer to this subject," John Harrington said with considerable animation.

"I can make that request," Philly said. "What if the request is denied?"

"Then we want to file a lawsuit to get the records permanently destroyed," John Harrington said.

Carpenter kept his peace. He had a strong opinion on whether to file a lawsuit in this situation, but this was Philly's case and she had taken charge of this client meeting.

"I'll make the written request," Philly said. "But I'd think twice about filing a lawsuit."

"Why?" John Harrington exclaimed, genuinely stunned by Philly's response.

"First," Philly said, holding up a finger, "if you file a lawsuit, the discipline given to Luke may become public. Also," she added, holding up a second finger, "even though we're talking about an anonymous report, the statements in the anonymous report are true based on what you told us. Lastly, some child welfare agency may get wind of all this and come to the conclusion that you acted inappropriately as parents." Philly held up a third finger and Carpenter was pleased that she had counted off the same reasons why he thought a lawsuit was ill-advised.

"Are you saying Luke could be taken away from us?" Naomi Harrington asked, horrified.

"I don't think that's likely but it's impossible to predict what some self-righteous, misguided, public official might do."

"This is incredible," Naomi Harrington said. "It's intolerable to us to have an anonymous letter be part of our son's school record."

Carpenter silently acknowledged that the Harrington's had a point. But he foresaw the Harringtons losing their case because the allegations in the anonymous letter were true.

"I would not recommend suing if your request is turned down," Philly repeated.

"Then maybe we need another lawyer," John Harrington said angrily.

"That's certainly your prerogative," Philly answered evenly. "But you need to be clear about something. I've just given you a recommendation. You're free to reject it. If you do and you still want to sue, I'll sue on your behalf and fight like hell to win. But one reason for my recommendation is that I think you'll lose the suit and that the trial will bring to light things that you are not going to want to be made public."

"Can't we have a non-public trial?" Naomi Harrington asked.

Philly nodded in his direction and Carpenter fielded the question. "That's problematic. Dixfield may want a public trial and, regardless of what the parties want, a judge may insist on a public trial."

"This is unbelievable," Naomi Harrington said.

"You need to understand something," Carpenter said, taking the opportunity to support Philly. "If the allegations in the anonymous letter were false, I think you'd have an excellent chance of getting the letter removed from your son's records. But the allegations are true. I know it's hard to think ahead right now but, in my opinion, at the end of a long and costly lawsuit, I believe that if the school wants to keep the letter in its records, it's going to be allowed to because the letter doesn't contain anything that's untrue."

The Harringtons were both glowering and appeared so irate that it occurred to Carpenter they were too worked up to get a word out. He wasn't particularly sympathetic. After all, they'd put their kid in a closet a number of times where he couldn't sit down. How old was a third grader? Eight? Nine? What the hell were these people thinking? They hadn't even talked to a doctor.

"Why don't I write the letter we discussed," Philly said. "Once I have an answer we can look again at your options.

"I guess that's a no-brainer," John Harrington said.

"I thought you handled that well," Carpenter said when Philly returned to the conference room after showing the Harringtons out.

Philly shrugged and dropped onto her chair, a defeated air about her. "All you can do is advise a client," Carpenter said. "In the end, a client will do whatever the hell he wants. I wouldn't want to predict what this couple will do."

"I saw my baby's heart beating today."

Carpenter swung with the abrupt change of topics. "Congratulations, good for you," he said. It would have been great to have seen that during any of his ex-wife's pregnancies.

"It really brought the pregnancy home to me," Philly said.

Carpenter was excited for her but the way she was acting and talking, he didn't think she would appreciate any show of enthusiasm.

"Then there's the trial of the kid who killed Philip coming up this month."

Carpenter hadn't given any recent thought to how the teenager's upcoming trial would be weighing on Philly, bringing back her horrible loss. "Do you want me to write the letter for the Harringtons?" he asked.

Philly shook her head. "I've had it. I'm going home. I'll e-mail you a draft of the letter. Right now, I'm beat."

Carpenter watched Philly leave the conference room. She was dragging. Maybe Maxine would know what he should be doing for her.

24

On Saturday morning Philly woke when it was still dark. The days were getting a little longer, but the sun still didn't rise until after seven. Last night she had gone to bed at eight and slept like a log. She put a wool sweater on over her flannel pajamas and made her way to the kitchen where she made a large pot of coffee. Usually Raul or Isabella was the early riser and had coffee ready by the time she woke.

She filled a mug three quarters and made her way up the stairs. At the second floor landing she paused and looked down the hall to Raul's and Isabella's bedroom. It was dark and silent at that end of the hallway. She pictured the couple nestled close together, Raul with an arm encircling Isabella, much the way he had held her for the brief time they were a couple. Some things didn't bear thinking about.

In her office at the opposite end of the corridor she started up her computer. Today was going to be full. First, she was going to knock off the draft letter to be sent on behalf of the Harringtons. Then she would make breakfast for Raul and Isabella, something she had yet to do since they moved in together. How hard could scrambled eggs be? Mid-morning, they were scheduled to interview four prospective tenants for the two third-floor units. Then, after lunch, she would follow Dr. Shumaker's advice and take Raul and Isabella for an outing. She had withstood Raul's entreaties and kept their destination secret.

Philly checked her e-mail messages. Cambridge police detective Paul Sullivan had sent her a message that the trial of Colin Feeney had been put off for two weeks. She didn't know how to feel. She wanted the kid tried, convicted, and put away so that some sort of closure would settle over Philip's death. The new delay made it feel like her life was moving in slow motion and she was an outsider watching it slip away.

Philly began drafting a letter on behalf of the Harringtons. One thing at a time, she told herself.

Ellie Wood was the third prospective tenant they were interviewing this morning. The young woman was a secretary. She was short, stocky, and blond and looked to be in her late twenties. Raul had taken the middle position on the couch between Philly and Isabella. Wood was seated in one of the living room chairs; a gold nose stud sparkled when she turned and it caught the light.

"If you select me, would I have a say in choosing the other tenant?" Wood asked.

Philly was amazed. Yet another question that she and Raul and Isabella had not discussed beforehand. Their first interview of the morning had been with a young man who had come armed with a written list of questions that had put the three of them off.

"It's a fair question," Philly said, "and we'll give it consideration. But in this market, we have to reserve the right to make a decision that may not be to your liking."

"If you choose me and someone else, maybe the two of us could meet."

Philly didn't like a prospective tenant making their lives more complicated, but Isabella preempted her by saying, "We will certainly keep that in mind."

"When will you be making a decision?"

"As soon as we can," Raul said. "How soon could you move in?"

"I'd need a week," Wood said, "maybe less. I'm living with my folks and I need to get out of their house."

That earned her a point with Philly. "Are you okay if the other tenant is a man?" she asked.

"To be honest I'd prefer another woman. But it's not a deal breaker for me."

Philly consulted her list. The next prospective tenant was a man. "Thanks for coming in. We'll get back to you shortly."

Thomas Morrison also sported a nose stud. A scraggly goatee and a soul patch exaggerated his already long angular face. Philly pegged him for late twenties, Wood's age, and found it somewhat unsettling that she was interviewing people younger than herself. Since when had she become the grownup? Morrison was the assistant manager of a music store in Allston and had held the job for two years. Isabella had been the one to show him the third-floor rental units.

"I like the rooms," Morrison said when he faced them in the living room. "Right now I'm living with my folks and it's driving me nuts."

"Would it be a problem if the other tenant was a woman?" Raul asked.

"Not really. It would probably take some getting used to for me."

"Have you ever lived in a rental unit before?" Philly asked.

"No."

Philly wondered whether Morrison had continually lived with his parents. He didn't look like a momma's boy; he had long hair and was dressed in black jeans and a black leather jacket.

"We expect any tenant to treat the property with respect," Raul said.

"I understand."

"We'll get back to you as soon as we can," Raul said. "How soon could you move in?"

"Is tomorrow soon enough?"

“That would work,” Raul said.

“I vote we offer the units to the last two we interviewed,” Raul said.

“What about having them meet first?” Isabella asked.

Raul shrugged.

“I think it makes sense,” Isabella said and while Philly agreed with her, she decided to stay silent.

“This is becoming very complicated,” Raul said.

“I’ll handle this,” Isabella said. “I’ll call each of them and get permission to exchange phone numbers.”

“We should e-mail them copies of the lease,” Philly put in. Carpenter’s Barrister friend, Morton, had drafted a reasonably intelligible lease as part of his legal services for the house purchase. If left to herself, Philly would have pulled a form lease off the Internet and trusted to luck.

“I’ll take care of that as well,” Isabella said.

They fell silent. Philly considered the living room. The furnishings weren’t much to look at, but she was getting used to the place. The house was beginning to feel more and more like a home.

“So where is it you are taking us?” Raul asked.

“Wouldn’t you like to know?”

“I very much would like to know. It is still very cold outside, and you want us to bring shorts and sneakers and a change of clothes. I have an uneasy feeling about this.”

You and me both, Philly thought. “Trust me,” is what she said.

The spinning class at Pedal Pusher Galleries was nearly full with fourteen of the sixteen bikes occupied. Raul and Isabella were on adjacent bikes slightly cattycorner to Philly’s. Isabella was giddy with excitement but Raul, to Philly’s dismay, looked put upon.

“We have two first timers today,” Kim, today’s instructor, announced, pointing to Raul and Isabella. “If they think we’re going to go easy on them they are sadly mistaken. I’m only joking,” she added when Raul and Isabella flashed anxious looks. “The best part of spinning is that nobody has to do a thing the instructor says. Go at whatever pace is comfortable but don’t be afraid to challenge yourself.”

Kim took them through a warm up and stretching exercises. Philly stared at Isabella. Her housemate was gorgeous: long, finely muscled legs, a thin waist. With her long black hair done up, her elegant neck was revealed. She was definitely into the class; when she caught Philly's eye she smiled broadly and gave a thumbs up signal. Raul, in contrast, didn't seem to have entered into the spirit of a heavy workout.

Suicide Blonde was blasting from the speakers as they started a hill climb and Philly closed her eyes. She imagined her baby sloshing around inside her and wondered if the baby could hear the music. When she was at home, iPod plugged in, could her baby hear the sounds?

"Turn the resistance knob one full turn to the right and come out of the saddle."

Philly kept her eyes closed and stood. Falling into a rhythm, she thought about the two prospective tenants. She wondered whether it made sense to interview more people. The four candidates they'd interviewed seemed the best of the uninspiring lot their Craig's List ad had drawn.

"Pick up the pace. We're going to race the last forty seconds to the top."

When Philly had rented her apartment in Brighton, she'd had no steady income, but the landlord had taken a chance on her. Maybe what she needed to do here was take a chance on Wood and Morrison.

"Nice job. Ease up a turn on the resistance. We're heading down the other side of the hill."

Philly opened her eyes. Both Isabella and Raul were pedaling effortlessly, their long legs moving in time to the music. Isabella looked happy. Raul looked intent as if in deep concentration. Philly vowed to thank Raul for being a good sport no matter how much he bitched and moaned about the class.

"Flat road. Get some water. We'll try some all-out sprints next."

Philly drank from her water bottle and slowed her pace. What would it be like to be spinning and feeling her baby move? She'd find out soon enough, she figured.

Later they sat in the Pedal Pusher Galleries juice bar showered and dressed. Philly embraced that hollowed out, mellow feeling that spinning always left her with, a kind of calm that was both physically and mentally soothing, not exactly zoning out but a suffusing peace that put her worries of the moment at a remove.

They were sipping purple fruit concoctions. The cold liquid going down was so sensual and satisfying that Philly wished she could replicate this routine every day.

"This is wonderful," Isabella gushed. "I always wanted to try spinning. What made you think of it?"

"I've been doing it for a little over two years," Philly said, and she explained how she had become acquainted with Pedal Pusher Galleries through a client. Raul, she noticed, was atypically silent, a worrisome sign.

"Raul, thanks for doing this," Philly said, finding it an effort to offer thanks. "I know it's not for everybody, but you were a good sport."

"This is not at all what I expected."

Philly remembered from their time together how wiry and strong Raul was. Yet at the end of the spinning class it was Isabella who looked as though she had better survived the exercise.

"I want to do this again," Isabella said.

Philly knew that Raul was not about to volunteer for a repeat performance. "Then we will," she said. She made a mental note to ask Dr. Shumaker how long it was safe to spin.

"Did Philip go spinning with you?" Isabella asked.

Philly was surprised by the question. Neither Raul nor Isabella had mentioned Philip before in casual conversation. In Raul's case, Philly believed that he was making a deliberate effort to avoid the subject.

"Yeah, he did. He liked outdoor biking more, but I managed to drag him down here a few times."

"This was a wonderful idea you had," Isabella said. "Thank you for letting us share this activity with you."

"It's not over," Philly said. "We still haven't seen the art. That client I was telling you about? He was always saying that the money was in the art."

Once inside the art gallery, Philly sat on a bench and watched Raul and Isabella roam about. The exhibits on display this afternoon didn't interest her: abstract paintings with striking colors that she couldn't make sense of even after reading the titles of the works, a series of photographs of ocean shorelines, and a second set of photographs of mountain settings with snowcapped peaks dwarfed by vast blue skies. Philly realized what she liked by what was missing: photographs of people and, in particular, their facial expressions when captured unobserved. Philip would have been attracted by the nature photographs. But since coming to the gallery, she had always been drawn to photographs of people in all their moods. This attraction perhaps explained why she and Carpenter liked representing individuals in the practice of law. The way a person revealed a problem couldn't fail to touch you in some way regardless of whether the problem was of the person's own making.

Philly sighed. It would have proved diverting if one of the art pieces had moved her, jolted her out of the day-to-day grind that was wearing her down. These days, Isabella might be the only person she had patience for, the only person whom she didn't have to make an effort to interact with.

Isabella took a seat beside her.

"The photographs are very nice but I don't understand the paintings," Isabella said.

"You and me both."

"When I see something that I don't understand, I can't shake the feeling that it's a failing on my part."

"Or your instincts could be right and what you're looking at is a lot of crap."

Isabella laughed and her face lit up. "This has been a lovely day."

Philly nodded, thinking that sometimes, lovely didn't cut it.

Raul was standing over them. "I think it's time to go."

Philly didn't need any urging. She hefted her gym bag and made for the door.

Philly dropped Raul and Isabella at the house saying that she had an errand to run and would be back shortly. She headed toward Allston and pulled into the first bar over the town line. The place was more brightly lit than Shredders, the Brighton bar she used to frequent. She took a seat at the bar where there was no television to view. The place was mostly empty except for two guys in ski parkas sitting at the other end of the bar. The bartender had to walk over to take her order and approached her as if he resented having to make the effort.

"A draft," she said putting a five spot on the bar, intending to make it one and done.

25

Daniel Catching, Jerome Singer's lawyer, hadn't wanted to talk on the phone, had insisted on a meeting. Carpenter was relegated to his office. Philly had preempted the conference room; she was scheduled to have a heart to heart with Frederick Chun, and Carpenter was hoping to catch the tail end of her meeting if he could make short work of Catching.

He'd made small concessions to make his office look presentable. The usual array of files on his visitor chair had been removed and there was a reasonably clear path to that chair. Otherwise, his usual clutter was in place.

"A Mr. Catching is here to see you," the receptionist announced over his intercom.

"Show him in," Carpenter said. He had wanted to make a point by not getting up and going to the reception area to greet Catching but, as Catching entered his office, he couldn't figure out what the point was.

Catching took in the surroundings without expression as he advanced to the visitor chair. Carpenter rose and the men shook hands before taking their seats.

"I like what you've done with this place," Catching said straight-faced, and Carpenter awarded him a point for his joke.

"I should have cut my decorator's budget, but I gave her free rein."

Catching's laugh was genuine and Carpenter silently bestowed another point, although puzzled by Catching seeming totally at ease. If a lawyer preferred to say something face-to-face, the something had to be grave or unpleasant. Yet there was an unmistakable hint of amusement in Catching's eyes.

"Thanks for seeing me," Catching spoke easily. "I thought I'd seen everything there was to see but this is a new one for me. I'm authorized to make you an offer in Ms. Smith's suit against Mr. Singer. But the offer comes with a condition that is beyond bizarre. It puts me in a very uncomfortable position and for all I know, may put you in a conflict of interest situation. I'll let you figure that part out."

Carpenter had no difficulty maintaining a blank look.

"Singer will agree to pay your client's business school tuition for two years. That's eighty thousand dollars."

Catching paused. Carpenter waited for the catch.

"The condition is that you take over representing Singer's company, Top Tier, in an investigation of the company being conducted by state regulators. So far, my firm has been handling that matter."

Carpenter couldn't suppress his surprise. Singer's condition for settling Michelle Smith's suit *was* bizarre. "The investigation into Singer's company has to do with Devonshire Plastics, right?"

Catching nodded. "I know you're somewhat familiar with that matter but let me lay it out for you so we're on the same page. Devonshire Plastics defaulted on its loan agreement with Top Tier. Devonshire's president, a guy named Norman Cassidy, illegally recorded a telephone conversation with Singer in which Singer arguably suggested that Devonshire would have ninety days to cure a loan default even though the loan agreement said the cure period was ten days. Singer consulted you. You advised him to honor the ninety-day cure period. You were concerned that Cassidy would file a complaint against Singer's loan company with state regulators. My firm, on the other hand, largely on my recommendation, advised Singer to sue once the ten days expired, reasoning that Cassidy wouldn't file a complaint with regulators since he'd be admitting to the crime of illegally recording a telephone conversation. Singer took my advice and sued after ten days. But I was wrong. Cassidy did file a complaint with regulators. We tried to get an injunction to freeze Devonshire Plastic's assets, but we lost that motion because of the recorded telephone conversation which was played in court. The judge ruled that Singer had agreed during the conversation to give Devonshire ninety days to cure any loan default. Based on Cassidy's complaint, the regulators want to take action against Singer's company's lending license and there's going to be a hearing on whether to revoke the license. The regulators take the position that Singer made false promises to obtain loan business by falsely telling prospective borrowers they had more time to cure a default than was set forth in the loan agreement." Catching paused. "That brings us to now. Singer wants you handling the regulatory case. He told me flat out that my judgment so far had been for shit and that yours had been on the money. I think that about covers the main points."

So Catching was being forced out of a case and had been assigned the task to arrange for his successor. In similar circumstances, Carpenter would never have matched Catching's forthrightness and calm.

"What happened in Singer's suit against Devonshire Plastics?"

Catching flashed a wry expression. "We ended up with the real estate to foreclose on and not much else. Cassidy used the ninety days to strip his company bare. Singer's company took a big hit on that loan."

"I need to think for a moment," Carpenter said. "This is a lot to take in."

"Take your time."

Carpenter remembered the advice he had given Singer, and Singer's angry reaction to it. He also remembered another smart move he had made. He had never billed Singer's company for the meeting they had had to review the Devonshire Plastics situation.

Carpenter looked past Catching to the man in the photograph whose typical stony stare was, for the moment, replaced by an amused gleam that flashed in the man's eyes.

Carpenter had never liked Singer. There was something slick and superficial about the guy. Plus, Singer didn't like to receive advice he didn't want to hear. The man was convinced of the infallibility of his own judgment. Yet Singer had linked the settlement of Michelle Smith's case to Carpenter representing Singer's company. Perhaps Catching's presence in his office meant that Singer had realized that he was as capable of fucking up as anyone else. Also, Singer was a vengeful prick. Carpenter didn't doubt that the offer to Michelle Smith would be taken off the table if he didn't agree to handle the regulatory case.

"When's the licensure revocation hearing?" Carpenter asked.

"In two months. You could probably get an extension as new counsel."

"Would your firm have any role in the case?"

"Only if you asked us to."

This was not Carpenter's first rodeo with Singer. In fact, it was his third. He had first met Singer and Michelle Smith two years ago. That time, too, Singer had rejected Carpenters advice and a lawsuit against his company had ended up costing the company more money than would have been the case if his advice been taken. At that time, Carpenter had hoped to be engaged by Singer's company so that he would have a steady, well-heeled client that would alleviate some of the worry about where his next case was coming from. Was Singer now giving him that opportunity?

"I don't know shit about loan companies and the regulations that apply to them," Carpenter said.

"Singer suspected that would be the case," Catching responded. "It's not a problem for him. There's a guy in my firm that handles the regulatory part of his business and he could get you up to speed in short order."

"Is the Devonshire Plastic loan the only loan that Singer's company didn't give the borrower ninety days in which to cure a loan default?"

"So far, that seems to be the case. But more files need to be reviewed. Also, you need to keep in mind that not every borrower was told orally about a ninety-day cure period."

Carpenter decided first things first. The offer to Michelle Smith needed to be dealt with before he could begin to consider representing Singer's company. "Here's what I'll recommend to Michelle Smith," Carpenter said. "One hundred fifteen thousand dollars as a lump sum settlement with mutual releases."

"That's more than her tuition payments will be."

"You noticed."

Catching grinned. "It's true what they say about you; you really are a card."

Carpenter didn't want to know who the *they* were.

"If your figure is accepted will you take over the regulatory case?" Catching asked.

"If Smith has no objections, I will."

"The money won't be a problem," Catching said. "Talk to your client. You can mention the one hundred fifteen thousand number."

"I could have gotten more for her, couldn't I?"

"That's for me to know," Catching said, his grin still in place.

Carpenter considered Philly's pregnancy and upcoming maternity leave and the broad outline of a game plan started to take shape. "If I take over the regulatory case, do I get to bring in who I want to help me?"

Catching didn't answer straightaway. "I'd say within reason. Singer's got a lot riding on this. I wouldn't say that money is no object. But if you're reasonable, I don't see him bitching about legal fees."

"Okay," Carpenter said. "I'm going to want a sit down with Singer if Michelle Smith signs off on this. I may be asking him for a retainer."

"I don't foresee a problem with any of that."

Carpenter studied Catching. The man had shown grace under fire. "Right now, I'm thinking you should stay involved in this."

"That's very gracious," Catching said.

No, Carpenter thought. That's just being smart.

Carpenter knocked, entered the conference room, and was greeted by Frederick Chun's grim expression.

Carpenter took a seat next to Philly. He debated taking Philly outside the room so they could talk privately and decided against that move. "Fill me in," he requested Philly, who looked as downcast as Chun.

"I've explained to Mr. Chun that his chances of getting his job back are slim. I've also explained that for us, taking his case on a contingency basis is unattractive because the likelihood of recovering substantial damages is iffy. Mr. Chun is disappointed with this advice."

"How are you doing with a job search?" Carpenter asked Chun.

"It's brutal out there," Chun replied. "Companies involved in finance aren't hiring. If anything, they're cutting back."

"Do you have any leads?"

"I've got an interview with a company tomorrow."

"How are you going to deal with being fired from your last job?" Carpenter followed up.

Chun shrugged. "Tell the truth," he said.

"I think that's the right move," Carpenter affirmed. "By the way, Ms. Piper has correctly assessed your situation in my opinion."

Chun breathed in deeply and emitted an audible sigh. "I guess we're done. Thanks for trying to help me."

Chun started to rise but Carpenter gestured for him to remain seated.

"Ms. Piper and I need to talk further about your situation," Carpenter said. "Even though your case is a long shot, it may be worth taking a chance filing a discrimination claim on your behalf. The theory would be that your company tolerated dirty jokes from its white and African American employees but fired you because you're Asian."

"How the hell would you prove that?"

"With difficulty. We'd file discovery, and we may get lucky. Maybe someone white or black had porn on his or her computer and nothing was done to the employee."

Chun's shoulders sagged. "Maybe I should just throw in the towel."

"If we decide to file a discrimination claim on your behalf are you prepared to see it through?"

"I guess so," Chun said without enthusiasm.

Carpenter glanced at Philly. She was looking at him as if he had taken leave of his senses.

"Now we are done," Carpenter said. "Ms. Piper and I will talk and get back to you on whether we're prepared to go with the discrimination case. Good luck tomorrow. Our brilliant legal advice is to kill the interview."

Chun offered a weak smile. "Thanks," he said.

"What was that about?" Philly said when Chun left the conference room.

"I'm willing to play a hunch in Chun's case," Carpenter said. "I like the guy and I think he got screwed over. Of course, I might be reacting differently if something else hadn't happened today."

Carpenter recounted his meeting with Daniel Catching. As he talked he watched Philly closely, troubled that although she showed interest, she wasn't excited. "That's a great result," Philly said when he concluded his account.

"I need to tell Smith and get her to sign off. It's not a done deal until that happens. But I'm pretty sure she'll go for it."

"What does this have to do with Chun?" Philly questioned.

Carpenter saw no way around his spelling things out. He would have preferred that Philly make the connection, see the big picture. "This regulatory case of Singer's could make our year."

"The trial's in two months," Philly pointed out. "The case isn't going to last long."

"If the case gets tried before the end of the summer, I'll be surprised. You're definitely going to be a mother before this case goes to trial."

At the mention of the word mother Philly frowned and Carpenter wondered whether she was having second thoughts about her decision to have a child. He had better remember to have Maxine give Philly a call.

"I'm trying to look at the big picture here," Carpenter continued. "I've never had a really big case with a well-heeled client willing to throw money at me. This could be that case. We've both got time on our hands so now we get to fill it and bill for it. There's going to be a lot of paper generated in this case, so I'm also thinking of bringing in those two Spenser School of Law lawyers I told you about. I can see assigning them document review. This case has paper written all over it."

Philly's frown remained in place.

"What!" Carpenter said. "I thought you'd be more excited."

"The truth is I'm not all that excited about anything."

"Then I'll be excited for both of us. If we play our cards right, this case could be very big for us."

"Why would you involve this guy Catching?" Philly asked.

"A couple of reasons. First, I liked the guy. He was straight with me and that couldn't have been easy for him. Plus, he's got big firm resources behind him which we may need to use."

"You're feeling flush and that's why you're willing to take on Chun."

"That's right," Carpenter said. Philly had him pegged. "I'm being a jerk and counting on money that hasn't come in the door and might never come in the door if Michelle Smith does something off the wall. But I'm thinking that this really is going to happen."

Philly sat in her chair looking forlorn. "Okay," she said. "We'll take on Chun after Singer signs an engagement letter with you."

"There's one other thing," Carpenter said. "I'm going to give Michelle Smith a break on the contingent fee agreement she signed. I'd be entitled to a third of one hundred fifteen thousand less the five thousand retainer she paid. I'm only going to take ten thousand more if she goes for the deal. I want her to get her full tuition taken care of plus a little walking around money. I'm going to split the ten thousand with you."

"That's not fair to you," Philly protested. "This was your case. It didn't involve me. You took the depositions. I think I looked over the court complaint, but I didn't draft it."

"The depositions were nothing," Carpenter said. "Besides, I don't give a shit whether you helped with the court complaint. This is not open to discussion."

"You're in a generous mood," Philly observed.

"Yeah, I am. You should try it."

26

Michelle Smith was grinning broadly, her relief evident. "I can't believe Jerome rolled over on this. I thought he'd fight me till his dying breath."

Watching a happy client was one of a lawyer's infrequent pleasures. In Michelle Smith's case, Carpenter's pleasure was doubled because the woman was a knockout: tall, thin, and elegant.

He had insisted that Philly attend this conference room meeting, counting on Smith's happiness, and the rare sunny day in March, to rub off on her. But Philly regarded Smith with a somber, neutral expression that he wished she'd lose.

"Here's another thing," Carpenter said. "I'm making a small change in our fee agreement," and he proceeded to tell Smith what he had in mind.

"That's very kind of you," Smith said, "but I made a deal and I want to stick to it. A deal is a deal."

"Don't fight me on this," Carpenter said. "If you agree to Singer's offer you'll be doing us a favor."

Smith became lost in thought. "I'll accept the offer and your change in our fee arrangement, but I want one more thing from Jerome."

Carpenter braced himself. Was Smith about to snatch defeat from the jaws of victory?

"I want Jerome to agree that I can have access to the papers in his regulatory case that you have in your office. I have to write a major paper to graduate, and I'm thinking this might be an interesting case to write about. I don't have to decide on a subject until my second year, but I want to keep the option open. You can tell Jerome that no real names would be used."

At least Michelle's proposition had gotten Philly to show some interest. Carpenter couldn't imagine Singer's reaction but if he gave his okay, Carpenter would be the first to admit that having Smith around in his life for a little while longer would be a plus. "What if Singer says no?"

"Then tell him there's no deal," Smith said.

"Jesus," Carpenter said, visualizing the plans he was counting on for the rest of the year spiraling down the toilet.

"If Jerome doesn't change his mind in a week, tell him I've reconsidered and the condition is off the table."

"You're not making this easy," Carpenter said.

"Didn't you tell me once that *nothing* was easy?"

"Shit!" Carpenter muttered. "Don't you just hate it when your words of wisdom get thrown back in your face?"

"Do you think I'm being foolish?" Smith asked.

"If you're really going to insist on this, make the week two days," Carpenter said. "Singer will get another lawyer; he needs to move fast on his regulatory mess and he's not going to let a week go by. He'll withdraw his offer. To be blunt, taking on his case would be a big deal for me. I don't want to lose the opportunity if it can be avoided especially where he's giving you what you want in terms of money."

Smith was looking at him seriously, and Carpenter considered whether he had crossed a line by putting his own interests before his client's. But it wasn't clear cut because Singer would only pay Smith if Carpenter ended up representing his company.

"Raise the condition I want," Smith said, "and if Jerome says no, make the deal without it."

"You sure?"

"Yeah, I'm sure. I don't want to be stupid about this. You're right about the money."

Carpenter glanced at Philly. She was giving Smith her hard stare.

"How's business school," Carpenter asked Smith.

"I love it. I should have tried it years ago."

Carpenter returned to the conference room after showing Smith out. Philly continued to sport a sour look. "You could have been a little more upbeat," he said taking a seat across from Philly. "Getting rid of Smith's case is a good thing particularly if it gets us a big case as an extra."

Philly shrugged, remained glum.

"What the hell's going on with you?"

"I kept thinking that here's this woman doing what she wants without a care in the world, and here I am about to be a mother and totally clueless about how I'm going to deal with that and a law practice. I think that covers it."

Carpenter caught himself, held back telling Philly to stop feeling sorry for herself. Motherhood would be a life-changing event for her and would seriously screw up her practicing law. But that was life. Somehow, they'd find a way to deal with the situation. With all the technology around today, there had to be a workable solution.

"I'm about ready to pack it in," Carpenter said. "What say we talk about your situation tomorrow?"

"Sure," Philly said. "Nothing will be different tomorrow except that another day will have come and gone."

27

At noon Carpenter leaned back in his desk chair and gave the finger to the man in the photograph facing his desk. "You're not going to be happy for me so fuck you," he said to the photograph. It was not the man's job to make him feel good, but Carpenter thought he had reason to be pleased. Jerome Singer had agreed to Michelle's condition as long as she sent him a copy of her paper. Documents would be signed today and money would change hands early tomorrow.

Carpenter consulted his calendar. Tomorrow the real fun would begin. A meeting with Jerome Singer was scheduled for ten thirty in Catching's office. The next day back to court to report to Judge O'Connell on how Jack Lawson was faring. Shortly he'd have to file an opposition to the motion to dismiss the case filed by Herbert Stanton and Millie Lane against Wise Computer Services. In the midst of this activity, he needed to prod Philly to bring Frederick Chun on board and file a discrimination claim against Crowe Investment Strategies. In a matter of weeks, he expected to hear from the Board of Bar Overseers about Marshall Hyde's blog. And there remained the possibility that John and Naomi Harrington would opt to do something stupid and take on the Dixfield school system if the system refused to remove documents from Luke Harrington's school record.

For the moment, life was good, Carpenter reflected. People were doing mean and stupid things to one another and some of the legal fallout was landing in his lap. True, the cases could turn to shit in a heartbeat, but there came a time when you had to rejoice that things were looking up. Well some things, anyway. If only Philly were back to her old self!

The knock on her door wasn't Carpenter's signature knock but Philly said, "Come in," without bothering to ask who it was.

"Shit!" she muttered when Maxine French entered her office.

"Nice to see you too," Maxine said, taking off her overcoat and draping it over a stack of files beside the visitor's chair she appropriated.

"You're here because of Carpenter, right?" Philly challenged Maxine. "He sent you to check up on me."

"Guilty as charged," Maxine retorted, unabashed. "So what the hell's going on with you? You didn't have to bite my head off just now."

Philly didn't want to unload her miseries on Maxine. Given her druthers she preferred to sulk and feel miserable. "I don't want to talk about it."

"Tough shit," Maxine countered, raising a hand above her head. "I have had it up to here with Carpenter telling me how you're not yourself."

Philly stood up and patted her belly. "I'm definitely showing," she said. "This is really going to happen and it's starting to freak me out." She recalled how over the weekend she couldn't wriggle into a pair of her jeans.

"You're changing the subject," Maxine said. "What can I do to help?"

"Nothing," Philly said, shaking her head.

"I'm not going to accept that," Maxine came back. "You are more pigheaded than Carpenter and that's saying something. I'm starting to wonder how you've avoided killing each other the past few years. He's worried about you. He can't put his finger on it, but he says he thinks it's something more than your pregnancy that's eating at you. You need to trust me and tell me."

Philly studied Maxine. The woman was slight and trim. With her gray hair, your first impression was that she was a non-threatening grandmotherly type. It was easy to forget that Maxine was tough as nails.

"I'm just feeling overwhelmed," Philly said.

"All right," Maxine replied. "If you're not going to talk to me, you're not going to talk to me. Let's think ahead. It's the middle of July. You've given birth and you're home from the hospital. How do you see your life?"

Philly had been studiously avoiding thinking about the future. But she decided to humor Maxine and try to visualize what lay ahead.

"I guess I'm going to be changing a lot of diapers and doing a lot of feeding the kid and not much else."

"Are you going to breastfeed?"

"I don't know. I think it's going to make practicing law more complicated."

"I recommend that you breastfeed," Maxine said. "It's good for the baby and it'll be good for you when it comes to bonding with your baby. I speak from experience here. I wasn't a great mother, but I did breastfeeding right."

"I don't know," Philly repeated.

"I'd like to hold a baby shower for you," Maxine shifted gears. "Give me the names and phone numbers of everyone you want to invite."

Philly began to think that Maxine was the female equivalent of Raul. Once she got up a head of steam, there was no stopping her.

"You're supposed to say thank you," Maxine reminded her.

"Thank you."

"Do you have a crib and bassinet?"

Philly shook her head. "What is this, twenty fucking questions?"

"Carpenter and I want that to be our gift to you. You don't have to worry about that."

"That's very generous."

Maxine waved the compliment away. "Do you have a home office in your new house?"

Philly nodded.

"Make sure you have a good printer. You'll also need a scanner, fax machine, and copier. Don't skimp on any of that. You can probably get all those features in one machine."

Philly considered the logistics of her second-floor office. The new equipment might mean that Philip's old desk would have to go and another tie with Philip severed.

"Can I ask you something?" Philly requested. "Do you think Carpenter would go ballistic if I gave up my Boston office?"

Maxine smiled. "Of course he will. But his explosion will be quick and then he'll simmer down. You need to do what you have to do."

"It won't be the same if we're not seeing each other," Philly said.

"Carpenter doesn't like change. He likes to go about practicing law in the manner he's become accustomed to over the years. He's always saying how he likes to eyeball people. But Carpenter's more resilient than he lets on. You, if anybody, should have learned that by now. He'll come to terms with whatever you need to do."

At last Philly raised one of the subjects she was fearful about. "Why would he want to keep our association going if I'm not around?"

"I think you know the answer to that," Maxine said. "Carpenter genuinely likes you. Also, you're a good lawyer. The two of you had a rather successful year last year or so he claims. Let us help you."

Philly wondered what it was inside her that made her resist the people who were trying to look out for her. "What are you doing right now?" she said, coming up with a diversion.

"Nothing."

"Let's get out of here and go shopping. I can't get into my jeans anymore."

"Deal," Maxine said. "I was wondering why you were wearing a dress. But while we're walking you're going to give me names for that baby shower."

Not a problem, Philly figured. It was going to be a short list.

28

Philly remembered Jerome Singer as a glib, arrogant dandy. He hadn't changed much. He was tall and slender, wore his dark hair slicked back and had a pencil thin moustache. Seated at the head of a long conference room table in Daniel Catching's Boston office, he didn't appear the least bit humbled by the regulatory mess he found himself in.

Catching was accompanied by another WilsonCrane lawyer, a young woman associate in a dark business suit. Catching made the introductions and Philly understood why Carpenter had liked the guy. Catching was down to earth, without airs, and that said a lot for a lawyer who was being shoved aside on a major case.

"We've put together an indexed compilation of documents," Catching said, once they were all seated. He nodded to his associate and, with some effort, she extracted from a litigation briefcase a pile of paper that Philly guessed was easily a foot high. Carpenter gave the stack a malevolent stare and removed a notepad from his own briefcase.

"Is the Devonshire Plastics loan the only loan where a borrower who was told about the ninety-day cure period didn't get the full ninety days?" Carpenter directed at Catching and Singer.

"No," Catching said. "Jerome can't recall with certainty all the borrowers he mentioned the ninety days to. But since you and I last talked, we've documented one instance where a borrower was told about a ninety-day cure period but was sued immediately after the ten-day cure period in the loan agreement expired."

Carpenter jotted a few words on his notepad. "When did this other instance occur?"

"This was an earlier loan that defaulted three years ago."

"Do the regulators know about that case?" Carpenter asked.

"Not yet, but they will once we reply to document requests."

Carpenter pointed to the stack of paper produced by Catching's associate. "Is that case in the papers you've put together?"

The associate shook her head.

"Get me the papers on that case," Carpenter instructed the woman. "What percent of borrowers were told about a ninety-day cure period?"

"Roughly twenty-five percent give or take," Catching said.

"Why did you mention ninety days to borrowers," Carpenter leveled his first pointed question at Singer.

Singer leaned forward in his chair and frowned. "Because I try to work things out when a borrower defaults on a loan. Working things out takes time, usually about ninety days."

Carpenter made another notation on his notepad. "I'm assuming that you didn't work things out with the earlier borrower you mentioned ninety days to."

"That's right," Singer said. "Right off it was clear that negotiations were going nowhere."

"I want to hear the tape of the conversation you had with Norman Cassidy," Carpenter said. "I understand you have a copy." Carpenter noted, with some relief, that Philly seemed alert and engaged. That was an improvement.

Catching's associate produced a tape recorder, plugged it into a console set in the middle of the table, and started the tape.

Philly wrote down Singer's exact words when it came to the language that mattered: *"Don't worry about the ten days, Norman. That's what the lawyers insist upon. I pretty much give my borrowers ninety days to cure. I try to work things out."*

Carpenter insisted that that part of the conversation be played back. Philly thought that Singer had lost some of his certitude as he listened twice to the words that had landed him in difficulty.

Carpenter stared at his notepad lost in thought. Philly had seen him get so caught up in trying to unravel a thorny knot that he'd forget he was with other people. But after a long moment, Carpenter pointed to the stack of paper produced by WilsonCrane. "Is the entire loan file for Devonshire Plastics in the papers you've put together?"

The associate shook her head and Catching said, "We'll get that for you before you leave."

"Why did Devonshire Plastics default on its loan?" Carpenter asked.

Catching and his associate turned toward Singer.

"The company ran out of cash," Singer said

"Was that a surprise?" Carpenter asked.

"We didn't see it coming, if that's what you mean."

"Why didn't you seeing it coming?"

Singer shifted in his seat and Philly figured that he wasn't used to being grilled. If he hung around Carpenter long enough he'd discover that grilling was the norm.

"The financials we had been getting showed some deterioration in the company's business but nothing to suggest the company was broke."

"What did Cassidy say about his company's downturn?"

Singer again shifted in his chair. "Not much really."

"Were the financials you were getting audited or unaudited?"

"Year-end financials were audited. Interim financial statements during the year were unaudited."

"Who were the accountants?"

Singer glanced at Catching.

"Miller and Huggins," the associate contributed.

"Just like the baseball manager," Carpenter said, and Philly took in the blank looks around the table that greeted his statement. She made a note to ask him about the reference.

"I never heard of Miller and Huggins," Carpenter said.

"They're a small firm in Wellesley," Singer explained. "Cassidy had been using them for years and we decided to let him continue to use them. I'm pretty sure we checked them out and found them okay."

Carpenter set his briefcase on the conference room table, opened it, put his notepad inside and then turned to Catching. "Daniel, I'd like you to do two things for me. First, find out whatever you can about this Miller and Huggins accounting firm. I'm particularly interested in whether any member of that firm is a personal friend of Norman Cassidy."

Catching nodded. "What's the second thing?"

Carpenter pointed to the pile of paper Catching's associate had produced. "Deliver that to my office along with the other things I asked for. I'm not about to lug that shit back to my office."

"That's it?" Singer said. "You mean we're done?"

Philly looked at her watch. The meeting had lasted thirty-five minutes.

"For now we're done," Carpenter said.

"What's my defense?" Singer asked.

"How the hell should I know" Carpenter came back. "I haven't done my required reading. And after Ms. Piper and I have waded through what you've put together, it may turn out that you don't have a defense."

"This is fucking great!" Singer exclaimed, and Philly thought he was close to losing it.

"Just because you don't have a defense doesn't mean you're going to lose," Carpenter pointed out.

"What the hell are you talking about?" Singer exploded.

Carpenter stood up and headed for the door. "To be continued," he said before exiting the conference room.

They were back in their own conference room and Philly was concerned that the walk to their offices had tired her. They had picked up sandwiches on the way, Carpenter's treat. She was ravenous. She arranged her new maternity dress as she unwrapped her sandwich at the conference room table. Buying maternity clothes with Maxine had been one of the most depressing afternoons of her life. *Expandable waistbands* were two words she never wanted to hear again.

"Who the hell are Miller and Huggins?" Philly asked, when her hunger had been partially satisfied.

"Miller Huggins was a famous major league baseball manager."

"Nobody seemed to get that."

"I noticed," Carpenter said. "The guy managed a long time ago, so I guess it's just another thing to show that I'm a geezer."

Philly strained to stop herself from laughing out loud. Carpenter's use of the word she silently called him was too much. "So what *is* Singer's defense?" she asked.

"I meant what I said before. I don't have a clue."

"How do you want to handle the paper?" Philly asked.

Carpenter checked his watch. "It's noon," he announced. "How about this? You go off to one of your asinine spinning classes while I put a call into the Lawsons. We're in court tomorrow and I need to find out how young Jack has been making out. Hopefully the little fucker didn't become a raving lunatic when his meds were cut. When you come back refreshed, the Top Tier papers should have arrived from Catching and we'll go through them together. I don't expect to finish them today."

Had Carpenter really suggested she go spinning in the middle of a workday? "Are you serious?" she asked.

"Yeah, I am. Also, when you get back, there will be a check for you from Michelle Smith's case. By the way, I hit Singer up for a twenty thousand retainer and he paid that and signed my engagement letter. But I'm not going to do anything with his retainer money right now if that's okay with you."

Philly continued to feel guilty about receiving any money from Michelle Smith's case. But she found herself nodding to everything Carpenter had put forward.

"Okay then," Carpenter said. "Get your sweaty ass back here by two thirty."

Carpenter sat in the office suite conference room thinking about tomorrow's court hearing in the Lawson case while he waited for Philly. He had tracked down Sylvia Lawson. She reported one pushing and shoving incident during recess in which a girl was pushed by Jack, landed on her ass, and began wailing. A monitor on duty at the time reported that the girl had grabbed a kickball from Jack, the two had engaged in a brief tugging match over the ball, and then Jack had given her the push that landed the girl on her backside. The monitor was not quite fast enough to prevent the girl from hitting the ground. It struck Carpenter as a harmless, run of the mill squabble. But no doubt, Stonington would paint Jack as a playground terror. On the plus side, Sylvia Lawson had reported that Jack's energy level was up the last two days.

Philly entered the conference room looking reasonably mellow. Carpenter filled her in on his discussion with Sylvia Lawson.

"Kids get into playground fights all the time," Philly commented.

"That's going to have to be my position," Carpenter said. "What do you see the judge doing?"

Philly was giving his question her full attention. Good. Carpenter probably had Maxine to thank for her change of attitude, although Philly still hadn't really opened up about what was bugging her.

"I'd say there's a decent chance the judge will leave things alone."

"That's what I was thinking," Carpenter said. He pointed to the stack of documents delivered by Daniel Catching. "Now we get to do what I've been dreading."

"What are we looking for?" Philly asked.

"I don't know. But it's like what that judge said about obscenity. We'll know it when we see it."

At four thirty, Carpenter began to lose focus. Philly, he observed, seemed to have more pep than he did so maybe there *was* something to the notion that exercise gave you energy. Maxine exercised several times a week and had more stamina than he did on their weekend hikes.

Carpenter figured that he and Philly had each gone through about a third of the documents delivered by Catching. He now had a decent grasp of the administrative process facing Top Tier Finance Company, and the regulations that applied to loan companies were reasonably straightforward. The gist of the complaint against Singer's company was that the company made misrepresentations to prospective borrowers about the time borrowers had to cure a loan default. A regulation prohibited misrepresentations. A case could be made that Singer was guilty of a misrepresentation to Norman Cassidy.

"I'm ready to pack it in," Carpenter admitted. "I want to be fresh for court tomorrow. Also, if you don't mind putting a halt to this, I'd appreciate it if you reviewed the pleadings I've done for Herbert Stanton and Millie Lane."

Philly leaned back in her chair and rubbed her belly in a circular motion. "Okay," she said. "Is it just me or is this stuff really boring."

"It's just you. No, I'm kidding. It's pretty deadly."

"We haven't come up with anything that's going to help Singer, have we?"

"No, we haven't."

"I think if we don't, he's going to fire us and go back to Catching."

"You're right," Carpenter agreed. "Singer has a short fuse and he's the kind of guy who would turn on a lawyer in a second. Look what he did to Catching."

"What's our plan here?"

"We do what we're doing. After court tomorrow, we'll keep going through this stuff. If we're lucky, we can finish it tomorrow."

"I can hardly wait," Philly said.

29

Philly willed herself to focus on Judge O'Connell and stop thinking about how much Stonington's attorney reminded her of Philip and what she'd be missing out on in upcoming years. The jurist was studying Craig Lannon's motion to dissolve the injunction that had permitted Jack Lawson to attend school with monitors in attendance while his medications were being reduced. Present in court were Max and Sylvia Lawson as well as the monitor who had witnessed the playground shoving incident that involved their son, Jack.

Judge O'Connell looked up. "Was the girl in the incident described in your motion injured in any way?" he asked.

"Not physically, Your Honor," Lannon replied. "But she became terribly upset and it took a long while to calm her down."

"Isn't that the kind of behavior Stonington school officials were afraid would happen if Jack Lawson's meds were reduced?" the judge directed at Carpenter.

"That's what Superintendent Burnside claims," Carpenter responded, rising. "But nothing untoward happened. Because Mr. Lannon's motion was presented to me just before Your Honor took the bench, there has been no opportunity for the Lawsons to respond in writing. But Mr. and Mrs. Lawson, are here in court today, and so is Ms. Nancy Kline, the monitor who observed the incident. I would ask them all to rise."

The Lawsons stood accompanied by a serious-looking, stocky woman in her early twenties who sported a short ponytail.

"The monitor is prepared to testify today. She will relate that the playground incident involved a tug of war over a ball that the girl took from Jack. There was grabbing back and forth and Jack pushed the girl and she landed on her rear. I suspect the only thing injured was her dignity. If this incident had occurred with any other student, it would have passed unremarked upon. The fact is that reducing Jack's medication levels has improved his socialization dramatically. If he had still been on full doses, his mother will tell you that he wouldn't have been out on the playground playing. Instead he'd have been sitting off by himself in a daze."

"Why didn't the monitor prevent the push?" the judge followed up.

"Again, Your Honor may ask her for her account. She will testify that she arrived a moment too late to prevent the push. She will tell you that she was watching Jack closely but the back and forth between Jack and the girl took a matter of seconds."

The judge turned to Lannon. "What do Jack's teachers have to say about his socialization?"

"I don't have that information," Lannon said.

Judge O'Connell sat back in his chair and gazed thoughtfully at counsel. "Let me see my calendar for next week," the judge asked his clerk.

"Here's what I'm going to do," Judge O'Connell announced. "I'm not going to dissolve the injunction. The two monitors are to remain in place and the medication reduction can proceed as previously ordered. The first Thursday of next month at two in the afternoon, I will hold an evidentiary hearing. I want present in court Mr. and Mrs. Lawson, Jack's teacher or teachers, the two monitors, and everyone who has submitted an affidavit in this case. Anyone who hasn't submitted an affidavit already should do so. We'll engage in cross-examination. I want counsel to exchange copies of affidavits two days before the court hearing. I want counsel to work out a further extension of the hearing on Jack's IEP. Any questions?"

"Thank you, Your Honor," Carpenter said.

"No questions," Lannon said.

"The court will be in recess," the judge declared.

Carpenter held court while the Lawsons and Nancy Kline looked on uncertainly. "So far we're winning. Ms. Piper will be working with you on affidavits. The points we are going to hammer home are that Jack is more alert, more interactive, and less lethargic. Ms. Piper will work with Ms. Kline and the other monitor as to what they might be able to say in affidavits." Carpenter paused and his glance focused on Kline. "How do you see things going with Jack?" he asked the monitor.

Kline colored. "He's definitely become more animated as the week progressed. She paused, apparently thinking through how to phrase what she next wanted to say. "I don't think the shoving on the playground was any big deal. But to be honest, I'm a little worried that he might become more aggressive. It's nothing I can pinpoint; it's just a feeling I have."

Carpenter studied Kline. "Okay," he said. "Ms. Piper will be following up with you shortly." He turned to Sylvia Lawson. "You'll need to e-mail me contact information for Ms. Kline and the other monitor. We've got some work to do here."

The carton and the plastic utensils that had accompanied their pizza and salad orders had been pushed to an edge of the conference room table. Philly marveled that she and Carpenter had made their way through the mountain of paper related to Devonshire Plastics. Her back ached slightly and she wondered whether in another month, her pregnancy would permit her to sit for a protracted period without pain settling in. Carpenter seemed no worse for wear. There were times recently when she had noticed him showing his age but tonight wasn't one of them. He was focused, intense.

"Any thoughts?" Carpenter asked.

Philly wondered why Carpenter had spent so long going over the Devonshire Plastics loan file maintained by Top Tier Finance Company. Maybe he had seen something in those documents that offered Singer's company a glimmer of hope. "I don't think Singer's company has much of a defense. Nothing's jumped out at me."

"I agree," Carpenter said immediately. "What would be a win for Singer's company?" he asked.

"To keep its license," Philly said.

"Exactly. That's what we need to focus on. Singer's company is going to be punished. I don't see a way around that. Singer probably misled Norman Cassidy and nothing we've read will change that."

Philly thought of Singer's reaction to this glum assessment. "But what do we do with our client?"

"Tell him the facts of life. He's not going to like it and he may fire us on the spot. But that's the way it goes."

"What kind of punishment were you thinking about?" Philly followed up. She didn't believe Singer would be amenable to any sanction that was more than a slap on the wrist.

"A hefty fine," Carpenter threw out. "Maybe he agrees to a period in which he employs an internal auditor to review Top Tier's lending practices."

"Singer will love that," Philly said.

"Singer will hate everything about it. We'll have to listen to him bitch and moan about how unfair it is that he's being picked on. He'll refuse to recognize that his own stupidity landed him in the mess he's in."

"Do you really see the regulators going for something less than taking away the company's license?"

"I don't have a read on that. The timing of all this sucks. In this down economy, with the newspapers constantly reporting about home owners and businesses battling evil lenders to avoid foreclosure, regulators might want to make an example of Singer's company and come down hard."

"So what's the game plan?"

"We blame the victim."

"Cassidy?"

Carpenter nodded. "The man already broke the law by illegally taping a telephone conversation. What if the financials Cassidy produced when Devonshire Plastics took out the loan were rigged?"

"How the hell are we going to prove that?"

"*We're* not," Carpenter said. "But we both know someone who can. Lily Tompkins does the books for Singer's company. She first introduced me to Singer and Michelle Smith. Our job is going to be to get Devonshire Plastic's financials and backup to the financials so that Lily can review them."

Carpenter had unlimited faith in Lily Tompkins' abilities; he had consulted her on his own dime to review financials in a class action case they had settled last year. "There's just one problem," Philly said. "When Singer lied to Cassidy he had no reason to believe that Cassidy's financials were false, assuming that they were,"

"That's a big problem," Carpenter conceded. "I haven't thought through that yet. I believe that if someone illegally records your telephone conversations you can sue that person."

"I'm not sure," Philly said, wondering where his sudden detour would lead them.

"I want to get those Spenser Law grads to do some research on illegal recording of phone calls. I think it's a good way to spend some of Singer's retainer."

Philly tensed. There were entirely too many new people entering her life. She had two new tenants to deal with—Wood and Morrison had met through Isabella's efforts, decided they could tolerate each other, and had signed leases. And now Carpenter wanted to involve two new lawyers in a major case which could be pulled away from them if Singer behaved like he had always behaved when told something he didn't want to hear.

"What the hell," Philly said. "Go for it."

"Now you're talking."

April

Philly's Untitled Playlist

Like a Rolling Stone

Bob Dylan

30

Late Sunday morning Philly felt that she was floating in her expandable waist jeans as she took the stairs to her second-floor home office. She had gone for an early morning bike ride out by Boston College, luxuriating in the unexpected warm air, not quite certain whether halfway through the ride there was a baby's kick. Now, back at her desk, she was conscious of noise above her; that would be Morrison given the layout of the third-floor rental rooms.

Philly turned on her computer and decided to methodically pick off the items on her to-do list. First, she fired off an e-mail to Frederick Chun telling him that she would take on his discrimination case on a contingency fee arrangement. Carpenter's willingness to take on Chun's case still puzzled her, but she decided to trust his hunch that there was a payoff to be had.

Next, Philly reread the letter sent to her by an attorney representing the Dixfield school district. Dixfield refused to delete any document from Luke Harrington's file; the documents the Harringtons wanted to delete contained important information that would assist administrators and teachers in meeting Luke's educational and other needs.

Philly saved the letter in PDF form and attached it to an e-mail to the Harringtons. She suggested that they call her to set up a time for a conference call or a meeting, certain the couple would opt to wage a losing battle to have documents removed from their son's school records.

After that was done, Philly took her time going over Carpenter's pleadings in the Herbert Stanton and Millie Lane suit. The motion to dismiss their clients' suit asserted that Stanton and Lane had no claim for damages because, as employees at will, Wise Computer Consultants had an absolute right to fire them at any time and thereby cut off their wages and benefits.

Philly thought that Carpenter had done a good job of driving home the point that an employer's right to fire an employee at will couldn't be based on an employer illegally violating the employee's right to privacy. Wise Computer Consultants claimed that keeping track of mobile employees was an employer's prerogative. But the company had no good answer to Carpenter's argument that it concealed from employees what it was up to, and never limited its GPS employee monitoring to work hours. Philly made a few wording changes to

Carpenter's efforts and then did some on-line research which produced two cases she thought would support the legal arguments he had come up with.

Turning to the Lawsons' case, Philly sent an e-mail to each of the monitors hired to keep an eye on Jack. She requested that they share with her their observations of Jack and point out any facts that showed he was not a danger to other students and teachers. That left just one more item on her list: affidavits for Mr. and Mrs. Lawson. Philly started with Mrs. Lawson. Ladies first, she reasoned.

31

Simon Jeffries and Rachel Boyle hadn't made much of an impression on Philly during the law school honor code case she had helped Carpenter with last year. He must have picked up on qualities that she had overlooked. During introductory small talk, each recent graduate from Spenser New England School of Law, despite exhibiting a certain understandable diffidence, had a quiet confidence and self-possession. Jeffries seemed the more intense of the two. He was painfully thin with slicked back dark hair. Boyle had short blond hair and a round face and Philly gave her a point when her serious expression gave way in the face of Carpenter's joking around. Philly couldn't believe how young and earnest the recent law school grads looked.

"Here's a brief rundown of a case that Philly and I have taken on. If you know what's good for you, you'll refer to Ms. Piper as Philly when we're being informal."

Philly tried for a genuine smile but suspected her product was weak. There was definitely movement inside her and she gave her belly a circular rub.

As Carpenter discoursed on the plight of Top Tier Finance Company, Boyle seemed intent on taking down every word he uttered. Jeffries, in contrast, jotted down a word or two occasionally but for the most part regarded Carpenter intently.

"Your job," Carpenter wound up, "is to research whether in Massachusetts, Jerome Singer has a cause of action against Norman Cassidy because Cassidy recorded their telephone conversation without telling Singer he was doing so. If the answer to that question is no, you don't have to do anything else. If the answer is yes, I want to know what kind of damages Singer can recover. For example, if

Singer's company is brought down because of the telephone conversation Cassidy recorded, can Singer sue Cassidy personally for that loss?"

"I think Massachusetts has a statute that allows a person to sue somebody who illegally records the person's telephone call," Boyle chimed in.

"You need to set us straight," Carpenter said, "and your conclusions need to be right. This is important."

The young lawyers were unfazed by Carpenter's admonition.

"Here's another issue to look into," Carpenter continued. "If someone violates a statute that makes it a crime to secretly record a phone conversation, can the person reveal the recorded conversation to regulators as a whistleblower?"

Carpenter's last question got Jeffries to match Boyle when it came to taking notes.

"And while you're thinking about that question, a related question is whether a regulatory agency that receives information that was obtained by committing a crime can use that information in an administrative proceeding against someone who is regulated."

Carpenter paused until the young lawyers finished writing.

"Keep track of your time. I'm proposing to pay you each one hundred dollars an hour for your time. When you come up with a work product that addresses the questions, send us an email with a memorandum attached. State the question, your conclusion, and then provide a brief discussion. You don't have to cite us a million cases. But if there's case law against any conclusion you reach, we need to know what the opposing case law is. Consider yourselves a team. Philly and I are not interested in how you divide up work, but we expect the finished work product to come from both of you."

Jeffries and Boyle eyed each other. Philly thought that Carpenter's assignment required only one person, but he must have had his reasons for bringing the two of them in on Singer's case.

"I know that each of you has other work you're involved with," Carpenter said. "I'd like to hear from you a week from today. Will that present a problem?"

Jeffries and Boyle shook their heads.

"We appreciate this," Boyle said.

"Don't mention it," Carpenter replied. "Philly and I are the ones who are grateful."

Carpenter showed Jeffries and Boyle out and returned to the conference room in what was, for him, a good mood.

Philly considered that he'd be a fool if he didn't take advance steps to have backup available while she was dealing with a newborn. But she couldn't dismiss feeling threatened by their displacing her when Carpenter needed help with work. "Why bring both of them in on this?" she asked.

"When I talked to them on the phone, I thought they had different strengths. I decided to play a hunch and use both of them. They're going to have to talk to each other and defend positions against the other. Let's see what happens. We can always cut our losses if it doesn't work out. But I'll tell you one thing. Those two will charge a lot less than you or me or Catching's firm."

Philly stopped off at a package store several blocks from the house. The clerk looked at her oddly when she presented one large bottle of beer for checkout, but Philly gave the clerk her hard stare and he took care of business. At least I still have the evil eye, Philly thought as she buried the cold bottle in her leather work tote.

32

For this meeting on the following day, Carpenter's instincts told him that the mountain should go to Muhammad so here in his conference room were Jerome Singer and Daniel Catching and Catching's associate whose name he had forgotten upon hearing it. Philly didn't look as together as he would have liked. If she wasn't on her game, he would have to play around her.

"We've gone through the documents Daniel sent over and we have some initial observations that we wanted to share with you sooner rather than later," Carpenter began. Catching and his associate were all attention, but Singer seemed to be only partly focusing, as if mentally distancing himself from bad news.

"First, the licensing board rules prohibit misrepresentations. The taped conversation contains a statement that Mr. Cassidy didn't have to worry about the ten-day cure period in the written loan agreement. It turned out that Mr. Cassidy and Devonshire Plastics did have to worry about the ten-day cure period in the agreement because Top Tier held them to that shorter time to cure a loan default. A superior court judge came to the same conclusion. Therefore, it's our opinion that Top Tier Finance Company is going to receive regulatory discipline of some kind because of the statement made by Mr. Singer to Mr. Cassidy."

Carpenter paused. Singer stared at the conference room tabletop. If Catching had communicated a similar conclusion, it would mean that Singer was now hearing from a second lawyer that his company was at major risk.

"The worst regulatory discipline would include loss of Top Tier's license to make loans," Carpenter continued. "So a victory in this case would be for Top Tier to keep its lending license and end up with some other kind of discipline instead."

Carpenter saw Catching nod but Singer's expression was unreadable.

"Daniel, did you have any settlement discussions with the regulatory board lawyers?"

Catching shook his head. "Mr. Singer was not disposed to negotiate."

"Does that still stand?" Carpenter directed at Singer.

"Let me hear the rest of what you have to say," Singer said peevishly.

Carpenter turned to Catching. "When you foreclosed on Devonshire did you obtain that company's financial records?"

"No," Catching said. "Devonshire never contested that it was in default under its loan. The only financials are in the papers you have. Those financials are what Devonshire sent to Top Tier under its loan agreement."

"Ms. Piper and I want all of Devonshire's financial records," Carpenter said. "Do you think the regulators will help us get them?"

Catching shrugged. "I don't know. You could try to subpoena the records."

"Why do you want all the financial records?" Singer grumbled.

"I want to try to figure out whether Devonshire's financials were false."

"What's that going to prove?"

"I'm not sure," Carpenter admitted. "The problem is that you never believed that Devonshire's financials were false when you made the loan to Devonshire Plastics and when you started foreclosure proceedings against the company. But if Norman Cassidy misled you, my instincts tell me that the regulators will be more amenable to resolving your case short of de-licensure."

"How are we going to figure out whether Devonshire's financials are tainted?" Singer asked, with a little less hostility.

"If we get our hands on the financials, I want you to have Lily Tompkins take a look at them."

This suggestion engaged Singer. He leaned forward in his chair and ran his fingers down the sides of his moustache. "What else do you have?"

"I'm having some research done on some other issues. I'll fill you in if anything bears fruit."

"Who the hell do you have doing research?"

"Freelancers," Carpenter said.

"Why not have Daniel's firm do the research?"

"I'll bring Daniel in when appropriate," Carpenter fired back, sick of Singer's interrogation.

"I don't like this," Singer grumbled.

Carpenter turned to Catching. "Did you find anything out about Norman Cassidy and his accountants?"

Catching nodded at his associate and the woman colored. "Paul Huggins and Norman Cassidy live in Cherryfield on the same street. Devonshire Plastics is located on the outskirts of Cherryfield. Also, when you go to the Miller & Huggins website, it appears that Devonshire Plastics is the accounting firm's major client. Of course, that's no longer true since Devonshire went bankrupt."

Carpenter remembered that Cherryfield was somewhere south of Boston down around Middleboro. "What are the chances we can take this Paul Huggins' deposition?" he asked Catching.

"The rules of procedure don't permit depositions unless you get a prehearing order that gives you permission. You might have better luck getting an order requiring Huggins to turn over his firm's financial documents on Devonshire."

Carpenter thought Catching's assessment was probably correct. He turned to face Singer. "Is settlement still off the table?"

"No," Singer said, and it seemed to Carpenter that the word had been surgically removed from his client.

33

Philly sat beside Cambridge Police Detective Paul Sullivan in Room 560 in the new Cambridge Superior Court building in Woburn. Sullivan had e-mailed her that a plea agreement had been reached and would be heard in court today. Colin Feeney was scheduled to plead guilty to involuntary manslaughter and would be on probation for five years if the plea agreement was accepted by the court. Reading the e-mail, Philly had barely controlled her rage. Colin Feeney was going to walk. The little shit who had wrecked her life was going to parrot a few magic words that his attorney would have beaten into his thick skull and leave the court a free man. The months of waiting for Feeney to get what he deserved were going to result in no justice at all. Philly had been so furious after reading about the plea deal that in a manner of minutes, she'd knocked off the warm beer she had squirreled away in her bedroom. The slight buzz she had experienced had done nothing to dampen her fury.

"The Commonwealth versus Colin Feeney," the clerk called out.

The cast that had been present when she first laid eyes on Feeney reassembled. Judge Irene Caffrey pushed her wire rimmed glasses back on her nose as Evan Blake moved forward with Colin Feeney. Blake's athletic bearing and evident energy contrasted with his client's hangdog demeanor and stooped posture. On this occasion, the prosecutor, Heidi Greenbaum, had only one file folder in front of her.

"I understand that the defendant wishes to change his plea to guilty," Judge Caffrey said.

"That's correct," Blake said as Greenbaum nodded her accord.

"Please proceed, Miss Greenbaum," the judge directed.

Greenbaum spelled out what the commonwealth intended to prove at trial. Although the information was painfully familiar to Philly, the tale Greenbaum recounted lacked immediacy, as if a story that had unfolded in a distant past was being dusted off and repeated.

Judge Caffrey fired off a series of questions designed to ensure that Feeney agreed with the facts Greenbaum had recounted and was entering his guilty plea voluntarily. Feeney replied yes to the judge's questions, keeping his head lowered as he delivered his responses.

The judge's next set of questions were directed to Blake. Blake provided assurances that Feeney had been fully advised of the rights he was waiving by agreeing to plead guilty.

The judge's interrogations had lasted twelve minutes. Philly realized that if she remained silent, the plea agreement would be a done deal.

Philly stood and moved toward the gate that separated the lawyers and the judge's bench from the gallery. "Don't do this," Sullivan whispered shrilly, but Philly pushed on the gate and entered the attorneys' area. "May I be heard, Your Honor?" she called out.

Judge Caffrey startled at the interruption. "And who might you be?"

"Philomena Piper. Philip Sizemore was my fiancé."

"And what is it you expect to accomplish by this interruption?" the judge demanded.

"I want to be heard," Philly said, trying to keep her anger under control. She didn't know whether her baby's movements were a sign she was doing the right or wrong thing.

"I'm not inclined to take any victim statement in this matter," the judge said.

"You'll take mine," Philly said. She felt a hand on her shoulder. Paul Sullivan was by her side. "Please," he whispered.

"I'm going to ask the court officer to escort you out of the courtroom if you don't take your seat."

"I'm not the only one that will be escorted out of the courtroom," Philly came back. She undid her coat. "The other person leaving the courtroom will be a baby that will never know its father. I can't believe that this kid gets to mouth a few yes answers that have been pounded into his head and he walks away from what he's done. Where the hell is justice here?"

"You're out of line Ms. Piper," the judge cautioned. "Are you by any chance an attorney?"

"I am."

"Then I would be very careful what I said and did from this moment on."

"I'm not afraid of you, Your Honor. I'd never be able to live with myself if I just sat and said nothing and let this travesty unfold. For this kid to get a slap on the wrist is incredible."

Judge Caffrey said nothing. Philly met the jurist's hard stare without flinching. Sullivan's hand was still on her shoulder. "You're messing with the wrong judge," he whispered.

Evan Blake started to rise and sank back in his chair. Colin Feeney, sitting beside Blake, lowered his head into his hands.

"Not another word out of you, Ms. Piper," the judge said. "I'm going to accept the plea agreement. Mr. Feeney will be on probation for five years. He will report to an assigned probation officer. During the probationary period, he is not to ingest any alcohol at all. No exceptions. A condition of probation is that he receive counseling approved by his probation officer."

The judge paused and glared at Philly. Sullivan's grip tightened on her shoulder.

"In accepting the plea agreement, I've given careful attention to the probation report," Judge Caffrey directed at Philly. "Until his mother's death some years ago, Colin Feeney had not been in any kind of trouble. After his mother died, trouble has seemed to follow him. He took up drinking. Home visits disclose that his father is not able to control him. One upshot of Mr. Feeney's behavior is the tragic death of Mr. Sizemore that brings us to court today. Mr. Feeney. Look at me."

Feeney raised his head and Philly saw in his eyes the same terror that had been present at the court session that occurred months ago.

"Let Ms. Piper's presence today and her grief be a lesson to you. True, you have owned up to taking responsibility for your act. But you now no doubt realize how many lives you harmed by your conduct. You now have an opportunity to turn your life around. Don't squander the opportunity. The plea agreement puts in place helpful resources that will assist you in this task. We can't undo the tragedy you caused. But you need to make sure that from here on out, nothing like this ever comes close to happening again. Do you understand me?"

Feeney nodded and lowered his head.

"I need you to look at me and answer me so I can hear you."

Feeney's head inclined upward. "Yes," he said barely audibly.

Judge Caffrey paused and turned to face Philly. "I'm sorry for your loss, Ms. Piper. Let Mr. Sullivan escort you from the courtroom if you know what's good for you."

Sullivan turned her around, one hand remaining on her shoulder, his other hand at her waist. They moved back through the swinging gate to the rear of the courtroom. Philly was struck by a large, pale complexioned man dressed in work clothes who lowered his head when they passed. Although there was no close resemblance, she knew she had gotten her first look at Colin Feeney's father.

In the courthouse cafeteria, Paul Sullivan silently sipped his coffee. Philly let her tea cool and braced herself for Sullivan's I told you so. But when Sullivan remained silent, Philly spoke first. "Go ahead and say it," she challenged the detective.

Sullivan shook his head. "I'm not playing your game."

"You would have done the same thing in my position."

"If it were some years ago, you're right," Sullivan said. "But today, knowing what I know, I would have shut the hell up."

"And just what is it you know?"

Sullivan's soulful dark eyes were fixed on her as if he were seeing something inside her that he found unsettling.

"I know that Colin Feeney will in all likelihood drink again and do something incredibly stupid that will land him in jail. It's going to take something out of the ordinary to prevent that. And as for you, doing something stupid is a definite possibility."

"Is that it?"

Sullivan shook his head. "I hope I'm wrong here, but you and Feeney . . ." Sullivan paused, breathed deeply. "You're alike in some ways."

"What the fuck are you talking about?"

"Think about it," Sullivan said as he pushed his coffee mug to the middle of the table. "I've got to hit the road. If you ever need to talk, call me anytime. That offer is always open."

"Why are you saying things like that?" Philly asked as Sullivan stood up to leave. She never expected to see Sullivan again. "What the hell is there left to talk about?"

Sullivan smiled for the first time since they had sat down. "That's another thing you can think about."

34

As Philly addressed John and Naomi Harrington in the conference room, Carpenter thought that she was doing a good job of holding herself together. She'd given him the short version of what had happened in court yesterday and he thought it was a tossup whether Philly would succumb to tears or fly into a rage. In the end she did neither, settling for a string of profanities that had surprisingly little force behind them. In describing her run in with the presiding judge Philly had looked abashed, but Carpenter had been relieved. That was the fearless Philly he respected who wasn't going to back down before anybody, even a judge.

"Mr. Carpenter and I are of one mind on this," Philly summed up to the Harringtons. "We don't think you should pursue any legal action in connection with your son's school records."

Here were two other clients who were getting advice they didn't want to hear. In terms of reaction to bad news, Carpenter preferred Jerome Singer's sullen anger to the Harringtons' disappointed, incredulous looks.

"They think we abused Luke," John Harrington said. "They cited that law about abuse. We can't sit back and let that go unchallenged."

"Yes, you can," Philly said with authority. "You believe that you did nothing wrong. But someone, an outside third party such as a judge, might come to a different conclusion. Or a judge might decide that whether what you did was improper or not, Luke's records should be left alone. The point you need to understand is that there is nothing untrue in the records you want removed from Luke's file. That makes any lawsuit you bring problematic at best."

In unison, the Harringtons folded their arms across their bodies, a synchronized signal that Philly's common sense advice hadn't changed their predisposition to file suit.

"We're disappointed that you don't believe in our cause," Naomi Harrington said. "We're in the right here."

"It's not a question of believing in your cause, Philly said evenly. "We've done our duty to advise you. You've decided on a different course of action and, if you wish us to represent you, we'll fight like hell to get you what you want. We're simply giving you our opinion that it is unlikely you will get it. Since you've obviously rejected our advice, our next step will be to draw up a court complaint on your behalf. We'll try to turn around a draft document in a few weeks."

The Harringtons didn't appear mollified in Carpenter's opinion. "How much is this going to cost?" John Harrington inquired.

"This is an estimate," Philly said. "Probably around five to ten thousand dollars to draft a complaint and supporting affidavits, and to seek an injunction on your behalf."

Carpenter saw Naomi Harrington wince at the figure, but John Harrington never flinched.

"What about after the complaint is filed?" John Harrington followed up.

"If I were on the other side," Philly said, "I would consider taking your depositions. We'd have to prepare you for likely questions and sit in at the depositions. If you testified at your depositions confirming that Luke's records contained only true information, the Dixfield school district will probably file a motion to dismiss your suit. You would have to oppose that motion. That would involve legal briefs, affidavits, and a court hearing. We might have to take a deposition of our own to try to prevent the case from being dismissed. You're talking many thousands of dollars. If the case is not dismissed, the case would need to be tried. One decision you will have to make is whether you want that trial to be before a judge or a jury."

The Harringtons probably saw dollars flying out of their bank accounts. Carpenter believed that a jury learning how the couple had disciplined their son would take about a minute to tell the Harringtons that their parenting techniques left a lot to be desired.

But ultimately, the couple seemed undeterred by either the cost or the advice they'd received. "Go ahead and draft the complaint," John Harrington declared firmly. "We're in this for the long haul."

After work, Philly had stopped at a deli for a dinner sandwich which she ate at a small table in the deli's dining area. With each bite she felt more bloated. She had asked for her roast beef to be medium but, staring at the sandwich before each bite, she was greeted with a blood red smile.

Now, entering her house, all she wanted to do was shed clothes, get into her flannel nightgown, and lie in her bed with her feet raised by a pillow. Raul was pacing in the living room and Isabella was also present. Philly sensed they'd been waiting for her which had to be a bad sign.

"Hi," Philly said as she wriggled out of her coat. Raul glanced briefly at Isabella and received a nod in turn. "What's going on?" Philly asked.

Raul held out an empty beer bottle. "I found this when I was putting out the trash. Isabella and I do not drink beer. Did you have this beer?"

Philly silently cursed her stupidity. She should have tossed the bottle in a street trash receptacle on the way to work.

"You need to answer Raul," Isabella said, unsmiling.

"How about you two butting out. What's the big deal? So I had one fucking beer. Who gives a shit!"

"This is very bad," Raul said. "You should not be drinking anything at all in your delicate condition."

Philly remembered telling Raul that she would have to kill him if the words *delicate condition* again passed his lips. "Fuck off, Raul."

"Raul's right," Isabella weighed in. "What's going on, Philly?"

"I don't want to talk about it so butt out."

"No!" Isabella practically shouted, and Philly was taken aback by how upset and angry she was. Isabella began to pace as if she was working herself up to deliver a tirade. But Isabella abruptly deflated, collapsing on one of the living room easy chairs.

"Raul and I are not going to let you do anything that you will hate yourself for later on," Isabella said softly. "If you need some kind of professional help, I will help you get it. If you are too stubborn to help yourself, Raul and I will intervene. I haven't figured out how exactly. But we are not going to let you do anything to harm your baby. You need to be very clear about this."

If Raul had delivered such a speech, Philly would have tuned out half way through. But the speech had come from Isabella and Philly had listened.

"This is *my* life and *my* baby. I know you mean well but you need to butt out."

Isabella shook her head. "No," she repeated. "We will soon be starting childbirth classes. I will assist you as I promised but if you now wish a different partner, I understand. What *you* need to understand is that Raul and I are united on this. We refuse to let you do something stupid that will hurt your baby."

"We're done here," Philly said, as she headed toward her bedroom. "I'll get back to you on the childbirth classes."

35

The legal memorandum prepared by Simon Jeffries and Rachel Boyle was three pages single spaced and Carpenter appreciated the young lawyers' brevity. If the memorandum was a joint effort, it showed that both could write.

Recording a telephone conversation surreptitiously was a crime, they wrote. A Massachusetts statute provided for a civil cause of action against a person who recorded another's telephone conversation without the other's consent. If a person suing under the statute couldn't prove damages, the person could nonetheless be awarded twenty-five dollars for each illegally recorded telephone call. Jeffries and Boyle had found cases in other states in which, under similar statutes, plaintiffs had been awarded substantial damages. In one case, an illegally recorded phone conversation torpedoed a business deal, and the plaintiff was awarded the money he lost because the business deal fell through. Carpenter made a marginal note on the memorandum to read the out-of-state case.

Carpenter had expected the other conclusions that Jeffries and Boyle had reached. Someone who illegally obtained information could use the information to be a whistleblower. Also, an administrative agency could use illegally obtained information in a regulatory proceeding so long as the agency did not itself illegally obtain the information or encourage someone to do so.

Carpenter considered next moves. He was now counsel of record for Top Tier Finance Company in the license revocation hearing pending before a state agency known as the Loan Company Licensure Review Board. Shortly he was scheduled to speak with Louise Fuller, the lawyer who was prosecuting the case to revoke Top Tier's lending license. That telephone call would be his first chance to explore settlement of the case.

Carpenter e-mailed Jeffries and Boyle their next assignment: draft a motion to exclude from evidence the telephone discussion that Norman Cassidy had illegally recorded. The motion was contrary to the legal conclusion the young lawyers had reached but so what? The sooner a lawyer learned not to let the law stand in his way, the better.

Philly returned from work well after the dinner hour again dead on her feet, wondering if it were possible to avoid running into Raul and Isabella for an entire evening. But as soon as she entered the living room she realized that Raul and Isabella were the least of her problems. Rainy and Mace, her former drinking buddies at Shredders, the Brighton bar she used to frequent, were sitting in the living room easy chairs. They stopped talking when she entered and got to their feet. Philly could hear Raul and Isabella chatting in the kitchen. "Isn't this an unpleasant surprise," Philly said.

Isabella appeared from the kitchen and stopped short. Philly figured that either Isabella or Raul had told Rainy and Mace what had gone on the preceding evening. It had been months since she had seen either of them, and the situation was beyond awkward. Two years ago, she and Rainy had been in a relationship which she had broken off. Mace was simply bad news dangerous, a woman with a violent streak that could erupt without warning.

Rainy looked good. He was dressed in black—black silk shirt, black slacks, a black sports jacket—perhaps the outfit he had worn to teach at middle school today. Even though they had broken up, Philly knew that she and Rainy would always be friends. True, he was looking at her with a somewhat uncomfortable expression, but she attributed that to his seeing her pregnant and the news he had received from Raul and Isabella.

Mace was another story. Tall, thin, and dark complexioned, the woman's most striking feature was her long hair dyed nearly white. Philly tried to ignore Mace's angry stare and to forget the fact that Mace was a karate expert.

Raul came out of the kitchen and moved beside Isabella. Philly figured it wasn't often that you ended up in a room with two guys you had slept with while pregnant with the child of a third man.

"Don't let me interrupt anything," Philly said as she started for her bedroom door.

"Wait," Rainy said.

Philly stopped as Rainy drew beside her, helping her off with her coat. He guided her to the easy chair he had vacated and motioned for her to sit. His unease had vanished and Philly was impressed that he'd taken charge. Usually Rainy let someone else do the heavy lifting.

"Isabella and Raul stopped in at Shredders," Rainy said. "We got to talking and they told us they were worried about you. Mace and I are worried about you, too. We think you need help."

Philly played out the argument that had yet to begin and felt she lacked the energy to go through it. She decided to say nothing and wait Rainy out.

"You know I'm your friend," Rainy said. "Friends look out for each other." He glanced at his watch. "There's an AA meeting that starts in an hour. I'll drive you to it. It's not very far. Why don't you get changed and I'll run you over? I'll go in with you this first time."

Philly wasn't going anywhere. She opted for a measured, calm response. "I appreciate your concern, I really do. But right now, what I need is space and some time to lie down and put my feet up. I know you all mean well, but this is my decision. I need you to respect that."

"I told you you'd be wasting your time trying to talk sense to her," Mace intervened.

"Please," Rainy said, his eyes never leaving Philly's. "Do this for me."

"I'm going to lie down," Philly said, getting slowly to her feet.

Philly couldn't believe how fast Mace moved. One second the woman was standing behind Rainy, and the next she was in front of her pushing her hard back onto her chair.

"You stupid bitch!" Mace shouted. "Talking nice to you is fucking useless. Rainy and I are taking you to this AA meeting whether you like it or not. End of discussion."

Philly again stood up. "Out of my way."

Philly never saw the blow coming. Mace's open right hand came out of nowhere and caught her hard on her left cheek sending her back onto the chair. Mace hadn't held back. Philly put a hand to the cheek that stung. Rainy was staring wide-eyed and Raul and Isabella looked shocked. Mace leveled her gaze at Philly.

"Do you know how lucky you are? You're going to have a kid for Christ's sake. There are some of us who can't have kids. Did that ever fucking occur to you? All right, you had a tragedy in your life. Get over it. I will slap you silly before I let you do anything to harm that baby of yours. And you know I mean that."

Mace had barely raised her voice but Philly saw the menace in her eyes.

Mace asked Rainy for the time. "We're leaving in ten minutes. If you want to change or grab something to eat now's the time. Ten minutes."

Philly thought of taking out her cell phone and dialing 911. Mace would probably stomp the phone into pieces. So Philly sat. The ten minutes inched by. Philly wondered whether there was some hidden away part of her that was secretly grateful that Mace had thrown a nutty and taken charge.

"Times up," Mace announced.

Philly remained seated and then Mace was behind her, putting her arm in some kind of pressure hold that hurt like hell. She was on her feet—standing was the only way to make the pain stop—and being herded to the door. "Get her goddamn coat," Mace hissed at Rainy.

Philly looked over her shoulder. Isabella and Raul were nowhere to be seen.

The basement in Saint Sebastian's Church in Allston had seen better days. There were nicks in the pale green paint that coated the walls, the overhead lighting was dim, and the gray metal folding chairs that faced a table of the same color looked to Philly like used surplus office furniture that had been bought in bulk on the cheap. Mace forced Philly to sit, keeping hold of her arm but letting up on her pressure grip so the pain was gone for the moment. Rainy stood beside her giving her occasional weak smiles. He had draped her coat over her shoulders.

"Let's come to order!"

The speaker was tall and thin with long, greasy, brown hair and a scraggy brown moustache. The guy looked familiar; Philly suspected that she had seen him around Brighton. There had to be two dozen people taking seats although the chairs that had been set up could have accommodated twice that number.

The attendees spanned broad race and age spectrums; there were more men than women.

"I'm Charlie," said the man who had called for order. "I'm an alcoholic."

"Hi, Charlie!" came a weak chorus.

"Do we have anyone new here this evening?"

Rainy raised his hand. "I'm Rainy. My friend and I have brought Philly here against her will. I believe that's not the way you do things, but we didn't see any alternative."

Philly had lowered her head when Rainy pointed her out, but now she looked up and regarded Charlie. With any luck, Charlie would say she couldn't be kept in this depressing place if she wanted out.

"Would you prefer to leave, Philly?" Charlie asked.

"You're damn right I would."

"Let her go please," Charlie said, and Philly waited for an explosion. Mace disliked taking direction from anyone.

"I said to let her go."

Mace released her grip and Philly rubbed her arm where Mace had taken hold.

"You're free to go, Philly," Charlie said evenly. "But I would ask a favor of you. Please sit for ten minutes before you leave. I can't help noticing that you're pregnant. If you give us ten minutes, there's someone who might have some words for you that you might find interesting. So please take a seat."

Philly was about to head for the door when Rainy put an arm around her. "Ten minutes," Rainy whispered. "If you want to go in ten minutes, I swear I'll drive you home. You have my word."

Philly forced herself to sit. Rainy took an adjacent chair and waved Mace away.

"Melanie," Charlie said, and Philly followed his gaze to a young woman sitting in the front row who was painfully thin with washed out blue eyes. "I know we're taking things out of order," Charlie continued, "but it occurred to me that if you were willing to share with Philly some of the things you've shared with the rest of us, Philly might benefit from what you had to say. It's up to you."

Melanie slowly rose keeping her eyes on Charlie. She hugged herself as if she were cold, but Philly knew that the temperature wasn't responsible for the woman's gesture; she had already shrugged off her own coat because the steam heat was overpowering.

"I'm Melanie and I'm an alcoholic."

"Hi, Melanie!"

"I drank when I was pregnant with my daughter. She developed fetal alcohol syndrome. She almost died. I almost killed by daughter with my drinking. I didn't kill her but I sure as hell gave her problems she didn't deserve. I still haven't come to the point where I can forgive myself and move on."

Melanie sat down abruptly.

"Thank you, Melanie," Charlie said. "Since that took less than ten minutes, Philly, you should feel free to leave now if that's what you wish to do. Thank you for listening to Melanie."

Philly felt all eyes upon her. Rainy placed a hand on her shoulder pushing down gently, without any real force. It wouldn't take much of an effort to stand and displace his hand. But the downward pressure had just enough impact to give her pause. She remained seated, momentarily unable to move. Rainy's hand left her shoulder. Philly thought of getting up. Instead she moved closer to Rainy and leaned her head against his shoulder. She closed her eyes.

"Does anyone else have any new business?" Charlie asked.

May

Philly's Untitled Playlist

Shattered

O.A.R.

36

Carpenter hadn't been able to sleep so here he was in his Boston office at seven in the morning sipping at a black coffee and consulting his calendar to get a sense of how May would play out. The next hearing in the Lawsons' case had been pushed back to mid-month. Affidavits had been exchanged and he needed to prepare to cross-examine the witnesses for the Stonington school district, and to prepare his own witnesses for Craig Lannon's questions.

Before the Lawson court hearing he would have his first meeting with Jason Gerber, the Board of Bar Overseers lawyer who was handling the Board's complaint against Marshall Hyde. Carpenter believed that Hyde's case was heading for an evidentiary hearing, but perhaps Gerber would broach a settlement.

At the end of the month there would be a court hearing on the motion to dismiss the GPS-privacy rights lawsuit brought by Herbert Stanton and Millie Lane. He'd block out a half day to prepare for that hearing.

He made a note to remind Philly to get a discrimination claim filed on Frederick Chun's behalf in the next two weeks. He was considering farming out any work that needed to be done on that case in Philly's absence to Jeffries and Boyle. Hopefully the young lawyers would be quick studies when it came to discrimination law.

This afternoon, Carpenter would have his first discussion with Louise Fuller, the lawyer representing the Loan Company Licensure Review Board in Top Tier Finance Company's license revocation hearing. He settled down to review his notes, predicting that the afternoon call would leave him in a foul mood.

In Brighton, Philly stepped out of her bedroom to find it was business as usual. Raul and Isabella had brewed the morning coffee and Raul had made a large omelet and toast. She wondered whether they'd all pretend that last night never happened.

"Sit Philly," Raul said, pointing to the dining room table. As she settled in her chair, Raul placed a mug of coffee and a plate with eggs and toast on her placemat.

Sipping at her coffee, Philly felt a semblance of awareness cutting through the fog that enveloped her. Last night Rainy had told Mace to wait in the car, and he had walked her inside the house. He seemed reluctant to leave her alone as if he were afraid she'd harm herself if left unattended. She finally had to tell him that she was all right and he needed to leave. She should have thanked him, too, but the cussedness that lay at her core prevented her from freeing up the words.

"There is another AA meeting tomorrow night," Isabella said. "I will be taking you. Raul and I are very proud of you. We know it was not easy for you last night. I hope you are not angry that we talked to Rainy and . . . Mace." Isabella laughed. "That is such a horrid name for a woman."

Not in her case, Philly thought. Ordinarily she'd be bristling at the presumptuousness of people planning and running her life. But when it came to Isabella, she no longer had it in her to tell her housemate to leave her alone.

They ate for a time in silence, Philly thinking about the tales of woe she had heard last night. Jobs lost. Relationships destroyed. Families torn apart. People trying to gain a small foothold on what was left of their lives. It was awful. But surely that wasn't the fate of everyone who had a beer now and then. Even during pregnancy. But she'd barely slept, thinking about Philip, thinking about the baby, simultaneously rationalizing her behavior and beating herself up about it.

She spied Raul giving her surreptitious glances, his dark, soulful eyes making momentary contact and then focusing on his food.

Philly glanced at the clock in the kitchen. She needed to get a move on. The time it took to get ready before leaving for work seemed to have doubled recently, and she was exhausted from her restless night.

Philly realized that she had cleaned her plate. Raul may be a pain in the ass, but he could cook. She hadn't thanked Rainy but the least she could do was acknowledge Raul and Isabella.

"Thanks Raul. The breakfast was delicious."

Raul smiled uncertainly. "You are very welcome."

Philly turned to Isabella. "I've made a decision. You're still my coach for childbirth classes."

"Thank you," Isabella said. "It's still an honor."

"I don't see why you need a continuance," Louise Fuller said. "This is a straightforward case. Either Top Tier represented to borrowers that they had ninety days to cure a default or it didn't. Why do you need an extra month?"

Carpenter breathed deeply and tried to loosen his death grip on the telephone. "I've explained this to you. I'm new to the case and there's a lot of paper involved. I need time to get up to speed."

"Mr. Singer should have given more consideration to his initial choice of counsel. I think this change of counsel is stalling on his part."

Carpenter accepted that he was an anachronism. During the early years of his practice, extensions and continuances were granted by lawyers routinely, explanations for such requests rarely asked for. Lawyers were busy. They understood that personal lives intruded on work. There-but-for-the-grace-of-God-go-I was the unwritten rule that lawyers lived by. Carpenter continued to be guided by those precepts which meant he truly was living in the past.

"I don't see what the big deal is about a month's extension," Carpenter said. "Are you agreeable or not."

"You can ask for an extension," Fuller said. "I won't oppose it."

"May I put that in my motion?"

"No."

"Well, thank you for your time," Carpenter said, biting the words off. "Has the Board given any consideration to trying to settle this case without a trial?"

"What did you have in mind?" Fuller came back.

"Nothing," Carpenter said. "I simply wanted to know whether this was a case the Board was interested in resolving informally."

"Is Mr. Singer prepared to give up his company's license for a time?"

"I very much doubt he'd agree to that." Some conversations started out bad and progressed to worse.

"Then I don't think we have anything to talk about as far as settlement goes," Fuller said.

Carpenter paused several beats. "Thanks for being direct with me," he said. "If the Board ever changes its position and wishes to consider a settlement with terms that don't involve loss of license, let me know."

"What sort of terms?" Fuller asked.

"Given the Board's apparent position that Top Tier would have to lose its license in any settlement, a discussion of terms would likely not be productive. But I think you know that creative lawyers often are able to work out a compromise that their clients can live with. For example, there are other penalties besides loss of license. Off the top of my head I can think of fines, oversight monitoring, and compliance agreements."

"You're right," Fuller said. "A discussion of terms such as the ones you've mentioned would be unproductive. Anything else?"

"No, thanks for your time."

Carpenter hung up and addressed the photograph facing him. "Off the record. Is it just me or was the woman a bitch?"

The man said nothing, and staring at the photograph, Carpenter's thoughts turned to Fred. The latest blood test he'd had since being diagnosed with CLL showed an increase in his white blood count, a sign that Fred was on the rise. Doctor Specter, his oncologist, was unconcerned; she had told him that when it was time to worry, she'd tell him. This advice provided him with no comfort. It was the same advice he occasionally gave clients when he tried to allay their legitimate fears.

37

Philly wasn't really listening as Charlie made some introductory remarks at the AA meeting that night, but then he mentioned her name.

"We have someone new with us this evening. I know that she was here two nights ago, but that doesn't count because she was brought here against her will. Welcome Philly."

Philly squirmed as a few people clapped.

"Would you like to introduce yourself, Philly?"

Isabella had been holding her hand and gave her hand a gentle squeeze. If anyone other than Isabella had been here tonight—Raul or even Rainy—she knew that she'd never get the words out that she needed to speak aloud. But she got them out, thinking of that phrase from the Lady Gaga song, *chewing on pearls.* "My name is Philly and I'm an alcoholic." She still wasn't sure she was. But she knew she had to say it, so she did.

"Hi, Philly!" the chorus came back.

"Do you wish to tell us a little about yourself?" Charlie prompted.

Isabella again gently squeezed her hand.

"I'm a lawyer. I've got a baby coming sometime in July probably. The baby's father was killed by a drunk teenage driver just after we learned I was pregnant. We were engaged. I haven't had a drink in about four days. I'm worried about how I'm going to deal with being a mother and keeping my law practice alive."

Philly paused, taken aback that she had revealed anything to these strangers in the depressing atmosphere of a rundown church basement. The people in the folding chairs regarded her earnestly. But Christ! She didn't know these people!

"Say a little more," Isabella whispered.

"When I get worried I feel like having a drink. I know a drink will only relieve the worry for a moment. But it doesn't matter to me if the problem isn't going to be solved and go away permanently. Washing away the worry for the moment is all I can think about."

Philly fell silent. From the little she'd observed at the last session, she guessed that someone would soon be offering her advice. Instead the silence lengthened.

"We've all been there, Philly," Charlie said. "We know exactly what you're talking about."

"Do you have anyone looking out for you?" a man with thinning gray hair asked.

"There's Isabella who's with me tonight. There's her boyfriend Raul. The three of us just bought a house together. I'm worried about paying for everything when I'm out on maternity leave."

Philly teared up momentarily. She took a deep breath, trying to get back in control.

"There's this other, older lawyer who has an office next to mine. He's promised he'll keep on top of my cases. Plus, he's got a lady friend who's been really nice to me. There's my fiancé's family. I'm not that close with my parents but they're around."

Philly paused. She couldn't bring herself to mention Mace and Rainy but if it weren't for the two of them, she wouldn't be here tonight.

Melanie raised her hand and Charlie acknowledged her.

"You have a lot of people to help you," Melanie said. "My advice to you is let them help you. I was a jerk. I couldn't stand it when people were being nice to me. I didn't know how to say thank you. The best thing I can say to you is take whatever help you're given."

Philly heard "amen" from several directions. Melanie had been talking about herself, but Philly knew that Melanie could have been talking about her. Like Melanie she recoiled from people offering comfort.

"Thank you Philly and Melanie," Charlie said. "Would anyone else like to speak now?"

When the meeting adjourned, Philly wanted to make an instant escape, but Isabella insisted on coffee. While Isabella drank from a steaming mug off to the side of the coffee table, Philly stood by impatiently, rubbing her belly, feeling movement inside.

"May I feel," Melanie said, holding out a hand.

Melanie had appeared out of nowhere. There was something so desolate about the woman that Philly wondered whether bad vibes would be transmitted to her baby if Melanie touched her belly. There was almost a pleading look in Melanie's eyes.

"Sure," Philly said, and she guided Melanie's hand to where she had last felt movement.

"Wow!" Melanie exclaimed. "The kid's awake."

Melanie's expression had turned rapt as the baby continued to put on a show. Philly didn't have it in her to remove the woman's hand. "I don't remember much of my daughter moving around inside me," Melanie said. "I was pretty much out of it during my pregnancy. I know I missed out on a lot."

Melanie removed her hand and Philly touched the vacated spot which had settled down.

"If you want," Melanie said, "I could be your sponsor."

Philly knew that she needed a sponsor, someone to turn to in weak moments when she wanted a drink. She had vaguely hoped that Charlie would fill that role.

"I've never sponsored anyone before," Melanie said. "I don't even know if Charlie would let me do it."

Isabella approached, regarding Melanie with interest. "What do you do, Melanie?"

"I'm a waitress."

"It was very kind of you to share your experience with Philly."

Melanie reddened, gave an embarrassed shrug. Philly remembered how hard it had been for Melanie to speak. The woman didn't strike her as a person who would respond well in a crisis. And just what kind of support could a mousy, depressed waitress have to offer? Even as she thought it, Philly knew this was unfair and prejudiced. So maybe the question was what kind of help would Philly accept from anyone?

"Will you be at the next meeting?" Isabella asked Melanie.

Melanie nodded, avoiding eye contact.

"Philly will let you know then," Isabella said. "The two of us need to talk about tonight's meeting. This is all new to us."

"Okay," Melanie said, not at all put out that the subject of sponsorship had been tabled.

Isabella returned her empty coffee mug to the coffee table. "We've got to go, Melanie. See you at the next meeting."

Melanie gave a half-hearted wave and Philly wondered how she could say no to the woman.

38

Jason Gerber was a humorless, young lawyer with black curly hair and black framed glasses. He was a small guy who looked like he assiduously avoided exercise of any kind. Carpenter distrusted anyone on a mission and from Gerber's initial remarks, the Board of Bar Overseers' attorney seemed hell bent on severely disciplining any attorney who crossed a line that Gerber had drawn in his mind.

"We can't have lawyers publicly calling judges pigheaded," Gerber said with a smile Carpenter found condescending.

"Of course we can," Carpenter retorted with what he hoped would pass for equanimity. "Some judges are pigheaded and need to be told that fact."

"But not by a lawyer," Gerber qualified.

"Especially by a lawyer," Carpenter volleyed back. "Who knows judges better than the lawyers who try cases before them? Mr. Hyde was accurately reporting Judge Porter's temperament and conduct based upon personal experience and observation. We need more of that."

Carpenter was dismayed that Gerber's shocked expression was genuine. He wondered whether Gerber had ever tried a case.

"Mr. Hyde hasn't even apologized to Judge Porter," Gerber pointed out.

"Nor has Judge Porter apologized to the criminal defense bar of Middlesex County."

"You really don't see how outrageous your client's conduct was, do you?" Gerber asked, an incredulous expression firmly in place.

Carpenter silently counted to ten. There was no point in pissing Gerber off. What he said next would color their relationship for the remainder of the case.

"I've tried a lot of cases in superior court," Carpenter said. "This Judge Porter was abusing his power and Mr. Hyde called him on it. Mr. Hyde had a first amendment right to do so."

"The Board isn't impressed with first amendment claims in this case."

Thinking that a brief change in focus would diminish the chance he'd tell Gerber to fuck off, Carpenter deliberately took a moment to study his surroundings. They were in a small windowless conference room in the offices of the Board of Bar Overseers. The small wood table they were seated at was scarred. The wooden chairs they were seated on were beat up and Carpenter's listed when he sat forward. A fair number of his most unpleasant experiences practicing law were spent in rooms similar to this one.

"I have no authority to propose any settlement," Carpenter said. "Would the Board consider a reprimand?"

"I wouldn't recommend a reprimand in this case. I would recommend a sixty-day suspension."

I'm sure you would you pompous little shit, Carpenter thought. "Thank you for meeting with me," is what he said.

"If your client isn't willing to accept a suspension, I really don't think a settlement is possible."

You've got that right, Carpenter thought.

Philly had decreed that tonight she was going to handle the cooking. Raul and Isabella had protested and with good reason; they had sampled her cooking. Philly had resorted to her death ray stare to bring them in line and was now in the process of deciding whether the chicken she was broiling was done. With her luck, she'd be dealing with desiccated, barely chewable chicken parts that were blackened beyond recognition. Philly stuck a fork in a thigh, saw clear juices run, and decided that the bird parts had endured enough.

Isabella chose that moment to check on her progress and Philly delegated serving duties to her. When Philly got to the dining room table, Isabella was already dishing out the chicken and baked potatoes and steamed green beans. She eased herself onto her chair breathing hard. Pregnancy was hard work, and she felt increasingly out of shape in every sense. At best, she was only good for about one or two further spinning sessions. Assuming she found the time to fit those in, she'd have to dial back on the routines.

Raul sampled the chicken and nodded approvingly. "This is very good."

"Don't sound so surprised."

"I'm sorry, I . . ."

"Raul! I was teasing you. I'm as surprised as you are."

Raul was watching her warily. Philly couldn't blame him. She'd given him cause to tread lightly around her.

"I wanted to say a few things to you guys," Philly said, after confirming Raul's assessment that the chicken was edible. "First, I know you two are responsible for dumping some money in my Fidelity account."

Raul colored, lowered his head, and studied his food. Isabella's expression became guarded.

"I know you both felt that you had to pay me something for trying to help Isabella's uncle Santiago last year. You didn't have to do that. I thought I'd been clear about that. For a while I was thinking of ways to return the money to you. But I'm not going to fight you on this. The only thing I'm going to say is thank you."

Raul's relief was evident. Philly suspected that he'd been anticipating another bitter, exhausting argument. Isabella's guarded look vanished; she was smiling. Isabella raised her wine glass in a silent toast. At least she and Raul weren't giving up alcohol in her presence.

"Can we agree that the book is closed on Santiago?" Philly asked.

"Yes," Isabella said, and Raul nodded his assent.

Her baby moved, stirrings that like clockwork occurred during dinner. Philly rubbed her belly to let the baby know that she had picked up on the movements.

"The second thing I need to say is that I don't have any hard feelings that you told Mace and Rainy about my . . . drinking. I actually need to thank you for doing that."

"You are very welcome," Raul said, and the way he said it, spontaneously and directly, Philly entertained the hope that Raul would be his usual aggravating, obnoxious self around her from here on out.

"I'm sorry I've been such a bitch lately," Philly soldiered on, determined to get through her mental list of what needed to be said. "I'm going to try and work on that. But you need to tell me when I'm out of line. I don't want you to be afraid of hurting my feelings."

Isabella nodded and sipped from her wine glass. Raul's eyes came alive.

"The chicken is actually a little tough," Raul said, grinning.

"I know," Philly said. "That's another thing I need to work on."

39

Watching Carpenter do battle against Craig Lannon on behalf of the Lawsons, Philly wondered when she would muster up the courage to tell him she had started attending AA meetings. Would he applaud her for getting help and repeat that he'd be there for her? Or would he regard her as damaged goods he couldn't rely on and sever their relationship. She forced her attention back to the courtroom.

With the return of warm weather, activities on the Stonington school playground had ratcheted up. Jack Lawson had gotten into two further playground scuffles since the last court hearing, and currently Lannon was doing his best to beat Maryanne Fairmount over the head with these recent events.

"Would you agree, Ms. Fairmount, that Jack Lawson is averaging one playground altercation for every five school days?"

Fairmount regarded Lannon evenly. "I wouldn't characterize any of the incidents as an altercation. There was an argument and some pushing involving a ball. The more recent events involved some jostling for position when forming lines."

"Jostling?" Lannon raised his voice. "Isn't it true that in each incident Jack Lawson pushed another student who ended up on the ground?"

"Jack was also pushed on each occasion," Fairmount said. "But I've read the reports and you are correct that the other students ended up on the ground."

"Would you agree that before Jack began cutting back on medication there were no incidents involving Jack where other students ended up on the ground?"

"That's my understanding but I need to add something."

"There's no question before you," Lannon said promptly.

"Objection!" Carpenter thundered.

Judge O'Connell regarded Carpenter and Lannon with the resigned expression of a jurist who recognized that he was dealing with two experienced litigators who were going to make him rule on repeated objections.

"Mr. Lannon, your objection is noted. What did you want to add?" the judge directed to Fairmount.

"I wanted to say that I have read the affidavits of the monitors. They witnessed four other shoving incidents where students ended up on the ground none of which involved Jack Lawson. When children of Jack's age are out on a playground, pushing and shoving will occur. There was nothing dangerous with respect to the incidents involving Jack or with the incidents involving other students."

"Do you encourage or discourage pushing and shoving at the Wilton Center?" Lannon continued immediately."

"Discourage."

"Is that because someone could get hurt?"

"That's one reason."

"So pushing and shoving isn't a good thing, correct?"

"Correct. I wouldn't call it a good thing. But it is something that children do."

"While the current Stonington IEP was in effect, isn't it true that there were no pushing and shoving incidents involving Jack?"

"Based on what I've reviewed, that's correct."

"Nothing further," Lannon said.

"Is the current plan involving reduced medications working?" Carpenter asked.

"In my opinion, yes."

"What do you base that opinion on?"

Fairmount considered Carpenter's question with the same deliberateness she exhibited in responding to Lannon's questions. Philly believed she was coming across as a thoughtful, believable witness.

"Jack's academic performance hasn't suffered as his medications have been decreased, and his monitors have noted his increased participation in class discussions. The monitors' affidavits confirm that as Jack's medication dosages have dropped, he's appeared less lethargic. The monitors note that the playground incidents that Mr. Lannon asked me about didn't involve any threatening or violent behavior on Jack's part."

When Carpenter paused and leaned toward her, Philly held up her notepad to shield their faces from the judge.

"I like that last answer," Carpenter said. "I think it's the best I'm going to get out of her. Can you think of anything else I should ask?"

Philly reviewed her notes and shook her head.

"No further questions," Carpenter addressed the judge.

"We'll take a short recess," the judge announced.

Philly assessed that Lannon's cross-examination of the monitors had been a standoff. The monitors acknowledged the pushing and shoving incidents involving Jack Lawson, but stuck to their positions that the incidents were run of the mill and no student was in danger of serious injury. Now Lannon was questioning Sylvia Lawson. When Lannon looked up from his notes and squared his shoulders, Philly expected Philip's voice to emerge from his mouth.

"Has Jack broken anything at home in the last three weeks?" Lannon asked.

Lawson registered surprise and glanced at her husband seated in the first row of the gallery. "He broke a model airplane."

"How did that happen?"

Lawson again looked at her husband. Philly wondered whether Lannon had launched a probing question he didn't know the answer to and was now about to hit pay dirt.

"He was working on the model with my husband and he must have gotten frustrated because he threw it on the floor."

"Did you see this happen?"

"No. My husband told me about it."

"Was there any incident involving Jack breaking anything at home in the three months before his medications began to be reduced?"

Philly had a new appreciation for the expression *racking one's brain* as Lawson knit her brows. "Nothing that I can think of."

"Have Jack's sleeping habits changed since his medication dosages began to be reduced?"

Lawson shifted in the witness chair. "Somewhat," she said.

"What has been the change?"

"He's staying up later and has a tougher time settling into sleep."

"Does that mean he fell asleep more quickly before the reduction in medications?"

"Yes."

"Would you agree that since the medications began to be reduced, Jack is more agitated?"

"No. I wouldn't say he's more agitated."

"Is it the word agitated that you disagree with?"

"Yes."

"Why do you disagree with that word?"

"Because it's not accurate. The word I would use is alive. Jack's become more alive since the medication doses have been reduced."

"I move to strike that answer," Lannon addressed the judge.

"Motion denied," Judge O'Connell ruled.

Ten minutes later Lannon concluded his cross-examination, and then Carpenter stood to address Sylvia Lawson.

"Do you recall your testimony about Jack breaking a model airplane?"

"Yes."

"As a parent, did that action trouble or concern you?"

"No."

"Why not?"

Sylvia Lawson smiled briefly at her husband before turning her attention to Carpenter. "Max had bought Jack the model airplane kit about six months ago. Max had tried to interest him in building the airplane, but Jack showed no interest. But about ten days ago when Max took out the kit and asked Jack whether he wanted to work on the model, Jack said yes. That surprised us. They worked on it for about an hour and had pretty much gotten the airplane put together when Jack got frustrated and threw the airplane down. I know this may be hard to understand, but Max and I were thrilled that he finally showed an interest in putting the airplane together even if he did get frustrated in the end."

"How would you describe Jack's ability to concentrate since the dosage of his medications has been decreased?"

"In my opinion it's slightly better. It's like I said. He worked with Max on that airplane for about an hour."

"You mentioned that Jack's sleeping habits have changed. Does the change concern you?"

Sylvia Lawson offered a weak smile. "Yes and no. Yes, because it means that Max and I don't have as much uninterrupted time together as we used to have. But no because Jack's got more energy and he's . . . I don't know. It's like I said before. He's more alive."

The next witness, Florence Jefferson, was giving Carpenter all he could handle. The Stonington school district's expert witness paused before answering each of his questions, never raised her voice, and threw in references to educational research studies at every opportunity. Philly figured Jefferson for a professional witness who had testified in IEP cases numerous times.

"You didn't design Jack Lawson's IEP, did you?" Carpenter asked.

Here was a question Philly thought that Jefferson shouldn't have had to think about, but she still paused before answering.

"No."

"In your affidavit, you state that Jack Lawson's current plan with reduced medication dosages isn't working. Do you remember that statement in your affidavit?"

"Could I look at my affidavit, please? I have a copy with me."

Carpenter muttered, "Christ," under his breath and Philly was heartened by the sharp look that Judge O'Connell gave the witness.

"Go ahead," the judge said.

"Yes, that summarizes one of my statements."

"You point to the playground incidents as the reason why it's not working, correct?"

Jefferson studied her affidavit. "Yes."

"In terms of Jack's academic performance, the current plan with reduced medication is working, isn't it?"

"From the documents I reviewed, I didn't see any significant change in Jack's educational performance after medications were reduced."

"Then the current plan is working as far as educational performance goes, isn't it?"

"As I said, there has been no significant change in Jack's educational performance."

"Is the current plan working as far as Jack's academics go?" the judge intervened. "It's a straightforward question and I'd like you to answer it."

Jefferson was unperturbed. She was a middle-aged woman with a studious expression and Philly suspected it would take a lit firecracker shoved up her ass to get a rise out of her.

"Yes, as to academics it's working as effectively as the Stonington IEP."

"Why in your opinion do the playground incidents show the current IEP with lowered medication dosages isn't working?" Carpenter resumed.

"Because the incidents show that Jack is now acting inappropriately."

"Was Jack engaged in playground activity before the medications were reduced?"

"I recall reading that Jack stayed pretty much to himself during recess."

"Since medications began to be reduced is that still the case?'

"I don't know."

"One of Jack's monitors has reported that Jack's participation in playground activity has increased steadily. If that is true, isn't that evidence that Jack's socialization has improved since the reduction in medication dosages?'

"It could be, but I couldn't say for sure."

"Was Jack the one who initiated the playground incidents that you rely on in your affidavit?"

"I don't know. I do know that in each incident a child ended up on the ground."

"Move to strike the last sentence," Carpenter said, not bothering to hide his irritation.

"Allowed," Judge O'Connell said. "Please just answer the questions put to you Dr. Jefferson."

"The affidavits submitted by the monitors state that in the two most recent playground incidents, Jack was pushed first and responded to the pushes. Doesn't the fact that Jack wasn't the aggressor in those two incidents show he wasn't acting out but instead was responding to inappropriate acts of other students?"

"Not necessarily. In each incident, Jack got sufficiently worked up so that the force of his pushes landed students on the ground. That suggests aggression and anger to me, none of which occurred while his medications were at the originally prescribed levels."

Carpenter stared for a long moment at Jefferson. Philly had to admit that Jefferson was smooth; the woman refused to be pinned down and seemed capable of wriggling out of any corner Carpenter tried to paint her into. She pulled at Carpenter's suit jacket.

"What?" Carpenter said, leaning over.

Philly again used her legal pad to shield their colloquy from the judge. "I think she's coming across as too slick for her own good. I've been watching the judge. I think he's fed up with her qualifying every damn thing she says."

Carpenter was staring at her, his jaw muscles working as if he were literally trying to digest her advice.

"Thanks," Carpenter whispered. "No further questions."

Clarissa Webb, Jack Lawson's fourth grade teacher, probably wished to be anywhere else than on the witness stand. She was young and athletic looking with long blond hair and blue eyes. The way she kept her head lowered looking at her clasped hands, highlighted her nervousness and discomfort.

"How's Jack doing academically?" Carpenter asked.

"I would say he's doing okay," Webb said to her hands.

"Have you noticed any changes in his academic performance in the last three weeks?"

Webb glanced in Carpenter's direction before redirecting her attention to her hands. "No."

"How's Jack doing socially?"

"Again okay."

"Have you noticed any changes in his socialization in the last three weeks?"

"Yes."

"What changes have you noticed?"

Webb took a deep breath. Philly noticed that her knuckles showed white. "He's interacting more with other students."

"Do you regard that as a positive development?"

"Yes."

"Have the monitors caused any disruption in your class?"

"Not really. It's just taken some getting used to having them around."

"Have you observed Jack direct any threatening conduct toward any other student in the last three weeks?"

Webb colored but this time she met Carpenter's gaze. "No."

"No further questions."

"Do you have any safety concerns about Jack being in your class?" Lannon asked.

Webb didn't respond immediately. She shifted in her chair and glanced about the courtroom as if seeking an escape route.

"This is very hard for me," Webb said in a soft voice. "Jack's a lovely boy. I'm delighted to be his teacher. But I do worry about him. Maybe I'm overreacting to the monitors being in the class and the knowledge I have that his medications are being reduced. But the truth is that I am concerned that something may set him off where he does something unfortunate. Do I have any objective evidence that will happen? No. But I do have an uneasy feeling about him. I wish I could be more specific, but I can't."

"No further questions," Lannon said.

"Do the monitors allay the concern you just expressed?" Carpenter asked.

"Somewhat. Now that I'm used to them, I like it that they're around."

"The concern you expressed is based solely on a subjective feeling you have, is that correct?"

"Yes, pretty much."

"Are you saying that you would prefer it if Jack went back to higher doses of medication?"

Philly heard Webb's heartfelt sigh from where she was sitting.

"I don't know," Webb said. "This whole thing is a mess."

Judge O'Connell was back on the bench after declaring a short recess. All witnesses had remained. Even if her baby weren't now doing calisthenics, Philly knew that her insides would be roiling over the tension in the courtroom.

"As I understand it," the judge began, "there is to be one further reduction in Jack's medications. I'm going to permit that last reduction to take place with the proviso that the medications be returned to their present level if there is any difficulty due to the last reduction. Is there a hearing date for the IEP?"

Lannon rose. "Next month."

"Everything is to remain as is. I still want two monitors in place."

Philly glanced at Lannon. The lawyer for the Stonington school system showed no disappointment over the judge's ruling.

"We just had a witness describe the current situation as a mess," the judge continued. "Well, most cases involve a mess. Life is messy. I would urge the parties to try to resolve this situation informally if that is possible. I'm impressed that both parties have Jack Lawson's interests at heart. It might be productive if Dr. Fairmount and Dr. Jefferson confer. Stonington needs to consider that the reduction in medication has not adversely affected Jack's academic progress and has measurably improved his socialization skills. The Lawsons need to consider that a full-time monitor may be necessary for Jack and that at the IEP hearing, Stonington does not have to prove that its IEP is best, but only that it is adequate. If there is a change in the situation, I will make myself available to entertain an emergency motion. Any questions? Then court is adjourned."

Carpenter was driving and Philly decided it was now or never. They had picked apart the court hearing and had been driving for a time in silence. "There's something I need to tell you."

"Sure," Carpenter said, his eyes on the road.

"I've started going to AA meetings."

Carpenter flashed her a quick look before immediately refocusing on the road. But the way he was holding the steering wheel, told Philly he'd been taken aback by her news.

"For how long?"

"A couple of weeks."

"What brought that on?"

"You could say a bunch of people decided to hold an intervention. I'd been having a beer or two on occasion."

Carpenter remained focused on the road, his jaw muscles working. "This goes back to the end of last year when you took a sip of my beer."

"I guess you're right," Philly conceded.

"How's AA working for you?"

Philly took her time before responding. "I'm not sure," she said. "I think I need to do it. I do have a problem. I've got this sponsor who's probably more dysfunctional than I am. The group leader is pretty good. I don't like it, but also I do. The bottom line is I need help so I'm going to stay with it."

They entered the City of Boston. Carpenter was driving slowly, intent on the road, his expression still unreadable.

"Say something," Philly said.

"Remember when Maxine and I said we were there for you?" Carpenter said.

Philly nodded.

"That still goes."

40

On Sunday morning, Philly rose early, made the coffee, and slowly mounted the stairs to her second-floor office. Getting up the stairs was now slow going and not merely because she had to balance her coffee mug and plate of toast lathered with peanut butter and jelly. She was big; the baby made moving painstaking. The most recent spin class she had gone to would be her last during her pregnancy. She'd had to take the entire class sitting.

Philly logged on to her office computer and was relieved that her Inbox only contained a few, new, unopened messages. Lately she felt that she was on a treadmill. AA meetings and childbirth classes took up three nights a week and left her exhausted. Last week there had been an OB-GYN visit thrown into the mix. Two days last week she had worked from home, unable to face the commute to and from her office. She didn't want to face the fact that working solely from home was fast approaching.

Philly cleared out her Inbox and forced herself to again read through the motion of the Dixfield school district to dismiss the suit of John and Naomi Harrington. The dismissal motion had been filed by a lawyer she knew. George Norris was a middle-aged man with a put-upon attitude who showed little animation, and Philly had never been able to figure him out. When they had been on opposite sides of a case the previous year, the jury deadlocked.

Norris' motion was direct and to the point. The Dixfield school district should not be required to remove any record from Luke Harrington's files. Norris pointed out that the Harringtons' complaint did not dispute the accuracy of the information in Luke's record. The information, if true, was disturbing and school officials needed the information to ensure that Luke was monitored for any signs of mistreatment or abuse.

To oppose the motion to dismiss, Philly felt her only recourse was to focus on the fact that the document the Harringtons wanted removed from Luke's files had come to school authorities anonymously. Did parents have a right to exclude from their child's school record a document delivered anonymously? Even if such a right existed wouldn't the parents have to claim that the anonymous report was untrue? Norris' motion to dismiss had basically challenged the Harringtons to dispute the accuracy of the anonymous letter.

Philly spent an hour of on-line research that produced little help. Luke Harrington's school record was confidential; only school personnel on a need to know basis could view the record. None of this helped the Harringtons.

Philly sent the Harringtons a copy of the motion to dismiss without comment. Remembering their rigid view that standing Luke upright in a closet was appropriate without doctor input, she doubted the couple would drop their suit. The Harringtons apparently knew as little about parenting as she did.

That afternoon Philly sat in one of the easy chairs in the living room-dining room area overwhelmed by the turnout at her baby shower. There was an impressive pile of baby shower presents to her immediate left and the pile didn't include the crib and bassinette that Carpenter and Maxine had brought and were already placed in the baby's room. Maxine and Isabella had assembled snacks and drinks on the dining room table and people were digging in.

Philip's parents had driven down from North Andover and had sprung for a year's diaper service, handing her an envelope with the information. The couple stood off to the side, ill at ease. They had aged. It had to be hard for them to go through this moment without their son.

Philip's sister Pamela was another story. She mingled easily, currently engaged in conversation with Raul, while her daughter, Geneva or Genie as Pamela called her, had focused in on the cookies arrayed on the snack table. Genie had to be approaching three. Philly tried to picture her life when her baby would be almost three. She couldn't.

Her own parents hadn't come and Philly was okay with their absence. The baby clothes they had sent were largely winter garments.

Rainy had come accompanied by a gorgeous, statuesque black woman he introduced as Monica. The couple was now talking with Carpenter. Philly recalled Monica's first words to her. "I've heard all about you," Monica had said. "Rainy says you're the one I have to thank for drawing him out of his shell." Rainy had taken the remark without comment, smiling shyly.

Mace had shown up, was now chatting up Maxine. Philly couldn't imagine what the two of them had to say to each other.

The presence of Tom Grange and his sister Heather had been a wonderful surprise. Heather was a former client. Tom had been Philip's best friend growing up and he had missed Philip's funeral because he had been aboard a ship doing oceanographic research. Philly tried not to stare at him. He was not quite as tall as Philip but he had Philip's blond hair and blue eyes and sinewy build. Maybe it was something in the North Andover water: Philip, Tom, and Heather were all beautiful people.

The front door opened and Melanie entered, her hand clasped by a thin, blue-eyed girl who was probably a few years older than Genie. Melanie's presence had to be Isabella's doing. Isabella greeted Melanie, relieved Melanie and the little girl of their coats. On the way to the snack table, Isabella dropped to one knee and introduced Genie to the newly arrived little girl. When Melanie looked her way, Philly waved, still unsure whether Melanie was the right person to be her sponsor.

The front door opened again and Thomas Morrison held the door for Ellie Wood. The two seemed to be friendly and Philly wondered if there was anything going on between their third-floor tenants.

Maxine struck a fork against a drinking glass and the pinging produced silence. "I think it's time we got down to business," Maxine announced.

Philly read out the gift card before opening each gift. She felt self-conscious holding up booties, jumpers, and one-piece pajamas, the items of clothing so small and cutesy. The gift givers had stayed away from pinks and blues and Philly was glad that she still hadn't succumbed to the urge to find out the sex of her baby. Better to keep people guessing because she couldn't stand pink. Then there were the play things: a mobile to hang over the crib, blocks, toys, and thick-paged baby books. Pamela's gift was last—something for the baby to grow into Pamela said—and when Philly tore away the gift wrap paper to reveal a small red tricycle, she couldn't imagine a time when this gift would be put to use.

It was during a moment of calm when Philly succumbed to tears. Suddenly she was no longer the center of attention. People were orbiting about her easy chair, their conversation background noise. But then she looked at the small tricycle and flashed on an image of Philip stooping to hold their baby secure on the tricycle seat while he gave the baby her first bike ride on some sunny May day just like this one. She envisioned a little girl. It was the thought of Philip trying early on to instill in the baby a love of his favorite sport that brought about her tears for it was the sport that had gotten him killed.

"You are such a fucking wuss," Mace said as she made her way to the snacks and drinks.

"Bite me," Philly said through her tears.

"Welcome back," Mace retorted. "Good to see you're back to your old self."

Most guests had departed when Tom Grange plopped down on the floor beside her easy chair, his long legs stretched out in the direction of the facing sofa. "You hanging in there?" he asked.

"It's a little bitter sweet," Philly said.

"I still can't believe he's gone."

"Maybe it's harder because you couldn't come to his funeral," Philly offered. She remembered a comment Heather had made once, about how Philip was the steady one and Tom the wild one in their friendship. Tom had a roguish air, accented by a nose that obviously had been broken at some point giving him an off-kilter appearance as if he weren't properly centered.

Philly started at her baby's kick.

"What?" Tom asked.

"The baby's kicking up a storm."

"May I feel?" Tom asked, as he moved to his knees and held his hand out.

Philly placed Tom's hand where the last kick had exploded. Nothing happened for a long moment but then the baby let loose with another burst of movement.

"That is so cool," Tom said, grinning.

Philly didn't say anything. She was struck by how much more time Tom had had with Philip than she had had.

"Don't take this the wrong way, but I never would have pictured Philip falling for someone like you," Tom said. "He certainly broke the preppy mold."

Philly shifted in the easy chair, said nothing. For the moment the baby was in constant motion, a pleasant distraction.

"You know he wrote me about you," Tom said. "I remember the first e-mail he sent about you. He said that he had run into this girl and he couldn't get her out of his head."

Philly welled up again. She closed her eyes and tried to picture her baby floating inside her.

"If you ever need help with your kid, let me know. I'll be at Woods Hole for a stretch so I'm around."

"Thanks," Philly managed to say without her voice breaking.

"Don't mention it. It's the least I can do. I never got to say goodbye to him."

41

When he represented plaintiffs, Carpenter usually preferred to attend court hearings alone to give the presiding judge the impression that his plaintiff client was a poor working stiff who couldn't afford a battery of lawyers. But for the hearing on Wise Computer Consultants' motion to dismiss the lawsuit he had filed on behalf of Herbert Stanton and Millie Lane, Carpenter made an exception. Seated next to him were Simon Jeffries and Rachel Boyle. Hours before the court hearing he had had the young lawyers fire questions at him to prepare for oral argument. It had been a fun session and valuable to boot. There had been moments when Jeffries and Boyle had given him a hard time.

Wayne Anderson sat alone at the defendant's counsel table. Wise Computer's lawyer was young and appeared confident. Watching his opponent, Carpenter wondered whether today's litigators were required to spend time working out. Anderson had broad shoulders and a powerful build that his gray pinstriped suit didn't hide.

"Court!"

Judge Carmen Fielding took the bench, another recent appointee to the superior court about whom Carpenter knew nothing. As Fielding's piercing green eyes appraised the lawyers in front of her, Carpenter knew there would be no opening pleasantries at this hearing.

"How can the plaintiffs claim damages, Mr. Carpenter, when they could have been fired for any reason or no reason," the judge started in.

Carpenter rose slowly to his feet. He didn't mind a judge's pointed questions right out of the gate. He did mind being deprived of an opportunity to introduce his clients.

"I would respectfully disagree with your statement, Your Honor. My clients are in the courtroom and I would ask them to stand." Carpenter turned around as his clients rose reluctantly. When Carpenter turned back to face the judge he was dismayed to find her frowning.

"My clients couldn't be fired because they were over forty. They couldn't be fired because of their religion or race or sex. Nor, I submit, could they be fired because their former employer, Wise Computer, elected to violate their privacy rights. Therefore, I would dispute that the plaintiffs could have been fired for any reason."

Carpenter turned and gestured for his clients to resume their seats. "In this case, Herbert Stanton and Millie Lane were fired because their former employer secretly and surreptitiously invaded their privacy and then claimed that the invasion of privacy permitted the company to give them the sack. Since when does wrongdoing of such an egregious nature become an excuse to deprive competent workers of their jobs? Never one would hope."

"That's a fine jury speech, Mr. Carpenter," Judge Fielding came back. "But as Mr. Anderson correctly points out in his legal memorandum, an employee at will can be fired for any reason. That translates into the hard reality that the plaintiffs are not entitled to their jobs back and cannot claim damages."

Carpenter didn't like the judge's tone and knew that he'd better watch himself before he sounded off fueled by emotion. "Again, Your Honor, I have to take issue with the conclusion you just presented. There was an oral employment contract between the parties. Wise Computer breached that agreement by violating Mr.

Stanton's and Ms. Lane's privacy rights. Under contract law, they are entitled to damages for that breach. Also, even if there were no contract which is not the case, we have a Massachusetts statute which protects privacy rights and provides that someone whose privacy rights are violated may obtain damages from the violator. Surreptitiously implanting a GPS tracking device in a cell phone the plaintiffs were required to carry violated the plaintiffs' privacy rights."

The judge turned to Anderson. "Is Mr. Carpenter correct that the plaintiffs were required to carry the cell phones given to them?"

"While they were on the job, yes," Anderson said as he rose to address the judge. "On their own time they were not required to carry the phones."

"Why didn't your client tell employees about the tracking device so they could make an informed decision about whether to carry their work cell phones on their own time?"

"That would defeat the purpose of the tracking devices."

"What purpose would that be?"

"To verify their location during work hours."

"You didn't answer my question. Employees were not told of the tracking device so had no reason to replace the phone on their own time."

"They were told that the only time they were required to carry the phone was during work time."

"As I understand it, your client fired the plaintiffs when the tracking devices showed them to be at the same location which was often a motel. Do I have that right?"

"Yes, Your Honor," Anderson said. "That was the precipitating event."

"Were the plaintiffs paid for any of the time that they spent in motels together?"

Anderson paused. Carpenter was developing a sudden fondness for this judge. As long as questions rained down on his opponent, he and Her Honor might get along.

"I don't believe they were paid for any of that time," Anderson acknowledged.

"Which means they weren't doing anything on company time when they were . . . what's the legal term I'm searching for here? I've got it—shacked up."

"Jesus," Boyle whispered.

"They were on call," Anderson pointed out.

"So what?" the judge rejoined. "If one of them got a call they could un-shack up and respond to the call. They claim they never failed to timely respond to a call. Is that true?"

"On this record, it is true," Anderson conceded.

"So essentially the plaintiffs were fired for something they did on their own time," the judge observed. "I think I've heard enough."

Anderson took his seat. Jeffries and Boyle stared at the judge wide-eyed.

"Here's my ruling on Wise Computers' motion to dismiss. The motion is allowed in part and denied in part. The motion is allowed as to plaintiffs' contract claims. The motion is denied as to the plaintiffs' claims that their rights to privacy were violated. I'll enter an order today and you should have it shortly. When can you be ready for trial?"

Carpenter and Anderson stood. Carpenter consulted his pocket calendar. "I think discovery can be completed in ninety days," he said.

"Ninety days! What's to discover? I'll give the parties sixty days to complete discovery. We'll have a pretrial conference in ninety days. I'll deal with discovery issues then. Anything else?"

Carpenter was sure he was missing something. Anderson also looked a bit uncertain.

"Very well. The court will be in recess."

In the corridor outside the courtroom, Carpenter introduced Stanton and Lane to Jeffries and Boyle.

"What just happened?" Millie Lane asked.

"You get to go to trial on your privacy claims, but your contract claims were dismissed," Carpenter explained. "Your former employer may decide to take your depositions. I might decide to take your former boss' deposition, Bruce Bolton. This judge is going to move this case."

"Is any of this good?" Lane questioned.

"I'd say it's good," Carpenter answered. "With your contract claims gone, you're never going to get your jobs back. But getting your jobs back wasn't going to happen anyway. By the way, what's your job situation?"

"We didn't have much luck getting a new job," Stanton said, "so we decided to go out on our own"

"Are you making as much as you made at Wise Computer?"

"Not yet but we're getting close," Lane said with a big grin. "Some of Wise Computers' clients have sought us out."

"Did you ever sign a contract saying that you couldn't work for Wise Computer clients if you were fired?" Boyle asked.

"No," Stanton said.

"Okay," Carpenter said. "That's good to hear. We'll keep in touch."

"I can't believe the judge used the term shacking up," Boyle said as they made their way back to Carpenter's office.

"Neither could I," Carpenter confessed. "Especially after the way she started out on me."

Carpenter explained the fee arrangement he had with Stanton and Lane. "I need to clear this with Philly but what would you say to Philly and I splitting the contingency fee with you two if you decide to work on this case? The contingency would only kick in if we won."

Jeffries and Boyle exchanged a look that Carpenter couldn't read. "We're in," Jeffries said.

"If Philly gives her okay, I'm going to want you to take Bruce Bolton's deposition," Carpenter said, nodding in Jeffries' direction. "And you," he said to Boyle, "can come up with a demand to produce documents and interrogatories."

"You realize that we haven't done any of this before," Boyle pointed out.

"Don't let that stop you. It's never stopped me."

"Why are you doing this for us?" Jeffries asked.

"You've got it ass backwards, kid," Carpenter said. "You're the ones doing me and Philly a favor. And by the way, Philly has started working from home. When we get back to my office, I'm going to give each of you a key to her office. She's okay with that."

"This is a lot to take in," Boyle said.

"Get used to it," Carpenter replied.

42

Carpenter stared at the Top Tier case documents he had spread across the conference room table. It was seven in the morning, he had a large Dunkin' Donuts coffee steaming next to him, and he wouldn't hear his phone ring. It was time to fish or cut bait and make some final strategy decisions in the regulatory proceeding involving Jerome Singer's finance company.

Jeffries and Boyle had done a good job drafting a motion to keep out of evidence the telephone call that Norman Cassidy had illegally recorded. Carpenter signed the motion; it would be mailed today. He knew that the gesture was futile; the recording of the telephone discussion would be allowed into evidence. But some acts of futility needed to be pursued.

He considered the next futile task he needed to get done. The Loan Company Licensure Review Board regulations only permitted depositions in extraordinary circumstances such as when a person couldn't be subpoenaed for trial. Top Tier Finance Company couldn't fairly point to any circumstance that was dire or extraordinary. Norman Cassidy and Paul Huggins, the named principal in the accounting firm of Miller and Huggins, lived in Massachusetts and could be subpoenaed to any hearing before the Board. Still, Carpenter wanted to get a crack at Cassidy and Huggins before the hearing began. He also needed to get Devonshire Plastics' financial records.

On his notepad, Carpenter outlined the next task he would inflict upon Jeffries and Boyle: drafting a request to take the depositions of Norman Cassidy and Paul Huggins. The deposition notices would require the production of any and all financial records relating to Devonshire Plastics. The assignment was one that he would have given to Philly if she were around. But she had her own priorities and problems. At least she was doing what she could to help herself. There was a part of him that saw her drinking problem as a weakness. When he had made the mistake of voicing this feeling to Maxine, she had bit his head off, rightly he supposed. Still, he hated the double standard: women were constantly bitching about men not sharing their feelings but when sharing occurred, the feeling shared had damn well better be politically correct and sensitive. Unkind feelings, however genuine, were best kept to oneself.

On a fresh sheet of notepaper, Carpenter began to outline a court complaint that Jerome Singer would be filing seeking damages against Norman Cassidy for illegally recording the telephone conversation that had come to haunt Singer and cast a cloud over his company's ability to stay in business. It was time for Singer to go on the offensive. Although they didn't know it, Jeffries and Boyle were going to take the first crack at a superior court complaint.

Philly sat at her home office desk thinking that sometimes coming up with a defense was blind luck. Last night she'd watched the HBO film *Temple Grandin,* a sappy biopic that held her interest. The autistic woman of the movie title had come up with breakthrough techniques in animal husbandry. To deal with her autism, she had devised a machine that hugged her close, calmed her, satisfied a need for contact that she couldn't get from other people because she couldn't bear to be touched by another human being. Seeing Claire Danes squished into the machine, she had thought of Luke Harrington standing upright in a narrow closet. The first thing this morning she had called Naomi Harrington.

Harrington described in more detail the first time Luke had been placed in the closet. It was a chance event. Luke was acting out physically, twisting and writhing, screaming at the top of his lungs, and it was all John Harrington could do to keep hold of him. They were in the front hallway of their house, Luke wriggled free, and John's reaching out for Luke had landed the boy in a small open closet across the hallway from the principal closet used to hang coats and jackets. John had been angry, had reflexively slammed the closet door shut, and the result had been instant silence. "It was weird," Harrington had recalled. "One moment Luke was shrieking like a banshee; the next there was no sound from him at all. When we finally opened the closet door, Luke walked out as if nothing had happened. It was almost as if he didn't remember the whole incident."

Harrington had given Philly the number for Luke's pediatrician, Dr. Anne Cooper, who had agreed to give her fifteen minutes this afternoon.

When Dr. Cooper picked up, Philly gave the physician a brief summary of the pending litigation. Dr. Cooper listened without interrupting. "What's your read on this from a medical point of view?"

"Luke has had some medical tests done regarding his explosive behavior at home, but the tests haven't turned up anything like a tumor or a hormone imbalance, so there's been no diagnosis. This is the first time I'm hearing about the closet." Cooper paused. "This may sound glib and too general, but I'm of the view that if parents find something that works for a child, they should go with it."

"Would you say something to that effect in an affidavit?"

"Probably. I would need to see the affidavit and give it careful thought. Obviously, I'd need to see Luke."

"Of course," Philly said. "When's the last time you saw Luke?"

"I think it was two to three months ago."

"Would it be possible for you to fit him in for a brief office visit in the next few days?"

"I'm sure something could be worked out."

"I'm curious," Philly said. "In layman's terms, how's Luke doing?"

"I would say generally okay. My understanding is that he's doing reasonably well in school. But there's obviously something new that's entered the mix and needs to be evaluated."

"Should the Harringtons have told you about their putting Luke in a closet?"

"Yes. It would have been helpful to me if they had brought it up. There's no such thing as irrelevant information when it comes to a child's behavior that causes parents concern."

"If you give me your e-mail address, I'll send you a draft of the affidavit I'm thinking about."

Talking to Carpenter about cases on the phone, Philly missed watching his face. True, reading his expressions was problematic since there was little to distinguish among his many grouchy looks. But Philly believed that in the years they'd been working together, she had gotten a handle on assigning meaning to the subtle gradations of his irritability.

"Okay," she said, after Carpenter went through his proposal to share any contingency fee in the Stanton and Lane case with Jeffries and Boyle.

"I've got a hunch a jury is going to stick it to Wise Computers," Carpenter said.

"Let's hope you're right."

"What are you up to?" Carpenter asked.

"I'm becoming totally round."

"I mean as far as work is going."

Philly filled Carpenter in on the Harringtons' case.

"Why don't you use Jeffries and Boyle to write your legal memorandum?" Carpenter suggested.

"I can't see bringing both of them in. If you had to choose, who do you think I should use?"

"I'd say Boyle," Carpenter answered after a long pause. "But I don't think you should choose. I think they complement each other. They seem to work well together."

"You think anything's going on between them?"

"Who the hell knows? I don't really give a shit!"

Philly considered her options. She had already agreed that the two young lawyers could use her office. If they were going to take over her legal life maybe she should give them free rein.

“Okay, I’ll send them an e-mail and tell them what I want. I’ll copy you on the e-mail so you can give them a hard time.”

“You know,” Carpenter said, “I’ve been thinking I could get used to this delegating shit.”

Philly didn’t want to get used to it. But she didn’t have much choice. Carpenter seemed to think that Jeffries and Boyle could handle anything. He’d better be right.

June

Philly's Untitled Playlist

Uprising

Muse

A Bully

43

Looking out the window of her second-floor office, Philly was heartened that the few trees lining the street were fully leafed out and that sunshine played on the steeply sloped roofs of the neighboring houses. This perfect day for a bike ride would mostly be spent putting the finishing touches on the affidavit of Dr. Anne Cooper, the pediatrician who was treating Luke Harrington. When that chore was concluded, she vowed to get off her increasingly fat ass and take a walk.

An incoming e-mail message put her plans on hold. Daniel Spring had called and had left a call-back number. Timing was everything, she thought. If her major referral source was calling with a new case, she might have to turn it down.

"I hope you're well, Ms. Piper," Spring said when she returned his call. "I just gave your name to a family that is sorely in need of legal representation."

"I am well," Philly said, which wasn't a flat out lie. All things considered, she was hanging on. "What's the matter about?"

"Student bullying."

Philly had read the recent news stories about two teenagers who committed suicide after enduring relentless physical and cyber bullying. "What happened to the student?" she asked.

"The bullied student was beaten up and was hospitalized for a stretch," Spring explained. "The family that will be contacting you is the family of the kid who administered the beating."

Any uplift from the sparkling spring day vanished. The last thing Philly wanted to do was represent some young thug. "I may have to decline. I'm pregnant and if the doctors are right I'll be delivering next month."

"Congratulations. That's wonderful. Didn't you work with another attorney?"

"Yes."

"Then maybe he could fill in for you. The family's name is Hatch, Wendy and James, and the son is Gerald. I think the Hatches are going to call you. At least hear them out before you make a decision."

"Of course," Philly said. "I'll be happy to talk with them. Thank you again for thinking of me." She wasn't happy at all but turning away Spring out-of-hand wasn't a good idea.

Spring paused. "The injured kid was hurt pretty bad. This won't be an easy case. I'd fully understand if you decide not to take it on."

"I'll let you know what I decide."

"Just a minute," James Hatch said. "My wife's going to get on an extension."

Philly had managed to wedge her office window upwards. A cool June breeze filled the room but thinking ahead to the height of the summer, Philly expected her office to be a steam bath. The room wouldn't get the direct heat of the sun, but it would be stifling nonetheless. She didn't think that she'd be able to get by with just a fan.

"Okay, I'm on," a woman's voice announced

"Thanks for talking with us," James Hatch said. "We've been sued and our son Gerald has been sued. Did Daniel tell you what the case was about?"

"He gave me a brief outline. He described it as a case of bullying."

The word *bullying* produced a brief silence.

"Gerald badly injured another student," Wendy Hatch said.

"We've been to a lawyer," James Hatch continued. "He wasn't comfortable representing all of us. He recommended that Gerald have his own lawyer. Would you be interested?"

Philly hadn't expected this twist. Her pregnancy gave her a ready-made excuse to decline the matter. Still, she had given her word to Daniel Spring. "I need to hear a little more about what happened."

"Gerald's finishing his junior year at John Adams High School in Cambridgeport," Wendy Hatch said. "He won't tell us much of anything, but from what we've been able to find out, he pretty much picked on this other junior most of the school year. They had been lab partners in a chemistry class. During a chemistry test, Gerald tried to copy off this other boy's paper. We think there's more to that story, but Gerald won't share what went on. We're told that Gerald harassed the other boy—pushing him, calling him names, punching him—that kind of thing."

Philly recalled the taunting and challenging that went on during her own high school years. But bullying had taken on a more sinister dimension since then. "What caused the fight?" she asked.

James Hatch fielded the question. "According to the principal, Gerald had pushed the other student, knocked his books to the ground, and was swearing at him. The other student charged Gerald and Gerald punched him in the face. Gerald kicked the other boy while he was on the ground. I don't know what would have happened if a teacher hadn't come along and pulled Gerald off. Gerald was much bigger and stronger than the other boy."

"How badly was the other student hurt?"

"Pretty bad," James Hatch acknowledged. "He suffered a bruised spleen and a broken clavicle. His face was pretty banged up."

"Were the school authorities aware of what was going on?"

"The school and the principal are also being sued," Wendy Hatch advised. "The boy who was hurt had complained numerous times. Other than split Gerald and the boy up as chemistry lab partners, I don't believe the school did anything."

"Did the other boy's parents complain to you?"

"No," James Hatch said.

"How do you explain your son's actions?"

"We can't," Wendy Hatch said immediately. "We're appalled by what Gerald did. Our lawyer probably wouldn't want us telling you this, but we've been unable to control Gerald. He's nothing like his younger sister and younger brother. He can be angry and mean."

Philly rubbed her belly. What did it take out of parents to admit openly that their kid was mean? "Would you be able to send me a copy of the complaint filed against you and your son?"

"If you give me your e-mail address I can do it when we get off the phone," James Hatch said.

Philly provided her contact information. "I'm pregnant," she told the Hatches, "and I'm due to deliver next month. So if you hire me, I may not be directly involved in your son's defense for a number of months. There's a lawyer I work with who's an accomplished litigator and he'll be looking after my cases."

"This is unexpected," Wendy Hatch said.

Philly didn't say anything. She listened to the birdsong outside her window. She took in narrow, short breaths.

"Would we get to meet with you and this other lawyer before we decide?" James Hatch asked.

"I could arrange for that," Philly said.

"Why don't you set that up?" James Hatch instructed. "I'll e-mail you the complaint."

"Will you be paying for Gerald's representation?"

"We've been paying for Gerald for years," James Hatch said with the first indication of bitterness Philly had picked up on during the call. "This is nothing new."

44

Carpenter led the procession into Philly's living room-dining room area, followed by Simon Jeffries and Rachel Boyle. He hoped his expression hadn't given away his amazement at how huge she'd become. She'd been big during the baby shower but now she was enormous.

"I've got coffee on in the kitchen," Philly announced. "It's self-service."

Simon saw to the coffee orders.

Carpenter took a seat at the head of the dining table, anxious to get started. Simon and Rachel had juggled their schedules to attend this meeting and he was intent on making their time together productive. "Let's come to order. We've got a lot of ground to cover before the Hatches get here."

"I'll start," Philly said as she eased herself onto the chair at the opposite end of the table. From Carpenter's point of view, pregnant women by and large were put upon, irritable, and eager to put the experience behind them. He suspected that any glow they emitted was fanned by anger and fueled by hormonal changes. Yet Philly did seem reasonably composed and together, and she looked surprisingly good. Her white skin had more color than usual and her black curls looked . . . well, lustrous was probably the right word.

"I need to thank you," Philly said to Simon and Rachel. "The legal memorandum you did for me in the Harringtons' case was great. I think we have a good chance of keeping their case alive. I've made a few changes that I want Carpenter to look at and he'll make sure it gets filed. That was a big help."

The two young lawyers were soaking up Philly's compliment. Carpenter had always told Philly when she'd done a good job, and he was pleased to see that she knew how important it was to give praise when praise was due.

Carpenter brought Philly up to date on the cases that didn't require much discussion. Simon and Rachel were handling the discovery in the case brought by Herbert Stanton and Millie Lane; Simon would be conducting a deposition of Wise Computer's president. Crowe Investment Strategies had filed its position paper with the Massachusetts Commission Against Discrimination denying that the company had discriminated against Frederick Chun. Rachel would be drafting discovery requests in that case. Carpenter's preparation for the appeal hearing concerning Jack Lawson's IEP was under control, and lawyers were coming forward as potential witnesses in Marshall Hyde's disciplinary action before the Board of Bar Overseers.

"Next on my list is the Top Tier Finance regulatory matter," Carpenter changed the subject. "This week we'll be filing suit against Norman Cassidy. You guys did a good job on the first cut of the court complaint," he said to Simon and Rachel. "We're trying to keep out of evidence the damaging telephone call that Cassidy recorded but that's not going to happen." He saw no dissent to his assessment.

"Any thoughts about the Hatches?" Carpenter inquired. He had given copies of the complaint filed against the Hatches to Simon and Rachel. The victim, Martin Mercer, had sued everyone in sight: Gerald Hatch and his parents, the high school principal and assistant principal, each of Mercer's high school teachers, and members of the Cambridgeport School Committee. The Mercer kid's lawyer, Donald Fanning, was a flamboyant litigator with an over-the-top style that Carpenter found off-putting, but which apparently connected with jurors. There were numerous emotional heart strings to be tugged on Mercer's behalf, so Fanning would be in his element.

"Isn't a jury going to think it's a little weird that Gerald has one lawyer and his parents another?" Rachel asked.

"I'm sure you understand why the lawyer for Mr. and Mrs. Hatch wants Gerald to have his own lawyer," Carpenter responded.

Rachel nodded. "The parents need to distance themselves from their son to avoid personal liability."

"Right," Carpenter concurred. "If the parents paint Gerald as this uncontrollable, wild kid, we've got our work cut out for us defending Gerald."

"I really haven't come up with a defense for Gerald," Simon interjected.

"Yeah, there's that," Carpenter muttered. "As we've discussed in the Top Tier case, there's always blame the other guy as a last resort."

"You mean blame the school defendants and the Mercer kid?" Rachel questioned.

Carpenter nodded. It wasn't much of a defense to claim that someone else should have prevented a client's wrongful act, but sometimes a lousy defense was all you had. "Let's see if the Hatches come up with something we can work with. Right now, I need a little face time with Philly. Why don't we go up to your office?"

Philly eyed the stairs with misgivings, and Carpenter wondered whether he'd been inconsiderate without meaning to be. But then Philly pushed off from the table top, rose, and headed to the stairs.

Carpenter followed her to the second floor, worried as he did so that she would topple over backwards, careening into him like a bowling ball, and leave him a crumpled heap at the bottom of the stairs. But they gained the landing and at one end of a hallway Philly turned on the light in the room that served as her office and took the only chair in the room. Carpenter perched on a desk that had no chair.

"That was Philip's desk," Philly said, pointing to where he was sitting. "There's really no room for it, but I can't bear to move it to the basement."

It was warm in the room. Carpenter's view out the room's one window showed the sloping roof of a neighboring house. "I know you hate the question, but I'm still going to ask you how you're doing."

"I'm dreading giving birth, but I can't wait for this pregnancy to end."

"You're looking good," Carpenter said. "And you're sounding good. Is the AA helping?"

"Who the fuck knows," Philly muttered. "I just need to keep going to the meetings. I don't want to talk about it."

Carpenter preferred Philly's short temper to passivity or resignation. "I'm figuring you're going to be out of action for three to four months," he said. "I think with Jeffries and Boyle we can keep things going and keep money coming your way."

"That would bother me," Philly said. "I won't be earning any of it."

"You're looking at it the wrong way," Carpenter countered. "Let's say you bring in this Hatch kid as a client and his parents pay the kid's legal bills. Some of the money we bill out and collect is going to come back to you."

Philly frowned and Carpenter silently hoped that her stubbornness, pride, and independent streak didn't push her into a wrong decision.

"I won't be able to put anything in my pocket. Anything that comes my way will go to keeping up my Boston office. That's why I think I should give up the office."

"Don't do that yet," Carpenter urged. "From the day you go into the hospital, I want to pick up half your office nut."

Philly's eyes widened and then she sullenly shook her head. "I'm not a goddamn charity case."

"I know that. We've got a good thing going here. We can make money off Jeffries and Boyle, plus I like them. They're helping."

Philly shook her head. "A lot of what they're doing is on contingency work that may never pay off."

"I've got a hunch about the contingency cases. I think we're going to score on those."

"What's with the hunches," Philly grumbled. "You're one of the most pessimistic people I've ever run into. You never think anything will turn out well."

"I'm trying to change that. In a crazy way, having Jeffries and Boyle around has got me energized."

"Jesus!" Philly exclaimed. "You're talking like we're a law firm."

Carpenter scowled. Philly had made a telling point. He *was* making noises as if the four of them were a firm. But the truth was they were four independent lawyers collaborating on cases. "I'm not ready to use the word firm."

"You're halfway there as far as I can tell," Philly said.

A doorbell sounded.

"Time to meet the Hatches," Philly said, as she labored to her feet.

James and Wendy Hatch and their son Gerald were grouped around one end of the dining room table, Carpenter and Philly facing them at the other end. Simon and Rachel had settled on the easy chairs that Simon had moved closer to the table. Philly studied the Hatches and didn't like what she saw when it came to Gerald. The kid was six feet tall and rugged looking with a thickset build of mostly muscle. He had hard, unblinking dark eyes and thick, long, dark hair that hung along the sides of his face. She sensed you could look into Gerald's eyes till hell froze over and you wouldn't see a trace of kindness in the kid's gaze.

"Thanks for seeing us so quickly," James Hatch said.

Philly nodded. People thinking about hiring a lawyer had to be looking for some semblance of a law office, but the elder Hatches didn't seem to be bothered by meeting at her house. Their grim, resigned expressions made Philly wonder how many meetings they had attended where the subject was trying to make the best of something nasty that Gerald had done. James Hatch was an architect and his wife was an event planner. They looked to be in their mid-forties. Each sat hunched over as if their son's behavior literally weighed them down.

"Gerald," Philly said sharply. "Why don't you tell us about the fight you got into with the Mercer boy?"

Gerald regarded her is if she were road kill. Philly struggled not to laugh as she maintained her own hard stare. She remembered her teen years when she had posed in front of a mirror until her death ray glare was down pat.

"There's nothing to tell. The asshole came at me and I kicked the shit out of him."

"Any idea why he came at you?"

"You'd have to ask him."

"I'm asking you."

Gerald sulked, glaring at her. His parents stared at the tabletop.

"He looked at me funny and I gave him a push. His books fell on the ground and then he ran at me."

"What was funny about his look?" Philly demanded, resolving to cut Gerald zero slack.

"I didn't like it. I don't take shit from anyone, especially a loser like Mercer."

"Have criminal charges been filed against Gerald?" Philly asked the teen's parents.

"Not yet," James Hatch said wearily, "but it's a possibility."

"Why did you keep kicking the Mercer boy?" Philly said to Gerald.

"It's like I told you—he came at me."

"But after you hit him and he went down, why did you keep kicking him?"

"I just did."

"What do you weigh?"

"What's that got to do with anything?"

"Just answer my question."

Gerald fell silent and Philly judged it was even money whether he'd respond.

"A hundred ninety."

"What about the Mercer boy—how much does he weigh?"

Gerald colored slightly. "I don't know."

"Take a guess."

"I don't know. A hundred fifty maybe."

Philly glared at Gerald and it was the teen who broke off eye contact.

"Okay, Gerald. You've given us a feel for how tough you are. What do you have to say about the court complaint which states you were picking on Mercer pretty much all of the last school year? Is that true?"

"I don't like the kid," Gerald said defiantly. "He deserved whatever I dished out. He had it coming to him."

"Is that because he wouldn't let you copy his chemistry test answers?"

"I'm sick of your questions. I thought you were supposed to be helping me. Who the fuck needs you?"

Carpenter was about to intervene and Philly preempted him with a head shake. "You do," Philly replied calmly. "Here's what's going to happen to you if you don't knock the chip off your shoulder. Mercer is going to get a money judgment against you which he won't enforce right away but he will if you ever get a job. From what you've said so far, a criminal complaint might be filed against you and you may be convicted. That could mean jail time. If you go to jail, you'll have a chance to prove how tough you really are. So you need to give us something to work with to help prevent these things from happening to you."

Gerald sat smoldering and Philly decided to let him stew. It had felt good to let her frustrations out on this teen who didn't seem to have any redeeming quality. Carpenter wanted the case because it was a billable hour matter, but she didn't give a damn whether Gerald became a client or not. Maybe her hormones were overriding business sense, but she was damned if she was going to take a ration of shit from a punk kid.

"What do you mean something to work with?" Gerald said in a voice so low that Philly strained to hear. She counted slowly to ten taking short shallow breaths. Her diaphragm seemed up around her throat.

"By something to work with, I mean is there anything you can think of that justifies you getting into the fight with the Mercer boy. Or maybe you can think of something that casts you in a better light."

Surprisingly, Gerald was taking her questions seriously. His glower toned down and he was concentrating.

"That chemistry test," Gerald said. "It was multiple choice. The thing was, Mercer did let me copy the answers to a bunch of questions before he wouldn't let me look at his test paper any more. But I'm pretty sure the answers he let me copy were wrong answers. He must have changed them later."

"How do you know this?"

"The little shit got a hundred on the test. I failed."

Carpenter's jaw muscles were working; Gerald had given him something to chew over. Rachel was writing furiously on her legal pad while Simon was regarding the teen with a dark, unforgiving look. For the first time during this meeting the Hatches focused on their son.

"Why didn't you ever mention this before?" James Hatch asked.

"As if you give a shit!" Gerald railed at his father.

"We do give a shit," his father replied angrily. "If you'd show us a little more respect and stop locking us out of your life, we might be able to help you."

"Like that's going to happen," Gerald snapped. "You don't give a damn about me."

"You don't give a damn about yourself," Wendy Hatch intervened. "We've never understood why you've become so . . . mean. You weren't always like this. What happened to you?"

"Are we done?" Gerald raised his voice.

No." Philly was firm. "Do you want us to represent you? If you say yes, you need to understand that I won't be involved for a while for obvious reasons." She patted her stomach. "Mr. Carpenter will be handling your case until I come back from maternity leave and even then, he may be playing the leading role. You need to know that Mr. Carpenter will put up with less crap from you than I will, and I'm not about to put up with very much."

Simon and Rachel exchanged a glance, perhaps wondering whether all interviews with potential clients were nasty, belligerent affairs.

"I guess so," Gerald said.

"I'll take that as a yes," Philly said. "What do you have to say to your parents?"

"Nothing."

"How about thank you. They're paying for your legal representation."

Gerald glared at his parents. "They can afford it."

"Not the right answer," Philly said. "Is it that you really don't get it or is it that you're just being a jerk?"

"I don't have to take any shit from you."

"Yeah, you do. And it's going to keep coming at you until you change your act." Philly checked her watch. "Now we're done."

"I never thanked you for inviting me to your baby shower," Melanie said. "That was nice of you."

Philly shrugged noncommittally. Isabella had extended the invitation, but Melanie didn't have to know that. "Glad you could come."

The AA meeting had ended and Philly and Melanie were on folding chairs, sipping at coffees in a corner of the basement meeting room at Saint Sebastian's. Philly had become accustomed to the drab, rundown look and feel of the room. Even the pale sun of a June evening coming through its few high windows did little to brighten it. Listening to the tales of woe unfold at tonight's meeting, she continued to believe that she wasn't like the other attendees. There was no way in hell she was as pathetic as they were.

"You haven't talked at the last couple of meetings," Melanie said. "Is there a reason?"

"I just haven't had a lot to say."

"I don't think it's that."

"What do you think it is?"

Melanie sipped at her coffee unhurriedly. "You think the hardest part is over. You think by saying that first time you were an alcoholic, your business is done. That's not the way it works."

Philly held off from saying that Melanie had no business telling her what she was thinking. And Melanie was, uncomfortably, correct. Philly *had* embraced the mindset that after her initial revelation, her work was pretty much concluded.

"I try to say at least one thing every other meeting," Melanie continued. "Sometimes when you start talking, even if it's not about important stuff, somebody comes up with something that can help you."

Philly thought back over the past month. Part of her regarded the AA meetings as a chore. She had been making an effort to accept help from other people and that seemed to be working. But Melanie, she knew, was talking about something else.

"I want you to say something next meeting," Melanie said.

"I'll think about it."

"That's not enough," Melanie said. Her sponsor's sharp tone surprised Philly.

"You probably think you're smarter than me," Melanie went on. "You may have a lot more school than I have, but when it comes to what we're doing here, you don't know shit."

Melanie averted her gaze. Philly knew that it hadn't been easy for her sponsor to come down hard. She thought back to late morning when she had come down hard on Gerald Hatch, probably irrevocably alienating the teenager, but she knew in her gut that the only way to reach Gerald was to challenge and confront him at every turn. Carpenter had taken her aside and told her to lighten up with the kid and she had stood up to him, told him to butt out and that he'd thank her later. But the truth was she couldn't imagine Gerald ever admitting that he was wrong. It was sad to realize that she had that in common with the teenager.

"I told you before that if you want another sponsor it's okay with me," Melanie said.

People were starting to leave and Philly wanted to join the exodus. She was exhausted. The thought of plopping down on her bed with her feet up was so enticing, she wished that she could somehow be instantaneously transported back to the house.

"Okay," Philly said. "I'll say something at the next meeting. And I don't want a different sponsor. Do we have a deal?"

"Deal," Melanie confirmed, and the woman's smile told Philly that her sponsor was doing her best to help her.

"Then give me a hand so I can get up. I've got to get out of here."

45

Carpenter looked around the hearing room and said a silent prayer of thanks that Jerome Singer was not in attendance. If Singer knew that the first motions in Top Tier's regulatory case were going to be argued by a lawyer who had just recently passed the bar, his circuitry would short out. Carpenter, himself, had only a tenuous grasp on his reasons for letting Simon handle this hearing. Mainly, he wanted to see how the kid performed under pressure. Logic dictated that you don't give a lawyer fresh out of law school the opening litigation task in a case that you were counting on to make your year financially. Yet, here he was, playing another hunch; something in his gut told him that putting Simon forward was the right move. But it was the kind of hunch that could blow up in your face. While Simon had held up under his own questioning, when a hearing was for real and not a mock trial run, it was a different ball game

Precisely at ten, Serena Jones, the presiding hearing officer, took the seat in the center of a conference table that faced two tables at which the attorneys were seated. Jones was middle aged with short dark hair and dark eyes. "Good morning," she announced. "We're here to address certain motions filed by the respondent. I'd like counsel to introduce themselves."

Simon did the honors for himself, Carpenter and Rachel, his voice strong.

"Louise Fuller for the Loan Company Licensure Review Board."

Carpenter didn't like the fact that Fuller was also middle aged. She was stouter than Jones and looked less accommodating than the hearing officer. Carpenter feared that Jones would feel some bond with another woman lawyer of the same age.

"Let's start with Top Tier's motion to exclude from evidence the tape of a phone conversation. I've read the parties' legal memoranda. What do you say, Mr. Jeffries, to the Board's argument that nobody associated with the Board did anything illegal?"

"A crime was committed," Simon began, and Carpenter liked that opening salvo. "It is a crime for someone to record a telephone conversation without telling the other party to the phone conversation that recording is taking place. Therefore, we start with the undisputed fact that Norman Cassidy committed a crime."

Carpenter was pleased to see that Jones was writing.

"The Board's position is that it may profit from that crime in presenting a case against Top Tier because Norman Cassidy has nothing to do with the Board. That argument should not carry the day because the Board would be benefitting from the criminal act of another. There is no justification for letting the Board gain any advantage from the criminal act of another."

Simon paused while Jones continued to write. Fuller was regarding Simon without expression. Beside Carpenter, Rachel was writing as conscientiously as the hearing officer.

"Moreover," Simon continued, "Norman Cassidy committed the crime in question for personal gain. First, he used the illegal recording to strip his company of assets and thereby financially harm his company's principal creditor, Top Tier. And second, he used it to bring regulatory pressure on Top Tier in order to influence the lawsuit Top Tier brought against his company. We're all familiar with the principal that a party cannot threaten criminal action to gain an advantage in a civil suit. What Norman Cassidy did is directly analogous to that prohibited practice."

"What do you say to Mr. Jeffries' arguments?" Jones directed at Fuller.

"They're off the mark," Fuller replied without hesitation. "Mr. Jeffries ignores the public interests that the Board must protect. Mr. Cassidy provided the Board with information that showed Top Tier's president was making misrepresentations to borrowers. Specifically, Mr. Singer was falsely telling borrowers that they had ninety days to cure a loan default when in fact his company enforced a loan agreement that provided for only a ten-day cure period. If Mr. Cassidy committed a crime, Mr. Singer is fully capable of filing a criminal complaint against him."

Jones looked inquiringly at Simon.

"There's no 'if' about it. Mr. Cassidy did commit a crime. Also, when it comes to the public interest, how is the public interest served by permitting regulators to benefit from a crime committed by a third party? The public interest is not served in that situation, because criminal conduct is not only being condoned; criminal conduct is being rewarded."

Jones became lost in thought. Carpenter thought Simon was enjoying himself. So far, he had stayed composed and had answered the hearing officer's questions.

"Let's turn to Top Tier's motion to take the depositions of Mr. Cassidy and an accountant, Paul Huggins. Under the Board's rules, Top Tier needs to show good cause to take any deposition. What is the good cause to take the depositions of Mr. Cassidy and Mr. Huggins?"

Simon turned over a page in his litigation notebook. "This case is about the loan from Top Tier to Devonshire Plastic. Anything concerning that loan is relevant to the regulatory hearing before the Board. Top Tier needs to examine all of Devonshire's books and records to prepare for trial before the Board. The Board complaint claims that Mr. Singer orally informed Mr. Cassidy about a ninety-day cure period and then Top Tier proceeded to bring suit against Devonshire under the ten-day cure period in the loan agreement. No suit was brought against Devonshire until after Mr. Cassidy revealed that he had committed a crime by illegally recording a phone conversation he had with Mr. Singer. Since it is a given that Mr. Cassidy is capable of criminal conduct, Top Tier needs to determine what, if any, additional crimes were committed by Devonshire and its president. For example, was the financial information false that Devonshire provided to Top Tier to obtain and continue its loan? Top Tier cannot determine the answers to such questions without obtaining and reviewing Devonshire's financial records, and without deposing Mr. Cassidy and Mr. Huggins."

Carpenter noted that Jones was no longer writing. Still, the hearing officer appeared attentive.

"What does any of that have to do with the simple issue in this case?" Jones asked. "The issue is whether Mr. Singer orally told Mr. Cassidy he had ninety days to cure a loan default and then gave Devonshire only ten days to cure."

"The issue," Simon responded, "is whether Mr. Cassidy's criminal conduct cancelled out anything Mr. Singer may have said. Faced with admitted criminal conduct by the borrower's president, Mr. Singer could have properly concluded that his own company may have been defrauded and that his company needed to act promptly. Mr. Singer's actions will come out at trial. What Top Tier is entitled to before trial is to learn whether an admitted criminal may have committed additional crimes in obtaining a loan for his company."

Carpenter liked Jeffries' repeated references to Cassidy as an admitted criminal, but he couldn't tell whether Jones was buying that characterization.

"What do you have to say, Ms. Fuller?"

"Your Honor has correctly identified the narrow issue in this case. It's whether Top Tier's president induced borrowers to take out loans by telling them they had a more lenient cure period than was set out in the loan documents. The Board regards such conduct as abhorrent. Mr. Singer did tell Mr. Cassidy that Devonshire had ninety days to cure a default but he didn't give Devonshire anywhere near ninety days. Mr. Singer expressly told Mr. Cassidy not to worry about the ten-day cure period in the loan agreement. Whatever financial information Devonshire gave Top Tier is beside the point."

When Simon leaned toward him, Carpenter held up his notepad to shield their mouths from Jones. Rachel leaned in to join the huddle.

"I don't really have anything to add," Simon whispered.

Rachel shook her head. "Drive home the point that any statement made by Singer was made with the understanding that Cassidy was law abiding and that no fraud was committed by Devonshire. Once Cassidy admitted he broke the law, anything Singer said became beside the point."

Carpenter nodded. He liked the way Rachel had put the additional argument.

"One last point," Simon said, and he repeated Rachel's suggested approach.

"Anything else?" Jones inquired. "In that case, I'll take the motions under advisement and you can expect a decision shortly."

"Nice job," Carpenter said to Simon as he led the procession back to his office. "You're next," he added to Rachel.

"I'm not sure that I want to do any actual litigating," Rachel said.

"How will you know unless you try?" Carpenter came back. "Don't sell yourself short."

"I enjoy research and writing," Rachel explained.

"You're surprising me here," Carpenter said. Rachel had impressed him with an ability to spot legal issues and come up with creative arguments. Yet litigation was not for everyone; some lawyers were happy never to set foot in a courtroom. Carpenter decided not to press Rachel. He'd give her a litigation assignment when the time was right and leave it up to her to turn it down.

"I'm Philly and I'm an alcoholic."

"Hi Philly!" the chorus came back.

"I haven't had a drink since I've started coming to meetings."

The light round of applause was underwhelming. Philly had no idea what she was going to say. When her silence became awkward, Charlie asked a question.

"How's the pregnancy going?"

"I wish it was over," Philly admitted. "But I'm also scared about it being over."

"Why are you scared?" Charlie followed up.

Philly studied the long-haired group leader and the attendees at tonight's meeting. Some of them had bared their souls in her presence. But Philly was possessive about her privacy and the rules of AA meetings cut against her grain. Melanie's hand was in motion, a circular movement signaling her to talk.

Philly took a deep breath. "I guess I'm afraid that I'll be a lousy mother and that motherhood will change my life in ways I won't like. I still don't know how I'm going to raise a baby and keep practicing law."

"I thought you told us you had people around to help you," interjected a bald man badly in need of a shave.

"Right," Philly acknowledged. "I did say that. But other people can do just so much. In the end, it comes down to you."

"But you're going to have a kid," said a woman wearing sunglasses and a baseball cap. "Think of how much fun that's going to be."

Fun was not the word that came to mind when Philly thought of motherhood. "Giving birth sounds like it's going to be hell," she blurted out, immediately regretting giving voice to her thoughts.

"It is," Melanie agreed. "But it's the kind of thing that you put behind you right after it's over."

Philly doubted that bit of wisdom. She still hadn't recovered from Philip's death. And lost in the shuffle was the need to find a lawyer who, on her behalf, would sue that miserable shit, Colin Feeney.

"Is there anything about being a mother that you're looking forward to?" Charlie asked.

"Nothing jumps out at me," Philly was forced to concede, wondering if she had morphed into someone gloomier than Carpenter. She was taken aback by the depths of Charlie's look of concern.

"What about that fiancée of yours you were telling us about?" the bald man brought up. "Think how happy he'll be looking down on you with his child."

Really? He thought Philip was sitting on a cloud in the sky? That was delusional.

"Brian has a point," Charlie said. "Joy is about to enter your life. You might try to embrace that."

Philly stared at the group leader, saw Melanie nodding out of the corner of her eye. Even the woman in shades was bobbing her head. What filter was blocking out the bright promise these people saw? What the hell, she thought. "Okay. I'll give it the old college try."

46

Philip's old desk was in the hallway outside her home office, replaced with a low file cabinet on which rested a new combination copier, scanner, FAX, and printer. Raul had offered to get a friend to help him move Philip's desk to the basement, but Philly couldn't yet bring herself to consign this piece of her short life with Philip to a place out of sight. So here she was fully equipped and set up to practice law from a home office, and she had nothing to do. Carpenter was dealing with her cases and his own. Simon and Rachel were playing a bigger role in their pending cases, picking up any slack, and Philly had to admit that the two young lawyers were helpful. She felt that she was the odd man out.

Philly started when her cell phone rang. "Philomena Piper."

"Hi. It's Paul Sullivan. I thought I'd check in with you. Are you a mother yet?"

"Not yet. Right now, I'm a dirigible."

Sullivan laughed. Philly pictured his moody, dark eyes flash amusement.

"You want some company before the big event?"

"Are you asking me out?"

"I'm thinking. I'm not sure I want to formally ask a dirigible for a date."

"What did you have in mind?"

"What are you doing right now?"

Outside her office window, the sun hadn't reached the sloping roof of the neighboring house. It was one of those cloudless days that would become unbearably hot once the sun was overhead. She really was going to have to get an air conditioning unit for her window, ruining her limited view. "Nothing."

"How about I stop by your house in an hour and bring lunch."

"Is this a date?"

"Yes," Sullivan said after a long pause.

"Okay," Philly replied after taking her own time. If Sullivan had to think about whether they would be having a date, so did she.

"Any preferences on food?"

"Surprise me."

"I can do that. Where do you live?"

Paul Sullivan had to be off-duty unless he was on an undercover assignment that was beyond weird. He was wearing cutoff jeans and a wife beater. He was lean and hard-muscled. If she hadn't become totally round she might have been able to summon up a modicum of desire. Instead Philly had to focus on the more immediate need of easing herself down on the front steps. Sullivan set out paper plates and began loading them up with Chicago hot dogs. He had brought along two twenty-ounce bottles of ginger ale and he broke the seal on each and removed the caps before setting the bottles down on the top step.

"You better like these," Sullivan said, pointing at the hot dogs. "I love the stuff."

"Look at me," Philly said. "I love everything edible these days and I get to justify feeding my face by saying I'm eating for two."

"You sure it's not three?"

"Very funny."

They ate for a time in silence. Philly felt sweat pouring off her. Her hair had to be a matted down mess. Sullivan had brought six hot dogs, three apiece. After the first one she wondered whether three would be enough.

"Can we get the serious stuff out of the way?" Sullivan asked.

Philly was brought up short. She and Philip would always air out everything when one of them announced they were having a serious discussion. In a serious discussion, the unwritten rule was to hold nothing back. "Whatever," she said, ambivalent.

"I was worried about you that day in court," Sullivan said. "I'm still worried about you. I'd like you to tell me truthfully how you're doing."

Philly was half way through her second hot dog and had no intention of slowing down. The hot dogs were good. Sullivan was looking at her thoughtfully and she debated whether to put him off. At the AA meetings, not knowing anybody's last name made it easier to let your guard down. Here, one on one with someone she knew slightly, Philly wasn't sure she could open up.

"Please," Sullivan said, and Philly remembered the earnest way he had entreated her in court not to confront the judge who had accepted Colin Feeney's guilty plea.

"I've been better," Philly said. "In no particular order, I'm scared about giving birth, motherhood, and practicing law with a baby."

"That's a lot to deal with," Sullivan said.

Philly gave him a point for not trying to cheer her up. The last AA meeting had given her enough joy-of-motherhood speeches to last a lifetime.

"Who's picking up your cases?"

"This older guy I share space with. He's brought in two young lawyers to help out."

Sullivan swigged his ginger ale. Philly wanted to pour half of what was left of her drink over her head.

"I checked in with Colin Feeney's probation officer," Sullivan said, and Philly's stomach knotted.

"I don't want to hear about it!"

Sullivan set down his drink and took Philly's hand. She tried to pull away but he held tight, meeting her gaze.

"I know you don't, but this is important."

"Let go of me!"

"The kid's been going to counseling but he won't go to AA meetings," Sullivan said, keeping hold of Philly's hand. "The probation officer says it's hard to say how the counseling's going. He also says that for the moment he's not going to push the kid on the AA meetings. As the judge said, the kid basically fell apart when his mother died. He took up with a tough crowd and started drinking. His father couldn't control him. The kid was headed for a fall and . . . well, we know what happened."

Philly wanted Sullivan to stop but couldn't force the words out. She drew into herself much as Gerald Hatch had withdrawn from his parents.

"The kid's wracked with guilt over the accident. He's having a tough time in school, but he seems to have stopped drinking, at least for now. The probation officer thinks it's a tossup whether Feeney is going to do something else stupid or turn himself around."

Sullivan let go of her hand and Philly hugged herself, for the moment feeling a tingling chill. "Did anyone ever tell you you're a shitty date?"

Sullivan didn't smile. "We're talking now," he said. "This isn't part of the date."

Philly closed her eyes and hugged herself harder, on the verge of shivering.

"There's one more thing," Sullivan said. "After you give birth and settle down, I want you to think about doing something you're not going to want to do."

Philly didn't like the sound of that request.

"Look at me," Sullivan said, and Philly forced herself to look into the detective's soulful, dark eyes.

"I wouldn't be asking you to do this if I didn't feel something for you. That first time I saw you in the hospital, my heart went out to you, but I was also attracted to you. I still can't figure out what the hell was going on."

Philly stayed silent.

"Even when you took on that judge against my better judgment, I had to admire your guts. You're a real piece of work."

Philly waited for the punch line, for Sullivan to say whatever he was going to say that was sure to make her anger flare.

"If you can find it in you," Sullivan said, "think about going to see Feeney and forgiving him."

Philly stared at Sullivan too stunned to speak. What the hell was this guy doing laying this on her less than a month from her due date? She wanted to lash out at him, but the way he was looking at her, concern in his eyes, she couldn't say a word.

"My timing's not great, is it?" Sullivan said.

"I think you better go."

"I probably should have done this months ago. There's never a good time for some things."

"Please, you need to go."

Sullivan stood up. He placed his third hot dog on Philly's plate and put the cap back on his bottle of ginger ale.

"I'm going to call you again," Sullivan said. "I hope you call me before I call you and especially if your baby comes. If there's anything I can do for you, all you have to do is ask."

Sullivan brushed crumbs off his clothes. He leaned over and gave Philly's dark curls a light pat, a gesture that was so reminiscent of Philip that Philly instantly teared up. And then Sullivan was down the front steps, turning to the left when he got to the sidewalk, walking at a brisk pace without once looking back.

47

Carpenter disliked retrials, and the administrative hearing on Jack Lawson's Individualized Education Program was basically a retrial of the hearing before Judge O'Connell. There were few surprises the second time around, just déjà vu all over again.

The hearing was being held in a rehabbed building near North Station in offices occupied by the Department of Administrative Law Appeals. This state agency assigned magistrates to hear and decide a host of administrative appeals ranging from retirement board cases and professional license revocation cases, to Medicaid rates and IEPs. The hearing officer, Benjamin Frye, was a senior administrative magistrate with white hair and a ruddy face. Frye seemed to have swallowed the rules of evidence in much the same way referees at a basketball game sometimes swallowed their whistles and let the teams play with no fouls being called. Carpenter had exchanged a wry look with Craig Lannon when, after a half hour, it became clear that Frye would overrule any objection and let into evidence anything that a witness wanted to say.

The administrative hearing had produced no surprises so far. The Stonington school district had quickly concluded its case presenting testimony from Superintendent William Burnside and Dr. Florence Jefferson. Carpenter had sparred with each witness but scored only the same minor points he had made in the court hearing before Judge O'Connell. Lannon's cross-examination of Maryanne Fairmount and the two monitors hired by the Lawsons had been equally uneventful. Fortunately, Jack Lawson's latest pushing incident was one of many pushing incidents that had occurred on the playground since the last court hearing.

Carpenter consulted his witness list. He had two further witnesses to present before he would be forced to make a major strategic decision. He decided to start with Jack Lawson's teacher, Clarissa Webb, who had been subpoenaed for the IEP hearing.

Webb was still uneasy in her role as witness, and her testimony was much the same as before. She reported that Jack's academic performance was satisfactory, and that although he was interacting more with his classmates, the other students didn't seem to like him any better.

Carpenter consulted his testimony outline. "When we were last in court do you remember testifying that Jack made you uneasy?"

Webb colored. "Yes."

"Are you still uneasy?"

"Yes, but not as much."

"What has contributed to the lessening of your unease?"

"I guess I'm more used to the monitors and the whole situation."

Carpenter decided to quit while he was marginally ahead. "No further questions."

During Lannon's cross examination, Webb repeated her now familiar opinions that when Jack had been on the higher medication doses his academic performance had been acceptable, and his socialization somewhat subpar. Three months ago, she had not seen any need for monitors.

Carpenter rose. "Isn't it true that three months ago, Jack Lawson wouldn't play with his classmates during recess?"

"Yes," Webb said coloring.

"That lack of interaction with classmates during recess wasn't satisfactory as far as Jack's socializing, was it?"

Webb lowered her gaze. "No, it was subpar as I said before."

"No further questions," Carpenter said.

"Call your next witness," Frye directed.

Carpenter called Sylvia Lawson to the stand. After several background questions, he focused on the issues.

"Have you noticed changes in your son since his medication dosages have been lowered?"

"Yes."

"Describe those changes, please."

Lawson took a deep breath and sighed audibly. "Jack is more lively, more engaged with everything around him. The lethargy he previously exhibited is gone. He sometimes complains if you ask him to do something he doesn't want to do. He's able to focus on things for a longer period of time than he used to." Lawson paused. "He's much more of a kid than he used to be."

Carpenter asked questions for another ten minutes and then took his seat.

Craig Lannon rose. "Three months ago, did Jack present any disobedience issues?"

"Not really."

"Since his medications have been reduced has Jack been disobedient?"

"I'm not sure I'd use the work disobedient. It's like he stands up for himself now if you tell him to do something he doesn't want to do. He's resisted the bedtime we've set for him. We've noticed that he refuses to eat foods he claims he doesn't like. He's become more stubborn over certain things. Last weekend we had a trip planned to visit his grandparents and he put up an argument about going. I'm not sure any of that qualifies as disobedience. It's just the normal give and take that goes on in a family, because Jack is not as blindly accepting of things as he was three months ago."

"It sounds like Jack's become more of a handful," Lannon observed.

"To which I say, thank God," Lawson replied.

When Lannon concluded his cross-examination of Lawson, Carpenter asked for a brief recess. He huddled with Sylvia Lawson and Maryanne Fairmount.

"We have a decision to make," Carpenter said to Sylvia Lawson. "Your husband has Jack available. Do we put him on the stand?"

"I would vote no," Fairmount said. "I think you've done as well as you can. Plus, we can't be sure what Jack will say."

"I'm conflicted," Sylvia Lawson admitted. "This hearing is our last chance. If Jack doesn't testify now, he never will."

"You were there when I talked with Jack," Carpenter said to Lawson. "He really couldn't describe whether he had changed for the better."

"I know," Lawson said as she shook her head in frustration.

"I'm leaning toward going along with Ms. Fairmount," Carpenter said to Lawson. "Sometimes doing nothing is the way to go when you don't know how something more proactive is going to turn out."

"I'm going to kill myself if we don't have Jack testify and the case goes against us. Should we ask Max?"

"Sure," Carpenter said. "Why don't you do that."

As Lawson left the room, Carpenter addressed the hearing officer. "Mr. Frye, I would request five minutes while Mrs. Lawson briefly confers with her husband."

"Very well," Frye said. "Five minutes."

When Sylvia Lawson returned to the hearing room, she looked shaken. Fairmount picked up on Lawson's mood change. "What's wrong?" she asked.

"We can't have Jack testify," Lawson said in a tremulous whisper.

"What's going on?" Fairmount inquired.

"Jack's a little out of control right now," Lawson whispered, on the verge of tears. "He's extremely agitated. Max had to take him outside."

Carpenter reflected that sometimes litigation decisions got made for you.

"What do you mean by agitated?" Fairmount pursued.

"He's thrashing about. Max has to hold him to keep him still. The Stonington people can't see him like this."

Frye resumed his seat. First things first, Carpenter decided. "Mr. Frye, the Lawsons rest their case," he announced.

Frye glanced at Lannon. "Any rebuttal witnesses?"

"No," Lannon said.

"Then the evidence is closed," Frye said, rising and gathering his papers. "You'll have my decision shortly."

In the lobby of the building, Sylvia Lawton didn't linger for small talk. "I've got to check on Max and Jack," she said, close to tears.

Carpenter watched Lawson hurry off. "What do you think is going on?" he asked Fairmount.

"I'm guessing here, but Jack may need more medication. Maybe the final reduced dosage amounts are too low and Jack is now reacting to that."

"The timing couldn't be worse," Carpenter said.

"The Lawsons have to tell the Stonington school officials," Fairmount said.

"Actually, they don't," Carpenter replied.

"What are you saying?"

"The Lawsons don't have to say anything to anyone."

"This is new information," Fairmount protested. "Jack could be dangerous if his medications are out of whack."

"I'll discuss the situation with the Lawsons and try to find out what's going on. But if they choose not to say anything to Jack's school, there's nothing I can do."

Carpenter understood Fairmount's shocked, stunned reaction. People oftentimes couldn't wrap their minds around the notion that lawyers were hired guns, duty bound to respect their clients' choices no matter how ill-advised or detrimental to others.

"This isn't a game," Fairmount said angrily. "If Jack's meds are off, he could hurt someone. I wouldn't put up with anything like this at the Wilton Center."

"We don't know for sure Jack is about to hurt anyone," Carpenter responded. "I said I'd talk to them, and I will. That's pretty much all I can do."

"What are you going to recommend?" Fairmount asked.

"I don't know," Carpenter admitted. "First I need to get a handle on what's going on with Jack."

"Tomorrow's a school day," Fairmount pointed out.

Carpenter didn't need to be reminded.

"What are you going to do?" Philly asked. Carpenter had just filled her in on the Lawson IEP hearing and she had welcomed the distraction of his phone call. She was bored.

"I don't know," Carpenter said. "I'll keep trying the Lawsons. If they're home, they're not picking up."

"It sounds to me like the Lawson kid needs to get checked out by a doctor."

"That's what I was thinking," Carpenter said. "I'm also thinking that the kid should stay out of school until this gets sorted out."

Philly thought about the ramifications of Jack staying away from school. "Stonington school officials will want to know *why* Jack was out of school especially if he stays out more than one day."

"Damnit!!" Carpenter muttered. "The Lawsons are going to want their kid back in school. They'll rationalize away Jack's recent acting out."

"Then read them the riot act."

"Somehow I don't think that's going to help. They've gotten a glimpse of their son the way they want him to be and they're not going to accept any other image."

"I wish I could help more," Philly said.

"Yeah, me too," Carpenter said. "I miss having you around."

"You better get used to it. I feel like I'm ready to pop."

"Now there's an image I could do without."

At six Carpenter heard his stomach growling. He decided to try the Lawsons one more time before he packed it in for the day.

"Hello," Sylvia Lawson picked up.

"It's Carpenter. I've been trying to reach you."

"We haven't been answering the phone. We've been a little frantic trying to figure out what we're going to do."

"What have you decided?"

"We're going to send Jack to school tomorrow. There are only a few days left. I've called the monitors and told them to be especially vigilant."

Carpenter was dismayed that his read on the situation had been pretty much spot on. "I'm going to advise you on what I think you need to do. First off, I wouldn't send Jack back to school until his pediatrician has fully checked out his medication dosages. Ms. Fairmount and I have talked about this. One reason for Jack's loss of control may be that his medication levels really are too low now."

"We're not going to risk keeping Jack out of school. Max and I feel we're so close to getting what we want that we can taste it. We've had our real son back for some weeks. I don't expect you to understand what that's been like for us."

Carpenter sensed that if he further disagreed with her, Sylvia Lawson would simply hang up on him. "How has Jack been since you got him home?"

The long pause by Lawson answered his question.

"He's down for a nap right now. We're going to wake him just before dinner. He's simply been overwrought. Driving into Boston was a big change in his routine."

Lawson hadn't answered his question, so Carpenter decided to push ahead. There was always guilt.

"If Jack goes back to school and injures another child, you will never forgive yourselves."

"That's not fair," Lawson bristled. "The monitors will be in place. Nothing's going to happen."

"You don't know that. The monitors can't prevent a sudden, unexpected physical action by Jack. There have been playground squabbles that they couldn't get to in time."

"Nothing's going to happen," Lawson repeated.

"At least keep him out of school tomorrow so his pediatrician can examine him."

"Max and I have discussed this. We don't want the school to ask any questions as to why Jack was absent."

"You and your husband are making a mistake here. You're not acting responsibly and you both know it."

"I have to go. I need to wake Jack and get dinner on the table."

The line went dead and Carpenter hung up his phone. His stomach continued to growl but he was no longer hungry. Just when, he wondered, had he acquired a conscience, and how soon could he give it back?

48

Firing questions about the Harrington case at Simon, Philly realized that she was playing the role for him that Carpenter had played for her. Somehow, Carpenter had convinced her to have Simon argue against the motion to dismiss the lawsuit filed by John and Naomi Harrington. True, Carpenter would accompany Simon to court and would take charge if he faltered. Still, Philly had envisioned Carpenter personally taking on any significant motion that came up in her cases. The Harringtons would be devastated if their lawsuit was thrown out. They hadn't sounded pleased about Simon stepping in to handle the matter and there had been a protracted, chilly silence when Philly revealed Simon's legal experience.

She and Simon were seated in her living room in the early morning, each in an easy chair. Philly had run out of questions. To his credit, Simon had an answer to everything she had thrown at him. Physically, Simon didn't inspire confidence. He was painfully thin and appeared unprepossessing. Yet when he opened his mouth there was a presence and confidence about him that couldn't be denied. Carpenter had already entrusted some key motions to Simon, so Philly figured what the hell; she'd go with another of his hunches. Carpenter was convinced that Simon was cut out to be a litigator, that he had *it*, whatever *it* was.

"How's Carpenter treating you and Rachel?" Philly opted for small talk.

"You guys have been great. I think you know how much Rachel and I appreciate the work you've thrown our way."

"You didn't answer my question."

Simon smiled weakly. "Okay, I guess. Does he ever smile?"

Philly laughed. "Not really. When he's amused, his frown changes slightly."

"You two are an odd pair," Simon said.

"We've been told that before."

"If it's not being too nosy, how come you didn't form a firm?"

"We've talked about it," Philly decided to be forthcoming. "But it's not something I wanted to do. I think Carpenter probably feels the same way, but you'd need to ask him."

If they had formed a firm, Philly realized she would now be feeling more beholden to him than she currently felt. She remained comfortable keeping their practices separate.

"Did you read over the discovery Rachel and I prepared for Frederick Chun?" Simon asked.

Philly nodded. "Nice job. I'll e-mail you some edits before the end of the day. Make sure Carpenter looks it over before it's filed."

Simon stowed his papers in a worn briefcase and stood up. "I'd better get going. Carpenter and I have to drive up to Essex for the hearing this afternoon."

"Tell George Norris I said hello," Philly said. "And make sure you give the guy hell," she added.

Carpenter remembered George Norris from Philly's first jury trial last year. The middle-aged lawyer reminded him of Peter Falk's Columbo character. His bedraggled, long-suffering pose made it seem as if he were carrying the world's woes on his shoulders. With his pasty complexion and stooped shoulders and brown suit that fit loosely about his frame, it seemed that Norris lacked the animation necessary for litigation. Yet Carpenter remembered that in doing battle with Philly, Norris had, in his phlegmatic way, scored points during the trial.

The Harrington case was the second case on the court's afternoon docket. Judge Karen White, a tall, imposing African American woman, was hearing arguments on the first case on the list and Carpenter tuned out the proceedings and turned to the back of the courtroom to observe the Harringtons sitting in the front of the gallery with grim expressions. The couple had given Simon curt greetings and had not reciprocated when Simon made friendly attempts at small talk. Carpenter figured that if he worked at it, he could probably piss off all of the clients he and Philly were currently representing.

"John and Naomi Harrington versus William Burnside, Superintendent of Schools for the Town of Dixfield."

Carpenter led the way to the plaintiffs' counsel table following the clerk's calling of the case. This was Simon's first superior court argument, but you would never know it from the way he carried himself. The young lawyer was composed and focused and Carpenter silently prayed that he was up to the task.

Judge White turned to Simon after counsel had introduced themselves. "I've read all the papers that have been submitted so I'm familiar with the facts. As I understand it, the case boils down to the Harringtons wishing to have the anonymous letter and related documents removed from their son's school record. Is my understanding correct?"

"Yes, Your Honor," Simon answered.

"From the affidavits submitted by Mrs. Harrington and by Luke Harrington's pediatrician, I understand that the statement in the anonymous letter that Luke has been placed in a closet is true. If that is the case, why should the letter be removed from Luke's school record?"

"There are two principal reasons," Simon said. "First, the letter is anonymous. That means that someone without courage and who is unwilling to identify himself or herself, gets to exert influence over Luke's schooling. The Harringtons regard that as both unfair generally and as an interference with their parenting role. Second, when the school district originally refused to turn over the anonymous letter, it did so on the ground that reports of abuse did not have to be disclosed.

Thus, the actions described in the anonymous letter are falsely characterized as abuse, and the Harringtons falsely characterized as abusive."

"The anonymous letter itself doesn't use the word abuse. Perhaps I should delete from the boy's record the letter from the superintendent using that word and leave the anonymous letter where it is."

"The superintendent's letter is another document that the Harringtons wish to have removed from their son's school record," Simon responded promptly. "But the anonymous letter should also be removed from Luke's record for the reasons I've stated."

"If Luke became agitated, would the Harringtons object to Luke's teacher placing him in a closet?"

"Yes," Simon said immediately. "As Luke's parents, Mr. and Mrs. Harrington need to make that kind of a decision. That is not a teacher's prerogative under any circumstances."

Judge White directed the next question at George Norris. "Why is the superintendent insistent on keeping an anonymous letter in Luke Harrington's school record?"

Norris rose slowly. "Because the letter contains true and accurate information that concerns a student's behavior and the way the student's parents discipline him to control that behavior. Everything in the letter is germane to helping teachers meet Luke's educational and emotional needs. This is not a case where an anonymous letter contains untrue statements."

"Is the superintendent willing to remove from Luke's file the letter she wrote that referred to the reporting of abuse?"

"No," Norris said. "While the student's pediatrician seems to be okay with putting this boy in a closet, the affidavit I've submitted from a psychiatric consultant to the school district finds this practice bizarre and unprecedented."

"Has Luke Harrington been diagnosed with a disorder that might bear on his behavior or how it is managed by his parents?" Judge White asked Simon.

"No," Simon replied. "By the way, Your Honor, the Harringtons are in the courtroom and would be pleased to answer any questions that you might have for them." Simon turned, motioned for the Harringtons to stand. Carpenter studied the judge's impassive features; if she thought that Luke's parents were nut jobs, you couldn't tell it from her expression.

The judge returned to Norris. "Does the superintendent regard the anonymous letter as a report of abuse?"

"Yes," Norris said. "Neither the superintendent nor the school district's psychiatric consultant believe that putting a boy in a closet is humane or medically justified."

"Has Luke ever acted out of control during school hours?" the judge questioned Simon.

"Not to the Harringtons' knowledge. They've never been told of any inappropriate behavior on Luke's part."

Judge White became lost in thought. Carpenter doubted that she would immediately rule on the motion to dismiss the Harringtons' case; more likely she would take the motion under advisement.

"Have the parties or counsel tried to resolve this matter?" the judge asked.

"No, Your Honor," Simon said.

"Here's what I'm going to do. I'm going to take the defendant's motion under advisement. Please don't take my next comments as any indication of how I'm going to rule on your motion, Mr. Norris. But my current inclination is not to dismiss this case. It's a novel case and there appears to be no clear-cut case law authority on the issues presented. I will not issue any ruling until at least two weeks from now. During the next two weeks, I would ask counsel to try to come up with a creative solution to resolving this matter. If you are making progress and need more than two weeks, let my clerk know.

"And here's one thought. I recently heard a case involving an employee's right to receive her personnel record. The statute permits an employee who disagrees with something in her personnel record to include in her personnel record a correction rebuttal statement. Why not come up with a joint statement that reflects each party's position and have that document remain in Luke's school record with all disputed documents removed?"

Carpenter resisted his natural inclination to reject the proposal out of hand because it came from a judge. Her suggestion was, after all, a creative way to resolve the case. Norris was looking at the judge as if she had presented him with something unpalatable. Simon was nodding and before Carpenter could stop him, he thanked the judge for her suggestion. Which was a shame really. Up until that moment, Carpenter thought that the young lawyer had performed well. When a judge made a suggestion, however sensible, Carpenter made it a practice to smile benignly and keep his mouth shut. But there was hope for Simon; he was still young and had time to learn from his mistakes.

49

Isabella was rubbing Philly's lower back and the massage felt so good that Philly believed she'd soon drift off into a blissful sleep. She was lying on her side in the living room totally relaxed. Isabella had taken her through her breathing and visualization exercises. Noon sunlight filled the room and she closed her eyes to shut out the brightness. A fan sent a cool current of air above her. Until Raul spoke, Philly had momentarily forgotten he was there.

"You two look too comfortable," Raul said.

Isabella laughed. "I'm the one doing all the work here. I'm working up a sweat."

"Don't stop," Philly moaned.

"Are you two ready?" Raul asked.

"I'm ready," Isabella said, and Philly realized that she was as well. This weekend might be her last weekend before the baby was born. "I'm ready," she echoed.

"Is your wish for a boy or a girl?" Raul asked.

"I want to be surprised," Philly said. She was pleased that she hadn't succumbed to the urge to learn the sex of her baby.

"I am very much looking forward to the new addition to our household," Raul said, and Philly let Raul's odd, somewhat formal phrasing slide. Raul had been a big help; singlehandedly he had repainted the baby's room, assembled the crib, and hung an assortment of mobiles.

"I do not mean to pry, Philly, but are you okay financially since you stopped working?"

Philly gave Raul the benefit of the doubt and treated his question as one of genuine concern. "I'm okay," she said, although in truth she was living off the savings she had socked away during last year's successful financial year. Carpenter continued to want her to keep her Boston office going, but that couldn't go on much longer.

"If you ever feel a need, Isabella and I would be pleased to help you during this time of transition."

"I said I'm okay!"

"Raul!" Isabella exclaimed.

"All right. I will say nothing further."

"I'll believe that when I hear the silence," Philly said, and that got Isabella laughing again.

"Do you miss practicing law?" Isabella asked.

If it weren't for the lack of money coming in, Philly would be content to focus on her baby. When had she stopped being a compulsive, driven workaholic? "In a way, it's nice not to have to focus on cases. I've never had a period of enforced idleness before."

"That's going to change very soon," Isabella said.

When she was juggling a variety of legal matters, Philly became focused and dealt with whatever needed to get done. With luck, a new baby could be juggled, too. Unless, of course, the baby turned out to be as demanding and stubborn as she was.

Isabella had kept up her back rub. Philly's eyes fluttered. This was the life, she thought.

50

Carpenter had made copies of the rulings made by Serena Jones in the Top Tier regulatory case and had distributed the copies to Simon and Rachel. They were seated around the conference room table and Carpenter waited until the two young lawyers had finished reading and looked up. His own assessment was that Top Tier had made out all right. Predictably, Jones had denied the motion to exclude from evidence the illegal telephone recording made by Norman Cassidy. But Jones had ruled that Top Tier could subpoena Devonshire Plastics' financial records from the company and the accounting firm of Miller & Huggins. Top Tier's motion to take the depositions of Cassidy and Huggins had been denied but without prejudice; therefore the motion could be re-filed if the documents provided grounds to take either man's deposition.

"I'd say this is a good result," Rachel said. "We knew we'd lose the motion to keep the telephone recording out of evidence. But we didn't lose anything else outright."

"Nice job, Simon," Carpenter said, then changed the subject and turned to Rachel. "Where are we on the answer to the complaint against Gerald Hatch?"

"I've prepared an answer to the complaint," Rachel said. "I reviewed the samples of answers that you gave me, and I think I've followed your style and approach."

"Are you having Gerald admit that he beat up the Mercer boy?" Simon asked.

"He's admitting that there was an altercation and denying that it was his fault."

"If you can get me a draft of the answer by the end of today, that would be a big help to me," Carpenter said.

Rachel nodded. "You've got us working on interesting cases," she said.

Carpenter agreed. "You guys doing anything exciting for the Fourth of July weekend?" he asked.

"Not really," Simon said, as Rachel shook her head.

"Remember what they say about all work and no play," Carpenter said.

"You need money to play," Simon said, and he immediately looked chagrined. "Believe me, we're very grateful for the payments we've gotten. I didn't mean that the way it sounded."

Carpenter considered Simon's comment. For the Top Tier case, he was paying the two young lawyers $100 an hour and billing their time out at $175 an hour, $25 an hour less than Philly's hourly rate. The spread was a way to get money to Philly. "You need to speak up if you think I'm being unfair to you when it comes to compensation."

"In this economy we can't complain," Rachel said. "I don't want to rock the boat."

"That's not the mindset you should be having," Carpenter said. "If the boat needs rocking, you need to rock it."

Rachel shrugged, plainly not convinced she should be more aggressive. Simon appeared poised to speak up on the money issue but seemed to think better of it. If the boat was going to be rocked, Carpenter was betting on Simon to do the rocking.

July

Philly's Untitled Playlist

Soul Sister

Train

51

Philly couldn't bear to leave Daisy in her bassinette. She wanted Daisy lying on her stomach where she could feel the baby's heart beat through the terrycloth one-piece the hospital staff had stuffed her into. Her nurse humored her and there was this scrunched up little creature with a full head of dark, wispy hair and blue eyes breathing evenly on her belly. She had won the gene war when it came to hair coloring, and Philip had won the gene war when it came to eye coloring. Melanie had been right. Now that Daisy was nestled on top of her, the ride to the hospital, the endless labor, and the painful delivery were dim memories.

Outside, the retorts of firecrackers were incessant. Philly thought back to previous July Fourths, to the times she'd had dinner with Carpenter, once with Connie and Raul, a second time with Philip and Maxine. Now the holiday would take second billing to Daisy. Already she was getting used to the name Philip had chosen. Daisy Sizemore Piper.

Philly closed her eyes. She was exhausted but couldn't sleep. She was going to have to think of something spectacular to do for Isabella and Raul. Isabella's presence throughout the delivery was a godsend; without her, Philly knew that she wouldn't have made it through the ordeal mentally. Raul had cried when he first saw Daisy and it was only when Isabella had taken him in her arms that he finally settled down.

With two exceptions, Isabella and Raul had handled the phone calls to relay the news of Daisy's birth, all seven pounds of her. Philly had been the one to speak with her own parents and with Philip's parents, and both grandmothers had broken down during the calls. Raul had been the one to call Carpenter and had ended that call laughing; Carpenter had said that Raul was the last person in the world he expected to deliver this news.

Philly reached for her cell phone without disturbing Daisy. It was ten in the evening, but she didn't think it was too late to call. This was one call she wanted to make herself, undisturbed.

"Hello."

"It's a girl."

There was a long pause Philly decided to wait out.

"Congratulations, said Paul Sullivan. "I'm thrilled you called. I thought I was on your permanent shit list."

"Tonight you're off the list. But don't get your hopes up. Tomorrow you're back on."

"Then I better make the best of what's left of the evening. How are you doing?"

Philly took her mental pulse. "I'm good," she said.

"And the baby?"

"She's lying on my belly. I think she's doing okay too. Her name is Daisy by the way."

"Not a name I would have guessed you would pick."

"Actually, Philip chose the name."

"Like I said, it's a great name."

Philly leaned forward and smelled Daisy's hair. "There's something I need to tell you."

"Sure."

"I'm in AA. I started over two months ago. I've got a drinking problem."

"When can I see you?" Sullivan asked without hesitation, and Philly mentally removed him from her permanent shit list.

"I'm here tomorrow and I'm going home the next day."

"Where's here?"

"Seacoast Regional Hospital."

"I'll see you tomorrow."

"Great. Good night."

"I meant it—thanks for calling."

Philly turned off her phone. Daisy stirred, letting loose with a full body spasm that quickly subsided.

"How's my favorite patient?"

Dr. Shumaker stood over her and leaned forward to stroke Daisy's head. Here was another person she needed to do something nice for. "I'm good and so is Daisy."

"You did a great job," Dr. Shumaker said.

"Thanks for everything. I don't think I can ever repay you."

"You already have or did you forget that you got me my job?"

Philly felt a preternatural calm, a restful, enveloping mellowness.

"There's something I need to tell you," Philly said. "It's something I should have told you about before."

Dr. Shumaker drew a chair up to the bedside. "Fire away."

52

Carpenter was sitting in the conference room with Rachel, feeling restless and edgy, his mind partly on the nine-day vacation he and Maxine would be starting next week. If left to his anal retentive, compulsive self, he would try to wriggle out of the vacation. But to Maxine, their vacation time alone together was sacrosanct; he'd be in deep shit if he tried to use work as an excuse to blow off their planned time away. So here he was trying to delegate work to make his life easier but was running into resistance from Rachel.

"I'm really not cut out to be a litigator," she protested. "Simon enjoys litigation. Why don't you have him do this?"

There were so many flaws in Rachel's reasoning that Carpenter found himself momentarily tongue-tied over where to start. "You won't know whether you're cut out to be a litigator unless you try it. I've got a feeling you're going to surprise yourself."

"I'm really not comfortable with trial work."

"Who the hell is?" Carpenter found his temper slipping off its moorings. "I still get nervous trying a case."

"Is that supposed to make me feel better?"

"It's not my job to make you feel better. My job is to turn you into the lawyer I know you can be."

"I still don't understand why you're insisting on this when Simon would be only too happy to take it on."

"For Christ's sake! If I wanted Simon to do this, I would have asked him. I want you to take this on."

"What if I say no?"

Carpenter glared at Rachel. If he weren't careful, something nasty and inappropriate would leave his lips. "Then you're not as useful to me and Philly as I know you can be," he decided to be frank. "With Philly out of action, I'm trying to put together a team that will fill her gap. Maybe something will come of this that's long term. If I can't use you for litigation, it's a problem."

Rachel frowned in concentration. Carpenter hoped that she would put her impressive reasoning ability into play and change her mind.

"This is not something I want to do," Rachel said. "If it means you won't use me anymore, then that's the way it's got to be."

Carpenter gave Rachel credit for sticking to her guns; it wasn't what he wanted to hear, but she had shown courage standing up to him.

"I have a proposition for you," Carpenter said, trying to hide his disappointment and lighten his tone. "Take on this one assignment. If you still feel the same way when it's over, tell me and I'll let the matter drop. But I'll have to give some thought about a continuing relationship. What do you say?"

"Why do you think I'm cut out to litigate?"

"You just stood up to me, didn't you?"

Rachel smiled. With her serious look displaced she looked younger, more at ease.

"Okay. We'll see how it goes."

"Do you understand the assignment?"

"I think so. Go over it one more time."

"Here's a list of the lawyers who have agreed to support our client, Marshall Hyde," Carpenter said, handing over the contact information. "The hearing before the Board of Bar Overseers is the week after I come back from vacation. I want you to handle the direct examination of the six lawyers. Here's a copy of all the papers that have been filed in the case. Read them first. Then come up with a testimony outline of the points you want to bring out on direct examination."

"I'd feel more comfortable writing out the questions," Rachel said.

Carpenter sighed. Delegation, he was discovering, could be hard work and plain annoying.

"I want you to trust me, Rachel. Use an outline. If you're reading questions, it's going to come across as scripted, boring, and stilted. An outline will force you to think on your feet. When you finish an outline show it to me. Before I leave on vacation I want you to use the outline on me. While I'm away, I want you to contact each of the six lawyers and take them through a trial run of their testimony. Try to get them talking. You'd be amazed at how many helpful ideas come up through conversation."

Rachel didn't look convinced of his approach, but Carpenter was determined to start her litigation experience by having her benefit from the lessons he had learned the hard way.

"I hope you know what you're doing," Rachel said. "This whole thing makes me nervous."

"I'll tell you what I told Philly before her first time in court. Nervous is good. If you weren't nervous I'd be worried."

"Then you have nothing to worry about."

53

Paul Sullivan pushed the stroller and Philly walked beside him, enjoying the cool evening temperature, glad to stretch her legs. Paul must have picked up on the fact that she was still sore and needed to take it slow because he was advancing the stroller at a snail's pace. He had driven over when his shift ended and borrowed her bedroom to change into shorts, a T-shirt, and running shoes.

Philly stooped to check on her daughter. Daisy was in a cocoon of wadded up bath towels. Her small fists were clenched in her lap. She'd been an easy baby. Very little crying. A three-hour feeding schedule give or take. Playful periods in the morning and afternoon. Philly had been surprised at how much she enjoyed breastfeeding. She would settle in the rocking chair that Rainy and Monica had given her, turn on one of her mixed tapes, and give herself up to Daisy. True the kid was a poop machine. But that was offset by baths and those moments when she would lie on her bed beside a sleeping Daisy and stare at her daughter for what seemed like minutes but often turned into an hour or more.

"She's still there," Paul said. "I don't think she's going anyplace."

Philly joined Paul pushing the stroller. She thought back to her last day in the hospital. Paul had visited as he had promised, and the first thing he did was kiss her, telling her he had been wanting to do that for a long time. Then he'd asked to hold Daisy and looked at the baby with a sloppy grin that had struck Philly as just right.

"I don't know anything about you," Philly said.

"You know I'm a police detective. I live in Cambridge in a condo that's pretty cramped. I'm thirty-seven. I'm divorced. I've got a daughter named Jennifer who lives with her mother and her mother's new husband in Concord. Jenny's nine. I see her most weekends but sometimes my work gets in the way. My ex's new husband seems like a decent guy. They have a kid of their own, a boy who's three." Paul paused. "That should get you started."

Philly recalled something she had read: police officers made lousy husbands. Well, there was no sense in getting ahead of herself. She was taking a walk for Christ's sake. For the moment she was grateful for Paul's company and decided to leave it at that.

"Do you like being a police officer?"

"I do. It's never boring. But there's a downside. There are times when the job is dangerous."

Philly winced inwardly. She could envision a future with Daisy that would help her put Philip's death behind her. But if she had to go through the death of another loved one . . .

"I try to be careful," Paul said as if reading her thoughts.

Philip, she reflected, had been one of the most careful people she had ever known. Shit happened and all the care and caution in the world were powerless to stop it.

"Let's change the subject," Philly suggested. "What do you do for fun?"

"I read a lot. I work out pretty religiously. I run. I can't say I'm a big party person."

"What are the chances of getting you into biking?"

"It's not something I would have tried if left to myself. But I'd be willing to give it a try."

"Biking was something Philip and I used to do together. I wanted to be up front about that."

"I see."

"But Philip or no Philip, biking is something I love. I'm not much into sports, but biking is fun."

"Like I said, I'd be willing to give it a try."

Philly remembered trying to puzzle out what it was about her that had attracted Philip. She had never come up with an answer. Now here was Paul, a handsome, thoughtful guy who apparently saw something in her that she didn't recognize.

"This is nice," Philly said.

54

On the phone, George Norris sounded just as put upon as he did in person. His tone suggested that it was a major, personal sacrifice for him to get on the line. This was Philly's first work-related call since Daisy had been born and she was surprised at how good it felt to get her head back into a live case. Daisy had just been fed and had settled into a contented sleep on an Afghan folded over double and spread on the floor of her second-floor office. Her window fan provided a cool breeze and the sun had moved so that no direct rays were heating up the room. Maybe, Philly thought, she could make it through the summer without a window air conditioner.

"How come you weren't in court when this case was heard?" Norris asked.

"I was very pregnant. I just had a baby. But I'm back. If you have a moment, I'd like to talk to you about the Harrington case."

"Sure," Norris said, and Philly couldn't understand how a man could be so bereft of any social graces. Not even congratulations from the guy.

"Is Dixfield willing to act on the judge's suggestion?" Carpenter had filled her in on Judge White's message to the parties. Norris was such a dour guy that Philly fully anticipated him to tell her to pound sand.

"What did you have in mind?" Norris inquired.

"I haven't discussed this with the Harringtons, but I'm leaning toward what the judge suggested," Philly came back, deciding not to spar with Norris and to make the first move. "We could draft a joint statement. Or we could put the affidavits filed in court in Luke Harrington's school record."

"Are you willing to have the word 'abuse' be in the school's submission?"

Up to this point, Norris' phlegmatic approach hadn't bothered her; now she thought he was being unreasonable. She wouldn't put it past the guy to deliberately try to put her in the same sour mood that he perpetually nursed.

"Let me ask you something George. Do you mind if I call you George?"

"I guess that's okay."

"So, tell me, George. What would it take to cheer you up? Last year we went through a long trial and I think you only smiled once."

"I thought we were going to talk about the Harrington case."

"We are," Philly said. "My question has to do with the Harrington case."

"No it doesn't. You're just trying to irritate me."

"I'm not trying to irritate you. You're always irritated. I'm trying to understand what would un-irritate you."

"You didn't answer my question about the word 'abuse.'"

Philly watched Daisy give one of her full body spasms that came out of nowhere. One moment she was thrashing about, the next in total repose.

"The use of the word 'abuse' is not acceptable to my clients. It pisses me off that you used that word in a settlement discussion. It sounds to me like you aren't serious about trying to follow up on the judge's suggestion on how to settle this case."

"I guess we have nothing further to discuss," Norris said. "Frankly I couldn't care less whether the case settles."

Philly doubted Norris' last disclaimer. Carpenter believed that no matter how tough a litigator, a lawyer was relieved when a case settled. A known result was usually preferable to rolling dice before a judge or a jury.

"I think you're full of shit, George, Philly said genially "The judge said that she was leaning toward denying your motion to dismiss the case. In your situation, I'd be a little more open to a creative solution to make the Harringtons' case go away. Here's what I'm prepared to recommend to the Harringtons. The superintendent's letter mentioning the statute about reporting abuse comes out of Luke Harrington's school record. The anonymous letter that brought about this case stays in the record. The affidavits submitted by the superintendent and the school district's expert stay in the record. The affidavits from Naomi Harrington and Luke's pediatrician stay in the school record. All of the documents are clipped together and a cover page entitled 'Documents Relating to an Anonymous Letter' is set in front of the documents. What do you say?"

"I don't think that's going to fly," Norris said dismissively.

"Here's what I'm going to do," Philly continued. "I'm going to send you an email outlining the proposal I'm prepared to recommend to the Harringtons. You can do what you want with it."

Norris didn't say anything. Philly knew that he would present her proposal to his client. A lawyer was duty bound to pass on a settlement proposal. If money for cities and towns were in as short supply as the newspapers reported, Dixfield town officials might prove more receptive to a settlement than Norris. Town officials would frown on the prospect of a lengthy, costly trial.

Philly glanced at Daisy. The baby was sleeping peacefully.

"I hear my daughter stirring," Philly said. "I've got to go."

55

Maxine had insisted that they rent bicycles on their second day on Cape Cod. The last time Carpenter had ridden a bike was when he had visited Connie in Africa at the end of 2007, discovering that bike riding *was* one of those things that you never forgot how to do. Today they were starting out in Falmouth, and Maxine had mapped out a ride to one of the beaches north of the town, a circuitous route that included several heavily trafficked main roads.

"How are you doing?" Maxine called out over her shoulder.

"Great," Carpenter hollered back. He remembered the bike he had as a kid, a blue and white Shwinn with thick tires. When it came to gears, his recollection was hazy: maybe three gears, maybe none. The red bike he was now on was some kind of hybrid. At least Carpenter was pretty sure that was the word used by the pimply teen who'd handled the rental. The tires were thin. And what the hell was he supposed to do with twenty-one gears? Maxine had seemed to understand the process of shifting gears, but Carpenter suspected that he was fated to make the ride in the one gear he was now in.

Maxine stopped at a traffic light and Carpenter pulled up alongside. "How do I change gears?" he asked, detecting a note of desperation in his voice.

Maxine rolled her eyes. "Weren't you paying attention?"

"Apparently not well enough."

"There's a gas station on the right once we get through this intersection. We'll pull in there and I'll show you."

Carpenter closed his eyes and counted slowly to ten. You're having fun he told himself. Remember to smile.

Carpenter couldn't see Maxine. She was far out in the water keeping company with other insane vacationers who had made a vow to get wet even though the water was bitter cold. There was no shade on this beach; a sweep of exposed white sand faced a hundred-foot breakwater and open water. Behind him was a vast parking area that was nearly full when they arrived. Carpenter had slathered himself with sun block and donned a Boston Red Sox baseball cap and T-shirt. By draping a towel over his legs, he was pretty much protected from the sun. Maxine could read him like a book but maybe, far off shore, her mindreading skills would be diminished and she wouldn't pick up on the fact he was thinking about work.

The last time he visited Philly, she looked good, relaxed, motherhood seeming to agree with her. Was it possible that she might do something off the wall like take a year off? The way she had breastfed in front of him—catching him off guard, never even asking if he minded—had driven home the point that law was no longer the most important thing in her life. Philly couldn't seem to get enough of her kid. It was as if she needed to be in constant physical contact with her daughter, hugging the baby, absentmindedly stroking the baby, leaning over to whisper to the baby. And what the hell was the story with the cop who had come over shortly before he left, made a beeline for Philly's bedroom, and emerged in cutoff jeans, a T-shirt, and sandals. Philly had plainly been glad to see him.

But it wasn't as if Philly had totally blown off work. She had called George Norris about trying to settle the Harrington case. She had completed revising the answer to the suit filed against Gerald Hatch, and her edits improved that pleading. Then she had listened attentively as he had explained Rachel's reluctance to litigate, and had backed up his approach to that problem, even going so far as to say that she didn't think it would be helpful to establish a relationship with a lawyer who wanted nothing to do with going to court. Her one negative comment was one that he had expected—due to money, August might be the last month she would keep her Boston office.

Carpenter pulled his T-shirt up in back so that his neck was covered from the sun. He took a beer from his backpack, pulled off the tab and took a healthy swig. The thought of biking back to Falmouth with a buzz was more attractive than making the return trip stone sober.

Maxine was coming out of the water. Damn, she looked good. She was wearing a dark blue one-piece bathing suit. She was thin and wiry and fine muscled and he could picture her as one of those active women who would be a force to be reckoned with into her eighties and nineties.

"Did you get your thinking about work out of your system," Maxine said as she positioned herself to let the sun dry her.

Maxine had to be freezing but her skin was free of goose bumps. If Carpenter had spent as much time in the water as Maxine had, he'd be toweling off vigorously in an effort to bring back circulation. "Yeah, I did."

"Anything you want to talk about?"

"No, I'm good," Carpenter said. Then he remembered his advice to himself and mustered up a smile.

56

Philip's sister Pamela had dropped in unannounced with her daughter Genie. They were wearing matching yellow sundresses and looked cool and collected in the mid-afternoon heat. Genie couldn't take her eyes off Daisy and nodded solemnly when Philly asked if she wanted to hold the baby. Then there had been a production that involved seating Genie in an easy chair and positioning a swaddled Daisy in her arms. That tableau had disintegrated after barely a minute and now Genie was sprawled on the floor drawing in a coloring book while Philly nursed Daisy in one easy chair and Pamela talked nonstop in the other. Philly let Pamela's words wash over her, her focus on the pleasure of the feeding, but when Pamela mentioned the words *unfinished business*, Philly tried to concentrate.

"You know about Philip's trust fund," Pamela said. "That's been taken care of and personally, I think you made the right move buying this house. But Philip also had money he had saved up. He didn't leave a will so we had a family meeting on what to do with it."

Philly tried to keep her expression neutral. She'd protest if the Sizemores had voted to send more money her way. The trust fund money itself continued to make her feel guilty.

"My parents are going to be setting up a trust fund for Daisy," Pamela announced. "Her education should be taken care of, so you won't have that to worry about. If anything happened to Daisy, the money would go in trust for Genie and any other grandchildren who might enter the picture."

Philly nodded. That sounded fair and generous.

"Fifty thousand dollars is going to go to you," Pamela said, and Philly stared at her sister-in-law wide-eyed, unable to voice the protest she needed to make.

"By the way, the principal in Daisy's trust fund will be one hundred fifty thousand dollars," Pamela said, with a casualness that reflected a comfort level with money that Philly knew she'd never have.

"I suppose I get no say in any of this," Philly said.

"You could say thank you."

"Of course I'm going to say thank you. But this is a lot of money. Why don't you and your brother take a share? Or why not put it all in the trust fund for Daisy?"

"It's the way my parents want things handled, and Jared and I are in full agreement. As for the money going to you, we talked it out and figured that

Daisy was going to put a crimp in your billable hours. In other words, we thought you could use the money. You've been really good about keeping my parents in your life. It means a lot to them. Don't fight them on this. They don't need the money and neither do Jared and I."

Philly knew that she had no say as to the education trust fund and truthfully, an extra $50,000 would relieve financial stress for the short term. With an extra $50,000, it might be possible to be a stay-at-home-mom for a time. The idea of hanging out with a little creature whose life so far consisted of sleeping, eating, crying, and pooping didn't seem so horrible at the moment.

Philly swallowed her objections. "Okay then, and thank you."

"Good. That takes care of business. You look good. How are you doing?"

Daisy's lip action was slowing but she was still working away. "Good," she said. "I think I could get used to motherhood."

"Don't worry, that's going to change. In a few weeks, cabin fever will set in and you'll be climbing the walls."

Philly idly watched Genie intent on her coloring. Work was going to prevent her from experiencing a lot of Daisy's growth to Genie's age, and the thought saddened her. She didn't want to think about day care or any other arrangement that would separate her from her daughter.

"I hope you're going to get out and socialize," Pamela said. "Philip would want you to get on with your life."

Philly couldn't bring herself to mention Paul Sullivan. Saying his name out loud would suggest that she had gotten over Philip's death and the mourning period was over. It wasn't over. It was different. Besides, she still hadn't figured out what was going on with Paul. She liked having him around, but if they were going to do anything more than kiss, she'd probably have to make the first move. "I'm working on it," she said.

57

The only positive for Carpenter was that Maxine was not giving him grief over calling his office. Rachel had left him a voice mail message on his cell phone. Jack Lawson had broken a kid's collarbone at a summer day camp. Somehow

Stonington school officials learned of the incident and Craig Lannon had filed two emergency motions: one to reopen the IEP hearing, and a second motion to dissolve the injunction that Judge O'Connell had entered in superior court. Judge O'Connell had scheduled a hearing at eight thirty in the morning this Friday, and had ordered that Mrs. Lawson be in the courtroom. He'd never hear the end of it from Maxine if he cut their vacation short. He had omitted to tell her about the Friday hearing when he explained the need to call his office.

"What do you want me to do?" Rachel asked after reading him Lannon's two motions.

If Philly were monitoring his cases, Carpenter would simply have had her cover the court hearing once they had talked through an approach. Asking Simon and Rachel to take on that task was not fair to them or to the Lawsons.

"Mr. Carpenter?"

"I'm thinking goddamn it!"

"You don't have to bite my head off. I'm trying to help."

"Sorry," Carpenter muttered while silently applauding Rachel for not taking his shit. "I want you to conference Philly into this call. Is Simon around?"

"Simon's away this week. He'll be back on Monday."

Carpenter cursed his stupidity. He should have had Simon and Rachel defer vacation time while he was away.

"Hello," Philly said.

"What happened to Philomena Piper, attorney at law?" Carpenter replied.

"She's on maternity leave."

"Rachel's on the line. We've had a development in the Lawson case. I'll shut up while Rachel fills you in."

"Do you want me to try to reschedule the motion for Monday?" Philly asked, when Rachel had concluded her account.

That was the sensible approach. He'd have Sunday to prepare for the hearing. It would be another instance where shit backed up while you were away on vacation and wiped out any relaxation the vacation had provided.

"Maxine will kill me if I have to leave early and cut our vacation short," Carpenter said.

"Then I'll ask for a continuance. Lannon might even agree."

"But I don't like the idea of trying to delay. The judge could view it as a sign of weakness or a delaying tactic and he obviously views this as a genuine emergency."

As the silence lengthened, Carpenter hated himself for wanting one of the women to volunteer and take charge. Philly had a new born to deal with and

Rachel had already made clear that she preferred not to litigate. This was his mess and he needed to be a man and talk with Maxine.

"Let me talk to Maxine and get back to you both," Carpenter said.

"I'll cover for you," Philly said. "I'm not sure what I'm going to do about Daisy, but I'll be in court."

"I suppose I could give it a try," Rachel said, and Carpenter picked up on her hesitancy.

"I don't think that's fair to either of you," Carpenter said.

"Perhaps if Ms. Piper . . . Philly . . . was present . . ."

"Rachel and I will work it out," Philly said. "You're off the hook. But I still think asking for a continuance is the way to go."

Carpenter's instincts told him that it was in the Lawsons' interests to stick with the judge's hearing date. "Okay, he said, relieved. "I'll leave it all to the two of you, and you should feel free to call me. I want it to appear that the Lawsons are not interested in delaying anything the judge finds important. You'll need to deal with Mrs. Lawson given what happened with Jack at the IEP administrative hearing."

"Okay," Philly said. "We're all set."

"Thanks by the way," Carpenter said.

"Don't mention it," Philly answered. "You'd do the same for me. In fact, you already have."

Carpenter set down the phone and peered out the window of the small kitchen of their rented bungalow. It was another perfect Cape day: blue sky, wispy clouds, the gray clapboard shingles on neighboring bungalows faintly glistening from last night's cleansing rain shower.

"Are you ready?" Maxine called out from the living room.

Carpenter joined her; she was on her knees fiddling with the straps on her backpack. For today, she had chosen a hike around a lake off the Cape Cod Bike Trail.

"A judge in one of my cases has scheduled an emergency hearing for eight thirty on Friday morning," Carpenter announced.

When Maxine looked up, he half expected her to go ballistic. Instead she shook her head resignedly and sighed. "I suppose with Philly out of action, you're going to cut out early."

"Philly said she'd cover for me. She hasn't figured out what she's going to do with her baby, but she's going to handle the hearing. She's taking one of the young lawyers."

"Could you have gotten a continuance?" Maxine asked.

"Probably. But I didn't think that was the way to go."

"Do you want to handle this hearing yourself?"

Carpenter nodded.

"But you're letting Philly deal with it because you knew I'd be pissed off if you cut our vacation short." It wasn't a question.

Maxine sat down on the living room floor, frowning, staring at their backpacks. Carpenter felt like a shit for offloading his problem on her.

"It's not right to make Philly deal with this," Maxine finally said. "If this is important to you, it's okay if you deal with it."

It wasn't okay, but Carpenter was grateful to Maxine for saying it was.

"I'm going to leave it up to Philly. I'll call her now."

Carpenter retreated to the kitchen and got out his cell phone.

"Hello."

"It's me," Carpenter said. "Maxine and I have talked. It's not right for me to throw this court hearing on you. Your daughter's what . . . three weeks old? I'll deal with it."

"No. Rachel's coming over with the case file. It's like I said, one of us will handle it. And if it's Rachel, I'll be in court ready to step in."

"This isn't fair to you."

"Life isn't fair or did you suddenly forget? If I have a change of heart after I meet with Rachel, I'll call you. I've got to start figuring out how to deal with these kinds of emergencies sooner or later, so it might as well be sooner."

"What are you going to do with your baby?"

"You don't want to know."

"What are you talking about?"

"I'm going to drop Daisy with Philip's parents in North Andover. I've got to express a lot of breast milk so they can do the feedings."

"Jesus!" Carpenter exclaimed. "Too much information!

"You asked."

"North Andover is way out of your way."

"I'll be gone three hours, four hours tops."

"Jesus!"

"Leave your cell phone on through Friday just in case. I may need to call you about how we're going to handle the hearing. I'll definitely call you after the hearing to let you know what happened."

Carpenter didn't say anything. He didn't think he could feel more miserable.

"I'm looking forward to this," Philly said, and Carpenter heard the fighter in her voice, a welcome sound. "But if you want to be helpful, think of something we can say to the judge."

Every time she saw Rachel, Philly regarded her as a sweet young thing. That perception probably had to do with her short blond hair and round, open face. They were seated at the dining room table and had gone through the Lawson case files. And Philly had briefed Rachel on Jack Lawson's behavior on the day of the IEP hearing. Daisy was asleep in her crib, but her naptime was just about up.

"Carpenter thinks we're on the losing end of this court hearing," Philly said. "Any ideas on what you'd say to keep the injunction in place." Philly hadn't come up with anything original and doubted Rachel would be of much help.

"I don't understand why Stonington is trying to get the injunction dissolved on an emergency basis," Rachel said. "It's summer. Jack Lawson made it through the school year. He won't be back in school until September. What's the emergency?"

"It's strategic," Philly explained. "Lannon wants to be able to tell the hearing officer in the IEP case that the injunction permitting Jack's medications to be reduced was dissolved. That supports the Stonington IEP that has Jack on higher doses of medication. Stonington's point is that Jack is dangerous without the higher doses."

Philly thought she heard a soft cry coming from Daisy's room. She strained to hear anything further and was greeted with silence.

"Why did you file the superior court suit?" Rachel asked.

"Why do you think?" Philly challenged Rachel. Talk about dumb questions.

"Please," Rachel entreated. "Humor me. Why did you file the lawsuit?"

"To get Jack Lawson in a school environment where his medications would be reduced prior to the IEP hearing. We wanted to be able to present evidence about Jack with reduced medications."

"Exactly," Rachel said. "The suit has achieved its purpose. You've had the IEP hearing."

"Where are you going with this?"

"Why don't you just withdraw the superior court suit? It's achieved its purpose. The injunction got you through the school year and through the IEP hearing."

Philly stared at Rachel thinking "out of the mouths of babes." She and Carpenter had taken the knee jerk reaction to oppose a hostile motion at all costs. Rachel had focused on a bigger picture.

"We can't just withdraw the case on our own," Philly said. "We'd need Lannon's consent because he filed an answer on behalf of Stonington, and there's no way he'll agree."

Rachel was unfazed. "Then we should file an emergency motion of our own to dismiss the case because the case is now moot. If the IEP hearing is reopened, the Lawsons can fight the battle over the summer camp incident before the hearing officer. Mr. Carpenter will be back from vacation to deal with that."

Philly picked apart Rachel's strategy and couldn't find a flaw in her reasoning. "Draft the motion," she said. Today or tomorrow they could fax the motion to the court and to Lannon.

"Then I better get back to your office," Rachel said.

"No. I've got an office upstairs. Turn right at the landing and you can't miss it. My computer's on. You're not leaving until the motion's done."

Daisy let loose with a piercing cry.

"Besides, there's someone I want you to meet."

Rachel sat on the living room floor talking baby talk to Daisy while Philly read over the motion. For someone with very little legal experience, Rachel had banged out a concise well-reasoned motion in about an hour. Philly made a few word changes and silently pronounced the motion done.

"Nice job. Do you want to argue the motion?"

Rachel stopped cooing at Daisy and her expression turned serious.

"I already told Mr. Carpenter that I'd prefer not to get involved with litigation."

"I know what you told him. But you haven't answered my question. Do you want to argue this motion that you drafted?"

"I have a feeling that you won't like it if I say no."

"You're right," Philly owned up. "I won't like it and neither will Carpenter. We want you and Simon to do everything that we do. You're not as valuable to us if you've got limitations such as no litigation."

"I really prefer the research and writing role."

"You still haven't answered my question."

Rachel looked torn but Philly wasn't feeling sympathetic. Carpenter had been right that Rachel would never know whether she was cut out to litigate until she tried arguing in front of a judge.

"I already promised that I would do some of the witnesses in the Marshall Hyde case," Rachel said, at last. "I suppose I could make another exception."

"Smart choice," Philly said. "You keep on playing with Daisy while I run upstairs and put this in final form. Then we're in for a treat. We get to call Sylvia Lawson."

"I'd rather play with your baby."

"That makes two of us."

58

On Friday morning, Carpenter and Maxine ate breakfast in Woods Hole, sitting outside under an umbrella with a cool breeze coming off the water. Carpenter had nixed going on a whale watching boat. The deal he had cut with Maxine involved parking their asses in Woods Hole until Philly or Rachel reported to him on the Lawson court hearing. Then Maxine got to choose what they did with the rest of their last full day on the Cape. She'd opted for getting him in a canoe, a craft that she knew made him nervous and cranky. But, then again, he was always nervous and cranky.

"They'll be fine," Maxine said as she added maple syrup to her order of waffles topped with strawberries and chocolate ice cream.

Carpenter moved scrambled eggs around on his plate and nibbled at a slice of whole wheat toast, fretting. The Lawsons would have a nervous breakdown if they knew that the fate of their son rested in the hands of a lawyer who had never argued a case in court before.

"You're doing the right thing here," Maxine added. "You're delegating. You're trusting the people you're working with."

Carpenter emitted an unintelligible grunt. The truth was that he liked what Rachel had come up with. The fact that he hadn't thought of her approach, made him suspect he was losing his fast ball.

"It sounds like Ms. Boyle is a first-class lawyer," Maxine went on. "Philly will be with her so stop worrying."

Carpenter couldn't stop worrying. In one worst case scenario, he imagined Judge O'Connell putting Sylvia Lawson on the witness stand and questioning her himself, getting her to admit that Jack Lawson had recently become dangerously unmanageable, something that Lawson had confessed to Philly and Rachel. He couldn't imagine Rachel dealing with that situation.

"Talk to me," Maxine urged.

"I can't," Carpenter said. "I'm too wrought up. I'm not going to relax until one of them calls. And if it's bad news, then I'll never relax."

"Suit yourself," Maxine said.

Carpenter took his cell phone out of a front pocket of his shorts and stared at it. Willing a phone to ring was the equivalent of watching paint dry. But it was all he could bring himself to do.

"I've got two emergency motions before me," Judge O'Connell announced from the bench. "Let's start with you Mr. Lannon. The plaintiffs say that their lawsuit is moot because the administrative hearing on Jack Lawson's IEP has concluded. "What's your response?"

"An injunction has entered in this case, so the case is not moot," Lannon said. "The injunction should be dissolved because Jack Lawson has acted violently since his medications have been reduced. Stonington believes that the injunction should never have entered in the first place but, since it did, it should now be dissolved."

"What do the plaintiffs say to that?" the judge asked.

Rachel slowly got to her feet. Philly had played judge with Rachel, firing questions at her, and she believed that Rachel was ready for this hearing. The question just asked by the judge was one they had gone over. Philly held her breath, waiting for words to leave Rachel's lips. Instead, Rachel took the cap off the water bottle she had brought to the plaintiff's counsel table, took several sips, and set the bottle down. When she spoke, her voice was firm.

"If the plaintiffs' motion to dismiss their case as moot is allowed, the injunction will no longer be in effect because there would be no pending case. Dissolving the injunction serves no purpose; the injunction achieved what the plaintiffs wanted which is to have Jack Lawson experience reduced medication levels prior to the IEP hearing. The IEP hearing has occurred. Mr. Lannon is free to seek to raise events that occurred after the IEP hearing before the IEP hearing officer. In fact, he's done just that and we have provided Your Honor with a copy of the motion Mr. Lannon filed with the hearing officer to reopen the IEP hearing."

"Why don't I do both?" the judge suggested. "Why don't I dissolve the injunction and allow your motion to dismiss the case as moot?"

"Because dismissing the case as moot automatically ends the injunction."

"It seems we're playing with words here," the judge observed.

"Dissolving the injunction won't change any of the facts that unfolded before and after the injunction was in place," Rachel said. "Those facts supported Your Honor's injunction order."

Judge O'Connell was frowning, and Philly wondered whether the issues in the case *had* evolved into semantic word play. Rachel leaned toward her. "I could suggest that if the injunction is dissolved it be dissolved because it is now moot," Rachel whispered.

Philly considered Rachel's suggestion. It was not a response she would have come up with. Philly wished Carpenter were here to advise them. Observing the judge, she sensed that he was ready to rule. "Go for it," she whispered to Rachel, playing a hunch.

"You're Honor, may I add something?" Rachel requested.

When the judge nodded, Rachel cleared her throat. "I want to assure the court that the plaintiffs' position was not based on word play. The plaintiffs have no objection to Your Honor issuing a separate order dissolving the injunction on the ground that injunctive relief is now moot because the IEP hearing has occurred."

Philly watched Judge O'Connell's expression brighten. "Will that do the trick?" he asked Lannon.

"Stonington prefers an order dissolving the injunction without mentioning mootness," Lannon responded.

The judge barely hesitated before ruling. "I'm going to adopt Ms. Boyle's suggestion. An order shall enter dissolving the injunction as moot. A separate order shall enter allowing the plaintiffs' motion to dismiss their action as moot. The parties are free to pursue any course of action they believe is appropriate before the hearing officer in the IEP case." Judge O'Connell consulted his watch. "The court will take a brief recess before the next case is called."

In the corridor outside the courtroom, Philly let Rachel explain to Max and Sylvia Lawson what had happened in court. The couple appeared dazed by her report.

"You mean our lawsuit is dismissed?" Max Lawson looked crushed.

"You won your lawsuit," Philly decided to intervene. "You got what you wanted by filing suit. Jack got to attend school in Stonington with reduced meds. It was actually dangerous to keep the lawsuit alive. We didn't want the judge to start asking either of you questions about the summer camp incident. As it is, the hearing officer might decide to reopen the hearing to take testimony on that issue."

Max Lawson looked unconvinced by her explanation. Philly decided to focus on the larger issues the Lawsons had to deal with. "I want to go over the summer camp incident," she said, and that statement reduced the Lawsons to silence. "Why did you send Jack to the summer camp without monitors? Did the camp even know of his medications?"

Max Lawson shifted uncomfortably while Sylvia Lawson stared at her shoes.

"You need to answer me," Philly pressed.

"We filled out a form listing Jack's medications," Sylvia Lawson said. "We didn't think monitors were necessary."

You didn't think period, Philly held off saying. Instead she took a deep breath and decided to read the riot act in a calm voice. "You need to face the fact that the reduced medications may not be working. You told us on the phone that Jack was acting up more and becoming more agitated than he had been. If the hearing officer decides to reopen the hearing, all of that will come out and the Stonington IEP for Jack will likely remain in place."

The Lawsons greeted this admonition with stony stares.

"The camper that Jack injured is probably going to sue the camp. When that happens, there's a fair chance that Jack's medications and the use of monitors while he was in school is going to come up. If the camp discovers that you didn't disclose Jack being monitored at school while his medications were being reduced, it's a pretty safe bet that the camp and maybe the injured camper will try to hold the two of you responsible for what happened."

Max Lawson colored slightly; his hands dropped to his sides. Sylvia Lawson continued to regard her feet.

"Your son hurt another child badly," Philly continued. "You need to make sure that doesn't happen again. You may like your son better when his meds are reduced but if he's dangerous when his med dosages are lowered, you have to face that fact."

"Whose side are you on?" Max Lawson challenged.

"I'm sorry you felt you had to ask," Philly said. "We're on your side, but you don't seem to want to hear anything that's contrary to the way you wish your son could be. That had better change damn quick."

On the ride to North Andover to retrieve Daisy, Rachel fell silent. Philly also didn't feel like talking. Her breasts were full and ached. The Lawsons had left a bad taste in her mouth even though Carpenter confirmed that she had said the right things to the clients. The geezer actually sounded upbeat about the way the court hearing had gone.

"So how does it feel to have your first superior court hearing under your belt?" Philly asked when she saw the first sign for North Andover.

"I feel relief."

"You did great. You won. Stop sounding like you lost."

Rachel shrugged.

"I mean it," Philly said. "You came up with stuff on the fly that I never would have thought of. You can do this kind of work and I think you know it."

"But what if I don't particularly like it."

"You'll get over that."

August

Philly's Untitled Playlist

Just Like Heaven

The Cure

59

After the AA meeting, Philly returned to the house bone tired but knowing that even were she able to lie down, the respite would be brief. If Daisy was asleep she would soon wake and want to be fed. The baby demanded at least two nighttime feedings and was alert and awake after the first.

Raul and Isabella were sitting close together on the couch, Raul holding Daisy, talking to her in Spanish, Isabella leaning forward to stroke the baby's cheek. A Spanish song played softly on the stereo. Philly experienced a twinge of sadness; if Philip were alive, the family picture would have been theirs.

Philly moved behind the couch. Daisy's eyes were open and she grinned whenever Isabella's finger passed near her mouth.

"This is one sweet baby," Raul said softly.

Philly collapsed on an easy chair.

"How was your meeting?" Isabella asked.

"Good," Philly said. She had addressed the group, telling about how good it had felt to get back into a courtroom. But most of all she had talked about Daisy and how the baby had consumed her life in a good way. She liked being around Daisy; it was that simple. She liked Daisy's touch and smell and the way she nursed. She liked talking to Daisy about Philip and her cases and Carpenter. She liked taking Daisy outside and holding her tight while she walked. She liked pushing Daisy in a stroller with Paul at her side, although recently an investigation had consumed his attention and he hadn't come around. Still Paul had called her at least once every day when he couldn't put in an appearance.

"Would you like me to get you something to eat?" Isabella asked.

Philly shook her head. She needed to get into her nightgown and rub a cool washcloth over her face. Life was going to be very different when winter came, she reflected.

Once upstairs, Philly looked at her reflection in her bedroom mirror. She was slowly losing the weight she had gained during pregnancy. She had two narrow stretch marks near her right hip. Her breasts were huge and made her look top-heavy. She played out a scene in which she stripped down in front of Paul. Would his desire be evident, or would he be turned off by how she looked?

Back in the living room Philly sat down next to Isabella. Daisy began to squirm as if she had suddenly remembered she was hungry. So Isabella took Daisy from Raul and passed her on to Philly. Daisy reached for a breast.

Philly slid her nightie off a shoulder and let Daisy's searching mouth find a nipple. Philly had quickly decided that if Raul and Isabella wanted them to be a big happy family they could put up with her nursing in front of them. Lately they had accepted her nursing as a matter of course. Besides, each of them had seen whatever there was to see.

Daisy was hard at work. "I know what I'm good for," Philly said, watching her daughter.

60

Carpenter decided to make the most of the next half hour before Simon and Rachel arrived and he had Philly to himself. Her daughter was awake and looking around. The kid was cute, in many ways a miniature version of Philly. Philly settled Daisy on a baby seat placed on the conference room table and tickled her feet. The baby squirmed and Carpenter thought he heard a faint gurgle.

"I need you to focus," Carpenter said, and Philly looked up reluctantly. "I've talked to Simon and Rachel. They're willing to pay twenty-five percent of your rent. Would you be willing to keep your office open if you and I split the rest?"

Philly didn't reply immediately. She produced a notepad and jotted down some figures. "Let me think about it," she said. "I'll let you know soon."

"The thing is," Carpenter continued, "my office is too damn small for me and them. Besides, I'd have to clean it up which isn't going to happen."

Philly nodded. "I said I'd think about it."

"We need more cases," Carpenter said. "If we had more work for Simon and Rachel, I bet they'd quit their part-time jobs. Plus, the more work they have, the more money we make. They're definitely trying to make a go of things. It's a big deal for them to offer to pump some of the money we're paying them back into rent."

Philly again nodded, glancing at Daisy. Carpenter couldn't tell whether she was giving him her full attention.

"What about you?" Carpenter asked. "Are you up for making a go of things?"

Philly now regarded him all business. "I'm enjoying being a mother," she said. "I didn't think I would, but I like hanging out with my daughter."

Carpenter could predict what was coming next. Philly was going to take some time off and put the law on a back burner.

"But when I went to court with Rachel," Philly continued, "I realized how much I missed being in court. I almost wanted to tell her to sit down so I could argue the Lawson motion."

"So where are you going with this?"

"I'm going to go for all of it," Philly said without hesitation. "Somehow, I'm going to raise this cutie pie and practice law. I haven't figured out the details and I'm sure there will be bumps in the road. But I'm with you on what you're trying to do."

Carpenter hoped that his relief wasn't obvious. He had seen things coming apart if Philly crapped out. He liked Simon and Rachel, thought they would make good lawyers. But when all was said and done he wanted to stay teamed up with Philly.

"I really appreciate what you've been trying to do to help me out," Philly said. "As for the rent deal you mentioned, let's discuss it next month."

"Okay," Carpenter said, no longer caring if his relief showed.

Philly picked up her daughter. "I know you've been dying to hold her. Here. Go ahead."

Carpenter took Daisy in his hands remembering to keep a supporting hand behind her head. She stared at him with interest, her eyes never leaving his. He remembered Philip's eyes, blue like his daughter's. It had to give Philly a jolt every time she made eye contact with her baby. Or maybe the kid's eyes reminding her of Philip's was an inspiration. Maybe it was the kid's eyes that made Philly want to do it all.

"You're right," Carpenter said. "You've got one cutie pie over here."

61

The hearing room in the offices of the Board of Bar Overseers was packed. It was not a large room but the twenty seats behind the counsel tables were full and Carpenter hoped that the gallery was weighted in favor of Marshall Hyde. Retired Judge Margaret Dorset had taken a seat in the last row. Rachel sat to his right and Hyde to his left. His opponent, Jason Gerber, seemed surprised at the turnout. Gerber shouldn't have been surprised. The parties had exchanged witness lists. Carpenter had presented a witness list of twenty even though he had narrowed the lawyers who would testify on Hyde's behalf to six. Better to keep Gerber guessing who would take the stand. A fair number of Hyde's colleagues who would not testify had come to the hearing to show their support. Gerber's witness list had one name. Carl Mickelson was an attorney who had written a book on legal ethics and codes of conduct for lawyers and judges. Mickelson was listed by Gerber as an expert in those fields.

Promptly at nine, Michael Dunn assumed the hearing officer's chair. Dunn was in his thirties and, with his blond hair, had that preppy look that had at first soured Carpenter on Philip Sizemore. A purple handkerchief that matched the color of his tie presented a triangular sail protruding from the jacket of his charcoal gray suit. Carpenter couldn't understand what possessed a lawyer to sport a pocket handkerchief.

Dunn introduced himself, stated the purpose of the hearing, and laid out the hearing ground rules. He didn't seem fazed by the filled hearing room.

"In these hearings," Dunn said, "the Board of Bar Overseers is the first party to present its case. Please call your first witness Mr. Gerber."

Carl Mickelson was as dry and humorless as the subjects he claimed to have mastered. He was a fifty-something, tall, stoop-shouldered man with a thin face and an unruly mop of salt and pepper hair. Gerber quickly established Mickelson's credentials and had Mickelson confirm that he had read Marshall Hyde's blog that was the subject of the hearing.

"Do you have an opinion as to whether this blog violated any provision of the code of conduct to which Massachusetts lawyers are subject?" Gerber asked.

"Objection!" Carpenter interrupted.

"What's the basis of your objection?" Dunn inquired.

"First, the witness is being asked to give a legal opinion on the ultimate issue in this case. The ultimate issue is for you to decide." Carpenter paused while Dunn wrote on his notepad. "Second, this witness is not qualified to give an opinion on anything to do with this case." Carpenter again paused, this time to take in Mickelson's genuinely shocked expression. "Mr. Mickelson has not practiced law in his life. None of his qualifications concern criminal law which is the underlying area of law involved in this case. Where it appears that Mr. Mickelson has never been before any judge in a court of law on behalf of a client, the witness is not competent to give any opinion in a case that concern's a sitting judge's actions and a practicing lawyer's response to those judicial actions."

Carpenter sat down gratified that Dunn was making further entries on his notepad.

"What do you say to Mr. Carpenter's objection?" Dunn directed at Gerber.

Gerber stood with alacrity. "The ultimate issue in this case is a mixed question of fact and law. Therefore, Mr. Mickelson can testify as to the facts leaving you to apply the law. Furthermore, the issue in this case concerns whether Mr. Hyde violated any standard of conduct when he sent out his blog. Mr. Michelson is a renowned expert on the rules of conduct that lawyers must obey. He is eminently qualified to give an opinion."

Dunn became lost in thought and, for a brief moment, Carpenter entertained the hope that he had a chance of torpedoing the Board's case at the outset.

"I understand your objections, Mr. Carpenter," Dunn said. "I'm inclined to hear Mr. Mickelson's testimony, but your objections are noted. Also, you may make a motion to strike his testimony once it is concluded. As you know, the rules of evidence are liberally applied in administrative cases such as this. On balance, I'm going to let Mr. Mickelson testify."

"Do you have an opinion as to whether Mr. Hyde's blog violated any code of conduct applicable to lawyers?"

"I do," Mickelson said firmly.

"What is your opinion?"

Mickelson glowered at Carpenter before turning to Dunn. "Calling a judge pigheaded, a tyrant, and a bully is simply unacceptable. It is conduct and language that is intemperate, shows no respect for the judicial system, and is unprofessional to say the least. In my experience, this is a rather egregious case of intemperate and unprofessional language that brings disrespect to the legal profession."

"Do lawyers have recourse when they believe that a judge has overstepped his or her authority?" Gerber followed up.

"Of course," Mickelson said. "There's a Commission on Judicial Misconduct. Any lawyer may file a complaint against a judge with that Commission. Also, a lawyer may lodge a complaint with the chief justice of the superior court."

"Are there any provisions of the lawyers' code of professional conduct that you have determined were violated by Mr. Hyde's blog?"

"Yes."

"What are those provisions?"

"Objection," Carpenter said.

"Overruled. I'll hear the answer."

Mickelson cited two sections of the code of professional conduct: one that required lawyers to act and conduct themselves so as not to bring disrespect to the legal profession, and a second that required lawyers to treat judges, opposing counsel, and litigants with respect.

"No further questions," Gerber said.

"Is it true Mr. Mickelson that you have never engaged in the practice of law?" Carpenter began his cross-examination.

"Yes. I've done some teaching stints at law schools and I've been a guest lecturer at law schools from time to time. I've also written a book about legal ethics and the codes of conduct that apply to lawyers and judges. But I've never practiced law."

"You've also testified at disciplinary hearings involving lawyers, haven't you?"

"Yes."

"How many times have you testified on behalf of the Massachusetts Board of Bar Overseers?"

Mickelson took a moment to consider the question. "Somewhere around a dozen times."

"Have you testified on behalf of boards of bar overseers in other states?"

"Yes."

"About how many times a year do you testify for boards of bar overseers?"

"Approximately two dozen."

"Have you ever testified on behalf of a lawyer facing a complaint by a board of bar overseers?"

"No."

"What do you charge for your testimony in a case such as this?"

"Objection," Gerber said.

"Overruled."

"Five thousand dollars a day."

"Do you charge an hourly rate for preparation time?"

"Yes."

"What is that rate currently?"

"Five hundred dollars an hour."

"So basically you've become a professional witness for boards of bar overseers, haven't you?"

"I wouldn't agree with that characterization."

"I didn't ask you whether you agreed with the characterization," Carpenter deliberately raised his voice. "I asked you whether you've become a professional witness for boards of bar overseers. Is it true you've become a professional witness for boards of bar overseers?"

"I've testified in cases on behalf of boards if that's what you mean?"

"What was your income last year?"

"Objection," Gerber interposed.

"Overruled."

"Approximately, three hundred thousand dollars."

"What percentage was derived from providing services to boards of bar overseers?"

"Probably eighty to ninety percent."

"Is a lawyer required to speak and write the truth?" Carpenter abruptly changed the subject.

"I would say that's correct generally" Mickelson said.

"You said generally. When is it permissible for a lawyer *not* to speak and write the truth?"

"Offhand I can't think of an instance."

"Have you ever testified in a board of bar overseers case where a lawyer was disciplined because the lawyer told the truth?"

Mickelson pondered Carpenter's question. "I can't think of an instance at the moment."

"Is it true that Judge Samuel Porter, the judge who was the subject of the blog by Mr. Hyde that you referred to, was pigheaded, a tyrant, and a bully?"

As Mickelson shifted uncomfortably in his seat, Carpenter thought he heard a stifled laugh from Margaret Dorset.

"Those are not words that a lawyer may direct at a judge," Mickelson said.

Carpenter addressed Dunn. "I move to strike the witness' answer and I request that you order Mr. Mickelson to answer the question I posed to him."

"Objection," Gerber said.

Dunn took his time. His ruling would reveal the kind of hearing officer he would be.

"I'm going to allow Mr. Carpenter's motion. Mr. Mickelson. You were asked whether it was true that Judge Samuel Porter was pigheaded, a tyrant, and a bully. Please answer the question."

"I don't know."

"Let me get this straight," Carpenter said. "When you gave your opinions in response to questions from Mr. Gerber, you gave those opinions without knowing whether the words used by Mr. Hyde were true. Is that correct?"

"Yes, but . . ."

"Thank you," Carpenter raised his voice. Your answer is yes."

"Objection," Gerber said raising his voice. "The witness was not allowed to finish his answer."

"Your objection is overruled. The question called for a yes or no answer. You can follow up on redirect examination."

Carpenter now viewed Dunn as a brilliant jurist. The man could have ten handkerchiefs sticking out of his suit coat pocket.

"At this time, following Your Honor's suggestion, I move to strike Mr. Mickelson's testimony."

"Motion denied," Dunn said promptly.

Carpenter took a moment to regroup, reflecting that Dunn's brilliance had dimmed a bit.

"Are you familiar with the Code of Judicial Conduct that judges must conform to?" Carpenter asked.

"Yes."

"Is it true that judges must treat the lawyers who appear before them with respect?"

"Yes."

"If a judge acts toward a lawyer in a manner that is pigheaded, tyrannical, and bullying, does that conform to the judicial code of conduct provision that a judge treat a lawyer with respect?"

"I would have to know all the facts before I could answer that question," Mickelson said smugly.

"What are you talking about?" Carpenter said, trying to keep his incredulous tone from going over the top. "You expressed opinions in response to Mr. Gerber's questions without knowing whether the statements on Mr. Hyde's blog were factually true. Why can't you answer my question without knowing the facts?"

"Objection," Gerber intervened. "Mr. Carpenter is bullying the witness."

"That's an interesting word for Mr. Gerber to use," Carpenter said. "His sole witness, Mr. Mickelson, condemned the word bullying on Mr. Hyde's blog without knowing whether Judge Porter had in fact engaged in bullying. Whatever bullying is, I'm certainly not doing that to Mr. Mickelson. I wouldn't want to get hauled before the Board for bullying a witness when the Board's expert witness might accuse me of something he knows nothing about."

This time Carpenter was certain that Margaret Dorset had let loose with a short laugh.

"That's enough," Dunn said. "I think you've made your point, Mr. Carpenter. Let's move on."

Rachel was writing furiously in her trial notebook looking a little shell-shocked. The post mortem with the young lawyer was going to be interesting.

"Can you give me an example of judicial bullying?" Carpenter asked, deciding not to leave the subject of bullying just yet.

Mickelson took his time considering the question. "I suppose judicial bullying could occur if a judge threatened a lawyer with being held in contempt of court when the lawyer had done nothing contemptuous."

Carpenter mentally kicked himself. Mickelson had come up with a good answer.

"Might judicial bullying also occur if a judge forced a lawyer to comply with an unrealistic deadline?"

"I suppose that's possible," Mickelson said grudgingly.

"Might judicial bullying occur against a criminal defendant if a judge required a defendant to waive a constitutional right if the defendant couldn't comply with an unrealistic deadline?"

Mickelson frowned. "I suppose that's possible," he said mincingly.

Carpenter leaned toward Rachel who started when he came near. "I'm thinking of leaving my cross-examination of this joker where it is," he whispered. "Can you think of anything else I should be asking?"

Rachel was taken aback by the question. Carpenter realized that she hadn't expected to be consulted. He'd set her straight after the hearing. He didn't want any lawyer sitting beside him during a trial playing the role of a potted plant.

"Has he ever represented judges in judicial misconduct cases?" Rachel whispered.

Carpenter weighed the pros and cons of asking Rachel's question. The pros won out. "Have you ever represented judges in complaints of judicial misconduct?"

"Yes."

"Have you ever represented anyone who filed a complaint alleging misconduct on the part of a judge?"

"No."

Carpenter decided against asking a follow up question. Mickelson had carved out a lucrative niche for himself. Without having to deal with the travails of a law practice, he had made a comfortable living representing parties with money—boards of bar overseers and judges. Hopefully Dunn had gotten the point that Mickelson was a hired gun.

"No further cross-examination."

Gerber was quickly on his feet. "Mr. Carpenter cut off your answer to a question. You were asked whether the opinions you presented were given without you knowing whether the statements in Mr. Hyde's blog were true. You answered yes and were then cut off. What did you want to add?"

Mickelson turned to Dunn. "I was trying to add that the words used by Mr. Hyde on his blog were insulting to a sitting judge and inappropriate. If I had been allowed to finish my answer, I would have pointed out that some words, such as the words Mr. Hyde used on his blog, are so intemperate, in such bad taste and boorish that truth is beside the point. That's the case here in my opinion."

"Are you saying that it doesn't matter whether Mr. Hyde's words were true?" Dunn inquired, and Carpenter held his breath.

"I'm saying that Mr. Hyde simply shouldn't have used the words he did. He could have used more restrained language but preferably he shouldn't have used any language at all. As I mentioned previously, any complaint Mr. Hyde had as to Judge Porter could have been directed to the Commission on Judicial Misconduct or to the chief justice of the superior court."

Dunn looked inquiringly at Gerber.

"Nothing further," Gerber said.

"What more restrained language would have been appropriate in your view?" Carpenter let loose as he rose.

Mickelson frowned. "As I said, he should have used no language. But if he felt compelled to use language on his blog about this, he might have simply said that he disagreed with the judge's rulings."

"And what would be an appropriate way of expressing the reasons for his disagreement with the judge's rulings?"

"In my opinion he shouldn't have gotten into the reasons in a blog."

Carpenter paused. "Then is it correct, Mr. Mickelson, that what you meant by more restrained language is that Mr. Hyde should simply have voiced his disagreement without providing any basis for that statement?"

Mickelson nodded. "Yes."

Rachel tugged on his sleeve, gestured for him to draw near.

"I'd stop here," Rachel whispered. "His last statement was stupid. So was his statement about the truth of statements being beside the point. Have your expert pick up on this."

Carpenter grinned at Rachel. She was a quick learner. He wanted her head to be in the case and she had gotten the message.

"No further questions," Carpenter said.

"We'll take a short recess," Dunn announced.

Rachel had finished questioning the last of the lawyers she had prepped for the hearing. Carpenter leaned over and patted her shoulder. "Nice job," he said. In direct examination and redirect examination, Rachel had been matter-of-fact and composed. She listened to her witnesses' responses to her questions and departed from her testimony outline when an answer required a follow up question that was not on her outline. She had none of Philly's feisty aggression, but in her calm, deliberate way, she had her lawyer witnesses drive home the point that Judge Porter was pressuring criminal defendants into giving up their right to a speedy trial. Carpenter had been watching Dunn while Rachel held forth and had sensed that the hearing officer had responded positively to her measured, focused approach. Rachel had not spent more than seven minutes with any lawyer witness.

"Can we comfortably conclude with another witness before the lunch break?" Dunn inquired.

"I believe we can," Carpenter replied. "The Honorable Margaret Dorset."

Carpenter quickly elicited the retired judge's background information.

"How would you characterize Judge Porter's practice of setting prompt trial dates?" Carpenter addressed the reason for the hearing.

Gerber began to rise to lodge an objection before resuming his seat, apparently making the decision to abandon a leadoff objection.

"In my opinion," Judge Dorset said sharply, "busy defense lawyers would have found it impossible to prepare cases for trial given the trial dates Judge Porter was insisting on. I can tell you that when I ran the first superior court criminal session in several counties, I never imposed the early trial dates that Judge Porter was ordering. In my opinion, Judge Porter was forcing criminal defendants to accept an early trial date without any thorough case preparation, or to object to the early trial date and give up their right to a speedy trial because their cases would move to the back of the trial list. That's flat out unfair."

Carpenter waited until Dunn had concluded writing on his notepad. "Have you read Mr. Hyde's blog taking issue with Judge Porter's trial date directives?"

"I have."

"Did you listen to the testimony of the six attorneys who testified before you took the stand?"

"I did, with interest."

"Is there anything in Mr. Hyde's blog that you regard as untrue?"

"No. I regard the statements in his blog as truthful and accurate."

"What about the language in the blog referring to Judge Porter as pigheaded, tyrannical, and a bully?"

"If the shoe fits, wear it," Dorset said. "This judge was bullying the defense bar. We just heard lawyers testify that Judge Porter wouldn't listen to legitimate complaints about his scheduling trial dates. When you don't listen when someone points out reasonable problems with what you want the person to do, I believe pigheaded is an accurate description for you. Judge Porter was being a bully and, by the way, almost by definition, a bully is a tyrant."

"Did you hear Mr. Mickelson testify that Mr. Hyde should have filed a complaint before the Commission on Judicial Misconduct or complain to the chief justice of the superior court?"

"I did."

"Do you share Mr. Mickelson's view?"

"I think Mr. Mickelson's view is a lot of horse feathers. By becoming a lawyer, a person doesn't give up his first amendment rights to complain about offensive conduct. Mr. Hyde had a right to complain about Judge Porter's conduct in precisely the way he chose to do so. The Commission on Judicial Misconduct has nothing to do with this case. If a judge makes stupid rulings, does that mean the judge has been guilty of judicial misconduct? I don't think so. If that were the case, any disgruntled lawyer or litigant could lodge a case with the Commission. And when it comes to writing a letter to the chief justice of the superior court, when I was practicing law I would never consider going over a trial judge's head to the chief justice. That just isn't done."

"In your opinion, was Mr. Hyde, in his blog, being disrespectful to either Judge Porter or to the legal profession?"

Judge Dorset shook her head. "Mr. Hyde criticized a practice of a superior court judge that in my view needed to be criticized. The words he used were strong and appropriate for the occasion. Disagreeing with a judge is not tantamount to showing the judge a lack of respect. And I have never heard of the legal profession being disrespected by statements that were true. I don't know why . . . what was his name, Mickelson? . . . said that the truth of Mr. Hyde's blog didn't matter in this case. In my opinion, a lawyer speaking truthfully has not shown disrespect to anyone. Mr. Mickelson said that Mr. Hyde should have used more restrained language. Why? If you're trying to drive home a point, why not use strong language? I know I would."

Carpenter paused. Dorset had delivered for his client. But there was still one item on his direct examination checklist.

"Can a judge be too thin-skinned when it comes to criticism?"

Dorset smiled, her double chin rippling. "I believe that many judges are too thin-skinned as you put it. In preparing to testify, I gave a lot of thought to what I was called by lawyers in the course of trials. I was called an old fart, an old bag, a battle-ax, and probably worse. I never held a lawyer in contempt of court and I never reported a lawyer to the Board. My practice was to tell the lawyer that I was sure I didn't hear him or her correctly but that my hearing would improve if anything further was said. I believe in every case I got an apology. Lawyers get caught up in the course of a trial and I would cut them some slack because I remembered from my trial days how stressful and demanding trial work was. When a lawyer goes public with criticizing a judge's practice, I believe the lawyer should be cut similar slack and that it's not a matter for the Board of Bar Overseers if what the lawyer said was true."

Carpenter looked down at Rachel and grinned when she drew a finger across her throat.

"No further questions."

Gerber promptly stood. "So it's okay in your view for a judge to be called an old fart. Is that correct?"

"You weren't listening to me," Dorset snapped. "It's not okay and I never said it was. What I said was that when a lawyer feels strongly about something and says something in the heat of the moment that might have been better left unsaid, the lawyer should be cut some slack. I also said that judges need to be more thick-skinned given their job."

"Would you agree that a judge other than yourself might reasonably seek to discipline a lawyer who called the judge an old fart?"

"No. I don't think that would be reasonable for the reasons I just stated. If you meant to ask me whether a different judge might react differently than I did to being called an old fart, that's certainly possible."

"Do you think it's okay for a lawyer not to be disciplined when the lawyer uses profanity to refer to a judge?"

Dorset pondered the question for a moment. "I guess I do. As I said, it was my practice to give lawyers a mulligan if they swore at me. But if they kept it up, I probably would have taken stronger action."

"Such as filing a complaint with the Board of Bar Overseers?" Gerber asked.

"No. Some kind of sanction more likely."

"Do you agree that a judge might reasonably adopt a less tolerant attitude toward profanity directed the judge's way?"

"Again, I don't think a less tolerant attitude is reasonable, but I do understand that not every judge would respond to profanity as I would. And by the way, no profanity was used by Mr. Hyde."

Gerber consulted his notes. He had to know by now that Dorset would try to zing him at every turn. In Gerber's place, Carpenter would opt to shut his mouth.

"No further questions," Gerber said.

"We'll break for lunch," Dunn said.

Carpenter took his seat after concluding his direct examination of Marshall Hyde. He had grown to like and respect his client. All in all, Carpenter believed that Hyde had acquitted himself well. Hyde was a brusque, no-nonsense kind of guy with a somewhat short fuse, but had come across as sincere. Now Gerber rose to cross-examine.

"Why didn't you deliver your pigheaded, bully, and tyrant remarks to Judge Porter in court?" Gerber asked.

"I just didn't," Hyde replied.

"But you regard it as appropriate to level those terms at a sitting judge in the judge's courtroom, don't you?"

Hyde glowered at Gerber and Carpenter feared that his client was about to lose control. But Hyde gathered himself with several deep breaths.

"I don't know if you've ever tried a criminal case," Hyde said. "Probably not from the looks of you. My answer to your question is that I do think there are circumstances when using the terms I used in my blog would be appropriate to direct at a sitting judge. That doesn't mean I would do that. You have to remember that when you're before a judge you have a client with you. You don't want to have a judge take anything out on your client because of what you did as the client's lawyer. That's why a blog is so useful."

"If you were so displeased with Judge Porter's trial date practices, why didn't you complain about them to the Commission on Judicial Misconduct or to the chief justice of the superior court?"

Hyde shrugged. "I never gave those options any consideration. I felt that this was a matter that the defense bar was concerned about and a blog was the appropriate way to voice that concern. Besides, after this experience I'm going through, I wouldn't want a judge to have to defend himself before the Commission on Judicial Misconduct. It's expensive and nerve-racking."

"Have you ever used the terms you used to describe Judge Porter in connection with any other judicial officer?"

"I don't believe so."

"Did you ever publicly criticize a judge's ruling that went against one of your clients as a travesty of justice?"

Hyde became lost in thought. "I think I did once. I was representing a defendant accused of rape. The judge allowed into evidence an eyewitness' identification of the defendant as the assailant when the evidence showed that the eyewitness could not have seen what he claimed to have seen. When the defendant was convicted, I answered questions outside the courtroom and I think I said there had been a travesty of justice. If I didn't say that I should have. My client's conviction was overturned on appeal."

Gerber glanced at his trial notebook. In Carpenter's estimation, the Board attorney had yet to land a damaging blow.

"Was the purpose of your blog to ridicule Judge Porter?" Gerber asked.

"The purpose of my blog was to criticize the judge's trial scheduling practices for the reasons I've stated."

"But you wanted to embarrass the judge, didn't you?"

"I wanted him to stop screwing over defendants' right to a speedy trial."

"Pigheaded, tyrant, and bully aren't flattering terms, are they?"

"No, they're not flattering."

"In fact, you used those words to humiliate Judge Porter, didn't you?"

"I didn't think of my blog in that way. I thought I was doing the defense bar a service by complaining about a judge's practice that was forcing defendants to give up their right to a speedy trial."

"Why didn't you appeal Judge Porter's trial scheduling orders in specific cases if you were so unhappy with them?"

Hyde threw up his hands in exasperation. "Because the scheduling orders aren't appealable. A scheduling order isn't a final decision."

Gerber banged away at Hyde, trying to get the criminal lawyer to acknowledge that his blog was a personal attack on Judge Porter, but when the cross examination ended, Hyde was visibly angry but unbowed.

Carpenter leaned toward Rachel and held up his notepad to shield their colloquy from Dunn.

"I don't think I should ask any question," Carpenter whispered.

Rachel nodded. "That's what I was thinking."

"No redirect examination," Carpenter said. "That concludes Mr. Hyde's case."

"Any rebuttal witnesses?" Dunn inquired of Gerber.

"No."

"The evidence is in and that concludes the hearing," Dunn said. "The parties can have two weeks to submit post-hearing legal memoranda. Please try to keep those submissions brief. You don't have to repeat legal arguments made in the pre-hearing memoranda. Any other business? Then the hearing is concluded, and we are adjourned."

Even with the afternoon heat and humidity, Carpenter was glad to be outside and in motion. He tended to walk fast but Rachel had no trouble matching his pace. He tried to think if he could have scripted the hearing any better than it had unfolded and didn't think he could. Hyde had taken him aside and congratulated him on a job well done. Judge Dorset hadn't stayed to chat but had given him a thumbs up sign before departing.

"Any thoughts?" he asked Rachel.

"I thought things went well."

"So did I. Which makes me nervous. I'm trying to figure out what I'm missing."

"I don't think you're missing anything. I'm curious about one thing though. What would you have done in Gerber's place?"

"I would have had a judge as a witness," Carpenter said. "I might have put Judge Porter on the stand. I wouldn't have left my case in the hands of Carl Mickelson."

They walked for a time in silence. Carpenter began to relax. It felt good to let his game face dissolve.

"I want to thank you," Rachel said.

"What for?"

"For pushing me to get involved in this case."

"Don't mention it."

"I wouldn't say I loved it, but it wasn't as bad as I thought it would be."

Carpenter considered his next comment. Maxine once told him that a lawyer starting out needed to be told when she did a good job. Maxine had been referring to Philly.

"You've got a thoughtful, focused way about you," Carpenter said. "Like I told you, you did a good job. Be yourself. Don't try to turn yourself into someone you're not."

"I don't think I could ever have gone after Mickelson the way you did," Rachel said.

"You'd be surprised at what you can do when you need to do something. You would have gone after Mickelson in your way. And for all we know, your way might have been better than mine."

"I don't know about that."

"Take my word for it," Carpenter said. "I think you've got what it takes. Besides, you don't want Simon to have all the fun, do you?"

62

"It's just you and me, kid," Philly said as she clicked a ball point pen for Daisy's amusement. Daisy was loosely strapped into a baby seat positioned on Philly's home office desk, staring at her with Philip's blue eyes. Daisy was now more than a month old. If anything, her daughter's disposition had improved with age. Daisy smiled a lot, often gurgled happily when left alone, and seemed to be interested in anything that crossed her plane of vision. She had chunky arms and legs that Philly was hard pressed not to constantly squeeze.

When the phone startled her, Philly needed a moment to segue into business mode. "Philomena Piper."

"It's George Norris. Is this a good time?"

"For you, George, anytime is a good time." Philly blew a kiss at Daisy and tickled her daughter's feet.

"I seriously doubt that."

"What can I do for you?"

"Dixfield will go along with settling the case along the lines you discussed."

"I'm pleased to hear that. Now I have to get the Harringtons to agree."

"Do you see that as a problem?"

"It could be."

Daisy let out a squeal and jerked her arms upward.

"Is that your baby?" Norris asked.

"It is."

"How can you get any work done with a baby around?"

"Who said I wanted to get work done?"

"Very funny. Give me a call when you hear back from your clients."

"I will. May I ask you something, George?" Philly hoped that the repeated use of Norris' first name would loosen the man up.

"Sure."

"Did you recommend the settlement to Dixfield?"

Norris didn't respond to the question and Philly figured that she had crossed a line into territory where his irritability reigned.

"Why do you want to know?" Norris asked.

"I'm curious," she said. "You're a hard guy to read and I'm trying to understand what makes you tick."

"In that case, I'd prefer to remain a man of mystery," Norris said.

"Have it your way, George. I'll get back to you."

Philly put down her phone. Daisy let loose with a loud whine and squirmed in her baby seat so Philly released her. She held Daisy under the shoulders and stood the baby on her desktop, making sure her fingers supported Daisy's neck. Daisy cheered up immediately when her feet rested on the flat surface.

"That was an asshole, Daisy. They come in all shapes and sizes but they're not hard to miss. The first clue is when they open their mouths. With assholes, nothing useful comes out."

Daisy's right fist went to her mouth.

"Aren't I a good mother? I'm already giving you useful advice."

Daisy had nursed and was asleep on the floor, lying face down on a mat. Philly decided to use the time to deal with the Harringtons. It took some doing but she got them together on a conference call. Neither interrupted as she outlined the potential settlement she had reached with George Norris.

"We never authorized you to talk settlement with the other side," John Harrington led off. "How did this come up?"

"Attorney Norris and I were talking and I brought the matter up. I decided to be frank with him and let him know what I was willing to recommend to you. I explained very clearly to him that I didn't have your approval to settle the case."

"I don't like this," John Harrington said. "I don't like the idea of anything about the way we treat Luke at home in his school record. It frosts me that this all came about through an anonymous letter. And I don't like it that you initiated discussion of a settlement. Dixfield will think it's got us on the run."

Philly paused a beat to remain calm. "Here's why I recommend that you settle your case. First, there's nothing in the anonymous letter that's false. Second, the letter that mentions the abuse statute will be removed from Luke's school record. Third, the judge is likely to issue an order along the lines of the settlement since she was the one who suggested the approach that Dixfield is now prepared to accept. Fourth, I don't think you will do better than the settlement if you go to trial and rack up a lot of legal fees. Fifth, there is something to be said for putting this matter behind you." Philly paused as she decided how to deal with John Harrington's most galling comment. "Lastly, since the judge said she was not inclined to dismiss your case, you're the ones who have Dixfield on the run. The time to raise settlement is when you have the upper hand which you do for the moment."

"What would happen if Luke started acting out at school," Naomi Harrington asked.

Philly considered the Lawson case which was rapidly heading downhill. "If Luke were determined to be a student with special needs, the school would have to come up with a plan to meet those needs. Why do you ask?"

Naomi Harrington didn't respond immediately. One of the Harrington's labored breathing sounded over the phone.

"Lately, Luke has needed more time out periods," Naomi Harrington finally said. "He's still doing okay in school. It's at home when he gets agitated on occasion. But Dr. Cooper still can't make a diagnosis."

"We're drifting away from the court case," John Harrington said.

"Actually, I think this bears on the court case," Philly countered.

"I don't want to go along with the settlement," John Harrington said.

"Does the closet still calm Luke down?"

"Yes," said Naomi Harrington.

"Then maybe you want to make sure Luke's teachers know about the technique in case he does act out inappropriately while at school."

"That's ridiculous!" John Harrington exclaimed.

Philly stayed silent waiting for another country to be heard from.

"How could you even think such a thing?" John Harrington continued.

"Because I know how much you love your son and want to do the right thing for him."

"Oh, for Christ's sake!"

"Maybe she's right, John."

"What the hell are you talking about?"

"I'm afraid that Luke will do something at school and nobody there will know what to do. What if Luke doesn't get any better but only gets worse?"

"I can't believe you're giving up."

"I'm not giving up. I'm trying to do the right thing."

"Jesus H. Christ!"

When she was reasonably sure the Harringtons were talked out, Philly intervened. "I want to talk to both of you tomorrow when you've had some time to think about this. You need to talk this out. I don't want you to make a decision at this moment. What time works for you tomorrow?"

The Harringtons consulted their calendars. Philly agreed to place the early morning call. After hanging up her phone, she succumbed to a long sigh. She stared at Daisy. There was no way to gauge how your kid would turn out. Your high hopes for your kid could turn to dust. You could try like hell but sometimes your best wouldn't be enough.

Philly scooted down to the floor beside Daisy and inserted a forefinger into her daughter's tiny fist. Daisy knew what to do; she held on tight.

63

Philly set down her phone trying to gauge whether her astonishment had to do with the Harringtons' decision to accept her advice, or with John Harrington's apology. The Harringtons had approved settling, but naturally wanted to read the final agreement. John Harrington had apologized for coming on like a jerk on yesterday's call. He had explained that he was worried about Luke, was a nervous wreck over Luke's situation, and hadn't been himself. Philly assured him that yesterday's stressful call was now behind them. But when John Harrington had said that he hadn't been himself, Philly tried to assess *her* true self. Was it the mother who couldn't get enough of her baby? Or was it the stubborn, self-destructive woman who had decided to drink during her pregnancy?

Daisy was fed and napping on her mat in a clean diaper. Philly wished that there was a way she could exercise. Right now, in a spinning class, she wouldn't last fifteen minutes. Her weight was down but she felt like she didn't have a muscle in her body. Somehow, she was going to have to get herself into shape. In twenty minutes, she'd be dialing Carpenter for a conference call that included Simon and Rachel. Take the time when you can, she decided. She moved her desk chair and slid Daisy's mat under her desk. Then she hooked her feet under a side of her desk, left her knees bent, and began to do sit-ups. Pushups would be next.

As she brought Carpenter, Rachel, and Simon up to date on the developments in the Harringtons' case, Philly pictured them seated at the Boston office conference room table staring at the phone that had been set on speaker. She wondered whether they were finding it as disconcerting as she was to interact with disembodied voices. Daisy squirmed in her lap but so far, since waking from her nap, was not demanding to be fed. She had given Daisy a ball point pen to hold and the baby seemed content to resist her gentle efforts to pull the pen away.

"I'll draw up a settlement agreement that George Norris and the Harringtons can review," Philly wrapped up. "It's something I can do while Daisy's napping."

"Send me the draft before you send it to the clients," Carpenter said. "I may have some thoughts."

"Okay," Philly agreed.

"It's funny," Carpenter said. "When the Harrington and Lawson cases were starting out, I would have bet the Harrington case was going to be more difficult to work out. I was wrong. The hearing officer in the Lawson case has reopened the IEP hearing to take more evidence. I can see the Lawsons going down in flames."

Philly agreed with Carpenter's assessment. When it had come out that Luke Harrington had been placed in a closet, she had figured that she was dealing with parent whack-jobs who would never get anywhere in court. The Lawsons had seemed reasonable in comparison.

"Any thoughts on how we deal with the reopened hearing?" Carpenter threw out. "The hearing officer wants all the witnesses who previously testified to be present. If Sylvia Lawson is truthful, the hearing officer will be treated to testimony that Jack Lawson is becoming more unmanageable both at home and out of the house."

"And if Sylvia Lawson lies, we've got an ethical problem," Philly responded. "We can't represent her if we know she's downplaying Jack's behavior."

"Then we have to assume that she'll tell the truth," Simon reasoned.

"The Lawsons have already withdrawn their court suit," Rachel said. "There's nothing to prevent them from dropping their challenge to the Stonington IEP."

"I only see one way out," Carpenter said in a dispirited tone. "I don't know if there's enough time to work on this, but I think Jack Lawson's meds need to go up. Maybe the correct dosage is somewhere between what Stonington wants and where the med levels are now."

"I don't think the Lawsons are going to be receptive to that," Rachel said. "They want their son to be totally off all medications."

"Well, that's not going to happen," Carpenter said. "Rachel, try to get them in here tomorrow. If they won't come in, we need a conference call. Don't take no for an answer."

Daisy had lost interest in the ball point pen. Philly produced a pencil and a little fist grabbed hold.

Carpenter brought Philly up to date on other matters. He had assigned Simon the task of drafting a court complaint to force Norman Cassidy and Paul Huggins to honor the subpoenas they had so far refused to comply with. In Frederick Chun's case, Crowe Investment Strategies had produced documents that the Massachusetts Commission Against Discrimination had ordered be forthcoming, and Rachel would be analyzing them. Simon would soon be taking the deposition of Bruce Bolton, the president of Wise Computer Consultants who had fired Herbert Stanton and Millie Lane. Lastly, Gerald Hatch would have to respond to discovery requests in the suit brought by Martin Mercer. Philly wanted to review the discovery requests before deciding on who would draft the responses and Carpenter promised to fax her the papers.

"Sounds like we're busy," Philly observed.

Carpenter mumbled something unintelligible. Philly knew he was thinking they weren't busy enough. If it were just the two of them, they might be stretched too thin. But with two new lawyer mouths to feed, Carpenter was right—they needed more cases.

"Thanks for the update," Philly said, ready to hang up the phone. She had another mouth to feed.

64

Prickly, uncomfortable client meetings were a fact of legal life but that didn't mean a lawyer had to like them. Privately, Carpenter shared the Lawsons' obvious desire to be elsewhere. There were dark circles under Sylvia Lawson's hazel eyes and her reddish-brown hair hung listlessly. Normally Max Lawson presented a rugged exterior but on this occasion he seemed to be diminished, as if the anxiety of dealing with his son had worn him down.

Carpenter was glad to have Rachel seated beside him at the conference room table, confident she would speak up if she had something useful to say.

Carpenter outlined what he expected to happen at the reopened IEP hearing. The Lawsons listened to his account without expression. "The bottom line," he concluded, "is that I think we need to get an order from Jack's physician increasing the medication levels. The current levels don't seem to be working."

"That's not the direction we want to go with Jack," Max said sullenly.

"Is Jack's doctor aware of the camp incident and Jack's having more difficulties at home?" Rachel asked.

Sylvia Lawson shook her head.

"Neither Ms. Boyle nor I is a doctor," Carpenter said. "But our sense is that for the moment, Jack needs medications. Perhaps, as he gets older, that will change. But right now, he's acting out of control. We think you need to face that fact. This is important for Jack's health and safety and the health and safety of others."

"You're right," Max Lawson said confrontationally. "You're not doctors."

"You need to consult with Jack's doctor then," Rachel came back. "His doctor won't be able to help Jack or you if he's not brought into the picture."

"She," Sylvia Lawson said. "Dr. Carol Reed."

"When's the last time Jack was seen by Dr. Reed?" Rachel asked.

"When the medications started to be lowered," Sylvia Lawson replied.

"You need to get an emergency appointment with Dr. Reed, fill her in on what's been happening, and leave the medication issue to her," Carpenter put forward, suspecting that he was being tuned out. "At the hearing, you need to come across as reasonable if you want to prevail. Not bringing in your physician to consult on Jack's changed behavior is going to make you appear unreasonable and might cause you to lose. Dr. Reed may conclude that modest levels of medication work best for Jack and a hearing officer might accept her opinion."

The Lawsons remained silent. Carpenter found himself losing patience. "Will you do what I asked?"

"We'll think about it," Max Lawson said.

"You don't have much time," Rachel put in. "The hearing will be reopened next week."

"We know the schedule," Sylvia Lawson said testily.

"Quite aside from the public safety issues here, there are strategic issues related to your case," Carpenter said. "I'm going to have to brief Maryanne Fairmount, and she's going to be asked whether the new facts about Jack change her opinion."

The Lawsons became more downcast by this news. The couple seemed intent on toughing out an untenable position.

"Anything else?" Carpenter asked.

Sylvia Lawson rummaged in her purse. "We got this letter the other day."

Carpenter positioned the document so that Rachel could read it with him. It was an attorney letter written on behalf of the child whom Jack Lawson had injured at camp. The letter requested that the Lawsons supply the attorney with the name of their insurance company.

"I'll make a copy of the letter before you leave," Carpenter said. "You need to immediately send a copy of the letter to your insurance company. Your insurance coverage may provide you with legal representation in this matter. If not, we can talk about us handling this matter for you."

Sylvia Lawson nodded reflexively.

Carpenter decided what the hell; he was damned if he was going to sit back and let the Lawsons wallow in a sullen funk. He banged his fist on the table and it was Rachel who started.

"You two need to snap out of whatever the hell is bugging you and start getting your heads back into this case. All Rachel and I can do is advise you. You have to make some decisions here and take action. We've pointed you in a direction that we think is helpful given what's happened with Jack. You're free to reject that advice and, if you do, our legal opinion is that you're going to lose the IEP hearing. If you want a chance to win that hearing, we don't think you can let things go on as they have been. You've got to do something proactive."

Rachel appeared the most shocked by his outburst. Let her live and learn, Carpenter thought. What troubled him was that the Lawsons regarded his strong words without affect.

Max Lawson rose. "We'll get back to you," he said, motioning for his wife to join him. "You can keep the letter; we already made a copy."

"Is it all right to speak to a client like you just did?" Rachel asked after the Lawsons had made their getaway.

"It is and maybe it isn't," Carpenter said. "When I was starting out, I probably wouldn't have reacted to the Lawsons the way I just did. But I'm getting on in years and I put up with less than I once did. I've learned that typically the worst a client can do is fire me. At my age, that's not the end of the world. I don't get ticked off if a client has a good reason for disagreeing with me. But the Lawsons were just being stubborn. They never came up with a reason for ignoring our advice."

Watching Rachel consider his answer, Carpenter wondered whether he was a suitable role model for her. She seemed almost too sweet and nice. He found it easier to mix it up and level with Philly who had visible hard edges.

"I just don't think I could ever get angry at a client," Rachel said. "I mean I could get angry at a client, but I just don't think I could express that anger to the client in a face-to-face meeting."

"Just wait," Carpenter said. "You haven't been at it that long. You'd be surprised at what you might say to a client."

Rachel looked unconvinced. She slowly shook her head.

"A client doesn't hire you to be a friend," Carpenter continued. "You've got to tell a client what you think even if the client doesn't want to hear it. Sometimes, to get a point across, you have to come on strong."

"I know what you're saying makes sense," Rachel said. "I just don't think I could do it."

"Give it time," Carpenter suggested.

Walking with Paul Sullivan behind the stroller, Philly enjoyed the warm, summer evening. But even now, nighttime was coming on earlier. In winter, would she ever get out? Somehow, she was going to have to find a reliable babysitter or two.

"I got shot at last week," Paul said out of the blue. "I was debating whether to tell you about it and decided I should."

"Jesus!"

"I'm trying to be honest here. Honesty is the best policy, right?"

Philly thought about her relationship with Philip. She hadn't had a desire to hear every intimate thought he had. But when one of them wanted to have a serious discussion, the rule was that the truth was the only acceptable currency. That rule had worked.

"I'm glad you told me. Thanks. How are you dealing with it? I can't imagine what it feels like to be shot at."

"I'm doing okay," Paul said. "It was a wild shot but it was still scary. The department has a psychiatrist on consult and I talked to her about what happened. That helped."

If she took things further with Paul, Philly had no way to gauge how she would live with the possibility that every time he went to work he might not come back. Hadn't she read somewhere that police officer marriages played out on shaky ground because either the spouse couldn't live with the danger of the job or the police officer needed to relieve stress in ways that harmed the marriage?

"May I ask you a personal question?" Philly said.

"Sure. It doesn't mean I'm going to answer."

"Why did you and your ex get a divorce?"

Paul remained silent. They typically walked in a square and had just reached the halfway point. A refreshing breeze flooded the corner where they gave the stroller a quarter turn and started the walk back to the house.

"It's complicated," Paul said. "For the years right after we got married, I knew April was behind me. But after Jenny was born, April grew to dislike my job because of the danger. That started a vicious cycle of sorts. I was dedicated to my job. I still am. But I felt that I didn't have April's support any longer. Resentment built up on both sides and the short version is that it eventually overwhelmed us. We couldn't recapture the earlier years."

Philly thought she'd been lucky. Philip had always been in her corner.

"What are you thinking?" Paul asked.

"I was thinking about two things. I was thinking about Philip. And I was thinking about asking you whether you wanted to spend the night with me."

Paul put his hand over Philly's where she held onto the stroller. "Thinking about asking me and asking me are two different things. But if you were to ask me, the answer would be yes."

"Then consider yourself asked. I don't think I'm quite ready for intercourse, but we can still fool around."

"Fooling around is good."

Her heart was pounding, but Philly felt that she was doing the right thing. The test was that she didn't feel guilty, didn't feel she was betraying Philip or his memory. "Let's pick up the pace."

65

"Here's the thing, Fred," Carpenter said. "I've been too busy to think about you. Sometimes I think that if I keep up a frenetic pace I won't have to deal with you because you won't be able to keep up."

The expression of the man in the photograph morphed into the sour look he presented whenever Carpenter made a statement based more on hope and prayer than fact. Carpenter was resigned to the man refusing to cut him any slack. Still, it took something out of him whenever the man called him on wishful thinking.

But was his thinking wishful? His last blood test showed a decrease in his white blood cell count. It was the first time that the reading had dropped below a previous reading. Carpenter had expected an inexorable rise in his white blood cell count leading to a bout with chemotherapy and whatever other misery his doctors would prescribe. He had experienced such elation at the reduced reading that he had called Maxine immediately with the news. But when Dr. Specter had called him about the latest blood test results, she wasn't as upbeat about the lowered reading as he expected her to be. "The important thing," Specter had told him, "was your white blood cell count hasn't suddenly spiked."

Carpenter sipped his morning coffee. It was not yet seven o'clock. He hadn't been able to sleep and figured that if he was going to be awake it might as well be at his office. Now he wondered what the hell he had been thinking when he decided to block out some quiet time to pay attention to Fred. He had nothing to say to Fred really; recently, his conversations with Fred were forced. As long as he was symptom free, he wanted to delude himself into thinking that Fred wasn't important.

Carpenter glared at the photograph. "You haven't come up with one constructive thing I could talk to Fred about. You're useless!"

The man was impervious to criticism.

"Fuck you both!" Carpenter let loose. It was time to return to the real world. Norman Cassidy had filed a motion to dismiss the illegal wiretapping suit brought by Jerome Singer. Carpenter resolved to take the initial cut at an opposition to that motion. Then he needed to take Simon through a trial run of Bruce Bolton's deposition in the Herbert Stanton and Millie Lane case which was around the corner. Stay active, Carpenter counseled himself. Don't think about the elephant in the room. And there was another thing he didn't want to think about: Delaney's prediction to the Barristers on whether the Red Sox would make it to the post season. "Not a chance," Delaney had opined. "Too many injuries, no hitting, no bullpen, and an erratic closer."

The Red Sox playing in October was something else he wouldn't be able to look forward to.

Philly had to hand it to Raul and Isabella. They had come downstairs for breakfast, showed no surprise that Paul was present, and went about their morning rituals as if nothing was out of the ordinary. Philly had previously introduced them to Paul and they had seen Paul on some evenings, but she'd given them no indication that Paul was something more than a friend.

Daisy lay back in her baby carrier which served as a seat. The carrier was in front of her placemat and Philly found herself making faces at her daughter. Paul leaned over and offered silly faces of his own.

"This is nice," Isabella said, and it was nice, Philly reflected. The sun was coming in through the living room window, Daisy looked fat and happy, Paul had a hand on her thigh under the table, and Raul wasn't prattling on about anything. Raul appeared serious.

"We have some news," Isabella said. "I'm pregnant."

"Wow!" Philly said. She was on her feet, hugging Isabella, genuinely happy for the woman who had gotten her through her own pregnancy. Then she went to hug Raul who seemed self-conscious for some reason.

"I guess there are going to be some changes around here," Philly said as she resumed her seat. "This is great news."

"I am a little nervous," Raul confessed.

"Don't worry about it," Philly assured him. "If I can get through it, the two of you can."

"When are you due?" Paul asked.

"Next April or May."

"Our children will be less than a year apart," Raul observed.

"Speaking of children," Paul said to Philly. "Is it okay if I bring Jenny around this weekend? I want you to meet her."

"Of course."

Philly considered the ramifications of Isabella's news. Next spring, she should offer to switch rooms with Raul and Isabella, so Isabella could avoid the stairs. Soon, they were going to have to start thinking about childproofing the house. Also, she wouldn't have the house to herself during the nine to five workday and would have to figure out a way to block out chunks of time for legal work. And if Paul was going to be a permanent part of her life—something she hoped would be the case after last night—she'd have to make time for their relationship. Life would be easier if she didn't have to sleep.

"I've got to hit the road," Paul said, giving her thigh a squeeze. "I'll wash these dishes up before I go."

"Leave them," Philly instructed. "Off you go."

"I will join you, Paul," Raul said. "I have an early meeting with a prospective client."

Isabella was in no rush to get to work. When the men left, Philly studied her housemate. If the future brought them and their children closer together, Philly saw the development as a big plus. Her affection for Isabella was genuine.

"Raul seemed a little subdued," Philly threw out.

"He's a little worried about money. We haven't decided whether I'll keep my job after the baby is born. I won't be able to work from home the way you can."

"I'm not exactly working," Philly admitted. "I'm going to need babysitting very soon."

"You look happy," Isabella said. "Paul seems very nice."

"I am happy," Philly said. "I'm trying to enjoy the moment. I don't have a clue how I'm going to manage in the future. And yes, Paul *is* very nice." She blushed. Fooling around with Paul last night had been intense. She needed to remember to call Dr. Shumaker about when she could resume sex.

"I'm glad we have this house together," Isabella said. "It makes me less nervous to know that you will be here when Raul is not around."

"Ditto for me," Philly said, thinking that it would be heaven if the summer never ended and Daisy and Paul filled up her life.

66

The atmosphere in the conference room was decidedly chilly. Jeannie Smith, Carpenter's stenographer of choice, had finished setting up and nodded to Simon that she was ready. Beneath her mop of unruly white hair, her sour expression matched Carpenter's. Neither Wayne Anderson nor his client, Bruce Bolton, looked like he had smiled in weeks. Carpenter had forgotten what a big guy Anderson was; the broad-shouldered lawyer with thick, dark hair and dark eyes behind rimless glasses had an imposing presence. In contrast to his lawyer, Bolton was a thin, pasty-faced man with thinning hair.

Simon agreed to the deposition ground rules with Anderson, and Carpenter thought that Anderson would never suspect this was Simon's first deposition. It occurred to him that Simon could use a little of Rachel's measured thoughtfulness, and that Rachel would benefit from some of Simon's self-assurance.

Bolton presented background information in clipped responses. The president of Wise Computer Consultants had started his company eighteen years ago, and had built the business up steadily to the point where it was a solid, profitable concern.

"At some time did you provide company employees with cell phones that contained a tracking device?" Simon asked.

"Yes."

"When did that occur?"

"I don't remember exactly. A little over a year ago."

"Had you previously provided employees with cell phones?"

"No."

"Had you previously supplied employees with any piece of equipment that contained a tracking device?"

"No."

"When you decided to provide employees with cell phones containing a tracking feature, did you consult with any attorney about the tracking feature?"

Bolton glanced at Anderson before replying. "No."

"Did you consult with anyone about the tracking feature?"

"No."

"Where did you come up with the idea of putting a tracking feature into employees' cell phones?"

"I read an article about it."

"Did you save the article?"

"No."

"Do you remember where the article was published?"

"No."

"Was the tracking device in your company's cell phones a GPS tracking device?"

"Yes."

"Did you tell employees about the GPS feature when you presented them with the cell phones containing GPS?"

"No."

"Why not?"

Bolton again glanced at Anderson. His attorney met his gaze, but Carpenter saw no sign of any signal or coaching passing between them.

"I didn't think I had to, and I wanted to be able to keep track of my employees while they were on the job."

"Did the GPS permit you to keep track of your employees when they weren't on the job?"

"Yes."

"Did you in fact keep track of your employees' whereabouts when they were not on the job?"

"Not during normal business hours."

"What are normal business hours?"

"Roughly eight in the morning to six at night."

"Do you routinely pay your employees from eight in the morning to six at night?"

"No."

Simon stared at Bolton for a long moment. "You've identified a ten-hour span, Mr. Bolton. Typically, within the ten-hour span you mentioned, how many hours would you pay an employee?"

"It would vary."

"Then please provide me with a range of variation," Simon requested, and Carpenter noted with satisfaction that Simon's voice had turned hard.

"I'd say on average six to seven hours during the ten hours were paid."

"During the three to four hours employees were not being paid, were they on the job to use your phrase?"

"They were on call."

"While an employee was on call, was the employee required to be any particular place?"

Bolton paused. "No. I believe it was commonly understood they would be within the company's service area."

"What is the company's service area?"

"Boston and the surrounding suburbs. Particularly the suburbs west and north of Boston."

"Being on call is different than being on the job, isn't it?" Simon asked.

Again Bolton paused. "When an employee is on call, he's not being paid if that's what you mean."

"Is it permissible for an employee to run personal errands while on call?"

Bolton turned toward Anderson and sighed. "I suppose so."

"If an employee was on call and was running a personal errand and got a call to go to one of the company's customers, what was the employee supposed to do in that situation?"

"The employee would be expected to service the customer."

"Who else at Wise Computer knew that employee cell phones contained GPS?"

"Nancy Prince and Ruth Fine."

"Who are they?"

"Nancy is the office manager and Ruth is her assistant. They run the office and direct employees to respond to our customers' calls."

"Did you instruct them not to tell employees about the GPS?"

Bolton hesitated a beat. "Yes."

"While they worked for your company did either Herbert Stanton or Millie Lane ever fail to respond to a Wise Computer customer in a timely manner?"

Bolton took his time considering the question. "Not that I recall."

"Did you ever mention to either of them that they were untimely getting to an assignment?"

"Not that I recall."

Simon reached for a stack of papers. "You provided performance evaluations for Mr. Stanton and Ms. Lane. Is it correct that their employee evaluations were uniformly positive?"

Bolton shifted in his chair. "I would say that's correct."

"Did you perform their evaluations?"

"Yes."

"Why did you fire Mr. Stanton and Ms. Lane."

"Nancy Prince and Ruth Fine reported to me that their GPS readings had them at various motels."

"Does that mean you fired them because GPS reports had them at the same place at the same time?"

"It was because they were at motels. It wasn't as if they were meeting for coffee."

"How did you know they were at motels?"

"We looked up the locations."

"What were they meeting for?"

"It looked to me like they were having an affair."

"Before you fired them, did you know for a fact that they were having an affair?"

"I didn't ask them, but it was pretty obvious."

"Then you didn't know for sure they were having an affair when you fired them. Is that correct?"

"It was pretty clear to me."

"But you weren't one hundred percent sure when you fired them, were you?"

"Not one hundred percent sure but it was pretty obvious what was going on."

"What do you mean by an affair?" Simon asked.

"A sexual relationship."

"Was there a Wise Computer rule that stated employees couldn't have a sexual relationship?"

"Not as such."

"Was there such a rule or not?"

"No. But some things are just obvious."

"When you fired Mr. Stanton and Ms. Lane, did you mention the GPS in their cell phones?"

"Yes."

"Did word of the GPS get out to other employees after Mr. Stanton and Ms. Lane were fired?"

"Yes."

"Did any employee have a negative reaction to the GPS?"

"Two employees quit when they found out."

"Would that be Mr. Sam Reynolds and Ms. Lucille Stone?"

"Yes."

"What did Mr. Reynolds say to you when he quit?"

"I don't remember exactly. He was very angry."

"Isn't it a fact that Mr. Reynolds called you a sneaky bastard and told you to shove the company cell phone up your ass?"

Bolton colored. Carpenter noticed no change in Simon's demeanor or tone of voice.

"He probably said something like that."

"Does Wise Computer still place GPS in employees' cell phones?"

"Yes."

"Are employees currently advised about the GPS feature?"

"Yes."

"After Mr. Stanton and Ms. Lane sued your company, did you consult with legal counsel about whether employees should be advised about the GPS in their cell phones?"

"Objection," Anderson said. "You may answer."

"Yes."

"Would that be Mr. Anderson?"

Bolton looked at Anderson who was busily writing. "Yes."

"Let's break for ten minutes," Simon said.

"I've pretty much gone through my outline," Simon said, after they had retreated to Carpenter's office. "Is there anything else I should be asking him?"

Carpenter consulted his notes. He couldn't think of any major point Simon had failed to cover. "You did well. I like the way you handled the deposition. You listened to his answers and followed up on them. You weren't wedded to your outline."

"Thanks. I have to say this is fun."

Simon clearly was enjoying himself. Some people simply thrived on conflict. Carpenter knew he was one of those people.

"Ask him whether customers asked for Stanton and Lane after he fired them," Carpenter suggested. "We already know the answer to that, but let's see what Bolton says."

Simon nodded. "What happens after today's deposition?"

"Anderson will probably depose Stanton and Lane. My guess is that we'll get a lousy settlement offer before that happens."

"Define lousy."

"Ten thousand give or take."

"Define not lousy."

"Six figures."

Simon looked shocked. "They'd never settle for anything like that."

"You're right," Carpenter confirmed. "I've got a hunch they'll go as high as twenty-five thousand."

"The contingency would only apply to anything recovered above fifteen thousand," Simon stated the obvious, and Carpenter realized the young lawyer was focusing on the modest contingency fee a $25,000 settlement would yield.

"Would you recommend that Stanton and Lane accept a twenty-five-thousand-dollar offer?" Simon asked.

Carpenter shook his head. "I'd go over the offer in detail, but this is one of those cases where I'd roll the dice and see if a jury sticks it to Wise Computer."

"I don't have a feel for any of this," Simon confessed.

"What makes you think I do," Carpenter said. "No matter what anyone tells you, whether to settle a case is a little like flying blind. You end up going with your instincts on what to recommend to a client. It comes down to playing a hunch."

"They don't teach any of this in law school," Simon said.

"That's probably because they would never be able to come up with a title for the course. Something like 'Settling a Case—the Art of Reading Tea Leaves.'"

Simon grinned and looked at his watch. "I guess we better wrap this up."

67

Rachel was on the hardwood floor of Philly's living room playing with Daisy. Philly had shown Rachel how to make Daisy inch forward when she was on her stomach on a smooth surface. You took your hand and put mild pressure on Daisy's feet and Daisy would respond with what struck Philly as some atavistic frog kick against the hand exerting pressure. Paul had showed her that little game and Daisy never tired of it when she was fully awake.

Rachel had organized the documents that Crowe Investment Strategies had produced in Frederick Chun's case before the Massachusetts Commission Against Discrimination into neat stacks on the dining room table and as Philly reviewed the papers, she tried not to be distracted by Rachel's giggles and words of encouragement to her daughter.

Crowe Investment Strategies had produced an impressive number of personal employee e-mails containing off-color jokes ranging from dumb blonde jokes to Polish jokes to jokes of a sexually explicit nature that didn't leave much to the imagination and contained the f-word, the c-word, and several b-words.

Crowe Investment Strategies had fired only seven employees in the last three years—three white males, two white females, an African-American, and a Hispanic. No employee had been fired for sending or receiving off-color jokes via e-mail. Yet Chun had been fired because he had received a link to a web site that he never looked at.

"I think she's tiring of this game," Rachel's voice came from the floor.

"Try holding her."

Crowe Investment Strategies had requested that Chun's case be dismissed because there was no probable cause to support a conclusion that the company had discriminated against Chun because he was Asian. Philly played out a counter argument and then began to jot down key phrases on her notepad:

- *environment where sexual references and dirty jokes were permitted in company e-mails*
- *employees of non-Asian lineage permitted to work at Crowe despite receiving and sending sexually explicit jokes in Crowe e-mails*
- *one of only two Asian employees fired because of an e-mail containing a link with a sexually suggestive title*

Daisy was now reaching for one of Rachel's breasts and Philly decided to rescue the young lawyer. She moved to the floor and took charge of Daisy while passing Rachel her notepad.

Rachel reviewed Philly's notes and then became lost in thought. "Do you really think Chun was fired because he was Asian?"

"No. But we're damn well going to try to make that case."

"Isn't that . . . you know . . ."

"Dishonest?"

"Well . . . Overreaching is the word I would use," Rachel said.

"What if it is?"

"I guess I don't feel right about that."

"Do you think that Chun was treated unfairly?" Philly asked.

"Definitely."

"Maybe if Crowe Investment Strategies is treated unfairly, the unfairness will even out."

"Do you really believe that?"

Philly appreciated that Rachel was sincere in her misgivings about raising a claim that appeared to be borderline. "It doesn't matter what we believe. What matters is what some hearing officer is going to do. Which one of us is going to do the legal memorandum?"

"I'll do the memorandum," Rachel said.

"Keep it short and sweet. There's one other matter we need to discuss. I've read over the discovery requests that Gerald Hatch needs to respond to. I want you to take the first shot at preparing Gerald's answers to interrogatories. I'll deal with the documents Gerald has to produce. Okay?"

Rachel nodded. "May I ask you something?"

"Sure."

"Simon and I were talking. You've been throwing a lot of work our way and we're very grateful. But we were wondering where you saw this heading. Have you given any further thought to forming a firm now that Simon and I are in the picture?"

Philly was unprepared for the question. "I don't have an answer for you. Carpenter knew that with a newborn I'd be out of action and he thought of you and Simon to bridge the gap. Personally, I haven't thought about anything more than keeping my head above water while dealing with Daisy. But let me talk to Carpenter about your question."

"Okay," Rachel said deferentially, and Philly realized how hard it had been for her to ask her probing question.

"How's your paralegal job going?" Philly asked.

Rachel shrugged. "Truthfully, I wish I could give it up. But financially, I can't afford to do that. I'm just lucky they're flexible about when I do my work."

Rachel and Simon might force her to reconsider her position on forming a firm. And God only knew what Carpenter would say now. Nothing stayed anchored. Not a goddamn thing.

68

"Gerald and I are going to take a brief walk," Philly said. Neither Wendy Hatch nor Gerald looked pleased with that arrangement.

Gerald grudgingly helped her navigate the stroller out the front door. Philly's last look at Wendy Hatch before the door closed was of the woman sitting in one of the easy chairs, eyes closed, probably wishing she could be transported instantly elsewhere.

"Why do we have to walk?" Gerald complained. "It's hot out here."

Philly didn't respond. She decided to reverse the direction of the walk she took with Paul. Daisy was awake, comfortably supported by folded up bath towels, and the warm sun felt good. If she wasn't accompanied by a sullen teenager, Philly thought the outing would be just about perfect.

"Aren't you going to say anything?" Gerald asked when they turned at the first corner they came to.

"You've met Rachel Boyle. She's going to draft answers to the questions you have to answer. Have you read those questions?"

"Yeah."

"Did you understand them?"

"I don't know. Some of them had words I didn't understand. And I didn't understand all the directions on how to answer."

"Rachel and I will deal with the legalese. You need to think about what your answers are going to be to the questions about your fight with the Mercer boy. Have you given any thought to that?"

"I already told you what happened. How many times do I have to go over that shit?"

"You're going to have to go over the fight a lot more times. You're probably going to have your deposition taken. That means you'll be placed under oath and asked a lot of questions that you have to answer truthfully."

"Do I have to do that?"

Philly heard the fear in Gerald's voice. In her experience, under any tough kid's hard surface there were soft pockets that held hidden terrors.

"Yeah, you do. I'll be helping you with that."

"That sucks."

Philly believed that she could give Gerald a few pointers on all the things in life that sucked. Instead she focused on the lawsuit facing him. "It's been a while since we talked. Have you had any further thoughts about your fight with the Mercer boy?"

Gerald gave a violent kick to a small stone that was in his path. "Not really."

"You remembered how Mercer probably gave you false test answers to copy. Did anything else like that come to mind?"

In the summer heat, Gerald was wearing work boots. As he trod heavily beside her, Philly tried not to think about getting kicked with those boots. Gerald really was a stereotypical, hulking teenager.

"Not really," Gerald repeated.

"Do you know for sure that the Mercer boy got a hundred on the chemistry test?"

"Yeah. He showed me the paper."

"Did you show him your test paper?"

"No. Why would I do that? I failed the fucking test."

"How come he showed you his paper?"

"How the hell do I know? He just did."

They had come to the half way point and Philly turned the stroller to the left.

"Did he show you his chemistry test paper out of the blue?"

"Yeah, that's what I've been saying.

"Did he say anything to you?"

Gerald slowed and then had to pick up his pace to catch up with the stroller.

"He said, 'Look what I got.' Then he asked me how I did."

"What did you answer?"

"I told him to go fuck himself. I was ready to hit the little shit right then."

"Why?"

"Because of the look on his face. He was rubbing my nose in it."

"You mean he was gloating?"

"Yeah. Just because he's smart, he didn't have to rub my nose in it."

Daisy began to squirm and complain. Philly stopped the stroller and peeked inside. Daisy wasn't happy. Philly undid the straps holding her in and hoisted her into the sunshine. Freed of the stroller and in her mother's arms, Daisy began to look around.

"You mind holding her?" Philly said, presenting her daughter.

Gerald literally recoiled and Philly tried not to laugh. "Give me a hand here," she directed the teenager. She got Daisy settled in Gerald's arms and instructed him how to support her head.

"Thanks," Philly said as she started the stroller forward.

"Why don't you take your kid and I'll push that thing?"

Philly ignored the question. "Had Mercer ever showed you one of his test papers before?"

Gerald didn't answer. He was concentrating, trying to walk carefully while keeping up.

"Maybe. I'm not sure. The thing is, in homeroom class he was always boasting about his good grades."

"Really?"

"I used to tell him to shut his mouth, but he never did."

"This is helpful," Philly said, as she considered how to use the information. She changed subjects. "Why do you give your parents such a hard time?"

"That's none of your business. Come on, take your kid."

Philly pressed forward. "I need to understand you better, Gerald. I'm asking you to help me. When I was your age, I was a terror. You may find it hard to believe, but I was one of those high school girls who dressed punk. Back in those days I had blue hair, garish lipstick, you name it. I didn't talk to my parents about anything. I was pretty sure they wished they could ship me somewhere."

Gerald managed to keep up with the stroller. He continued to be careful where he stepped, trying to avoid tripping. His look of concentration softened his features. When they reached the final corner, Philly thought briefly of reclaiming Daisy. Instead, she made the turn and kept moving.

"They're always on my case about me doing lousy in school," Gerald said, when Philly had thought he had forgotten her question.

"Why do you do lousy in school?"

"Probably because I'm not too smart."

"Don't take this the wrong way," Philly said, "but I don't buy that. I did okay in school and if I could do okay, anyone can."

"I hate school."

"In high school, I didn't like school much either. Is there any subject you like even a little bit?"

Philly figured that Gerald would blow off the question but after they had progressed a little further he said, "Spanish is okay."

"No kidding." Philly hadn't expected that answer. "Do you do okay grade-wise in Spanish?"

"I get B's."

"You know, the two people I own my house with speak Spanish. Do you have anyone to practice on?"

"Not really."

They arrived at the house. "Let's switch," she said, and Gerald handed off Daisy who smiled. "The stroller folds up."

Gerald collapsed the stroller and hefted it easily.

"Can I speak frankly to you, Gerald, without you getting pissed off?"

"I guess so," Gerald said without conviction.

"Kicking the shit out of the Mercer boy was wrong. I think you know that. You could have injured him more seriously than you did and, if that had happened, I don't believe you'd feel very good about it. As far as the court case goes, the important thing is to tell the truth and put the case behind you. I'm going to help you do that. It's not going to be easy, but you're going to get through it with my help. Anything you want to say to me?"

"Not really."

"Do you have any interest in practicing your Spanish with my housemates?"

Philly turned to nuzzle Daisy, so Gerald wouldn't think she was staring at the way he was blushing.

"Maybe. I guess so."

"Good. I'll try to set that up. Thanks for coming over and talking. I'll be in touch. Let's go rescue your mother."

September

Philly's Attraction Playlist

Sex on Fire

Kings of Leon

69

In the early September morning, Philly was in her home office nursing Daisy, thinking that her daughter was coming up on two months old. The fact that she was now practicing law in a half-assed way, in fits and spurts, no longer bothered her. She wasn't being fair to the geezer, but she didn't care. Carpenter, bless his heart, hadn't laid a guilt trip on her, so she was determined to take advantage of the gift of time he was giving her. Things had a way of evening out; no doubt she'd be repaying him sometime in the future. His cancer could exert itself without warning.

Her office phone startled her, but Daisy showed no reaction to the sound.

"Philomena Piper."

"It's George Norris. Is this a bad time?"

"I've already told you, George, that no time is bad when it comes to you."

"Yeah, right. Listen, the last changes you made to the settlement agreement are okay. The document's done. We have a deal."

"That's great."

"Is the Harrington kid . . . Luke . . . okay? This business with the closet never sat right with me."

There were some lawyers you could have a frank, off-the-record discussion with. Philly didn't think that Norris was one of those lawyers. "He's been okay so far," Philly answered.

"That's all right," Norris said. "I didn't really expect you to answer my question."

Daisy was slowing down, but lulls were deceiving—a second wind could kick in at any time.

They made arrangements for the necessary documents, and then there was a pause. Philly wondered whether Norris had something else on his mind.

"Just so you know," Norris said, "I recommended the settlement agreement to Dixfield."

"Jesus, George, I hope you're okay. It's not like you to open up. I'm worried about you."

"Yeah, right. I've got to get going."

"Thanks for helping to get this resolved. It was good to work with you again."

"Don't push it," Norris said, before disconnecting.

Daisy had conked out. Philly moved her daughter to her shoulder. Burping Daisy had proved to be an adventure. You could never tell what was going to emerge.

As she gently rubbed Daisy's back, Philly thought about Carpenter's miserable task today. The IEP hearing in the Lawson case was scheduled to be reopened in thirty minutes. Labor Day was less than a week away, and it was unclear where, whether, and under what conditions Jack Lawson would attend school. The Lawsons had refused to talk to Jack Lawson's pediatrician about upping the dosages of the boy's medications. While Carpenter loved a challenge, Philly believed that the Lawsons hadn't left him with any cards to play.

Benjamin Frye, the senior administrative magistrate assigned to the Lawsons' case, called for order. "I've allowed Stonington's motion to reopen the hearing because there is newly discovered evidence that Jack Lawson seriously injured another child at a summer camp. I'm going to want to hear from Mrs. Lawson on what is currently going on with her son. I'm also going to want to hear from Maryanne Fairmount who testified for the Lawsons and Florence Jefferson who testified for Stonington. I don't require opening statements from counsel, and I'd like to start with Ms. Lawson."

Sylvia Lawson made her way to the witness chair near where Frye was sitting.

"She looks awful," Rachel whispered. Carpenter agreed. The dark circles under Sylvia Lawson's eyes were more pronounced and she appeared even thinner than she had in the past. Her haunted look boded ill.

"You are still under oath," Frye reminded the witness. "I'm going to ask you a few questions to speed this hearing up and then the attorneys may have further questions for you. Let's begin. Since school ended how has your son been behaving and acting?"

"He's much more active than he used to be," Lawson started off, her voice weak. "There's no sign of the lethargy he used to experience. He's more assertive." Lawson paused and faced Frye. "Is that the kind of information you're looking for?" she asked.

"Yes, thank you," Frye said. Carpenter sensed that the magistrate had picked up on Lawson's nervousness and was trying to put her at ease. "Could you also tell us whether since school let out, Jack's behavior has ever been difficult to control."

Lawson tensed in her chair. "He's gotten angry on occasion and we've had to send him to his room."

"What kind of things make him angry?"

"Being told it's bedtime. Being told he can't have dessert until he finishes his dinner. There were days when he didn't want to go to summer camp."

"Why did you decide to send Jack to summer camp without monitors?" Frye asked.

"Max and I didn't think it was necessary. This was a summer camp, not school."

"I don't understand. Why is that distinction important?"

"Because a camp is play and a school is mostly learning."

Carpenter liked Lawson's answer. Maybe she would surprise him with an ability to think on her feet. He didn't know what to expect from his client; the Lawsons had turned him down when he had offered to take Sylvia Lawson through a dry run of the questions she would likely be asked.

"Attorney Lannon mentioned that the camp was not told about Jack being monitored at school. If that is the case, why didn't you mention to the camp that Jack had been monitored at school?"

"The camp didn't ask. The camp had an information form that had to be filled out. The form asked for a listing of Jack's medications and we provided that information."

Frye frowned and wrote on his notepad.

"How do you explain Jack's hurting another camper?"

"I really can't explain it. For a while Jack didn't want to talk about it. When he did discuss it, he said that the girl who was injured and some of her friends were calling him names. They said he was a dork and a freak—things like that. I guess Jack took exception and there was some back and forth pushing and shoving. Things must have escalated beyond words."

Frye again wrote on his notepad. When he looked up, his frown remained in place.

Frye regarded Lawson for a long moment and then turned to Carpenter. "Do you have any questions for your client?"

"No," Carpenter said.

"What about you Mr. Lannon?"

"Just a few Your Honor," and Carpenter knew they were in for a long bout of cross-examination.

"When Jack has been sent to his room, have you or your husband had to take him to his room forcibly?"

Lawson colored. "Sometimes."

"On those occasions did he put up physical resistance?"

"He was kicking and writhing a few times, that kind of thing."

"On those occasions, what kind of force did you have to use to get him to his room?"

"We had to grab hold of him."

"Did you have to lift him off the ground?"

Lawson took a deep breath. "I think that might have happened on a few occasions."

"Before the medication reductions, did you ever have to take Jack forcibly to his room?"

"No."

"In fact, before the medication reductions, Jack didn't exhibit the physical resistance you just told us about, did he?"

"No, he didn't."

"What was your understanding as to why monitors were in place at Jack's school?"

Lawson shifted in her chair. Carpenter tried to think of a way to break Lannon's rhythm. He recognized Lannon's tactic because it was one he employed—sudden shifts in subject matter to try to catch a witness off guard.

"I believe the monitors were there to prevent anything dangerous happening."

"While the monitors were in place at school, isn't it true that they had to intervene in a number of playground incidents involving Jack?"

"Yes."

"Did the monitors ever have to intervene while Jack was in a classroom?"

"Not that I remember."

"Playground activity at Jack's school involved play, didn't it?"

"Yes."

"Yet you told us that you didn't think monitors were necessary at summer camp because camp was play and school involved learning. But isn't it true that when the monitors had to intervene at school it was during playtime?"

"Yes."

"So why weren't monitors necessary at camp which is also playtime as you've told us?"

Carpenter gave Lannon credit. He'd come up with an effective way to debunk the distinction that Lawson had drawn.

"Max and I just thought that camp was different from school."

Carpenter thought that Lawson's attempt at a saving answer sounded lame. Frye regarded her severely and then began writing on his notepad.

"Did it occur to you, Ms. Lawson, that the recent physical resistance Jack exhibited after school let out might be related to his reduced medications?"

"I don't remember thinking about that connection."

"To what did you attribute his physical resistance behavior that led to his writhing and kicking?"

"I don't know that I attributed it to anything," Lawson said, not sounding defensive. "To be frank with you, there was a part of me that was happy to see him respond physically when he objected to such things as being told to go to bed. At those times, he seemed to be more like a regular kid. It's hard to explain, but boys don't always like to be told what to do and Jack was behaving like a boy."

Carpenter silently applauded Lawson. She was getting hammered by Lannon yet was still often able to spin the facts in a way that supported what she wanted to accomplish for her son.

"Since the last hearing in this case, has Jack seen his pediatrician?"

"No."

"Did you inform Jack's pediatrician about the camp incident or any of the kicking and writhing incidents?"

"No."

"Have you talked with Jack's pediatrician since the last hearing?"

"No."

Lannon paused and regarded Lawson with a hard stare. Frye made some notes and again frowned.

"Isn't it true that you refuse to acknowledge the possibility that Jack's reduced medications make him a danger to others and perhaps himself?"

Lawson again colored and broke off eye contact with Lannon. "I wouldn't say that."

"Tell me, Ms. Lawson, do you agree that it's possible Jack's reduced medications make him a danger to others and perhaps himself?"

"Anything is possible."

"I didn't ask you whether anything was possible," Lannon raised his voice. "I asked you whether it was possible that Jack's reduced medications make him a danger to others and perhaps himself. Please answer *that* question."

"I suppose that's possible."

"What have you done to verify whether Jack's reduced medications make him a danger to others or himself?"

"I didn't do anything. Just because something's remotely possible doesn't mean I had to do something."

"You don't want your son on any medication, do you?"

"That's my hope for Jack, that he will be off medications entirely."

"To achieve that hope, isn't it true that you prefer to run the risk of having Jack harm someone else or himself rather than try to discover whether his reduced medications make him dangerous?"

"I don't agree with that."

"Will you agree to have the blood level of Jack's medication levels tested, and have his dosages reviewed by his pediatrician?"

"I'm not prepared to agree to that."

"Will you agree to have Jack's medication dosages reviewed by a physician chosen by the Stonington school system?"

"No."

"Why are you opposed to having Jack's medication levels and the dosages reviewed?"

"I don't believe it's necessary. Jack's been through a lot and I don't believe in putting him through anything that's unnecessary."

"Don't you want to rule out the possibility that Jack is a danger to others and himself?"

"I don't believe in the premise of your question. I don't believe Jack is dangerous to anyone."

"So why do you resist efforts that might confirm your beliefs."

"It's like I said. Jack has been through a lot and this testing you keep talking about isn't necessary."

"You have no medical training, correct?"

"That's correct."

"Nothing further," Lannon said, and sat down.

"Mr. Carpenter?" Frye asked.

"A moment please." Carpenter held up his notepad to shield his face from Frye and drew close to Rachel. "What do you think?" he whispered.

"I think she came across as unreasonable," Rachel whispered back.

Carpenter nodded. He didn't see an easy way to dispel the unreasonable label that Rachel had correctly identified. Maybe the thing to do was confront Lannon's strategy head on.

Carpenter rose slowly. He couldn't read Lawson's expression. Maybe she was sending him silent vibes to sit his ass down and shut his mouth.

"Tell me, Ms. Lawson. Did you get the sense from Mr. Lannon's most recent questions that he was trying to paint you as unreasonable for not wanting Jack's medication levels reviewed further?"

Lawson nodded. “Yes, I think that’s what he was trying to do.”

“Well then, help us out. Aren’t you being unreasonable by not agreeing to further evaluation of Jack’s medication levels?”

“I don’t think I’m being unreasonable.”

“Why not?”

Lawson looked to the rear of the hearing room. Carpenter turned briefly, followed her gaze, and saw Max Lawson leaning forward in his seat. “I’m Jack’s mother,” Sylvia Lawson said forcefully. “Mr. Lannon can suggest whatever he wants but he’s just a lawyer. He doesn’t know Jack. He doesn’t love Jack. Jack’s just a name to him. It’s true that I want what’s best for Jack. It’s not unreasonable for a mother to want what’s best for her son. Stonington wants to do what’s easiest for Stonington. They want Jack medicated so he doesn’t stand out, doesn’t make waves. That’s not what I want for my son. I want my son to be alive. I want him to get his life back even if that life is a little messy. I’ll tell you what this whole case reminds me of. It reminds me of that article in the newspaper recently that described how patients in nursing homes were on antipsychotic drugs to make them calmer. That’s what institutions do—they sedate people. I’m damned if I’m going to remain silent while Stonington tries to sedate my son.”

Carpenter didn’t know what he was expecting when he asked Lawson his open-ended question, but he certainly wasn’t anticipating the emotional response she had come up with. He again leaned down to confer with Rachel. “I’m thinking of shutting my mouth,” he whispered.

“Works for me,” Rachel whispered back.

“Nothing further.”

“Nothing further,” Lannon echoed.

“We’ll take a short recess,” Frye announced.

“Dr. Jefferson, you were present when Ms. Lawson testified,” Frye began after asking Florence Jefferson to take the witness chair. “Does anything she said change the testimony you provided at the previous hearing?”

“I wouldn’t change a word of what I said at the last hearing,” Jefferson said with smug satisfaction. “What I heard today from Ms. Lawson about the camp incident and about the way Jack Lawson has needed to be restrained physically at home simply confirms everything I said previously. The reduced medications aren’t working no matter how deeply Ms. Lawson wishes they were. There can no longer be any doubt that Jack Lawson presents a physical danger to others and likely to himself. He should not be allowed to return to any school with the reduced medications ordered by the court. And for the record, just to be complete, it was outrageous for the Lawsons to send their son to camp without monitors."

"Mr. Lannon—do you have any questions for your witness?" Frye asked.

Lannon regarded Jefferson thoughtfully for a long moment. "No, Your Honor."

"Mr. Carpenter?"

Carpenter rose slowly, wondering how he was going to earn his fee. Jefferson struck him as in immovable object and he had no irresistible force to direct her way.

"You're familiar with bullying in school, aren't you, Dr. Jefferson?"

"Very much so. Two student suicides attributable to bullying have been very much in the news and have been responsible for anti-bullying legislation."

"In your experience, may bullying manifest itself through words as opposed to physical conduct?"

"Oh, yes. Words can be very harmful and hurtful."

"In your opinion, should a student have to put up with harmful words in a school environment?"

"In my opinion, no."

"Would you agree, Dr. Jefferson, that one response a student might make to harmful words is to refuse to accept them?"

"That's a possible response," Jefferson conceded.

"So when Jack Lawson took exception to being called a 'dork' and a 'freak,' his taking exception to those hurtful words was appropriate, wasn't it?"

"It's not appropriate to break a student's collarbone."

"I move to strike the witness' answer," Carpenter directed at Frye.

"Denied," Frye ruled, and Carpenter was now sure which way the magistrate was leaning.

"Who started the physical altercation at summer camp?" Carpenter asked.

"I don't know."

"Isn't it true that a student who is subject to inappropriate physical contact or verbal bullying might respond physically?"

"That certainly happens."

Carpenter decided to give Frye another chance. "Your Honor, I again move to strike Dr. Jefferson's previous answer to the effect it is not appropriate to break a student's collarbone. The witness has no idea who started the physical altercation that occurred at the summer camp and has acknowledged that aggressive physical or verbal conduct may be responded to physically."

Frye regarded Carpenter evenly. "You've made your point, Mr. Carpenter. I'm again going to deny your motion, but I may choose not to give Dr. Jefferson's answer much weight."

Carpenter nodded. Frye had thrown him the only bone he was going to get.

"Should the girl who called Jack Lawson a 'dork' and a 'freak' be required to take medication so that she might behave less aggressively and stop using words in a bullying fashion?

"Objection!" Lannon was on his feet.

"Where are you going with this, Mr. Carpenter?" Frye inquired.

"I'll know when I get there," Carpenter fired back. "This is cross-examination and I request some leeway."

"I think you're moving far afield," Frye said. "But I'll allow your question. Do you need the question repeated, Dr. Jefferson?"

Dr. Jefferson shook her head. "It doesn't follow from playground insults that the student issuing the insults should be required to be on medications."

"Why not?" Carpenter thundered. "We've heard from you that harmful words constitute bullying. Why shouldn't someone who bullies by words such as 'dork' and 'freak' be on medication?"

"You're being absurd," Jefferson said.

"Answer my question," Carpenter demanded.

"Everyone calm down," Frye said. "Ask another question, Mr. Carpenter."

"In your experience, may bullying behavior be successfully addressed through medication?"

"That depends. It would depend on the situation but it's certainly possible."

"Bullying is dangerous, isn't it?"

"In my opinion it is."

"So why shouldn't any student who exhibits bullying behavior be tested to see if medication would curb the bullying and eliminate the danger the bullying presents?"

"Objection," Lannon said.

"Overruled."

"Not every epithet uttered in a school setting indicates a condition that requires medication for the student who uttered the epithet," Jefferson said.

"I'm confused," Carpenter said, hoping that by shaking his head he was exhibiting genuine bewilderment. "Without evaluating a bully for the need for medication, how would it be possible to determine whether medication might stop the bullying?"

"It wouldn't" Jefferson conceded.

"No further questions," Carpenter said, taking his seat.

Lannon rose. "Is it feasible or desirable to determine the need for medication for every student who utters a harsh word in a school environment?"

"No."

"No further questions."

"Nothing further," Carpenter said.

Maryanne Fairmount settled into the witness chair looking composed.

"Thank you for returning to testify Dr. Fairmount," Frye began. "You've listened to Ms. Lawson testify and I'm going to ask you the question I put to Dr. Jefferson. Is there anything you wish to change with respect to your previous testimony?"

"I'm glad to be here," Fairmount said equably. "Yes, there is one thing I'd add. I think it would be appropriate to have Jack be seen by his pediatrician after the pediatrician is briefed on the camping incident and Jack's behavior at home that has changed."

"Why is that?" Frye followed up.

"Because it seems to me that's the commonsense thing to do. The summer camp incident we've heard about strikes me as murky. There's no clear indication of who started it, what was said, the tone of what was said, and whether the injured girl simply landed wrong when she hit the ground, et cetera. It may be that medication changes would be appropriate for Jack and it may be that such changes shouldn't be made."

"If I understand you," Frye said, "you think that Ms. Lawson is off base by not having Jack seen by his pediatrician."

"I'm not saying Ms. Lawson is off base or on base. What I am saying is that in my opinion it makes sense for Jack Lawson to be seen by his pediatrician. As Jack's mother, Ms. Lawson's different view is entitled to serious respect."

"Knowing what you know, would you take Jack into your school if he was not seen by his pediatrician?"

"Probably not," Fairmount replied without hesitation.

"Is that because you think Jack would present a danger at your school?"

"No. It's because I regard it as prudent to have a medical evaluation of Jack take place. The reduced medications did a lot of good things for Jack. He became more engaged, more sociable, less lethargic. It may be that the medications need to be adjusted further. For all I know, the proper medication dosages may be somewhere between what Stonington is insisting on and the current reduced levels."

Frye regarded Fairmount intently and then began to write on his notepad. Carpenter glanced behind him. Predictably, neither Sylvia nor Max Lawson looked happy. Yet had Fairmount disagreed with Jack needing to be seen by a physician, she would have lost all credibility with Frye.

Frye looked up. "Any questions for Dr. Fairmount, Mr. Carpenter?"

"No, Your Honor."

"Mr. Lannon?"

Lannon stood and glanced at his notepad. "Is it correct that you disagree with Ms. Lawson as to whether Jack should be evaluated by a physician?"

"Yes, I do."

"Would you also agree that Mrs. Lawson's position suggests that she is not necessarily acting in her son's best interests in this case?"

"No."

"Why is that?"

"Ms. Lawson sincerely believes that a further physician evaluation of Jack is not necessary and not in Jack's best interests. She may be right; she certainly knows her son a lot better than I do. I simply disagree with her for the reason I've stated. I think it makes sense for Jack to be seen by a physician."

"Nothing further," Lannon said.

"Nothing further," Carpenter repeated.

"Does anyone have any additional testimony to present?" Frye asked.

Lannon rose. "The summer camp owner is present."

At the rear of the hearing room, an intense, wiry man with a salt and pepper buzz cut looked loaded for bear.

"It's your decision, Mr. Lannon," Frye said. "Keep in mind what Ms. Lawson acknowledged in terms of what she did and didn't tell the camp."

Shit, Carpenter thought. Frye had just announced that he had heard all he had needed to hear. An experienced litigator like Lannon would get the message.

"I believe it's not necessary to call an additional witness," Lannon said.

"In that case," Frye said, "I have one last question for Ms. Lawson. Would you please stand Ms. Lawson? There's no need to come back up here to the witness chair. My question is, are you still unwilling to have your son seen by a physician before I decide this case?"

Carpenter knew what his client's answer would be, but nevertheless held his breath.

"I'm still unwilling," Sylvia Lawson said.

Carpenter sighed inwardly. Sylvia Lawson was too myopic to see Frye's question for the last chance it was.

"I'm going to conclude this reopened hearing." Frye declared. "I don't require any further written materials from the parties. You'll have my decision shortly. Thank you all for attending."

When Frye left the hearing room, Carpenter made it a point to shake hands with Lannon. "Nice job," he said.

"You too," Lannon said. "It's nice to see you again Ms. Boyle."

Rachel smiled and offered her hand.

"Any predictions?" Lannon asked.

"I'd rather not go there," Carpenter said.

Carpenter told Maryanne Fairmount to beat a retreat so the educator wasn't around for what he expected to be a grim post mortem with the Lawsons. The Lawsons struck Carpenter as torn—they didn't seem to want anything to do with him, but appeared anxious to learn his assessment of the reopened hearing.

"How do you think it went?" Max Lawson inquired tentatively.

Carpenter knew that he should be feeling sympathy for his clients, but the truth was that he'd had his fill of them.

"You did an excellent job handling the magistrate's questions and Mr. Lannon's questions," Carpenter said to Sylvia Lawson.

"But?" said Max Lawson with bitterness.

"I think you know what the but is," Carpenter said. "The magistrate appeared to be concerned about your unwillingness to have Jack seen by a physician. That may have tipped the scales against you."

"Fairmount didn't help us," Sylvia Lawson snapped, as angry as her husband.

"Actually she did," Carpenter said. "The magistrate could adopt Dr. Fairmount's suggestion that Jack be evaluated before he makes a final decision." Carpenter didn't see Frye doing any such thing, but he was damned if he was going to let the Lawsons take shots at Fairmount because she was reasonable and they were not.

The Lawsons exchanged a quick glance. "We've got to get going," Max Lawson said, and the couple left without a thank you, or goodbye.

"They're not happy," Rachel stated the obvious.

"It's their own goddamn fault," Carpenter said. "But try to tell them that."

70

Philly regretted they didn't have much of a backyard. Raul had gone over the small grassy plot with a rusting hand mower, and they were able to position a number of folding chairs on the patchy grass. The concrete area where the grill stood was pitted and colored a dirty blackish gray. Philly figured that if it got too crowded, people could go up the back steps, pass through the kitchen, and hang out in the living room.

Many of the people who attended her baby shower were present for the afternoon Labor Day cookout: Maxine and Carpenter, Rainy and Monica, the third-floor tenants who had to be an item the way they held hands, Pamela and Genie, and Mace who Philly hadn't wanted to invite but Raul and Isabella did. Pamela's husband George was present as was Paul's daughter, Jennifer, who had Paul's dark coloring and soulful eyes. Both sets of Daisy's grandparents were in attendance; currently her mother was holding Daisy probably thinking that a granddaughter was the last thing in the world Philly would present her with.

Paul and Raul were manning the grill with hamburger, hotdog, and chicken smells coming from that direction. Isabella was keeping the bowls for salad, chips, and garnishes full. Philly liked having nothing to do.

Philly's mother handed Daisy off to Philip's mother and Philly took the moment to study the older generation. The two grandfathers were a mismatch: the elder Sizemore short, stout and balding, her father tall, thin, and with a full head of fair hair. The grandmothers were both tall, but her mother appeared painfully thin next to Philip's stout mother. In the baby's presence, Philly hadn't exchanged a harsh word with her parents so Paul's opinion that a grandchild could only change a lousy parental relationship for the good, had so far proven right. Daisy acted as a buffer.

Gerald Hatch paused at the back kitchen door, taking in the backyard scene with evident misgivings. Philly waved, caught his eye and gestured for him to come outside.

"I'm glad you came," Philly said when Gerald drew near. "Did you bike over?"

Gerald nodded, plainly ill at ease.

"I wish I had time to do more biking," Philly said. "Don't move, wait right here."

Philly appropriated Daisy, telling the grandmothers that she needed to borrow her daughter.

"You remember this character?" she asked Gerald.

Gerald nodded again, and Philly decided that there was a good chance he wouldn't get a word out.

"Do you remember how to hold her?" Philly said, and not waiting for an answer, she settled Daisy in Gerald's arms. "I'll be right back, stay right here. There's someone I want you to meet."

Philly returned to Gerald with Isabella in tow. Isabella had been briefed and greeted Gerald in Spanish. Gerald colored but managed a Spanish greeting in return. Gerald would have to multitask by figuring out how to keep hold of Daisy while conversing in Spanish.

Philly made her way to the grill where the heat was intense.

"Is that the kid you were telling me about?" Paul asked.

Philly nodded. Gerald was concentrating on Isabella but remembering to keep Daisy's head supported. "I didn't think he'd show."

"What's your plan for the kid?" Paul followed up.

"I'm winging it," Philly said. "I think he needs to get out of his own way and step outside his skin."

"Happy?" Paul asked.

"Happy and hungry. I've got dibs on the next piece of chicken that's done."

Philly had returned Daisy to her grandmothers and left Gerald to Isabella. The teenager didn't know it, but he wasn't going to hear a word of English from her housemate. In the living room, Carpenter and Maxine had appropriated the easy chairs. Jenny and Genie were on the floor playing with dolls and coloring books. Carpenter was sucking on a beer and Philly felt an overwhelming urge to have one.

"You going to tell me what the Hatch kid is doing here?" Carpenter asked, as Philly took a seat on the couch.

"No. You're off duty."

"Good luck to you," Maxine said, laughing.

"Do you want me to fill you in on the Lawson hearing?" Carpenter asked.

"No. I'm off duty."

Maxine was studying her. "You look terrific," Maxine said.

"No complaints," Philly said.

"You've got one sweet daughter," Maxine said. "I'd say that motherhood agrees with you."

"I'm enjoying it," Philly said. "I never thought I'd say that. And I have you to thank for it," she directed at Carpenter.

"What the hell are you talking about?"

"I'm talking about all the slack you're cutting me. You're giving me time to enjoy my daughter without making me feel guilty about work. And you were right about Simon and Rachel. They're terrific and it was the right move. So, thank you." Philly wished she had a beer bottle to salute Carpenter with.

"Don't mention it," Carpenter said gruffly.

"No. I'm going to mention it. It needs mentioning. You're really going above and beyond."

"Just stop it!" Carpenter protested. "You'd do the same for me."

"Don't be so sure," Philly said. "Excuse me a minute. I've got to play hostess."

"You need to learn how to take a compliment," Maxine said, after Philly departed for the kitchen.

Maxine was right. It couldn't have been easy for Philly to thank him the way she had. "Whatever," he said to Maxine, finding it mildly depressing to resort to an evasive slacker word.

The front door opened and Simon and Rachel came into the living room. "We're running late," Simon said.

"Not to worry," Carpenter said. "They'll never run out of food or beer and wine."

"I've heard a lot of good things about you two," Maxine said after Carpenter introduced her.

"They're all true," Simon said. "Obviously, any bad things you hear are false. Is talking business allowed?" Simon directed at Carpenter.

"Let me check," Carpenter said, turning to Maxine.

Maxine began laughing. "I need some baby time," she said before heading for the kitchen and the back door.

"Wayne Anderson left me a voice mail message," Simon said. "He wants me to call him after the Labor Day weekend."

"Then call him," Carpenter said.

"They agreed to reject Wise Computer's twelve-thousand-dollar offer. Wayne Anderson's going to take our clients' depositions. We've got the days picked out. Am I defending the depositions?"

"You are," Carpenter said. "What's going on with Frederick Chun?"

"There's going to be a probable cause hearing before the Massachusetts Commission Against Discrimination," Rachel said. "Crowe Investment Strategies is trying to get the case thrown out for lack of evidence that Chun was discriminated against because of his race."

Raul had referred Chun and Philly didn't want to let either down. Daisy let loose with a shriek and Philly debated whether to resort to a pacifier.

"Besides containing dirty jokes, do any of the emails contain links to pornography?" Philly asked.

"Not as far as I can tell," Rachel responded. "But some of the e-mails are pretty raunchy."

Philly was tempted to ask about the worst of the lot but didn't want to embarrass Rachel. "How's your legal memorandum going?" she asked.

"I'll get you a draft shortly."

"I think you should argue at the probable cause hearing," Philly said.

"Let's talk about that after you've reviewed my memorandum," Rachel said.

"What's going on in the Hatch case?" Carpenter asked.

"We've filed responses to Martin Mercer's discovery," Philly said. "I suspect Gerald will be deposed shortly."

"What's going on with the kid?" Carpenter pursued.

"He's actually coming over for dinner tonight for a Spanish lesson."

"Jesus!" Carpenter exclaimed. "What the hell are you doing with this kid?"

"I'm not sure," Philly admitted.

"I'll call you about that later."

Daisy began to wail.

"I'd better go," Philly said, and she hung up her phone.

"You trying to make friends with the kid?" Carpenter later asked over the phone. "That's never a good idea."

Daisy was down for a nap after feeding, and Philly tried to figure out what she *was* up to with Gerald Hatch. *Was* she trying to make friends with the teenager? "Maybe I am trying to make friends with Gerald. I want him to trust me. I think he's too angry to trust anybody."

"If it's about a settlement in Herbert Stanton's and Millie Lane's case, I thought you'd want to make the call."

"You thought wrong," Carpenter said, and immediately regretted sounding out of sorts. "Sorry, I'm just more cranky than usual."

"That's saying something," Rachel piped up.

"Very funny," Carpenter rejoined, smiling. It was good to see Rachel giving him some of his own medicine. Turning back to Simon, Carpenter said, "Hear him out. Tell him you'll get back to him. Also, he may be calling to schedule Stanton and Lane for depositions."

"Okay, I'll return the call," Simon said.

"I can't stop thinking about the Lawson hearing," Rachel said. "I woke up last night in the middle of the night and couldn't fall back to sleep because I was thinking about it."

"Whereas I slept like a baby," Carpenter said. "There's no point dwelling on that disaster."

Rachel didn't look assuaged.

"Look," Carpenter said. "We advised the Lawsons what we thought was best for their case. They refused to follow that advice. We know which way the chips are going to fall here. We did our best. End of story."

"I keep thinking we should have done more," Rachel said. "It's bugging the hell out of me."

"You've got to move on. All hell is going to break lose in the Top Tier litigation and you're going to need to focus."

Rachel became thoughtful and Carpenter hoped that she would sort through the Lawson debacle and obtain the necessary perspective.

"Where's that beer and wine you were talking about?" Rachel asked.

Philly thought that everyone was having a good time. Maxine sat beside her on the periphery of the small backyard holding Daisy. It seemed like every adult wanted a time with her daughter. Daisy accepted being passed around. She would study each new face wide-eyed and would reach for anything that struck her fancy: eyeglasses, earrings, even a moustache.

"Don't ever think you're letting Carpenter down," Maxine said out of the blue.

Philly knew better than to try to bullshit Maxine. "I am letting him down," she said. "I'm not pulling my weight. But I'm okay with that. I'm not feeling guilty in the least."

"Good. If Carpenter starts to feel put upon, he'll let you know."

"I've been putting off dealing with daycare," Philly said. "I'm going to have to deal with that pretty soon."

"You will," Maxine said. "How's the home office working for you?"

"It's actually great. I'm grateful I don't have to fight my way into Boston."

"I could have used a home office when I had kids," Maxine said. "The technology wasn't there and attitudes were different about letting women work from home. If I'd been able to do that, I think I would have been a better mother."

"I'm sure you were a great mother."

"You're wrong there," Maxine said with feeling. "You keeping up with the AA?"

Philly nodded. "When Carpenter was sucking on a beer I wanted one in the worst way. I guess I'm still in trouble."

"You always will be," Maxine said. "From here on it's a given in your life. You mind I ask you something?"

"Sure," Philly said with misgivings. Maxine was brutally frank and wouldn't hold back on any subject.

"What's the story with you and the police officer?"

Philly smiled. The question was an easy one. "The guy's great," Philly said, thinking of last night when she and Paul had had intercourse for the first time.

"Maybe that's why you're looking so good."

"It definitely helps," Philly said.

Philly had retreated to her second-floor office to nurse Daisy at her desk and was taken aback when Mace entered the room. The willowy blond showed no embarrassment at intruding on an intimate mother-daughter moment. Mace unselfconsciously stood in the doorway and watched Daisy nurse. Philly thought briefly about covering up and then decided not to bother.

"You still pissed off at me?" Mace said.

"I haven't really thought about you. But maybe I've got some resentment. I didn't want you to come today."

"Get over it," Mace said. "Rainy and I did you a favor and you know it. You're not angry with him so you shouldn't be angry with me."

Mace had a point. Still, Mace was so confrontational that Philly found it impossible to express a word of gratitude to her. Saying something nice to Mace was giving in to her, showing weakness. "We're not going to be friends," Philly said.

"I don't give a shit about that. Just be civil."

Mace was making an effort and Philly decided to reciprocate. "Truce," she said.

"Truce," Mace echoed. She looked about the office, taking her time. "Are you keeping up with AA?"

Philly hadn't minded the question coming from Maxine. Coming from Mace the question sounded like Mace was checking up on her. Philly moved Daisy to her other breast. What had Mace said? Be civil. "I've cut down on the meetings since Daisy was born. I'm only going once a week."

"What about the drinking?" Mace asked.

Philly thought the hell with civility. "What's with the third degree?"

"I'm checking up on you. I want to make sure you don't relapse and do something stupid."

Philly paid attention to her daughter and began to calm down. "I still feel like drinking," she said.

"I'm the last person who should be giving advice on this," Mace said. "But if you get the urge to drink, my suggestion is to think of your daughter."

"Point taken," Philly said, borrowing a Carpenter phrase.

"I've got to get going," Mace said. "Thanks for having me over. If you ever need anything I'm around for you. Don't ever forget that."

Mace was out the door when Philly found her voice. "Thanks for coming," she called out.

Monica held Daisy so Philly had her hands free to eat. Paul had used a spicy sauce on some of the chicken and it was delicious.

"I want one of these," Monica said, inclining her head toward Daisy.

"Tell Rainy to get on the stick."

"You know Rainy."

"I thought he was a changed man."

"That's true, he is. But for some things, you need to come at him the long way around so as not to scare him off."

Philly laughed. Monica seemed to have what it took to bring Rainy around on any subject she felt strongly about. Rainy had replaced Raul at the grill and he and Paul were engaged in conversation, knocking back beers. Paul had been a good sport about the cooking. "Rainy seems happy," Philly said.

"We both are. I'm trying to get him to move in with me, but he can't bring himself to move out of that house he's been living in."

"That house," Philly said, "gave me the idea to buy this house."

"Some other people went in with you, right?"

Philly nodded. Isabella was still talking Gerald Hatch's ear off and Raul had joined the discussion. Gerald was going to be fluent in Spanish by the time he got back on his bike. She pointed out Raul and Isabella to Monica.

"How has that worked out?"

"So far so good. Isabella is pregnant so it's going to get interesting in a short while."

Monica stroked Daisy's cheek. The woman was gorgeous, smart, and personable. Rainy would be an ass if he let her slip away. Philly didn't see taking Rainy aside and pointing out the obvious. But then again, what were friends for?

Philly had almost fallen asleep when she heard the door to her bedroom open. Paul was out of his clothes and beside her in an instant. He had gone off to return Jenny to her mother and had promised to come back.

"It's good to be alone," Paul whispered.

"Amen to that," Philly whispered back. "Did you have fun this afternoon?"

"Yeah. It was good to put faces with names. What I can't figure out is how you and Carpenter ever hooked up professionally. Talk about odd couples."

"It works," she said.

"I could see you and Rainy as a couple."

"That didn't work," Philly said, thinking that she and Rainy might have had a different ending if they had started up now.

"Good for me it didn't work," Paul said. "Last night was fun. I was thinking of a repeat performance if you're up for it."

"I know someone who's already up for it. That's not very subtle."

"I can't stop thinking about last night."

Philly pressed against Paul. "Me either."

71

In this morning's mail were two thick envelopes, one from the Department of Administrative Law Appeals, and one from the Board of Bar Overseers. Faced with the choice of which he wanted to hear first—the good news or the bad news—Carpenter usually opted for the bad news. Of course, two pieces of bad news might be facing him. But Benjamin Frye's decision was certain to be bad news so he started with that envelope.

Carpenter turned to the last page of Magistrate Frye's decision in the Lawsons' case and read the punch line. Frey had denied the Lawsons' challenge to the Stonington IEP for their son Jack.

Carpenter slit open the second envelope and again went directly to the punch line. Michael Dunn, the hearing officer in Marshall Hyde's case before the Board of Bar Overseers, had recommended that no disciplinary action be taken against Hyde. Carpenter's heart pounded, making him wonder whether he was getting too old for the litigation game. A different recommendation by Dunn would have been tough to deal with in conjunction with Frye's ruling.

Carpenter returned to Fry's decision and began to read carefully. The magistrate acknowledged that with reduced medications, Jack Lawson had shown improvement in several areas. However, there was considerable evidence that Jack had begun to act inappropriately and aggressively under the lowered dosages, something he had not done while the Stonington IEP had been in effect. Frye used the word "inexplicable" to describe the Lawsons' refusal to have Jack's medication plan reviewed by his pediatrician. He characterized the Lawsons' refusal as particularly troubling because—and here he cited Maryanne Fairmount's testimony—the ideal medication levels for Jack might well prove to be somewhere between what Stonington wanted in place and the current levels. In the end, Frye concluded that the Lawsons had failed to show that the Stonington IEP was contrary to law.

Usually when Carpenter received a decision in a case, he forwarded it to a client with an explanatory e-mail. But in this instance, he skipped the explanatory discussion and simply forwarded Frye's decision to the Lawsons, with an explanation of their appeal rights. He also offered to make himself available to discuss the magistrate's ruling. If the Lawsons decided to appeal, Carpenter thought it likely they would hire a new lawyer to pursue that effort. That was his hope anyway; he wished to be spared deciding whether to represent them on appeal.

Carpenter turned to the decision in the Hyde case. Michael Dunn described the words in Hyde's blog as strong and arguably abrasive. But Dunn viewed the blog as commenting on a matter of public interest and of concern to the Middlesex County criminal bar. In Dunn's view, Hyde's first amendment rights outweighed any claim that Hyde had showed a lack of respect to a sitting judge or to the legal profession. Although arguably abrasive, Hyde's words were true at their core because the practice of Judge Porter to schedule immediate, unrealistic trial dates was not supported by any witness. Dunn rejected Jason Gerber's claim that Hyde should have filed a complaint against Porter with the Commission on Judicial Misconduct because it was questionable whether a judge's rulings perceived as unfair rose to the level of judicial misconduct. Instead, Hyde elected to protest Judge Porter's rulings in a manner that has become usual and customary in the Internet age.

Again, Carpenter decided to forego an explanatory email; Hyde didn't need to be educated on what Dunn had ruled. True, Dunn's decision was merely a recommendation, but Carpenter didn't see the Board of Bar Overseers rejecting it. It was well reasoned and supported by the evidence. Hyde would be relieved.

Carpenter met the withering stare of the man in the photograph facing him. "What?" he exclaimed, acerbically. "One out of two isn't bad."

"How did you know what Wayne Anderson would propose to settle the Stanton-Lane case?" Simon asked, looking at Carpenter across the conference room table as if he possessed clairvoyant powers.

Carpenter shrugged, amused. Anderson had put a $12,000 proposal on the table and when Simon hadn't agreed on the spot, Anderson had immediately asked Simon to check with Stanton and Lane for suitable deposition dates.

"It was like you could read his mind," Simon said with unmistakable awe.

Carpenter decided to take himself down from the pedestal Simon had put him on. "Settlement negotiations are a kind of game. After you've played the game a while, the rules of the game get predictable. The twelve thousand is a low-ball offer. One way you can tell it's a low-ball offer is it's divisible by three."

Simon looked puzzled so Carpenter took him through the Barristers' divisible by three rule that he had considered when Wayne Anderson made an initial settlement offer of $3,000.

"Something else they don't teach you in law school," Simon said solemnly. "What should we do?"

"*You* are going to call the client and present the offer. Stanton and Lane are going to ask what you recommend."

"And . . ."

"You tell me. What do you recommend?"

"I don't know," Simon said. "I've never done this before."

"It doesn't matter that you haven't done this before. What do you recommend?"

Simon began to rock back and forth in his chair apparently realizing that he wasn't going to pass the buck back to Carpenter.

"I'm going to tell them that they can put the whole twelve thousand dollars in their pocket if they take the offer. They already paid five thousand and the contingency doesn't kick in until they recover something more than fifteen thousand. Right?"

"Right," Carpenter confirmed.

"But I'm also going to tell them that we recommend they reject the offer unless they have an immediate need for the money. I'm going to say that we think the other side is likely to offer a higher settlement figure. I'm going to tell them that we think this is one of those cases that makes sense to litigate on the chance that a jury could sock it to Wise Computers."

"That works for me," Carpenter said.

Simon smiled. "Are you ready for the Top Tier hearing," he changed the subject.

"Not yet, but I'm getting there."

"I've been thinking about the two decisions we got," Rachel said over the phone, calling from her paralegal job. "If Dunn had ruled the other way in Marshall Hyde's case, I would have been devastated."

"I would have felt the same way," Carpenter admitted. There was no reason to pretend he would have accepted a double loss stoically. "We knew what was going to happen in the Lawson case. But it would have been a major disappointment if Dunn had made a recommendation to discipline Hyde."

"If we had also lost Hyde's case, I sense you would have been able to move on without much difficulty. I'm not sure I would have been able to."

"I've already told you that you'd be surprised at what you can do when you have to. Don't sell yourself short."

"That's not the point I'm trying to make," Rachel said. "You're trying to turn me into a litigator. I'm not sure that's the right move for me. I don't think I can take losing the way you can."

"I understand," Carpenter said. "Losing is hard. How did you feel about Dunn's decision in Hyde's case?"

"Terrific."

"Me too. That's the other side of losing—winning. There's nothing like it. And I mean nothing."

"So it's agony or ecstasy with no middle ground?"

"That about sums it up," Carpenter agreed.

72

Norman Cassidy was going all out to oppose the civil suit filed against him by Jerome Singer, and to oppose document production in the Top Tier regulatory proceeding. In both cases, Cassidy had hired Herbert Brown, a seasoned litigator who had done battle with Carpenter and Philly last year in a class action case. The case eventually settled but Brown had almost torpedoed the settlement by digging in his heels on a trivial issue. Today, Carpenter and Brown would do battle in court over Cassidy's refusal to turn over the documents that the Loan Company Licensure Review Board had ordered him to provide to Top Tier.

Brown was a tall, muscular guy who didn't look fifty. "We meet again," he said, as he shook Carpenter's hand. "Where's Ms. Piper? I thought you two were joined at the hip."

"She's dealing with a newborn," Carpenter said, and proceeded to introduce Simon.

"We're the first case on the list," Brown said as he took a seat at one of the counsel tables where two of his associates were unloading litigation briefcases.

Carpenter took a seat at the other counsel table in the Suffolk Superior Court courtroom. He had read through Brown's pleadings and had to admit that big Boston law firms never failed to present a thorough, well-written legal argument.

At the rear of the courtroom, Jerome Singer was in attendance. Carpenter wasn't sure whether Singer had time on his hands or was simply checking up on him.

"Court!" the clerk announced. "All Rise!"

Judge Catherine Bard was short and trim with close-cropped graying hair and pale blue eyes. Here was another woman, Carpenter reflected, who might resemble Maxine in another ten years.

After the clerk called their case and Carpenter and Brown introduced themselves, Bard regarded them impassively for a long moment. "I've read all the papers," she said. "I have before me a motion by Top Tier Finance Company to enforce subpoenas issued by the Loan Company Licensure Review Board. The subpoenas are directed to Norman Cassidy, Devonshire Plastics, and the accounting firm of Miller & Huggins. In a separate case, Mr. Singer and Top Tier have sued Mr. Cassidy and Devonshire Plastics over the taped call. In this case, Top Tier wants various financial records because it believes Devonshire Plastics may have provided false financial information to Top Tier during the period the loan was in effect."

Bard paused. "Does either counsel quarrel with my summary? Admittedly, there's more to the case than I've stated but I believe I've got the basic facts straight."

Carpenter was not about to tell any judge that the judge's summary of a case was off the mark. Brown, too, elected silence.

"Very well then. Let's start with you, Mr. Carpenter. What information do you have that false financial information was given to your client?"

Leave it to a judge to start off with a loaded question that was beside the point, Carpenter thought as he rose. "The fact that Devonshire's president broke the law by illegally taping a phone conversation leads Top Tier to call into question the accuracy of certain financial reports submitted to Top Tier by Devonshire Plastics. But if I may, I'd like to respectfully suggest that it is not up to Top Tier to prove to you today that any Devonshire financial information is false. The Loan Company Licensure Review Board has determined that anything to do with the loan to Devonshire Plastics is relevant to the licensure regulatory proceeding. That's why the Board issued subpoenas. Top Tier could be put out of business as a result of the licensure regulatory proceeding. To present its case before the Board, Top Tier needs all financial information relating to Devonshire Plastics and a Board hearing officer agreed."

Carpenter paused. He couldn't read anything into the judge's expression.

"Mr. Brown," Judge Bard said. "I've read the Massachusetts statute that prohibits secretly taping a telephone conversation. Do you agree that Mr. Cassidy violated that statute when he recorded Mr. Singer's call?"

Carpenter gratefully took his seat as Brown rose.

"No, I don't agree. There has been no criminal complaint filed against Mr. Cassidy. There hasn't even been any investigation of a criminal or other nature in connection with the taped conversation."

"That's not my question," the judge came back. "Simply because Mr. Cassidy hasn't been charged with a crime doesn't mean he hasn't committed one. My question to you is, did Mr. Cassidy's conduct violate the statute prohibiting the surreptitious recording of telephone conversations?"

"Mr. Cassidy has never acknowledged doing anything surreptitiously. If he is a witness before the Licensure Review Board, Mr. Cassidy might well testify that he stated he would make a record of the conversation."

"Is that what you expect his testimony to be?"

"Testimony to that effect would not surprise me."

Was Brown actually suggesting that Cassidy might lie? Carpenter glanced at Simon. The young lawyer was looking at Brown with a mixture of astonishment and anger.

"Usually when someone announces in advance that he is going to record a call, the person repeats that announcement as the first order of business once recording has begun. I've read the transcript of the taped call. At no time did Mr. Cassidy state that he had given Mr. Singer advance warning the call would be recorded. Nor did he submit an affidavit in this case in which he states that he would record the call."

"That may be," Brown said, "but there was no obligation on Mr. Cassidy's part to follow what Your Honor has described as the first order of business."

"Mr. Carpenter. What do you say to the defendants' claim that you are trying to use the regulatory proceeding to obtain discovery in the suit that Top Tier and Mr. Singer have filed against Mr. Cassidy and Devonshire Plastics for illegally recording a call?'

Carpenter had sensed the judge's negative reaction to Brown's evasive wordplay when she tried to pin him down as to the legality of the taped call. "Mr. Brown has a point," Carpenter said, "insofar as issues in the other lawsuit you mentioned and issues before the Review Board overlap. Therefore, discovery produced in response to the Review Board's subpoenas may also be relevant in the other lawsuit. That can't be helped. If Mr. Brown believes that evidence produced before the Review Board shouldn't be in evidence in Top Tier's other lawsuit, he can make a motion to exclude that evidence in the other lawsuit. Just because two legal proceedings have common facts doesn't mean that one proceeding is being used to obtain an unfair advantage in the other."

Carpenter was pleased Judge Bard was writing in her trial notebook. The judge was deep in thought, seemingly oblivious to the many lawyers seated in the gallery who were waiting for their cases to be called.

"I'm going to allow Top Tier's motion to compel enforcement of the subpoenas," Bard announced, breaking whatever spell she was under. "A hearing officer of the Review Board approved the subpoenas over the objection of the Board's prosecuting attorney. The regulatory board hearing concerning Top Tier is of great importance to that company since its lending license is in jeopardy; any information deemed relevant by the hearing officer should be discoverable in the regulatory proceeding and the hearing officer can determine whether to admit the evidence. Devonshire Plastics and Mr. Cassidy are defendants in a suit brought by Top Tier alleging illegal recording of a telephone discussion. In that other lawsuit, those parties are free to object to any evidence whatsoever, including evidence presented in the regulatory proceeding. Therefore, allowing the motion to enforce the subpoenas doesn't harm Mr. Cassidy or Devonshire Plastics in any material way. The clerk will prepare an order allowing the motion to enforce. Next case."

Carpenter quickly gathered his papers and whispered to Simon to do the same. As soon as a judge ruled in his favor and called the next case, Carpenter believed that the wisest course of action was to get the hell out of Dodge. Brown was taking his time packing up and was probably seething inside. But, to Brown's credit, he showed no emotion.

Jerome Singer was waiting in the corridor outside the courtroom. "Nice job," he said. "What's next?"

"We wait for documents."

"How long will that take?"

"If you're lucky," Carpenter said, "till hell freezes over."

"What are you talking about?"

"Top Tier's currently lending money. Every day that Top Tier stays in the lending business is a victory of sorts. The hearing isn't going to begin until the subpoenas are complied with. The hearing officer in the regulatory case can't fault Top Tier for dragging its feet on enforcing the subpoenas. That means more days of lending money, pure and simple."

"You have a point," Singer said, grudgingly.

"Of course, if Cassidy wants to stick it to you, he'll comply with the subpoenas tomorrow. Also, we learned something very important today."

"What's that?"

"Mr. Cassidy is prepared to lie. He never told you that he was going to record your telephone conversation, did he?"

"No," Singer said after a few beats had passed, hardly a vigorous denial. Cassidy was trying to destroy Singer's business; if Cassidy was lying, Singer should be ballistic. In fact, Carpenter didn't understand why Singer hadn't started this discussion by complaining bitterly about Cassidy's willingness to lie.

"Clear your decks," Carpenter said to Singer. "I've got a hunch the pace is going to pick up in the cases involving Devonshire Plastics."

73

A warm but not oppressive September sun was coming through Philly's office window, and Daisy was fussing, letting loose with high-pitched squawks. Philly pictured Carpenter fuming at these distractions. He was all business during conference calls in which cases were reviewed. Rachel and Simon would be less disturbed by Daisy's interruptions since each had had some personal time with her daughter and Rachel particularly enjoyed those moments.

"The good news is that the Board of Bar Overseers has accepted the hearing officer's recommendation and will not be taking any action against Marshall Hyde," Carpenter summed up as Daisy fell quiet for a moment.

"That is good news," Philly echoed. "Nice job."

"Next we have the Lawsons, my favorite couple," Carpenter continued. "They asked me to file an appeal from Magistrate Frye's decision. I told them I didn't think there were any grounds for appeal. They didn't sound surprised. I think they sounded out other lawyers and were told the same thing. They said that they still wanted to appeal. I told them I'd get back to them in a day or two. I'm inclined not to handle the appeal. It's a loser."

"If you say no to the Lawsons, what do you think they'll do?" Philly asked.

"There's always the hope that they'll come to their senses," Carpenter said. "But barring that, I think they'll end up finding a lawyer willing to take their money to pursue a hopeless cause."

Carpenter was making the right decision; yet Philly was troubled by her desire to keep an hourly rate paying client on the hook.

"Simon needs to tell us about Herbert Stanton and Millie Lane," Carpenter said.

"Say you make friends with the kid and he trusts you. Then what?"

"I'm not sure," Philly said. "Maybe the only thing I'll accomplish is getting Gerald to survive his deposition without falling apart. I think if he trusts me, he'll let me prepare him for the deposition."

Carpenter's sigh whistled over the phone. "I'm going to shut up about this," he said. "What the hell do I know? Keep in mind we can't bill his parents for Spanish lessons."

Philly laughed, then changed the subject. "Rachel asked me something a while back. She asked me whether we were thinking about forming a firm."

"What did you tell her?"

"I didn't tell her anything. I said I'd talk to you. I guess they want to know what their future is with us."

"I wish I had an answer for them. I guess I'd like to keep things the way they are."

"I don't know if that's going to be enough for them. I'm assuming that Rachel and Simon have talked about this and we're dealing with both of them."

"Would they be on salary?" Carpenter asked. "I don't think we have enough billable hour work to make that happen."

"Especially with me not around," Philly threw in, deciding to beat herself up a bit.

"We can always tell them the truth," Carpenter said.

"What might that be?"

"That we're too fucked up to think about forming a firm and we want to keep the current arrangement as it is for a time."

"If we had more business would you be looking at this differently?"

Carpenter didn't answer right away. "I don't like feeling responsible for keeping another lawyer busy," he said. "I think that's a big reason why I've stayed solo all these years."

"But you were willing to go into business with me," Philly reminded Carpenter.

"Point taken. But remember, I told you I had mixed feelings. When you said no to the firm idea, a part of me felt relieved. It was one less thing I had to think about."

Philly considered their options. "I think we should be upfront about this with Simon and Rachel. We should tell them when we're both there in person."

"Works for me," Carpenter said.

Paul was all muscle. When he held her the way he was doing now—encircling her with his arms from behind as they lay in bed—Philly wondered whether he wished she were some hard-bodied physical fitness freak. She had been sticking to her regime of pushups and sit-ups, but it didn't feel like the exercises were doing any good. She felt chunky, out of shape. The only time she hadn't felt chunky in recent years was when she was heavy into spinning and biking with Philip.

"If you're not drifting off, what are you thinking about?" Paul whispered.

"I was thinking about how I need to get in shape and how there's no time for me to do that." Philly knew that if she ever came up with a babysitting solution, it wouldn't be fair to Carpenter if she used her freed-up time to work out as opposed to dealing with legal work. Assuming there was any legal work to do.

"Just wait until Daisy becomes mobile. She'll wear you out. Exercise will be the last thing you'll think about."

"*You* work out."

"That's because my ex has Jenny. If I had to be there for Jenny twenty-four-seven, I wouldn't have a life."

Philly promised herself that tomorrow she'd begin to investigate babysitting options. It was time to pull her head out of the sand when it came to child care.

"I was thinking about one of the things you said about the way you and Philip would have serious discussions."

Philly tensed. She took the way Paul referred to Philip without hesitation as a sign that Paul didn't feel threatened by the relationship she'd had with him. But if Paul was about to suggest a serious discussion under the ground rules she and Philip had used, she imagined an unpleasant subject being broached.

"I want to bring up a subject you're not going to like."

"Shit. You really know how to kill a good mood."

Paul began to rub her back. "April and I had gotten to a point when we never talked to each other. I was partly at fault. I like the serious discussion idea. What do you say?"

"Okay, serious discussion." Saying no was not an option.

Paul was now massaging her shoulders. He had strong fingers and their pressure soothed.

"I went to see Colin Feeney's probation officer," Paul said, and Philly shrugged his hands away. She turned to face him.

"Why the hell did you do that?"

"Hear me out," Paul said softly. "This isn't easy for me either."

Philly closed her eyes, silently fumed.

"The Feeney kid is doing lousy in school. His teachers say it's as if he doesn't give a shit about anything. I'm paraphrasing. His father still can't control him. The kid stays out late and the father has no idea where he's been."

"Why the fuck are you bringing this up?"

"I'm not a psychiatrist," Paul said, "although I sometimes play one on TV."

Philly tried not to smile but she couldn't maintain her anger. "Not funny," she said, although in the moonlight coming in through her window Paul had to have seen her change of expression.

"If you say so. I thought it was funny. Anyway, the kid is hauling around a ton of guilt. It's overwhelming him. I've seen this happen before. A kid does something tragic and can't get out from under the guilt."

"So what am I supposed to do? Forgive the little shit?"

Paul didn't say anything. He reached out and touched her face with the backs of his fingers.

"It's pretty amazing what you're doing with this kid Gerald," Paul said. "When you give him Daisy to hold he becomes a different person. You could see it at dinner tonight. When you dumped Daisy on him he forgot about keeping up an attitude. And Raul and Isabella are great with him and that's your doing."

"The thing with Gerald is different."

"No, it isn't. Not really."

"Gerald didn't kill Daisy's father."

"It's not that different," Paul persisted.

"Are we done?" Philly demanded.

"No. I want things to work between us. I think there's a better chance of that happening if you're not carrying around a load of rage directed at the Feeney kid. That's a feeling I have based on what I've seen on my job."

Philly repressed the urge to make a cutting remark. What she really wanted right now was a beer or two or three.

"I can't just forgive the Feeney kid," Philly said. "I just can't."

"You're not still thinking of suing the kid, are you?"

"I haven't ruled anything out."

Paul's eyes closed and just when Philly thought he was drifting off, Paul opened his eyes, his gaze both intense and concerned. "Now we're done," he said, again brushing her cheek.

A Hockey Player

74

The sound of her office phone caused Philly to start and Daisy to let out a squeak. Philly had been turning the pages of a picture book, pointing out pictures of common objects, saying the word that matched the object, describing colors. Daisy had been absorbed in the exercise, but the telephone broke the spell. Now Daisy fussed, arched her back, and Philly had to juggle her daughter and the book so she could reach for the phone.

"Philomena Piper."

"This is Joe Baird. Do you remember me?"

The name was familiar but no face came to mind.

"Think of a baseball player and a sports agent," Baird prompted.

"Of course!" Philly exclaimed, remembering. Baird had represented a sports agent that Carpenter had brought suit against on behalf of a young baseball pitching prospect. In Carpenter's absence, she had come up with a way to settle the case. "How's that pitcher doing? Derek Morgan, right?"

"You remember the kid's name but not mine. That should tell me something. I guess I'm not all that memorable."

"That's not true at all," Philly said, recalling a thick-set, blond man with a dimple centered in his chin. Baird used to be a hockey player and the sports agent that Carpenter had sued was one of his major clients as well as a former hockey player.

"Derek Morgan is making steady progress. I wouldn't be surprised if the Mets called him up next year."

"This is a surprise," Philly said.

"Do you have someone with you?"

Daisy was gurgling. A corner of the thick-paged picture book had found her mouth and drool was discoloring the corner a dark gray. "That's my daughter. She's not quite three months."

"You working at home?"

"For the moment."

"Does this mean you're not practicing law?"

"No."

"Are you and that guy Carpenter still a team?"

"We are."

Baird paused. Philly guessed that he had been about to sound her out on a case and was now thinking better of it.

"I was thinking of throwing a case your way but if you're out of action . . ."

"I've got a kid for Christ's sake. I'm not a fucking invalid."

"You haven't changed," Baird said, laughing. "You're still a pisser."

"What's the case about? You know I'll tell you if I can't do it."

"Fair enough," Baird said. "You remember Andrew Harrington, the sports agent Carpenter sued? Most of Andrew's clients are hockey players and the case I want to talk to you about concerns a hockey player."

Philly hated sports. She'd never figure out how she had come up with the idea that led to the settlement of Carpenter's suit against Harrington.

"Gerard Gorman is fifty-five years old today. He lives with his wife in an assisted living facility and suffers from dementia. He played for the Merrimack Marauders. You ever hear of that team?"

"No. I think I told you that I don't follow sports much."

"The Marauders are a minor league professional team. They use a rink at the University of Lowell. Gorman played for them for about ten years beginning in 1976 before a leg injury forced him to retire. He never made it to the NHL. He became a high school physical education teacher until the dementia set in and he had to leave teaching in 2008. Gorman's doctor is convinced that his dementia is a result of the hits he took while playing hockey."

"Did he suffer concussions?" Philly asked.

"Probably," Baird responded. "But he didn't miss any games because of a concussion. The only injuries he had that prevented him from playing were leg injuries."

"Where are you going with this?"

"Gorman's wife wants to know if there's anything that can be done legally on his behalf. Andrew and I have talked extensively with Gorman's doctor, a Nancy Corrigan. What we've come up with is filing a workers' compensation claim on Gorman's behalf."

Philly followed Carpenter's practice of not admitting ignorance when it came to any area of the law. "Why me? Aren't there lawyers who specialize in workers' compensation?"

"This is a case that would break some new ground," Baird explained. "There's a statute of limitations problem. There's the fact that Gorman would be claiming a mental disability and not a physical disability. And finally, there's a causation problem. Although Dr. Corrigan is convinced the early onset of Gorman's dementia is related to his hockey career, proving that is going to be a bear."

The drawbacks Baird had pointed out were major. He probably wanted a lawyer to take the case on a contingency basis. Even if Simon and Rachel would agree to assist, Philly didn't see committing substantial time and resources to a case that even Baird agreed was iffy.

"You're not painting a rosy picture of success," Philly said.

"That's because the case may be a long shot."

"Are you talking about a contingency case?"

"Finding someone to take the case on a contingency basis would be ideal. But Andrew and I don't think that's fair. We're looking for a lawyer to take the case on a reduced hourly charge. We thought about a bump up in compensation if the case ends with a win, but we would prefer that the money go to Gorman and his wife."

"Who's paying for this?"

"There's a legal fund in place. Andrew and I have put up some money. The minor league players' association has put up some money. What is your hourly rate?"

Philly had been putting off upping her hourly charge. She thought briefly of presenting Baird with an inflated figure and decided to level with him.

"Two hundred an hour. But I need to tell you that it's going to go up. I just haven't gotten around to it." Daisy batted at the picture book and Philly almost dropped it. "I've had other things on my mind recently."

"What would your rate be going up to?"

"Two fifty. How much is in the legal fund?"

"Twenty thousand."

"Why are you and Mr. Harrington backing this case?"

"Because it's the right thing to do. We believe that Gorman's dementia was a result of the pounding he took playing hockey. There's a lot of workers' compensation activity on the subject of dementia in California that concerns football players. If you sign on for this, I can forward you that information. But when it comes to hockey players, there's really little to go on."

"If I took this on, what hourly rate would you be looking to pay?"

"Based on what you told me, probably one hundred twenty-five, half of where you would like to see your hourly rate go."

"I need to talk this over with Carpenter," Philly said. "While I'm dealing with a newborn, I need to explain to you how Carpenter and I are organized right now."

Baird didn't say anything as Philly detailed the arrangement she and Carpenter had with Simon and Rachel and her home office situation. "Carpenter and I work together and his billing rate is higher than mine. I'd have to talk to him about reducing his rate."

"None of that bothers me if Carpenter is on board," Baird said. "I'll talk it over with Andrew and the others, but I don't believe they'll have a problem with anything you've said."

"You still haven't explained why you contacted me on this."

"Call it a hunch. Andrew and I were tossing around possibilities and Andrew remembered Derrick Morgan's case. We looked at each other and thought why not."

"I'm appreciative. I'll get back to you shortly."

"By the way, congratulations. How's motherhood treating you?"

Daisy's right hand had found the soggy corner of the picture book.

"Great," Philly said.

75

Herbert Stanton's deposition was being held at Wayne Anderson's twenty-lawyer business litigation firm located on Federal Street in a small, windowless conference room that was as unadorned as Carpenter's own on Milk Street. Simon was defending the deposition and if things went well, Carpenter had decided to let Simon handle Millie Lane's deposition, scheduled for later in the day, on his own.

Stanton didn't seem intimidated by Anderson's size or appear worried by the prospect of being questioned by a seasoned litigator. Carpenter had left Stanton's preparation largely to Simon. In short order, he'd know whether the young lawyer had done his job.

"Is it true that you and Ms. Lane are seeking damages from Wise Computer?" Anderson asked, after eliciting basic background information.

"Yes."

"How were the two of you damaged by Wise Computer?"

"We got fired and lost our jobs. Also, Wise Computer spied on us. The company violated our privacy rights."

Anderson consulted his notes. "Did each of you collect unemployment compensation after being fired?"

"Yes."

"Are you currently employed?"

"We're self-employed. We've started up our own computer consulting company."

"How long were you out of work before you started your own company?"

"About three months."

"Are the two of you making as much money at your own company as you did when you worked for Wise Computer?"

"Last month was the first time that happened."

Carpenter remembered Stanton's and Lane's answers to interrogatories. The firing had cost them about $30,000 while they built up their own company.

"Besides being fired and no longer being on Wise Computer's payroll, did either you or Ms. Lane suffer any monetary loss as a result of Wise Computer spying on the two of you to use your word?"

Stanton scratched his head and turned toward Simon. Simon stared straight ahead, expressionless. Anderson's question was on Simon's list of potential questions; Stanton shouldn't have had to think about his answer.

"There's the violation of our privacy rights," Stanton said. "I look on that as a monetary loss."

"Outside of no longer being on Wise Computer's payroll, did what you call spying result in either you or Ms. Lane not receiving money to which you were otherwise entitled?"

"No."

"Outside of no longer being on Wise Computer's payroll, did what you call spying result in either you or Ms. Lane having to spend money which you would otherwise not have spent?"

"Could you repeat that please?"

As the stenographer read back the question, Carpenter studied Simon. The kid had the poker face that a litigator needed; his expression gave no clue whether Anderson had so far scored a point. Rachel's expression would likely be less inscrutable.

"No," Stanton said, "except we had to pay money to start up our business."

"In the months before you were fired, during the hours of eight in the morning and six in the evening, did you and Ms. Lane rendezvous at motels to have sexual relations."

"Yes."

"Isn't it true that the two of you were on call during those hours?"

"Yes, but we were also on call earlier and later than the hour span you mentioned."

"What did being on call mean?"

"It meant we might be called from Wise Computer's office to attend to a client of the company."

"Isn't it true that engaging in sexual relations with Ms. Lane while being on call hindered your ability and her ability to respond to an assignment?"

Stanton registered surprise. "Absolutely not."

"What happened if Wise Computer called one of you while the two of you were engaged in sexual relations?"

"Whoever was called would take the call."

Stanton had struck Carpenter as a mild-manned man who would be embarrassed by questions directed to his sex life. In fact, Stanton seemed unconcerned by Anderson's personal questions.

"And if the call required one of you to attend to a client of Wise Computer, would you resume your sexual activity before departing for the client?"

"No, that's not what happened at all. We would shower and check out. Whoever got the call would shower first and leave."

"Then the shower time represented a delay in responding to the client, correct?"

"I don't consider shower time a delay. I've taken calls at home where I had to shower before going to a client. Also, I've been grocery shopping when I've received calls from Wise Computer and I would return home to drop the groceries before going to the client. I didn't want the groceries to spoil. Being on call never meant you couldn't complete a matter of personal business before visiting a client."

Anderson frowned. Carpenter sensed that he had not expected Stanton to be combative in answering questions.

"Do you or Ms. Lane have any information that Wise Computer shared any information obtained from the GPS systems in your cell phones with any other person?"

"I don't have any information on that one way or the other. Millie can speak for herself."

"Have clients of Wise Computer become clients of your new company?"

"Yes."

"Did you or Ms. Lane solicit those clients?"

"No. In each case, the client contacted one of us."

"Did you send out notices of your new business to clients of Wise Computer?"

"No."

"How did you market your new company?"

For a moment Stanton appeared nonplused by the question. "Now that you mention it, I guess we didn't do a very good job of marketing. We took out ads in several newspapers. We did some cold calling. We left a lot of business cards around."

Anderson favored Stanton with a hard stare. "Let's break for five minutes he requested."

When Anderson left the room, Carpenter rose. "You're doing fine," he said to Stanton. "Keep it up."

"Is it okay to discuss the questions Anderson asked Mr. Stanton with Ms. Lane?" Simon asked.

"Sure," Carpenter said. "Anderson will ask Ms. Lane whether that discussion took place. Make sure Ms. Lane tells the truth. And by the way, you'll be handling her deposition alone."

76

Carpenter woke at five in the morning drenched in sweat. He had soaked through his T-shirt and his top and bottom sheets were damp. Night sweats were a symptom of CLL. Fred had made his presence known.

In the kitchen, Carpenter poured a large glass of orange juice and slowly drank it, shivering as he drained the glass. He had left the kitchen window ajar and it was cold in the room. He didn't want to think about fall having begun and winter on the way.

Carpenter paced in his living room, glancing occasionally at the empty wall space behind his couch. A shopping trip with Maxine had failed to come up with something that both of them liked.

Dr. Specter had said that CLL symptoms might occur but the time to worry was when you didn't feel that you were yourself. Should he call Dr. Specter with news of last night's sweat? He still felt okay so why not give it another couple of days? Maybe the night sweat was a one-time occurrence. When it came to unpleasantness, Carpenter thought, the master of procrastination had struck again.

Going back to sleep was out of the question. Carpenter headed for the shower. It would be an early start to the workday.

A light was on in the conference room and Carpenter entered before going to his office. Rachel was seated at the table which was covered with stacks of paper that Norman Cassidy, Devonshire Plastics, and Miller & Huggins had produced in response to the subpoenas issued by the Loan Company Licensure Review Board. He had assigned Rachel the task of organizing the documents. Herbert Brown's clients had papered Top Tier to death and seeing the mass of paper arrayed on the table, Carpenter now considered that he may have offloaded an overly burdensome task on the young lawyer.

"You're up bright and early," Carpenter said as he took a seat across from Rachel. It was not yet seven and Rachel looked as if she'd been at it for a while.

"There's an assignment for my paralegal job that I have to get done today so I thought I'd come in early."

Simon and Rachel had been so readily available that Carpenter tended to forget they had lives outside of the world they shared with him and Philly. "All of this stuff can wait," he gestured toward the table. "Don't kill yourself. Take care of your other assignment first."

"I don't really understand all these financial reports," Rachel said.

"Jerome Singer and I have an accountant in mind who will deal with the financial information. I have a pretty good idea how to read a balance sheet. But I don't trust myself to draw any conclusions from any financial information we've been given. What else is here besides financial stuff?"

"Mostly contracts," Rachel replied. "Devonshire Plastics has given us copies of the contracts the company had before it went bankrupt."

Carpenter discerned a straightforward job for Rachel. "Make a list of the contracts. Include the other party to the contract, and that party's address and telephone number. Also list the date of the contract and what the contract was for."

Rachel nodded. "They've also given us copies of bills they sent to clients and copies of bills they had to pay."

"Leave those alone for a while. Work on the contract list and let me know when it's done."

Rachel sat up straight and took a deep breath. She raised her arms over her head and stretched. Carpenter saw her relief and made a vow to pay more attention to the tasks he had been routinely delegating to Simon and Rachel. It made no sense to overwhelm either of them.

"I don't know how you do it," Rachel said, pointing to the papers covering the conference room table. "I was becoming panicked by all this, but you seem to take this and everything else in stride."

Carpenter was not about to tell Rachel that Fred's presence made everything else seem like a walk in the park. "Don't be deceived," he said. "I fret and worry and bitch about everything. You should know that by now. But as far as all this financial information goes, there's a reason God made accountants."

Rachel offered up a weak smile. "I keep thinking about the Lawson case. I know you told them that you wouldn't be handling the appeal of the IEP decision, and I keep feeling that if they wanted to appeal, we'd be letting them down by not doing the work. Some new lawyer will charge them a lot of money to get up to speed."

Carpenter was again seeing a side of Rachel that gave him concern. She agonized over decisions long after the fact.

"Sometimes a lawyer can best serve a client by being brutally frank and telling the client what the client doesn't want to hear. I don't like taking a client's money on a fool's errand and that's what the IEP appeal would be. The Lawsons wouldn't listen to reason when it came to trying the case and that cost them. And by the way, they will find some lawyer out there to take their money and be happy to do it."

"You've put their case completely out of your mind, haven't you?"

Carpenter nodded. "If you want to play at this game, that's pretty much what you have to do. With practicing law, it's easy to get stuck in the past and fret about what might have been. When you do that, you shortchange the future and your active cases."

Rachel presented another weak smile, stood up, and made ready to go.

"The Lawsons will come to realize that we correctly advised them about the appeal," Carpenter said. "But if you think they'd ever admit that to us, think again."

"I'm Philly and I'm an alcoholic."

As the chorus of, "Hi Philly," greeted her, she reflected on how much easier it had become to admit to her condition.

"I haven't had a drink since I started coming here," Philly continued, "but I was sorely tempted a few times recently. When someone tells me something I don't want to hear, it gets me worked up and that's when I start thinking about having a drink."

"Why didn't you call me?" Melanie asked.

Her sponsor looked crushed and Philly realized that she had let her down. "I probably should have. I'm sorry. But I'm stubborn and I don't like asking for help."

"Why do you think that is?" Charlie interjected.

Tonight, the group leader reminded Philly of an over-the-hill hippie who didn't have a care in the world. Charlie's long greasy hair was done up in a ponytail, his bright yellow Hawaiian shirt adorned with large, brown coconuts.

"Because asking for help is a sign of weakness and I don't like to show weakness."

"We've talked about these themes before," Charlie said. "We've all been there in varying degrees."

Charlie paused and his gaze wandered. Philly half expected him to zone out standing up.

"Here's a thought," Charlie refocused. "If you want to appear tough, then next time you feel like having a drink do the tough thing for you and call Melanie. Maybe being tough is doing what's hardest for you."

There were low murmurs of assent to Charlie' suggestion. Charlie had made a fair point. "I'll keep that in mind," Philly said.

Melanie sat forward on her chair, her skinny arms folded across her body. "What got you upset?"

"It's kind of personal," Philly said. "I'm not comfortable talking about it."

"Everything that's said here is personal," Charlie said.

Philly surveyed the gathering. She continued to feel superior to most of those in attendance. The motley, bedraggled souls that had assembled this evening looked incapable of offering help with the problem she was wrestling with.

"Try letting go," Charlie prompted. "We're all in the same boat here."

Philly sighed, hating being worn down, and Charlie and Melanie were doing a good job of stripping away her resistance.

"There's this guy I've been seeing," Philly began. "He's been urging me to forgive the kid who killed my fiancé while driving drunk. I told him that I didn't think I could."

"That is totally heavy," Charlie said solemnly.

"Why would your boyfriend ask you to do something like that?" a woman wearing a heavy gray hoodie asked. Philly couldn't make out the woman's face. The late September cold snap had receded, replaced by temperatures in the 80s again. It was stuffy in the basement and the woman had to be roasting. Philly had stripped down to her T-shirt soon after the meeting started.

"He said it was important to our relationship," Philly explained.

"I don't follow that at all," the woman said.

"He said I needed to let go of my anger at the kid so that the tragedy wouldn't get in the way of our relationship."

"But that kid ruined your life," a solidly built, dark-haired man with a cobra tattoo on each arm put in. "Why the fuck would you forgive him?"

"Exactly my sentiments," Philly said. Support from any quarter, even from a guy who looked like a biker gang reject, was welcome.

"This boyfriend is the police officer you told us about, right?" Charlie asked.

Philly nodded, wondering whether Paul would be pissed off that his serious discussion was now being picked over at an AA meeting.

"I've given some thought to forgiveness," Charlie said in the same serious tone he had used previously. "I haven't come up with very much that's original. But I've got this theory that before you can forgive someone else, you've got to forgive yourself."

"I don't follow that either," the woman in the sweatshirt said.

"What about you, Philly?" Charlie asked. "Did you follow what I was saying?"

"I understand the words," Philly said, "but I'm having trouble thinking of anything I need to forgive myself for."

"I've pretty much forgiven myself for almost screwing up my daughter's life," Melanie said.

"There's an example that we can all appreciate," Charlie said. "I've been trying to forgive myself for being a lousy father and an even worse husband. I don't know if I'm there yet."

Philly didn't have it in her to catalogue everything in her life that she wished she'd done differently. She hadn't been much of a daughter, going out of her way to piss her parents off. Her stubbornness seldom produced anything good in her life. Were these the kinds of things Charlie was talking about?

"I know one thing each and every person in this room can forgive himself or herself for." Charlie paused and Philly saw that she wasn't the only one hanging on what he would say next. "Each of us can forgive himself or herself for being saddled with this horrible disease that leaves us with the urge to engage in behavior that we know will bring us down."

Philly chewed on Charlie's words. If Philip hadn't died would she be in this situation? She'd pretty much stopped drinking when lovemaking, biking, and spinning had filled up her life. Then, when pregnant, she'd deliberately put Daisy at risk, maybe not as severely as Melanie had endangered her daughter, but deliberately just the same.

"I can see that I've given you a lot to think about," Charlie said. "Let's end a little early and have some refreshments. Tomorrow is another day."

77

Philly had deposited Daisy with Philip's parents in North Andover so she could be at Rachel's side for the probable cause hearing in Frederick Chun's discrimination case. The round trip between North Andover and Boston would likely separate her from Daisy for five hours. Philips' parents welcomed the time with their granddaughter, but Philly knew that their North Andover location made them an impractical resource.

Crowe Investment Strategies was taking Chun's case seriously. The hedge fund had engaged Williams, Nyland & Cross, a mid-sized Boston litigation firm. Jane Quick, a partner in the firm, had filed a lengthy position paper pointing out numerous reasons why there was no probable cause to find that Crowe Investment Strategies had discriminated against Chun. Quick was dressed in a dark blue suit and she radiated competence and authority. The woman's flaming red hair curled up at her shoulders and when she focused on you there was a steely resolve in her dark blue eyes.

Lewis Lightstone entered the room and took a seat at the desk facing the counsel tables. Philly thought that the MCAD hearing officer looked fresh out of law school; he had to be younger than Rachel. Lightstone was dressed in khaki pants, and a blue blazer. His red tie was loosened at the collar of his buttoned-down white shirt. Lightstone was built like a football linebacker but there was gentleness in his expression that toned down his ruggedness.

"I've read all the papers," Lightstone began. "This is a hearing to determine whether there is probable cause to find that Crowe Investment Strategies discriminated against Frederick Chun because of Mr. Chun's race and national origin." Lightstone nodded at the lawyers seated at the counsel tables. "I see that counsel for both parties are present. What about the parties themselves?"

Rachel stood and beckoned Chun to stand. "Mr. Chun is present."

Quick then rose and gestured for a stoop shouldered man wearing a dark suit to also stand. "Mr. Wayne Madison is the Director of Human Resources for Crowe Investment Strategies."

"I'll hear from you, Ms. Boyle, as to why there is probable cause."

Rachel stood and centered her one-page outline on the tabletop in front of her. "Thank you, Your Honor. Mr. Chun was one of two Asian employees at Crowe Investment Strategies. He was an exemplary employee. He received good performance reviews and raises on each anniversary date of his employment. He was fired abruptly because a company IT employee found that Mr. Chun had deleted an email sent to him by a friend that had a link to a website named Sexy Russian Vixens dot com. Mr. Chun had deleted the email without going to the link. He was told that he was being fired because he used his computer for personal use in connection with pornography."

Rachel paused and took a moment to regard Lightstone. The MCAD attorney had yet to write a word.

"Crowe Investment Strategies has produced in discovery a considerable volume of e-mail messages involving its employees. Many of the messages occurred close to the time Mr. Chun was fired. Mr. Chun's position paper summarizes our review of those messages. In addition, attached to Mr. Chun's position paper are examples of some of the e-mail messages.

"Here's what we know. Crowe Investment Strategies employees send personal e-mail messages on their work computers and receive personal e-mail messages on their work computers. Many of these back and forth e-mail communications contain dirty jokes. White and African American employees have sent or received personal e-mails using such words as shit, asshole, fucking asshole, dickhead, fuckwad, bastard, and cunt."

Philly tried not to smile at the stream of profanity that had passed the lips of her innocent looking colleague.

"None of these white and African American employees were disciplined in any way. Mr. Chun never clicked on the link that he was sent. A friend had sent him an e-mail with the link in question, and Mr. Chun took only a moment to permanently delete the e-mail after viewing the link's title.

"Crowe Investment Strategies has systematically tolerated personal e-mails exchanged by Caucasian and African American employees that contain lewd and profane language. Mr. Chun, in contrast, one of two Asian employees of the company, was fired unceremoniously for receiving a personal e-mail with a link that Mr. Chun never accessed."

Philly glanced at Quick. Opposing counsel looked unfazed by anything that Rachel had said.

"There's a double standard being applied here. The company's stated ground for firing Mr. Chun is self-serving and not credible. Given what the company has tolerated from Caucasian and African American employees who make up ninety-five percent of the company's workforce, the conclusion is inevitable that Mr. Chun was fired because of his race and national origin. Thank you."

"Nice job," Philly whispered to Rachel. She liked Rachel's straightforward, deliberate approach. So what if the hearing officer didn't take a single note!

Jane Quick rose smartly as soon as Rachel was seated. "The complainant's case is based on classic faulty logic. The syllogism goes that Mr. Chun is Asian, Mr. Chun was fired, and therefore Mr. Chun was fired because he was Asian. There is absolutely no evidence of any kind to support the conclusion that the complainant wishes the Commission to draw." Quick paused to consult her notes. She was unhurried, totally at ease.

"Since you have stated that you have read the papers, Your Honor, I won't repeat what was said in Crowe Investment Strategies' written position paper and the attachments to that paper. Ms. Boyle overlooks one crucial fact—none of the e-mail exchanges that she characterizes as dirty jokes contained links to any pornographic website. That fact alone distinguishes Mr. Chun's situation."

From Lightstone's expression, Philly couldn't tell how the hearing officer regarded the distinction Quick had just drawn.

"Even if Crowe Investment Strategies tolerated what Ms. Boyle calls dirty jokes, it was not required to tolerate Mr. Chun's e-mail communication that contained a link to a pornographic site. Very simply, Crowe Investment Strategies, by Mr. Chun's admission, terminated Mr. Chun's employment because of the pornographic link in the e-mail he received. That reason for firing Mr. Chun has nothing to do with his race or national origin. Mr. Chun was an employee at will and he was fired for a reason that had nothing to do with his race or national origin."

Quick resumed her seat.

"Is there anything you wish to say in response to Ms. Quick's argument?" Lightstone directed at Rachel.

"I'll try not to repeat what's before you," Rachel replied. "Ms. Quick made repeated references to a pornographic website. There is no evidence that the website was pornographic. Mr. Chun can't tell you what was on the site because he never visited the site. I have visited the site and saw no sexually explicit content. The only pornographic matters that have been disclosed to date involve the words in the dirty jokes that Crowe Investment Strategies tolerated for its Caucasian and African-American employees." Rachel glanced at her argument outline and then took her seat.

Lightstone turned his attention to Quick. The hearing officer still had not written down a word that had been said to him.

"I'm trying to understand why Mr. Chun was fired," Lightstone said. "A personal e-mail message came to him with a reference to a possibly racy link. Mr. Chun's response was to immediately delete the e-mail without reading it. Why fire him over that particularly where employees who used patently offensive language in personal emails—including the c-word—remained employed?"

"Let's take a step back here," Quick said when she got to her feet. "Crowe Investment Strategies didn't need a reason to discharge Mr. Chun or any other employee at will. Mr. Chun's friend who sent him an e-mail with a pornographic link obviously got Mr. Chun's work e-mail address from Mr. Chun. If Crowe Investment Strategies disapproved of that situation, which it did, the company was free to terminate Mr. Chun which it also did regardless of what it may have tolerated in connection with other employees. There is no dispute that the personal e-mail with a pornographic link led to Mr. Chun's termination. His race and ethnicity had nothing to do with Crowe Investment's decision to end his employment."

Lightstone clicked his ballpoint pen as he contemplated the lawyers before him. The man had given nothing away. "Thank you counsel," Lightstone said, as he rose and headed for the door. "I'll take the case under advisement."

"What do you think he's going to do?" Chun asked.

Quick had left the hearing room with her client's representative in tow. Philly nodded to Rachel that she should field Chun's question.

"I don't know," Rachel admitted. "He showed no expression and he didn't write down a word as far as I could tell."

Chun was discouraged. Viewed objectively, Chun's claim that his race entered into the decision to fire him was probably a stretch. Still, Philly believed that Lightstone had raised a fair question as to why Chun was fired at all. "Don't give up hope," she urged Chun. "The hearing officer seemed to be offended by a couple of the employees using the c-word and other profanity and remaining on the job, while you neither did nor said anything offensive and were fired. You just can't predict what a hearing officer will do. We'll know soon enough."

Chun's expression didn't brighten.

"Cheer up," Philly urged. "I hear you've found a new job that pays you a little more than you were making. Congratulations."

"Yeah, there's that," Chun said, his mood remaining glum.

78

Philly wheeled the stroller up the front walk of Astoria Manor Assisted Living Residences, negotiated the front door, and made her way to the reception area. Rachel had already arrived as had Joe Baird. They were joined by a middle-aged woman who had a beaten down appearance. The woman was standing off to the side as Rachel and Baird talked, severe worry lines creasing her forehead, her head lowered as she nervously shifted position.

"Sorry I'm running a little late," Philly said. She hadn't been able to face another trip to North Andover and had decided that Daisy was coming along to this meeting. If anyone didn't like that, tough shit.

Baird made the introductions. Lila Gorman didn't meet Philly's eyes when she offered a limp hand in greeting.

"They've got Gerry set up in a sitting room where we'll have some privacy," Baird said, and he led the way to a small room with comfortable chairs that afforded a view of the lawn and gardens abutting a side of the building. A large man was seated in one of the chairs accompanied by an attendant who promptly departed as they entered.

Philly noticed that Gerard Gorman didn't focus on the new arrivals. He stared straight ahead; his lips were moving but no sound came forth. Philly knew that the bigger hockey players played defense. That must have been Gorman's position. Baird was thick set with broad shoulders, but his upper body was not nearly as massive as Gorman's. Gorman's craggy face was topped by a full head of dark hair. He first seemed to register that he had visitors when his wife planted a kiss on his cheek.

"How's it going today, Gerry?" Lila Gorman asked in a tone that suggested no meaningful answer was expected.

"I'm doing good," Gorman said, offering a fleeting smile.

"You're *looking* good," his wife said. "Very dapper."

Gorman was wearing jeans and a red and green flannel shirt. Philly couldn't stop staring at his hands. They were enormous, the palms callused, the fingers thick and blunt.

"How long have you been living here?" Philly asked as she extracted Daisy from the stroller.

Lila Gorman stared at Daisy and seemed to have forgotten that she'd been asked a question. Philly decided to go with her instincts. "This is Daisy," she said. "Why don't you give me a hand with her for a minute?"

Joe Baird rolled his eyes. Philly figured he was now having second thoughts about throwing Gorman's case her way. But Lila Gorman was looking at her daughter with evident delight and Philly was counting on Daisy to help the woman relax. "How long have you been living here?" she repeated.

"About seven months," Lila Gorman replied, carefully holding Daisy and never taking her eyes from the baby's face. "We really can't afford it and I'm not sure how much longer Gerry can stay here. He may need a nursing home before too long."

"We ran a fundraiser for Gerry," Baird said. "That will only help for the short term."

Rachel was busily taking notes. Philly had explained in advance that she wouldn't be writing anything down at this meeting.

"What is your husband's diagnosis?" Philly asked.

"Dementia. It could be early onset Alzheimer's. I'm not sure it makes a difference."

"What are the symptoms?"

Daisy wriggled and Lila Gorman smiled. "He has a lot of difficulty remembering things. He understands less and less of what he's told. More and more he needs help doing simple things such as dressing. You can see he's a big guy and when he gets frustrated he can be physical. I'm living in fear he's accidentally going to hurt someone."

"Cute kid," Gerard Gorman said. "Can I hold the kid?"

Philly didn't hesitate. Despite Lila Gorman's worried frown and head shake, Philly reclaimed Daisy and settled him in Gorman's arms. "This is Daisy. You need to be careful with her."

"I'll be careful."

"When did the symptoms start?" Philly asked.

"About three years ago," Lila Gorman said as she kept an anxious eye on her husband. "Gerry was teaching physical education and people at the school began to notice that he wasn't acting quite right. Then I began to notice things at home."

Philly turned to Baird. "Do you have the list of former teammates?"

Baird produced a list and Philly counted ten names.

"I've listed the teammates in the order I think they can be helpful," Baird explained. "They all know what's going on and they're all willing to help."

"Did your husband ever complain at home about hockey injuries?" Rachel asked.

"Gerry never complained much about anything. He was one of those strong silent types." Lila Gorman's eyes glistened, and Philly wondered how many times she was reminded of the husband she would never reclaim. "Every once in a while, he'd make a comment like, 'I really got my bell rung the other night.' But he'd never complain. He really loved playing hockey in those days."

"Mr. Baird knows that I don't know much about sports," Philly said, "so forgive me if I ask a dumb question. Did your husband wear a hockey helmet when he played?"

"Yes."

"Just so you know," Baird said, "helmet safety design back then wasn't what it is today."

"Have any of your husband's former teammates experienced anything like what your husband is experiencing?" Rachel asked.

"Not that I know of," Lila Gorman replied.

"It's going to get cold soon," Gerard Gorman said. "I can't wait to lace up my skates."

Philly couldn't explain why she felt her daughter was secure in the crook of Gorman's arm. Call it one of Carpenter's hunches.

"Has your husband been on skates since his troubles started?" Rachel asked.

Lila Gorman nodded. "He's totally at ease when he's skating. You watch him skate and you wouldn't think that he has any problems. The exercise is good for him. He's a lot calmer when he's been out on the ice."

No one said anything for a while. Philly wondered whether the small talk and basic questions had been exhausted. The key to the case was Dr. Nancy Corrigan's ability to tie Gorman's condition to his hockey days.

"Are you aware of any incident in your husband's life outside of hockey that could have involved a head injury?" Rachel asked.

"Mr. Baird asked me that. The answer is no."

"Did you witness your husband take blows to the head while he played hockey?" Rachel followed up.

"I went to a lot of Gerry's games," Lila Gorman said. "Hockey's a rough game. Players were constantly being slammed against the boards. I saw Gerry's head hit the boards countless times. I saw a few slap shots bounce off his helmet. There were a couple of times I saw Gerry take a stick to the head, once accidentally by one of his own teammates."

Rachel signaled that she was out of questions.

"Here's what's going to happen next," Philly addressed Lila Gorman. "Rachel and I are going to talk to Dr. Corrigan. What she has to say will be very important to whether your husband will be able to bring a successful case. Rachel will contact the teammates Mr. Baird has identified and will take statements from them. We'll be filing a workers' compensation claim on your husband's behalf very soon."

"Thank you so much."

Philly stood. "Mr. Gorman. I need my daughter back. We've got to be going."

"I like holding her."

"I can tell you do," Philly said. "Would it be okay with you if I brought Daisy back to visit you so you could hold her again?"

"Okay with me," Gorman said as he handed Daisy back to Philly. "Cute kid."

Daisy had woken from an afternoon nap and Philly wanted to get out of the house. The afternoon was warm and there might not be many more afternoons with such obliging weather. She had briefed Carpenter by e-mail on the Gorman case and now had the stroller in motion on the loop she walked with Paul. She turned the corner at the halfway mark and moved along a street much like the one she lived on. Three story houses were set close together with no front yards to speak of. There was no activity in the street. On her right, a woman was sitting on the top step off the front walk of a house that could have been a clone of her own house. Philly nodded as she drew near.

"I've seen you walking this way a lot," the woman said.

Philly stopped and checked her daughter. Daisy was staring at the woman they had encountered. Philly lifted Daisy out of the stroller and kissed her forehead. "I'm trying to take advantage of the weather while I can," Philly said.

The woman didn't respond, although Philly found the woman's gaze at Daisy friendly. "Say hello to Daisy."

The woman offered a curt wave and a brief smile.

"I'm Philomena Piper. Everyone calls me Philly."

The woman nodded. "I'm Mrs. Ferguson," she said after a pause, as if she had been debating whether to introduce herself.

"Why don't we get on a first name basis?"

"The name's Sarah," the woman said without any warmth.

There was no denying that Daisy needed a diaper change. "You mind if I change Daisy?"

When Sarah Ferguson shrugged, Philly decided to take the ambiguous gesture as a yes. She got her changing pack out of the pouch at the back of the stroller and took a seat on the top front step.

Philly worked quickly and soon had Daisy cleaned up and presentable. She stuffed the used diaper in a plastic baggie.

"I live around the block," Philly said.

"I know where you live. You and a bunch of others moved in before spring."

"That's right. How long have you lived here?"

"About twenty-eight years," Ferguson said, the words sounding as if she was announcing a life sentence.

Philly was not put off by Ferguson's lack of friendliness. She didn't know any of her neighbors and now was a chance to learn something about the neighborhood.

"Maybe you can help me," Philly said. "I don't really know anybody in the neighborhood. Do you know anyone reliable who might be interested in babysitting? I'd like to stay away from teenagers if possible."

Ferguson frowned. Philly pegged her in her early sixties. She had fierce dark eyes and a thin face with prominent cheekbones. Gray had made inroads in her short dark hair.

"I wouldn't be trusting a baby to any of the teenagers that live around here," Ferguson said curtly. "You're right about that."

"Then who would you recommend?"

"I'd have to think about that. Maybe no one."

"I've really got to find someone close by." Philly held Daisy under her arms and balanced her on her knees. Daisy bent her own knees and gurgled appreciatively. Philly thought she saw the hint of a smile on Ferguson's face. She had dressed Daisy in a blue one-piece with a matching blue cap. Daisy's black hair stuck out from under the cap.

"By the way, I'm a lawyer."

"I've got no use for lawyers, I'll tell you that right off."

"A lot of people feel that way."

"For damn good reason," Ferguson added.

Philly gestured toward the house behind them. "Do you live here with family?"

"You're pretty nosy, aren't you?"

Philly decided that she'd had enough of Ferguson's sour attitude. "I'm just making small talk. I'm trying to be neighborly. What's your goddamn problem?"

Philly stood up and noticed that she had finally gotten a reaction other than hostility from Ferguson. The woman looked shocked.

"Thanks for letting me use your stoop." Philly moved to the stroller and stored away the changing bag and soiled diaper. "We've got to get going. It wasn't totally nice meeting you. Maybe that will change."

Philly lifted Daisy up and down several times knowing that her daughter liked to be put in motion. Daisy reciprocated with a smile and excessive drool. "Time to go home, munchkin."

"I live on the ground floor," Ferguson said. "I rent out the other two floors. My husband died three years ago."

Philly studied Ferguson. The woman's look hadn't softened but she had made an effort. Philly sat back down on the top front step.

"Sorry to hear about your husband. Do you have family around?"

"My kids live out of state. There was no way they were going to stay around Brighton."

Philly thought about asking Ferguson whether she wanted to hold Daisy and decided not to. She needed to get a better feel for the woman.

"This babysitting job," Fergusson said. "How much are you paying?"

"I don't know. Whatever the going rate is I guess."

"Do you know what the going rate is?"

"No."

"Why don't you get back to me when you find out what the going rate is? I might have someone in mind."

"Who's that?"

"Me."

October

Philly's Untitled Playlist

Enjoy the Silence

Depeche Mode

79

Carpenter gazed across the conference room table at Simon and Rachel and missed Philly. He missed her giving him lip and attitude.

"Philly told me that you did a good job arguing the Chun case," Carpenter directed at Rachel. "Do you mind my asking why you did a turnabout and agreed to do the argument?"

Rachel colored slightly. "I'm trying to be more flexible in my thinking. You and I talked about the highs and lows of litigation. I came to a decision that I was willing to experience the lows in order to experience the highs. I might change my mind tomorrow, but that's my position today."

"Glad to hear it," Carpenter said. "Philly also filled me in on the question you asked her about whether we were thinking of forming a firm. Is this a question you have as well?" he asked Simon.

"Rachel and I were trying to get a feel for where the four of us were headed," Simon said. "We're not sure where that might be."

"Philly and I wanted to talk to you together about this, but that's proving difficult, so I'm speaking for both of us on this. The truth is we don't know where the hell we're going. In the past, Philly and I have talked about formalizing our association, but that never happened. It may have been a mistake not forming a firm or it may have been the right move. We don't have a clue one way or the other. The answer to your question is we don't know where this is heading. We both like working with the two of you. You've been quick studies and of invaluable help. We'd prefer to keep things as they are. Philly needs to sort out how she's going to manage with a baby, and I need to understand what that means for me."

Carpenter paused and regarded the two young lawyers. Simon's expression gave nothing away. Rachel seemed disappointed by his response. "The thing is, you need to speak up if you're unhappy or have complaints about the way we're treating you. We're not mind readers. You've offered to make a financial commitment to some of Philly's overhead here in Boston which we deeply appreciate. We get it that your gesture shows a commitment to practicing law with us. But when all is said and done, we prefer for the moment to keep things as they are."

"There have been a lot of positives for me working with the two of you," Rachel said. "Simon and I have gotten more experience in the past months than most of our classmates have gotten in a year. But it's unsettling to have nothing permanent on the horizon. I'd love to get rid of my paralegal job and devote all my time to practicing law. But I realize there might not be enough business for that to happen."

"There's that," Carpenter said.

Simon ran his hands over his already slicked down hair. "Let me make a suggestion. Let's revisit this situation before the end of the year. Philly needs to sit in. I want to think about this a little more."

"Fair enough," Carpenter said, relieved that another difficult discussion was postponed for a later day. Chalk up another victory for procrastination. "Philly's doing some research on that new case we're taking on, the one about the hockey player. Rachel, you've met the guy, so you'll likely be the one helping her with that. Also, you're in for a treat tomorrow. You get to meet Lily Tompkins, the accountant who's going to lead us out of the wilderness in the Top Tier case. By the way, Rachel, thanks for the list of Devonshire Plastics contracts. I now need you to go on line and find out if the contractors are legit."

"Do you think they might not be?" Rachel asked.

"One can only hope."

On this evening walk, Philly paused the stroller in front of the house where Sarah Ferguson lived. "I want you to meet this woman," she said to Paul. "Like I said, I don't know what to make of her. I want a second opinion." Ferguson's sour disposition argued against using her for a babysitter. Still, Ferguson wasn't some spaced out teenager with the attention span of a flea. Also, Ferguson seemed to want the job and lived close by. Maybe money was an issue for the woman.

Paul marched up the front steps and rang the bell. The light was fading and there was a chill in the air. Philly eased Daisy out of the stroller and nuzzled her. Daisy had on Oshkosh overalls over a purple turtleneck. She wasn't wearing a hat and her fine black hair whipped about in the evening breeze.

Sarah Ferguson opened the door and moved onto her front stoop. Philly waved at her as Paul extended his hand in greeting. Ferguson led Paul down the front walk to the sidewalk.

"We were in the neighborhood," Philly said, "and I thought we'd drop by. I wanted you to meet Paul and I've got an answer to your question. The going babysitting rate appears to be between six dollars and seven fifty an hour."

Ferguson showed no reaction to the numbers. The woman's unsmiling, distant attitude again troubled her, so Philly decided on plan B. "Could you hold Daisy for a moment? I need to get something out of the stroller."

Philly handed off her daughter before Ferguson could object. She moved to the stroller, trying to think of what she could extract from the rear pouch. As she rummaged, she saw that Ferguson was regarding Daisy with interest. The woman had yet to smile but her expression had softened and with a free hand, she stroked Daisy's cheek with the backs of her fingers. When Daisy wriggled with pleasure, Ferguson held on with both hands.

"Are you still interested in babysitting?" Paul asked.

Ferguson nodded.

"Why?" Paul followed up.

Philly found a small stuffed animal underneath extra diapers. Daisy had never showed any interest in the toy.

"I guess I'm a little bored," Ferguson said. "And the pocket money would be nice."

"When's the last time you took care of a little baby?"

Ferguson gave Paul a sharp look and Philly was glad he was around to ask the pointed questions.

"I guess that would be my own kids which was a long time ago. But there are some things you don't forget."

"Do you have any references?" Paul asked.

"References?"

"Right. People who can vouch for you. We don't know you."

Ferguson appeared torn, part of her wanting to tell Paul to bug off, part of her wanting to keep her options in play.

"There's lot of people in the neighborhood who know me," Ferguson said. "I could give you some names."

"Philly says you know where she lives. Drop a list of names and phone numbers off at her house tomorrow. We'll get back to you."

"I'd be looking for the seven fifty an hour," Ferguson said.

"We'll keep that in mind. So, what do you think of Daisy?"

"She's definitely cute," Ferguson said. "She doesn't look anything like you."

"That might be because I'm not the father."

"Oh!"

"Her father died in an accident caused by a drunk driver."

As Ferguson turned to her, Philly felt like an idiot holding a powder blue stuffed elephant by a droopy trunk. She also sensed that Ferguson was seeing her for the first time.

"I'm sorry to hear that. You'll have that list tomorrow."

After nursing Daisy and getting screwed silly by Paul, Philly decided that she now knew what it was like to feel sexually replete. Paul's lovemaking was different from Philip's, slower and less energetic in some ways. She had settled into Paul's unhurried rhythms which took time to ramp up in intensity and the good thing was—at least she chalked it up as a good thing—she had yet to think of Philip when she was with Paul. But the not so good thing, a sad thing really, was the way Philip's lovemaking was becoming dimmer. She foresaw a time when the details would fade completely.

"What do you think I should do with Ferguson?" Philly whispered.

"Nothing," Paul whispered back. "Send me the references and I'll check them out. If the references are good, I'd be inclined to give her a trial run."

"That's what I've been thinking. I just wish she'd smile."

"You can't have everything."

"Right now, I pretty much have."

80

Lily Tompkins was an acquired taste. The accountant was loud, brassy, and opinionated. She never failed to dress in a manner that accentuated bulges she undoubtedly wished to conceal. Today her garish purple outfit made her look like a large, misshapen grape. Carpenter had become used to Lily leveling insults at him as part of introductory small talk, but Simon and Rachel seemed nonplused by Lily's manner.

"Christ, Carpenter, there ought to be a goddamn law preventing you from turning two, nice, innocent, young lawyers into the twisted, cynical wretch you've become. Did you at least warn them what they were in for before they signed on to help you?"

"I don't come with warning labels," Carpenter retorted. He wouldn't be living up to the role he played in their repartee if he took everything Lily dished out lying down.

"Well, you damn well should. It's not too late," Lily directed at Simon and Rachel. "You still have time to retreat from the dark side."

"We're sort of getting used to Mr. Carpenter," Rachel said in a soft voice.

"Take it from me there's no such thing as getting used to Carpenter. And if you think you're getting used to him, it simply means that you've already embarked on the road to ruin. You don't want to get used to Carpenter. Ever."

"Maybe we can talk about our mutual friend, Jerome Singer," Carpenter proposed.

"And another thing," Lily went on, her focus remaining on Simon and Rachel. "Don't buy for a minute Carpenter telling you that practicing law means you can't have a personal life. Just because he doesn't have a personal life doesn't mean it's normal for lawyers not to have one."

"I *have* a personal life," Carpenter objected, "thank you very much. If you're lucky, you'll meet Maxine someday."

"The woman must be a saint," Lily retorted. "But here I am giving you the insults you've earned, when all you want to do is get down to business and bill the hell out of Jerome Singer. Fine. I've read your e-mail. I take it these are the financial records that the other side produced." Lily gestured toward the stacks of documents that covered most of the conference table's surface.

Carpenter nodded. "I've had copies of most of the papers made and boxed up. I'll have them at your office today. It would be helpful if we can show that Devonshire Plastics misstated facts on its loan application or on financial information it gave to Top Tier."

"I don't see how that's going to help Jerome and his company," Lily said.

"Neither do we exactly," Carpenter admitted, grateful that Lily didn't mince words when pointing out any flaws she saw in a battle plan. "If Devonshire Plastics was shady, we think it tilts things back in Singer's favor. It's that simple."

"Don't give me that," Lily erupted. "Nothing's ever simple. You know that better than anyone."

"I didn't cover this in my e-mail," Carpenter said, "but Rachel can't find any information on two of the companies that Devonshire Plastics paid money to."

"E-mail me the details," Lily said to Rachel.

"What do you know about the accounting firm of Miller & Huggins?" Carpenter asked.

"Not a damn thing. Never heard of them."

"Make some inquiries. Huggins, one of the principals, is a friend of Devonshire Plastics' president, the guy who taped the call with Singer."

Lily made her first note on the notepad she had set on the table.

"What else should we be doing for Singer?" Carpenter asked.

"I don't know," Lily said thoughtfully. "Let me dig into the papers you're sending me, and I'll get back to you on that. There are two things you need to keep in mind here. First, I might not be able to help you. There might be no rabbit that can be pulled out of a hat. Second, Jerome Singer is an egotistical rogue. He thinks rules don't apply to him. You don't want to know what I go through when it comes to his personal tax returns and the tax returns of his company. I'm just telling you something you already know—watch your ass with Singer."

"Well this has been a cheery sit down," Carpenter observed.

"Put a sock in it, Carpenter. You know I've gone easy on you."

81

Philly couldn't remember the last time she'd been in her Boston office. When she entered, she almost didn't recognize the room. There was no clutter. The floor was clear, files were either out of sight or arranged neatly on a long rectangular work table likely introduced by Simon and Rachel. A second visitor chair had been added: a black, upholstered, straight-backed chair that looked nothing like its wooden brown mate. Her desktop was bare except for a monthly calendar centered in front of her desk chair.

"Neat freaks!" Philly grumbled.

Philly sat at her desk and turned on her computer. Paying a visit to her office was something Paul had encouraged her to do. "You've got to try it sometime," he had said, making sense, and so today was the first time that she had left Daisy in the charge of Sarah Ferguson. Ferguson's references had checked out. Paul had reported that neighbors regarded her as somewhat of a character who was levelheaded and caring under a crusty exterior. Listening to his description, Philly had thought that Paul could be describing Carpenter.

Her goal for the morning was to draft a claim for workers' compensation on Gerard Gorman's behalf. She had read pertinent statutes, scanned articles on web sites, and reviewed claim forms. If she concentrated, she could knock out a claim by noon, eat lunch, and return home by two to reclaim her daughter.

Studies linked sports concussions to dementia, but there was no clear-cut study that drew that connection when it came to hockey. Bike riding was the sport that produced more concussions than sports typically considered violent such as football, hockey, and lacrosse. That statistic made Philly think of Philip; the sport he had chosen and that she herself loved, was more dangerous when it came to head injuries than most people thought.

Philly began to type. She played up the violent nature of hockey and the pounding Gorman took during the years he played the sport. She described instances when Gorman had become disoriented after taking violent hits that drove him into the boards. She emphasized the fact that Gorman had no way of knowing there was a link between his dementia and his hockey career until Dr. Corrigan made the diagnosis of dementia and cited concussions while playing hockey as the cause.

She relished working at her desk without distractions. At home, even when her daughter was sleeping, Philly was constantly keeping an ear out for any noise out of the ordinary.

Close to noon, when she was wrapping up her draft workers' compensation claim, there were three short knocks on her door and Carpenter entered. "This must be a vision," he said. "I must be hallucinating."

"You should be so lucky."

"Get over here. I want a hug."

"Oh, Jesus. Don't get all mushy on me."

"Get your ass over here. I want a fucking hug."

Philly exited her chair and walked around to the front of her desk. She found the moment awkward, but Carpenter moved close and wrapped his arms around her. Then he pushed her away and stared at her.

"It's great seeing you. I've had it with these goddamn conference calls."

"It's good to be here. I'm trying out a babysitter. I hope it works out."

"Rachel and Simon won't be in today. They're going to be sorry they missed you."

"What the hell did they do to my office?"

"I couldn't stop them," Carpenter said sheepishly. "I hope you're not too pissed."

"I'll live. Anything new?"

"Yeah. The hearing officer found probable cause in Frederick Chun's case, although he said it was a close case. There's a hearing next month. And we've got a trial date next month in the Stanton and Lane case."

"Two contingency cases," Philly observed.

"We'll take what we can get. Tomorrow I've got Lily Tompkins coming in to share whatever the hell she came up with in the Top Tier case. That's the case that's paying our bills."

"Do you have time for lunch?"

"For you, I'll make time."

Gerald Hatch had stopped by the house in the late afternoon and had stayed for dinner. Philly felt excluded as Raul and Isabella prattled on in Spanish and Gerald appeared to hold his own. Gerald had related that his Spanish teacher had taken him aside and complimented him on his improved class participation. Listening to the teen impart the compliment, his expression a mixture of pride and embarrassment, Philly wondered whether any teacher had ever before singled him out for praise.

Now, with Gerald in charge of the stroller they were walking around the block, and Philly was trying to figure out the most painless way to turn the conversation to the lawsuit and the deposition facing the teenager. They passed Sarah Fergusson's house and the first floor was dark. Philly had arrived home exactly at two in the afternoon and Ferguson looked like she was ready for a changing of the guard. But as Ferguson was making ready to leave, she had moved close to Daisy, made a silly face, and given the baby a gentle chuck under her chin.

"That was great news about your Spanish teacher," Philly said. "You should be proud of yourself."

Gerald shrugged noncommittally.

"I'm serious. Listening to you talk with Raul and Isabella, I thought your accent was pretty good. My sense was you understood everything, too."

"I'm working with language tapes," Gerald said. "I'm spending less time playing video games."

"What about your other subjects?"

"I'm still not doing so hot in anything but Spanish."

"You know, if you put in the kind of effort on those subjects that you're putting in on Spanish, you might see improvement."

Gerald didn't say anything. Philly saw him close down, hiding behind the blank stare he had displayed when they had first met.

"It was just a suggestion," Philly said. "You don't have to get pissed."

"I wasn't getting pissed."

Philly decided that she had pussyfooted around Gerald long enough. "Yeah, you were getting pissed because you didn't like what I had to say. The truth is, I've been watching what I say around you so I wouldn't tick you off. That's going to stop. It's not my way and I'm fed up with it. I need to be able to tell you what's on my mind without you going ballistic if it's something you don't want to hear."

Gerald had slowed down; the stroller was now inching along.

"What do you say?" Philly followed up. "Can we start talking frankly with each other?"

"I don't know," Gerald said in a small voice.

"Fair enough. But let's give it a try. If we end up where we're ready to kill each other, we can reconsider."

Gerald didn't say anything, but he picked up the pace pushing the stroller. Philly watched Daisy taking in the sights, gurgling from time to time. The light was gone and a cool breeze was meeting them head on.

"Your deposition is coming up this month," Philly said. "I've told you on two occasions that we need to prepare, but you haven't said anything about it. Avoiding talking about the deposition isn't going to make the deposition go away."

Gerald stopped the stroller. He reached down, freed Daisy from the straps, and brought her up against a shoulder. Philly took charge of the stroller as they made the last turn on the way to the house.

"I don't want to do that deposition," Gerald said.

"You don't have a choice."

"It scares me," Gerald said, barely audible.

"It would scare me too. But since we're now being frank with each other, I truly believe that you will get through it okay provided you make time for me to prepare you."

"Can we put it off?"

"Maybe. But I'd rather not. Let's see how the preparation goes. If the preparation goes well, you may decide that you don't want to put it off."

"I want to put it off no matter how the preparation goes."

"Don't be so sure," Philly said. "Do we have a deal on preparation?"

"I guess so."

"Excellent." Philly decided not to overload Gerald's circuits. The subject of his apologizing to the Mercer boy she would leave for another day.

Daisy let loose with a full body wriggle and a piercing squeal. Gerald held on tight, a smile on his lips, and Philly marveled at how the teenager underwent a transformation whenever he held her daughter. If only you could bring a baby to a deposition for the witness to hold, Philly thought.

82

Lily Tompkins was in full roar, braying off color jokes and giving Carpenter the ration of shit she dispensed his way whenever they met. Today, Rachel and Simon were not as shocked by Lily's performance.

"But enough about you," Lily said abruptly, and Carpenter watched her game face materialize as she extracted a large accordion file from a carryall. "Let's start with the payments made by Devonshire Plastics to the two companies you couldn't find any current information on. The companies were both corporations that, according to corporate records, dissolved four years ago. Devonshire Plastics had contracts with the companies that were dated before the companies dissolved. The financial records show that Devonshire Plastics made very recent payments to the two companies after the companies were no longer in existence. By recent, I mean after Top Tier told Devonshire it was in default."

Carpenter wondered whether this was a gotcha moment, whether Lily had proven that Norman Cassidy had been siphoning money from Devonshire Plastics by paying non-existent bills. Simon was regarding Lily with interest. Rachel was busily taking notes.

"We're talking about some sixty thousand dollars going to these companies after they dissolved. That's not a lot of money given the amount of Top Tier's loan to Devonshire, but sixty thousand is sixty thousand."

"What possible, legitimate explanation would Devonshire have for making payments to dissolved companies?" Simon asked.

"I just push numbers and look up corporate records," Lily replied. "You're the lawyers. It's your job to figure it out."

"Well, it's conceivable that Devonshire owed the companies for work done before the companies dissolved," Carpenter offered.

"No," Lily said. "At the time the two companies dissolved, Devonshire didn't owe them anything."

"Anything else?"

"Yup," Lily went on. "There were five companies that Devonshire paid penalties to. The contracts that Devonshire had with these companies didn't provide for penalty payments. But the bills these companies submitted had added amounts that were listed as penalties. The penalty payments to these five companies totaled three hundred thousand dollars give or take and also occurred after Top Tier told Devonshire it was in default."

The only scenario Carpenter could think of that would benefit Devonshire Plastics involved a kick back of some of the penalty money. Which meant that the companies would have come up with false expense payments on their own company books. Carpenter knew that he was suspicious to a fault and believed the worst of his fellow human beings. But would five separate companies agree to what amounted to a kickback scheme? That conclusion was a stretch. Maybe Devonshire had been pressured into making the penalty payments. Maybe the five companies had threatened to take their business elsewhere if Devonshire didn't agree to pay penalties.

Lily must have said all she was going to say. She began shoving papers back into her accordion file.

"That's it?" Carpenter queried.

"That's all I've got. The rest of it looked clean. Keep in mind I didn't do a full audit, but I did examine different accounts at random and backup to the financials."

Simon and Rachel were looking at him expectantly, but Carpenter had no brilliant follow up for Lily.

"We might be able to do something with the payments to two companies that had dissolved," Carpenter said.

"Why would Devonshire make payments to companies that it didn't owe money to?" Rachel asked.

"Didn't Carpenter give you his sermon about people being scum and willing to do anything for a buck?" Lily fired back. "Maybe this guy Norman Cassidy wanted to put sixty thousand in his pocket. Who the hell knows?"

"This sucks," Carpenter said. "I was hoping for a multi-million-dollar smoking gun since Top Tier lost millions on the Devonshire loan."

"I couldn't find one," Lily admitted.

"What if Norman Cassidy didn't know about the payments to the two companies that dissolved?" Simon offered. "What if one of his financial people concocted a scheme to skim money away from Devonshire?"

"Cassidy signed his approval to pay the invoices to the two dissolved companies," Lily said.

Carpenter had to throw some cold water on that idea, too. "Cassidy will say he routinely initialed bills for payment without reading them."

"Maybe Jerome is going to have to face the fact that he went back on his word to Cassidy," Lily said. "That might be a first for Jerome."

"Shit!" Carpenter let loose. "We've got a lot of porous things we can throw at Cassidy, but he's got easy outs on what you've come up with. What's the story with that accounting firm, Miller & Huggins?"

"Not much," Lily said. "They've got a bare bones website that's filled with platitudes. Paul Huggins, the guy who lives near Cassidy, has had a bunch of complaints filed against him. Also, he was sued by two clients and each case settled."

"What kind of complaints?" Rachel asked.

"Excessive bills, missed tax filing deadlines, not returning client calls—those kinds of things."

"We've got squat," Carpenter concluded. "If the payments to those two dissolved companies were some kind of scheme, the amounts in question are too small in relation to the multi-million loan Top Tier made to Devonshire."

Lily was giving him a hard, all-business stare. "What?" Carpenter said.

"The payments to the dissolved companies don't pass the smell test. So what if the amounts are small. If the idea is to depict Cassidy as a greedy bastard, you've got something to work with. Maybe it'll be a few little things that trip him up."

Carpenter nodded, but he wasn't convinced by Lily's pep talk. Sixty thousand was a drop in the bucket compared to Top Tier's multimillion-dollar loss. Singer wasn't going to like it that Lily had come up with little. He now needed to make a client call that he wouldn't mind putting off.

"Thanks, Lily," Carpenter said. "We'll take it from here."

"Don't sound so enthusiastic. Aren't you the one who's always saying you have to play the hand you're dealt?"

"Thanks for reminding me."

83

For this evening's walk Philly left the stroller at the house. Gerald was carrying Daisy. Her daughter was stuffed into a white winter snowsuit. Even a warm October day could have a chilly night. Philly had thought of leaving Daisy with Isabella but sensed that her daughter's presence in Gerald's arms would make their discussion easier. Seeing Daisy in winter wear, Philly thought ahead to Halloween; Daisy was too young for trick or treating, but it sure would be fun to dress her up in something ridiculous.

"It's time to talk about your deposition, Gerald. You agreed to let me get you ready for it, and I thought we'd get started on this walk."

"Do we have to?"

"Yeah, we do. I'm holding you to your word. You said that the deposition scared you, and I'd like to start by asking you what exactly you're scared about."

Daisy reached for Gerald's nose and he let her take hold. They were such a mismatch, Philly thought, the solidly built, hulk of a teenager and the bright-eyed baby with crazy black hair peeking out of her snowsuit hood.

"What scares you?" Philly repeated.

"They're going to ask me about the fight and why I beat Mercer up. I don't want to have to deal with that stuff."

Philly was wearing a flannel shirt and she pulled the collar up to keep the chill off her neck. It was dark. Pale yellow street light bathed the sidewalk. Daisy had released Gerald's nose and was content for the moment to look around. Evening walks seemed to settle her. When they returned to the house she'd be ready for bedtime rituals.

"We've talked a lot about the fight. Are you now thinking that maybe you overreacted?"

"I probably shouldn't have kicked him the way I did. I was just so angry I . . . I don't know, I guess I just lost it."

"You're going to be asked about the kicking and everything else that went on. The important thing is to tell the truth. Don't make any speeches. Don't volunteer information. Just answer the questions you're asked and tell the truth. If you can, keep your expression neutral."

"I'm going to come out looking bad."

"Maybe, maybe not. The Mercer kid tricked you on that chemistry test and then he teased you about how badly you did. Some people might think that he had it coming to him, and maybe that explains why you were so angry. True, other people might think you overreacted and that his tricking you didn't justify you kicking him the way you ended up doing. But that's for a judge and jury to decide. You need to tell your story and let the chips fall where they may."

Gerald shifted Daisy to a different shoulder. Philly couldn't imagine what her daughter made of the sights and sounds around her. She looked like she was taking everything in. But maybe she didn't have a thought in her head.

"I don't know if I can do that," Gerald said.

"If the Mercer kid were here now, what would you say to him?"

Gerald frowned. "I'd probably tell him he shouldn't have tricked me the way he did."

"Anything else?"

"I don't know. Maybe I'd ask him how he was doing, if he was all better."

"Would you apologize to him for anything?"

"I don't know," Gerald said, giving Daisy a gentle nuzzle. "I really don't like him."

They had passed Sarah Ferguson's house. First floor lights were on, but Philly saw no sign of movement inside.

"You've met Paul, right?" Philly asked. "The Cambridge policeman I'm seeing?"

Gerald nodded.

"I can't remember if I told you about Daisy's father, Philip, and how a teenage drunken driver ran into his bike and killed him right after I knew I was pregnant."

"I didn't know that," Gerald said, suddenly as wide-eyed as Daisy.

"The thing is, Paul wants me to forgive the kid who ran Philip down. Paul thinks it's important that I put Philip's death behind me, and he thinks that my forgiving the kid will help me do that. Paul's been keeping tabs on the kid and says that the kid's a mess because he's racked with guilt over what he did. What do you think I should do?"

Gerald kept walking and Philly sensed that he had momentarily forgotten he was holding Daisy. He'd probably never been asked for advice on an important, complicated question that had no easy answer.

"Are you still angry at the kid?" Gerald asked.

"Yeah, I'm pissed as hell at him if you want to know the truth."

"So why would you forgive the kid?"

"You tell me. Paul keeps saying it's important because it would help the kid get on with his life which is something he can't do right now because of all the guilt he's feeling. I don't know what to do."

"Do you want to forgive the kid?"

"Not particularly."

Gerald didn't say anything. When they arrived at the house he jiggled Daisy gently, holding her securely as he moved her up and down.

"If I ever killed anyone while driving drunk, I don't know if I could stand myself. If it was just an accident, that would be one thing. But getting liquored up and going behind the wheel is something else."

"You still haven't told me what you think I should do," Philly pressed.

"If I was that kid you're talking about, I would want you to forgive me."

Philly held out her arms and Gerald handed Daisy off. There was something off about the way the teen was regarding her, and it took Philly a moment to realize there was concern in his look.

"Thanks for letting me know what you think," Philly said. "I appreciate it. I've got a lot more thinking to do before I make up my mind."

Gerald fidgeted, shifting his weight nervously. "I guess I better get going. Thanks for dinner. I really like hanging out with you guys."

Gerald began to unlock his bike. It was a pale gray mountain bike and Philly had treated him to a front light and one of those red blinking lights for the back of his bike. She didn't like him riding long distances in the night. "You watch yourself going home," she said.

Gerald straddled his bike but stayed put. "I was having trouble in my math class," he said, "and I remembered what you said about my other courses besides Spanish. I went to the teacher after school for some help. I'd never done that before."

"Good for you."

Gerald studied the sidewalk. "He explained things to me. This teacher is so strict in class, everybody's scared to death of him. It was weird because after school he was kind of laid back."

"Then it took a lot of guts to go see the guy."

Gerald shrugged. "I guess so. I was just sick to death of being dumb in the class and not understanding anything the guy was saying."

Philly held Daisy out. "Someone needs a goodnight kiss before she crashes."

Gerald kissed Daisy's forehead, gave a curt wave, and was off. Watching the blinking red light fade from view, Philly thought she had done the right thing by taking things one step at a time and not telling Gerald he'd be ready for his deposition.

84

Jerome Singer had him on a speaker phone. Carpenter had briefed Singer on Lily's conclusions and his client had yet to offer a response. The silence was becoming awkward, but Carpenter was prepared to wait Singer out.

"I was hoping for something better than this," Singer said.

Weren't we all, Carpenter thought. "We need to proceed on the assumption that we're not going to get anything better."

"What happens now?" Singer asked.

Carpenter consulted the list he had made of possible next steps. "We could try to take Cassidy's deposition and the deposition of his accountant. That's not a slam dunk because we're going to have to come up with a reason why depositions are necessary, and the general rule is no depositions if a witness can be subpoenaed so that he's available for trial."

"Depositions would delay the regulatory hearing, right?"

"Right," Carpenter confirmed.

"Then try to take depositions. You were right; the longer this drags on and I'm able to run my business, the better."

Carpenter scanned his list. "If depositions aren't allowed, then I see a trial coming up in November or December. The way this is shaping up, the Loan Company Licensure Review Board will probably call Cassidy as a witness. He might be the Board's only witness, but my guess is they'll bring in someone from the other company you held to the ten-day cure period after mentioning ninety days. For your side of the case the potential witnesses are you, Cassidy, Lily, and Cassidy's accountant, a guy named Huggins. I've done some asking around and I don't think we're going to come up with an expert who will bless what you told Cassidy on the phone. If you have any ideas as to an expert, let me know as soon as possible."

"What if I don't testify?" Singer said.

Carpenter had never considered that possibility. "We need your testimony. It's the only way to get on the record that Cassidy illegally recorded your phone conversation by not telling you in advance that he was going to record the call. Cassidy will probably testify that he told you the call would be recorded. Also, remember that you're suing Cassidy in a separate suit for the illegal recording, and your testimony will be needed in that case as well."

"I'll have to think about whether I want to testify," Singer said.

Carpenter cursed silently. "I don't think the hearing officer will view your not testifying favorably," he said, trying to sound diplomatic.

"I'm not interested in whether a hearing officer looks on me kindly. I am interested in keeping my business afloat."

"Keeping your business afloat is directly tied to whether the hearing officer likes you and rules in your favor. If you stay on the sidelines, my guess is that she'll hold it against you."

"I said I'd think about it," Singer said, and Carpenter knew that the subject was closed.

"Anything else?" Carpenter asked.

"I'll get back to you. I'm already late for a meeting."

When the line went dead, it took some self-control for Carpenter to gently put his phone down. Singer was either in denial or an asshole. Maybe both. What the hell had Michelle Smith ever seen in the guy?

Philly took a call from Wendy Hatch in her home office. When the phone rang, she had Daisy in her lap and had been gently jiggling her while studying Rachel's research in the Gorman case.

"We haven't talked in a while," Hatch said, "and I thought I'd check in with you. I know Gerald's deposition is scheduled for the end of the month. He won't talk to us about it and I'd like to know whether he's getting ready for the deposition."

Philly breathed in Daisy's baby smell thinking that someone was missing a trick by not bottling the scent.

"I've been talking with Gerald about the deposition. We haven't gone through a dry run of possible questions he's likely to be asked, but we're working up to it."

"There's not much time," Hatch said, worry in her voice.

"We're making progress," Philly said. "I believe he'll be ready."

Hatch didn't say anything while Philly worked an eraser into Daisy's small fist.

"I know that Gerald has been visiting you and been to dinner at your house. I hope he's not making a nuisance of himself."

"Far from it," Philly said. The evening walks she took with Gerald were something she now enjoyed as much as the teenager.

"My husband and I have noticed a change in Gerald. He's less angry than he used to be."

"That's excellent."

"He still doesn't share very much with us. He's still not very communicative. But we're not constantly fighting about things recently."

Philly let go of the eraser, ceding the spoils of the tug of war to her daughter.

"I believe that Gerald is smart. He told me that of all his subjects, he enjoys Spanish the most. My two housemates are native Spanish speakers and they only speak to him in Spanish when he comes over. I think it's one of the things he likes about coming to my house."

"He's never said anything about this."

Philly had never told her parents a blessed thing about anything going on in her life. "You might want to check in with his Spanish teacher and get a recommendation for a language tape that Gerald might be interested in. I think Gerald would like that. When he talks with my housemates, he sounds pretty good."

"It's so frustrating," Hatch said with feeling. "It's almost like you know my son better than I do."

"I doubt that," Philly said. "Gerald's a teenager and I've got an advantage over you. I'm not his parent."

Hatch laughed. "Good point. I've already taken up enough of your time. Let me know if I can be helpful when it comes to Gerald's deposition."

When Hatch disconnected, Philly worked her hands under Daisy's shoulders and pivoted her so that they were face to face.

"You're not going to be one of those teenagers who blows her mother off, are you, pumpkin? You're not going to be one of those teenagers who's going to give her mother a dose of her own medicine, are you?"

The eraser suddenly dropped to the floor when Daisy released her grasp.

"I'll take that as a no to both questions, but in my heart I know the answer is yes. You're going to drive me bat shit, aren't you? Of course you are! We both know that."

The size of Maxine's bed was a plus when Carpenter spent the night at her place. It felt like it was twice the size of his, though that wasn't quite the case. Maxine never complained about anything at his condo. Carpenter remembered Lily Tompkins joking that Maxine had to be a saint. Maybe she was.

"What's bugging you?" Maxine asked as she nestled against him.

"Who said anything's bugging me. We just had a good time. I'm happy, can't you tell?"

"We did have a good time. I like our good times. You just seem somewhat withdrawn as if there's something on your mind."

Carpenter suspected he gave off a scent—one of those pheromones—that revealed when he was in a funk. "I was just thinking that there's a lot in my life I don't control."

"That's true of everybody."

"Maybe. But I don't have to like it."

"What are you not controlling that you want to control?"

Carpenter had his mental list ready. "There's Fred for starters. Fred is a factor that I don't have a prayer of mastering. Then there are the cases I've got. This regulatory case with a loan company that I was telling you about? I was talking with the president of the company today and I realized that there wasn't a goddamn thing I could do with the lousy facts in the case."

"You poor baby!"

"Hey, I'm looking for sympathy here."

"You've come to the wrong place. Besides, if everything broke your way, you'd be miserable. You wouldn't have anything to complain about."

"Complaining is overrated."

Maxine laughed. "Not for you. Stop feeling sorry for yourself."

"Then there's me and Philly," Carpenter said, deciding that since Maxine had asked, he was going to unload everything that was bugging him. "With her working at home, it's not the same. I can't stand not seeing her."

"Skype," Maxine said.

"What?" It sounded as if Maxine had mentioned some exotic, aquatic bird.

"Buy it for your computers. Then you can look at each other whenever you talk."

"What the hell are you talking about?"

Maxine explained the Skype technology and Carpenter made her go through it a second time. "How do you know about this?" he asked.

"My kids live out of state and I have a law practice to deal with here. If I want to see my grandkids, Skype is my best bet."

In his love-hate relationship with computer technology, Carpenter accepted that hate held the upper hand. Modern computer innovations were necessary evils and another thing he had no control over. But when a new bit of technology worked for him the way it was supposed to do, he had to admit that the result was terrific.

"That shut you up," Maxine said.

"Just another goddamn thing to think about."

"Then shut up and think about it. Tomorrow, if you're lucky, I'll show you how it works."

"I can hardly wait."

85

It was raining and Gerald had taken public transportation to get to Philly's house after school. Philly took his showing up as a good sign. He could have used the rain as an excuse to blow off their meeting. They had the living room to themselves; Raul and Isabella wouldn't be arriving until dinner time. Daisy was asleep on a mat beside the dining room table, lying on her stomach, her bum in the air. Gerald had checked her out, smiled when he saw her position.

"I'm going to play the role of the lawyer who will be taking your deposition," Philly said. She was seated on one of the easy chairs facing Gerald who was sprawled on the couch. "The idea is to prepare you for questions you might be asked. Are you ready?"

Gerald nodded. Philly couldn't assess the teenager's mood. He didn't have the sullen, closed off look he presented with when she first met him. But there was unease in his close set, dark eyes.

"When did you first become acquainted with Martin Mercer?"

"He's been in all my homerooms since I started at the high school."

"At some time did you get into a fight with him over a chemistry test?"

"Yeah."

"Before that fight, did you have any physical confrontations with him?"

"Yeah."

"What were those about?"

Gerald took a deep breath. "Whenever there was a test in a subject he had, he would always say he couldn't wait for the test. That's probably because he's smart and knew he would do well. And whenever he got a good grade on a test, he'd wave his grade around and ask out loud how everybody else did. And you could tell by the way he asked that he knew nobody had done as well as he had. There were a bunch of us who'd bump him in the halls or give him a shove in gym class to try to get him to stop."

"Did he know why people were shoving him?"

"Yeah. I'd told him to stop bragging about his grades if he knew what was good for him."

"Did he stop bragging?"

"No. He got off on rubbing everyone's nose in how great he did on tests."

"Did he ever complain about taking shots or getting bumped?"

Gerald shrugged. "I don't know for sure. He never complained to me."

"When did all this bumping in the halls start?"

Gerald paused, thoughtful. "Probably toward the end of sophomore year."

"Does Mercer have any friends as far as you can tell?"

"I don't think anybody in his homeroom is a friend. Nobody can stand him. Maybe he hung around with friends outside of homeroom."

Philly studied Gerald. The teen was still sprawled on the couch, but he was attentive. Something was bugging her about Gerald's description of Mercer. Back in her high school days there were plenty of smart kids in her class, but she couldn't remember any of them boasting publicly about high marks. Most of the smart kids had a touch of nerd about them and preferred to fly under the radar. A kid who trumpeted his high grades was just asking to get picked on. Maybe the Mercer kid had a death wish.

"Did something happen during a chemistry test in your junior year that involved Martin Mercer?"

"Yeah. I was sitting next to Mercer and I was copying off his paper. It was a multiple choice test. He saw me copying and shielded his paper so I couldn't see it. So I went back to doing the test and when I looked up again I could see his test paper and I began copying again. After a while he turned and looked at me and he saw I was copying his paper. He gave me this sorry ass smile and hid his paper again. I finished the test and handed it in."

"How did you do on the test?"

"I failed."

"How did Martin Mercer do on the test?"

"He got a hundred on the test."

"How do you know that?"

"We were in homeroom waiting for the homeroom teacher to take attendance and Mercer asked in a loud voice how everyone did on the chemistry test. I remember he was looking at me when he asked the question. Nobody said anything and then he said that he got a hundred. Then he showed me the test paper. I remember the grade was circled in red at the top of the paper."

"What went through your mind when he said that and showed you his test paper?"

"I was pissed off. I figured he let me copy wrong answers and then changed those wrong answers before he handed in his paper. I had copied most of my answers from him."

"Did anything happen between the two of you after homeroom that day?"

"Yeah," Gerald said, lowering his eyes. "We ran into each other outside during a period change and I told him I was going to get him because of how he tricked me."

"What else happened?"

"He said I was so dumb I didn't even know how to cheat. So I gave him a shove and knocked his books down and then he charged me. I sidestepped him and punched him in the face. He went down and I started kicking him. A teacher pulled me off him."

Gerald lowered his eyes.

"How long were you kicking him?"

"I don't know," Gerald said, looking up.

"Did Mercer say anything while you were kicking him?"

"I don't think so. I don't remember anything he said."

"Did the school administration do anything to you after the fight?"

"I got suspended for the rest of the week."

Philly decided that further questions could wait for another day. "How do you feel?" she asked.

Gerald sat up straight. "I feel wiped out," he said, meeting her gaze.

"I know that was hard, Gerald. But you did very well. You answered every question truthfully and you didn't try to avoid any question. We've done all we're going to do today. I really wouldn't change any answer you just gave me. I do have a few small suggestions." Gerald was watching her expectantly, nervously. "These are minor points. I'm very proud of you, and I hope that you're proud of yourself. If you can, try to say yes instead of yeah. Yes, sounds better. Okay?"

"Yeah."

"Jesus . . ."

"That was a joke," Gerald said, sporting a sloppy grin.

"You had me going there," Philly said. "The other thing I wanted to suggest was that you look the lawyer who will be asking you questions in the eye. You need to trust me that you have nothing to be ashamed of or embarrassed about. Eye contact. Remember eye contact."

Gerald nodded. "What else?"

"That's it. 'Yes,' and eye contact."

Gerald became lost in thought. Philly heard Daisy stirring.

"I'd still like to put off my deposition," Gerald said softly.

"Let's not make a decision just yet. We'll have another meeting and then decide. But if you want my opinion, you're ready."

"I don't feel ready."

Daisy let out a sudden wail.

"That's not a happy sound," Philly said. She moved to the dining room table and lifted Daisy off her mat. Even at arm's length, Philly smelled Daisy's dump.

"Come on, Gerald. If you're going to hang out here, it's time you learned how to change a diaper. After that, a deposition won't seem so bad."

86

The office of Gerard Gorman's physician, Dr. Nancy Corrigan, was in a medical building on Longwood Avenue within easy access to several major Boston teaching hospitals. Carpenter had warned her that physicians kept strange schedules, but Philly had never expected to be interviewing a witness at seven in the morning. A disgruntled Sarah Ferguson had reported for duty an hour earlier and Philly had been thankful that she'd already brewed coffee. Ferguson had been dragging; Philly prayed that caffeine would provide a spark. She couldn't shake the fear that Daisy would wake to find a groggy babysitter too far out of it to meet her needs.

Philly now sympathized with Ferguson; she was barely conscious, but Corrigan and Rachel looked alert. The physician had already glanced at her watch twice, a signal to get down to business. Corrigan's cramped office had them seated in a tight triangle.

"We're concerned that there appears to be no medical evidence that Mr. Gorman suffered a concussion," Rachel said. Philly was grateful that her young colleague was taking seriously the instruction to lead this discussion.

"That doesn't concern *me*," Corrigan said forcefully. "Think about it. Dementia is rare in a man in his fifties. There's no history of dementia in Gorman's family. When it comes to the etiology of his dementia, you examine his life and see if there was any activity that might explain the early onset of his disease. His hockey days leap out at you."

Rachel frowned. "I'm having difficulty understanding why you would be allowed to testify that Gorman suffered concussions in his hockey playing days when he was never diagnosed as having a concussion back then."

"I've been an expert witness before," Corrigan responded. "The question is whether I can give an opinion to a reasonable degree of medical certainty. Just so we're clear, it is my opinion to a reasonable degree of medical certainty that Gorman experienced concussions while playing hockey."

"What's the basis for your opinion?" Philly chimed in. Philly was disposed to like Corrigan. They were physically alike. The physician had brown curls as thick as hers and a compact body. Corrigan's pugnacious air suggested that the physician would not be a passive expert witness, but rather a proactive expert looking to help her patient. Still, Corrigan had to know she couldn't pull an opinion out of thin air.

"First, as I already mentioned, there's the lack of a history of dementia in Gorman's family. Second, there's Gorman experiencing dementia at a young age. Third, studies of football players, the sport where studies are most complete, show that football players experiencing early dementia had been concussed while playing. Ergo, Gorman suffered concussions while playing hockey."

Rachel wrote furiously on her notepad.

"And fourth, we've got Gorman's teammates relating incidents where he took hits to the head and 'got his bell rung', and times when he took a hit and became disoriented. These observations are consistent with concussions."

"I understand your reasoning," Philly said. "But Gorman was never diagnosed with concussions when he played."

"So what if there was never a medical diagnosis? It doesn't mean he didn't have concussions. Just that Gorman was too pigheaded to see a doctor."

"Well, you convinced me," Rachel said jokingly.

"Just so we're clear, doctor," Philly said, slipping into Carpenter's doom and gloom mode, "you may not be permitted to give your opinion that Mr. Gorman suffered concussions. Hopefully, your evidence will come in but there's no guarantee that will happen."

"That's your job," Corrigan retorted. "I've got my opinion and I'm prepared to support it. It's your job to make sure I get to have my say."

Philly nodded. Corrigan had correctly identified the lawyers' responsibility. "I don't really follow sports," she said, "but from the little I've seen, I've been under the impression that hockey is more violent than football. How come there aren't medical studies of hockey players that support the conclusions that were reached in the studies of football players?"

Corrigan shrugged. "I don't have an answer for you. It probably just hasn't happened yet. Someone has to be first."

Rachel raised her hand as if she were a student asking a teacher for permission to speak. "The hockey team will likely come up with an expert who will say that there's no medical evidence linking Gorman's injuries to hockey. How would we discredit such an expert?"

"I know what I'd do," Corrigan said authoritatively. "I'd ask the expert what did cause Gorman's dementia."

"What if the expert says he or she doesn't know what caused the dementia?" Rachel asked. "Aren't there cases where people experience dementia at an early age and no one can explain why that happens?"

Rachel's question caused Corrigan to pause. "I'll concede that not every case involving the early onset of dementia can be explained," Corrigan admitted. "But in Gorman's case we have a reasonable basis for attributing his condition to his playing hockey. He's experiencing the same delay that we see in the football cases between his playing days and showing his first signs of dementia. Anyway, that's my medical opinion and I'm sticking to it." Corrigan again looked at her watch. "We need to wrap this up. I've got rounds to do."

"I don't have any other questions," Rachel said.

"Thanks for your time, doctor," Philly said.

"I've got to run. Feel free to use my office."

Corrigan left and Philly consulted her notes from the interview. "Any thoughts?" she asked Rachel.

"She certainly has a strong personality," Rachel observed.

"Did you warm to her?"

"Not particularly. But I'm glad she's on our side. I don't see her changing her opinion."

"Your next job is to interview Gorman's teammates," Philly instructed. "We want eyewitness accounts of Gorman experiencing symptoms that go with a concussion. For example, Gorman becoming disoriented after taking a hit. When that's done, review Gorman's workers' compensation claim with Joe Baird and get him to sign off on filing it."

Rachel nodded. "What does it mean to have your bell rung?"

Philly guessed that Rachel cared as little for sports as she did. "I think it comes from having a ringing in your ears after taking a blow to the head. Make sure you ask each teammate whether he saw Gorman get his bell rung. Use that phrase. Also, ask each teammate you talk to whether he ever had his bell rung. Try to write down the answers verbatim. The information might not be totally helpful. If these teammates had gotten their bells rung and are not suffering from early dementia, that might hurt our case."

"I'll tell you this," Rachel said as she packed up her papers. "My head is ringing right now."

87

Donald Fanning reminded Philly of a televangelist. He had a full head of white hair slicked back on the sides with a thick pompadour that drooped over his forehead. His ruddy face appeared freshly scrubbed. When Fanning smiled, he displayed an array of blindingly white teeth. Carpenter had warned her that Fanning was smooth and connected well with juries, but Philly was finding that hard to believe. Ingratiating folksiness turned her off.

"Make yourselves comfortable," Fanning said. "The stenographer is running a little late but we should be getting started soon. Can I get you any refreshments?"

"No thank you," Philly said as Gerald Hatch shook his head.

The attorneys representing Gerald's parents and the school officials who had been sued also declined Fanning's offer. Frank Price, the lawyer representing the Hatches, was a young solo practitioner with a relaxed manner and an amused expression. In contrast, Calvin Blaine, the lawyer representing Cambridgeport school officials and teachers, was all business. Blaine was short and trim; he had a brown moustache and light brown thinning hair. When it came to trial, Philly figured Blaine would be the more aggressive of the two.

Fanning left his office conference room and Philly studied her client. She didn't like Gerald's blank look that she associated with his closing himself off. Maybe she had made a mistake telling Gerald he was ready for his deposition. She reached into her purse and took out the picture she had been meaning to give him. Philip's father had taken a fair number of photographs at the cookout she had held during the summer.

"Here. This is for you. I keep forgetting to give it to you."

Gerald took the picture, stared at it for a long moment, and flashed a brief smile. "Can I keep this?"

"Yes. It's for you. But I want to get another picture of you and Daisy. Raul has a camera and I'm going to borrow it."

"Can I hold this during the deposition?"

"I don't see why not."

The stenographer entered the room, flustered and apologetic. "I got held up in traffic," she explained.

Fanning took a seat next to the stenographer across the table from where Philly sat with Gerald. "The usual stipulations?" Fanning asked.

"Agreed," Philly said as Price and Blaine nodded.

When the stenographer was ready, Fanning introduced himself and started in with background questions. Gerald had lived in Cambridgeport his entire life. So far in high school he had been a C student with no extracurricular activities. He had not considered going to college, and had no plans to get a job when he graduated. He was somewhat of a loner, but had a number of friends. He and his friends liked to play video games and not much else. Gerald delivered his answers in a put-upon teen mode. Philly figured that Fanning assessed her client as a discontented teen with little ambition and no prospects for a meaningful future.

"Do you understand that Martin Mercer is suing you because you beat him up and caused him injuries?" Fanning asked.

"I understand he's suing me," Gerald said, without looking at Fanning.

"You did beat him up and injured him, didn't you?"

"We had a fight and he got the worst of it."

"What injuries did you suffer in that fight?"

Gerald stopped to think. He glanced at the photograph which he held below the conference room tabletop. "He didn't hurt me."

"What injuries did Martin Mercer suffer?"

"I couldn't tell you exactly."

"Isn't it true that Mr. Mercer suffered broken bones?"

"That's what I heard."

"You said that the two of you were in a fight. How did the fight start?"

Gerald again glanced down at the photograph he was holding. He looked up and Philly was pleased to see that he held Fanning's gaze as he recounted his fight with Mercer.

"How many times did you kick him?"

"I couldn't tell you."

"Was it more than once?"

Gerald looked down as he twirled the photograph.

"Yeah."

"More than ten times?"

"I don't know."

"Was he on the ground when you started kicking him?"

"Yeah. It's like I said, he went down."

"What did you have on your feet when you were kicking Mr. Mercer?"

"Sneakers."

"How long were you kicking Mr. Mercer?"

"I don't know."

"Was it longer than a minute?"

"I don't know."

"At some point did you stop kicking Mr. Mercer?"

"Yeah."

"How come you stopped?"

"A teacher grabbed me."

"Were you suspended from school for this incident?"

"Yeah. I mean yes."

Gerald glanced her way. Philly kept her head down but made sure he could see her smile and nod of approval.

"For how long?"

"The rest of the week. I forget how many days were left in the week."

"How tall are you?"

"Six feet."

"What do you weigh?"

"About one ninety."

"You said that Mr. Mercer brought up a chemistry test. What's the story with the chemistry test?"

Gerald looked at the photograph for a long moment and then faced Fanning, and repeated what he'd told Philly during their prep.

"So why did you knock Mercer's books down and shove him when he brought up the chemistry test?"

"Why do you think?" Gerald said defiantly.

"I'm sorry but you don't get to ask questions," Fanning said equably. "You need to answer my question."

"Because the little shit tricked me. He let me copy wrong answers and then changed his wrong answers. When he asked me how I did on the test he was rubbing my nose in it."

Fanning studied Gerald impassively. If Fanning was surprised by this evidence of the background to the chemistry test fight, you couldn't tell from his expression.

"Isn't it against school rules to copy from another student's test?" Fanning asked.

"Yes."

"You keep glancing down. Are you holding something? Are you looking at notes?"

Gerald brought the picture to the table. "It's a picture she gave me," Gerald said, inclining his head toward Philly.

"May I see it?"

Gerald slid the photograph across the conference room table.

"Who's that you're holding?"

Gerald again inclined his head in Philly's direction. "It's her baby."

Philly met Fanning's questioning gaze. She noticed that Price was grinning and Blaine unsmiling.

"Cute kid," Fanning said returning the photograph. "Were you and Mr. Mercer chemistry lab partners?" Fanning directed at Gerald.

"Yes."

"How did that work out?"

Gerald placed the photograph on the table in front of him and stared at it for a long moment. "It was good and bad. It was good because Mercer knew a lot and we got good grades on our lab reports. But it was bad because he was sort of a hog. He wanted to do all the work himself. He never showed me how to do anything and he never explained anything to me. He made me feel stupid, and he did it on purpose."

"Were you content to let him do all the work himself?"

"Yeah. I mean yes. I realize now that wasn't the best way to go about things."

"Before the fight you told us about, did you and some of your friends ever shove Mr. Mercer in the school corridors."

Gerald nodded. "Yes."

"Why?"

"Because in homeroom he was always bragging about how well he did on tests, and then he'd ask you what you got on the test like he wanted to embarrass you because he knew you didn't do as well as he did. He was being a jerk."

"Did you think that made it okay for you to shove him?"

"I wanted him to stop bragging and to stop trying to put everyone else down because we weren't as smart as him."

"Did you think it was okay to shove him to get that message across to Mr. Mercer?"

Gerald stared at the photograph. Philly had told him to think before he answered a question and that instruction must have taken root.

"Before any of the shoving started, my friends and I asked him a bunch of times to shut up about asking us how we did on tests because it was none of his business. He gave us one of his smart-ass smiles like he was better than us and I knew he was going to keep on trying to embarrass us by asking about how we did on tests. When he kept it up, I guess I was hoping a few shoves would get him to stop."

Fanning consulted his trial notebook. "What's your response when someone shoves you?"

"I shove back. I don't take shit from anyone."

"Have you been disciplined during high school for fighting?"

"I think I had to do detention after a fight back when I was a freshman."

"What was that fight about?"

"A friend of mine was getting into it with another kid and the other kid's friend jumped my friend. I pulled the kid's friend off of my friend. A bunch of other kids joined in."

Fanning wrote on a notepad. "Were you involved in any other high school fight?"

"I may have been. But nothing I got punished for."

"Did you ever get in a fight over something that happened at school and the fight settled things off school property?"

Gerald nodded. "There was one time in freshman year that this big guy who was a sophomore called one of my friends a retard. My friend was a little guy and I told the big guy to lay off my friend and he told me to fuck myself. I said I'd meet him after school."

"What happened?"

"I beat the kid up."

"What kind of injuries did the kid have?"

"He had a broken jaw."

"Do you look at fighting as a way to settle disagreements you might have with another student?"

Gerald glared at Fanning, and Philly wondered if the teen was about to lose his cool.

"No," Gerald said. "But it sometimes comes down to a fight."

Fanning looked at his watch. "Let's break for ten minutes."

Philly walked Gerald to the reception area of Fanning's office where they took chairs out of earshot from the reception desk.

"I'm proud of you," Philly said. "You're doing great."

"This other lawyer is an asshole," Gerald said morosely.

"That may or not may be the case. It doesn't matter."

"Did I say anything bad for the case?"

Philly leaned forward and patted his knee. "No,' she said. "I've been trying to get you to understand that telling the truth can never be bad for the case. Just keep doing what you're doing."

Gerald's worried look told Philly he believed that he hadn't performed well so far.

"What's he going to ask me when we go back?"

Philly consulted her list of cross-examination subjects that she had gone over with Gerald. "Not a hell of a lot. But he'll keep it going for another hour just so he can hear himself talk."

"Another hour," Gerald repeated as if he were contemplating an eternity.

"It'll be over before you know it."

"Are you going to do this with Mercer?"

"You bet your ass I am."

88

"We're here this morning to consider Top Tier's motion to take the depositions of Norman Cassidy and Paul Huggins," Serena Jones announced. "I'll hear first from Top Tier. Mr. Carpenter? Or will it be Mr. Jeffries today?"

Carpenter rose. He had every confidence that Simon could hold his own against Louise Fuller and Herbert Brown, but decided to spare the young lawyer the chore of arguing a losing motion that a client insisted be filed.

"It is true that both Mr. Cassidy and Mr. Huggins may be subpoenaed to testify at trial," Carpenter began. "And it is also true that the Board's hearing rules disfavor depositions when a witness is available to testify at trial."

Jones' fixed stare confirmed that he had correctly zeroed in on the major obstacles that Top Tier had to overcome.

"That being said," Carpenter resumed, "there can be no argument that the hearing to be held before the Loan Company Licensure Review Board needs to be fair. Top Tier's ability to remain in business is at stake, so the interests of Top Tier in a fair hearing are substantial. We have cited in our motion questionable practices of Devonshire Plastics that were revealed in the documents that company furnished in discovery. Fairness requires that Mr. Cassidy, the president of Devonshire, and Mr. Huggins, that company's accountant, answer questions about those practices so that Top Tier is not ambushed by testimony it would be hearing for the first time. Moreover, Mr. Cassidy's deposition is crucial because he is the one who illegally taped a telephone call with Top Tier and, at a minimum, his credibility is in issue. By illegally taping a call, Mr. Cassidy committed a criminal act. This criminal conduct concerned Mr. Singer, Top Tier's president, and Top Tier was warranted in seeking to foreclose on the Devonshire loan because of Mr. Cassidy's illegal act. Additional illegal acts by Mr. Cassidy would further justify Top Tier's foreclosure efforts."

"The argument that you are making can be made in every case before the Board," Jones interrupted. "I'm concerned that depositions will delay the trial in this case. If you believe that Top Tier has been unfairly surprised by any testimony, you can make a motion to suspend testimony until you have a chance to do further research. Also, you can explore any alleged illegal conduct by Mr. Cassidy at trial."

"Respectfully, Your Honor," Carpenter said, "that's putting the cart before the horse. A party to a hearing where its ability to remain in business is at stake needs to be informed of and have access to all the facts *before* the hearing commences. Interrupting the hearing so that a party may deal with surprise testimony will only serve to delay the hearing more than would be the case if the hearing began after full discovery was allowed."

"What do you say, Ms. Fuller?" Jones asked.

Louise Fuller looked bored as if she had heard the arguments Carpenter had just advanced countless times before.

"The Board wants the trial of this case to conclude this year. The trial has already been delayed by the discovery Top Tier has been afforded. Plus, the accounting irregularities that Mr. Carpenter mentioned have nothing to do with whether Top Tier's president, Mr. Singer, made a misrepresentation to Mr. Cassidy, something a tape recording reveals he did. The motion before you is a delaying tactic on Top Tier's part."

"Top Tier is agreeable to a trial of this case this year," Carpenter responded. "Depositions in November would still permit trial in December. Also, it is not true that the accounting irregularities have nothing to do with this case. If Devonshire Plastic's books and records are erroneous, then Top Tier was lied to and could properly proceed to protect itself regardless of what Mr. Singer may have told Mr. Cassidy."

For a long moment, Jones studied the lawyers before her without expression. "I've heard enough," she finally said. "Top Tier's motion to take depositions is denied. The individuals Top Tier wishes to depose are available to testify at trial. Top Tier may make an appropriate motion if any testimony from these individuals comes as an unfair surprise. Thank you, counsel."

Jones left the hearing room abruptly. Fuller and Brown began conferring. Carpenter didn't want to think about the help Brown would be offering to Fuller. Simon's hand settled on his shoulder. "That was preordained," he said.

November

Philly's Untitled Playlist

Fear

Way Out West

89

Judge Carmen Fielding had just instructed the jury that opening arguments were not evidence. Carpenter remembered Philly's first jury trial and the way his heart had pounded until she took her position in front of the jury and began her opening argument in a firm voice. As Simon faced the jury in Herbert Stanton's and Millie Lane's trial, Carpenter didn't have a similar feeling of unease. Which probably meant that he had missed a trick and should be worrying in earnest. But there was something about Simon that inspired confidence. The young lawyer had sat in on several jury trials to gain experience, and Carpenter had been unable to find fault with the trial run of his opening argument.

After introducing himself and Carpenter, Simon asked Stanton and Lane to stand. Carpenter followed the jury's collective gaze. The couple nodded in the jury's direction and Lane offered a genuine smile. Carpenter had grown to like the couple. They had turned down Wayne Anderson's last offer of $24,000 and decided to roll the dice with a jury trial. "Anything we recover is found money," Stanton had said. "If we come away with nothing, so be it."

"What's the one thing we Americans value more than anything else?" Simon asked the panel. He paused a beat while his question hung in the air. Several jurors leaned forward in anticipation of his answer.

"It's our right to privacy. It's our right to be left alone. It's our right to go about our personal business knowing that our business is personal and private without any Big Brother tactic monitoring what we do or where we are on our personal time. We all treasure our right to privacy, don't we?" Carpenter saw two jurors nod. "Can you imagine the outrage we'd feel if an employer we worked for installed a tracking device to monitor our whereabouts on our personal time and did that without telling us? It gets my blood boiling just thinking about something like that. Yet, that is exactly what happened to Herbert Stanton and Millie Lane.

"Mr. Stanton and Ms. Lane had worked for Wise Computer Consultants for years going to clients of the company and dealing with the clients' computer problems. They were good at their job. Wise Computer Consultants gave them consistently high marks when evaluating their job performance and awarded them raises and bonuses each year they worked for the company. And then, without warning, Wise Computer Consultants fired them on the spot. 'What happened?' you're probably thinking. Here's what happened.

"Wise Computer Consultants gave its employees new cell phones and required its employees to use the new phones during working hours. Sounds generous, doesn't it? But what the company didn't tell its employees was that the cell phones had GPS tracking devices built into the phones so that each employee's location was known to the company at all times. I'm guessing some of you may use GPS when you're driving. For those of you who are not familiar with this technology—and until this case came along I wasn't familiar with it probably because I don't even have a car—a GPS or Global Positioning System keeps track of where you are. It's a sophisticated technology that uses satellites. I'm not going to explain the technology any further because I'd probably get it wrong. But what we can all understand is that Wise Computer Consultants, without telling its employees what it was up to, gave cell phones to its employees, demanded that the employees use the cell phones, and used the cell phones to spy on its employees during their personal time. Not telling employees what it was up to when it gave them cell phones to use was just plain sneaky on Wise Computer Consultants' part."

Simon studied the jurors, panning the panel. Each juror was regarding him intently, interested in the story he was unfolding.

"Some of you may have nine to five jobs and may even punch a time clock. That wasn't the way Mr. Stanton's and Ms. Lane's employment worked. They were paid only for time they spent on a job and for the time traveling to and from the job. They had to be on call in case a job came up and they needed to be contacted. But when they weren't on the job, they were on their own time free to do whatever they pleased. When they weren't on a job or traveling to and from a job, they weren't paid at all even though they may have been on call.

"Mr. Stanton and Ms. Lane often chose to spend their free time together. We've all heard about workplace romances, and that is exactly what happened between them. They fell in love. They still are in love and recently became engaged. There were occasions, when they were on their own time, that they would meet together at a motel to carry on the romance that had bloomed between them. Getting together never interfered with doing their jobs. If they got a call about a computer problem that needed attention, they would respond to the call without missing a beat. Wise Computer Consultants never complained that they were late to respond to a job. So I'm sure you're asking yourselves why did these valuable, competent employees get fired?"

Carpenter was pleased. The jurors seemed anxious for more details.

"Wise Computer Consultants used the GPS devices implanted in their cell phones to spy on their movements. The company used the tracking device and saw that the two of them spent time together. The GPS tracking device showed their locations and the company looked up what was at the locations and found that they were at motels at the same time." Simon paused and moved close to the jury bar. "But here's an important fact. Wise Computer Consultants had no rule or policy that employees couldn't see each other socially, or date, or be intimately involved. Yet, when he fired Mr. Stanton and Ms. Lane, Wise Computer's president, a Mr. Bruce Bolton, told them he was firing them because the company knew that they were spending time together in motels."

Simon moved away from the jury bar. He again made eye contact with each juror.

"Put yourselves in the position of Mr. Stanton and Ms. Lane. Mr. Stanton and Ms. Lane had no idea how Mr. Bolton knew they were spending time together. As you will hear, they wondered whether Mr. Bolton had had them followed. In any event, they asked Mr. Bolton how he knew they were spending their free time together. And *that* was when Mr. Bolton, for the very first time, revealed that his company had snuck tracking devices into the cell phones he had given them to use. Imagine finding out at the time you were being fired that your employer had been spying on your movements during your personal time, in fact, your *most* personal time. You'll hear from Mr. Stanton and Ms. Lane about the outrage and humiliation they felt over this secret surveillance by Wise Computer Consultants. Mr. Stanton and Ms. Lane are lucky to be in Massachusetts because in our state, the right to privacy is so strongly recognized that we have a statute here in the commonwealth that protects our right to privacy and permits citizens to sue under the statute when their rights of privacy are violated."

Talking about legal principles oftentimes left a jury staring at a lawyer with blank looks. But Carpenter thought that the jury seemed focused.

"Mr. Stanton and Ms. Lane are seeking damages from Wise Computer Consultants for the outrageous and clandestine violation of their right to privacy. After you hear the evidence, you're going to be in the position of putting a dollar value on just how much a violation of privacy is worth. I have no doubt that you will value the right to privacy enjoyed by Mr. Stanton and Ms. Lane as much as you would value your own right to privacy. Thank you."

Simon nodded to the jurors and again made eye contact with each of them before resuming his seat. Wayne Anderson waited a long moment and then took his position in front of the jury. Carpenter was struck by the physical mismatch between Anderson and Simon. Anderson was a big guy, muscular, an imposing physical specimen with the air of confidence that big guys often projected. If you stood Simon next to Anderson, Simon would appear to be the kid he was.

"The plaintiffs in this case have resorted to claims that their privacy rights were violated because they have no other claims that they can bring against Wise Computer Consultants. The plaintiffs had no employment contract with Wise Computer. They were employees at will and I'm sure many of you know what that term means. It means that their employment could have been ended at any time, for any reason or for no reason. And that is exactly what happened. Wise Computer didn't have to give the plaintiffs any reason for firing them. The fact that Mr. Bolton provided a reason doesn't mean that the plaintiffs are in any better position than if Wise Computer fired them without giving them a reason, as it had every right to do. While the plaintiffs emphasize that they were involved in a romantic relationship, Wise Computer was not required to be as impressed with that fact as the plaintiffs apparently are."

Carpenter considered it might be wishful thinking, but he sensed that Anderson, at least in his opening remarks, had not engaged the jurors' attention as Simon had.

"The plaintiffs want you to believe that their numerous rendezvous occurred on their personal time. That's just not the case. As the plaintiffs admit, their romantic trysts occurred while they were on call for Wise Computer. Wise Computer had an absolute right to know where its employees were during their on-call hours because they had to be available to Wise Computer when a job required attention. Nor was Wise Computer required to inform its employees that their on-call time locations would be monitored. That argument by the plaintiffs is simply the plaintiffs trying to come up with a way to get around the fact that they could be fired for any reason or no reason."

Anderson regarded the jurors in turn, totally at ease. Carpenter sensed that he was starting to score points with his counterattack on the arguments that Simon had made.

"Mr. Jefferies used the word spying a lot when he addressed you. Now there's a false characterization if I ever heard one. The only thing Wise Computer learned from the GPS feature in its employee cell phones was where an employee was. What an employee was doing at a particular location cannot be determined by GPS. Why was it important for Wise Computer to know where its employees were? I'm sure you know the answer to that question, but I'll spell it out just the same. Knowing an employee's precise location made it easier for the company to decide which employee was nearest to a job site where a computer needed to be fixed and which employee should be contacted first to address a client computer problem. Wise Computer had no information as to what an employee was doing at any location, and had no information as to how an employee spent his or her personal time or on call time. Nothing of a private or personal nature was revealed by the GPS feature of the cell phones given to employees."

Carpenter was impressed by the way Anderson had confronted the privacy right issue. Anderson had probably leveled the playing field after Simon had scored points in his opening argument.

"Now, the plaintiffs want you to believe that they were damaged by the GPS feature in their cell phones. But they weren't damaged in the slightest. We certainly haven't heard how they were damaged. The fact that the plaintiffs claim to be outraged and humiliated by being given a cell phone with a GPS feature doesn't translate into the fact that they were damaged. And, in fact, the plaintiffs were not damaged in any way, shape or form. When Wise Computer terminated their employment as it had an absolute right to do, the plaintiffs were in the exact same position they would have found themselves in if they had been fired for no reason at all which, I'll repeat, Wise Computer could have done. Also, after being terminated, the plaintiffs went into business for themselves and are earning more money than Wise Computer ever paid them."

Anderson paused as if to allow time for his remarks sink in. Then he briefly paced in front of the jury box before returning to a centered position.

"The plaintiffs may think they have the right to do whatever they want, and they may think that they had been given lifetime employment by Wise Computer. But they are wrong on both points. An employer is not required to accept how or where employees spend their time when the employees are on call for the employer. And certainly the plaintiffs are deluding themselves if they believed that they had jobs for life and couldn't be fired. They were employees at will which meant they could have been fired instantly in their employer's absolute discretion. That's what the law permits when it comes to employees at will. That's what happened to the plaintiffs and they have no cause to complain. The plaintiffs should be awarded absolutely nothing in this case."

Anderson returned to his seat unhurriedly. Carpenter cast a quick glance to the rear of the courtroom. Stanton and Lane didn't appear fazed by Anderson's performance.

Judge Carmen Fielding rose. "We'll take a short recess and proceed with the plaintiffs' case when we return."

When most witnesses had been deposed in a case, Carpenter found the actual trial to lack suspense. He was experiencing that feeling now as Anderson was cross-examining Herbert Stanton.

"You mentioned that you and Ms. Lane have gone into business together," Anderson said. "Is that business prospering?"

"I'd say so," Stanton said with evident pride.

"Are you and Ms. Lane currently making more money than you made when you were employed by Wise Computer Consultants?"

"That only happened about a few months ago."

"Is it true that you and Ms. Lane, in your new company, currently service clients that you used to service while with Wise Computer Consultants?"

"Yes."

"Would I be correct that as you are testifying here today, you regard your reputation and Ms. Lane's reputation as computer consultants to be excellent?"

"I'd say we're excellent at what we do." Stanton said, his pride again surfacing.

Carpenter wondered if Stanton understood the game Anderson was playing. In his closing argument to the jury, Anderson would focus on the fact that Stanton's and Lane's reputations hadn't been damaged by being fired or being tracked with a GPS device, and that financially, the firings had worked to their benefit.

"Did you ever inform Mr. Bolton that you and Ms. Lane had a romantic relationship?" Anderson changed the subject.

"No. If he had asked, I would have told him."

"You testified earlier that you were outraged and humiliated when you found out that a GPS feature was contained in your company phone. Do you recall that testimony?"

"Yes, that's what I said.

"Did you discuss those feelings of outrage with anyone besides Ms. Lane?"

"No."

"Is it correct that outside of Ms. Lane, no one knew of or shared in your feelings of outrage and humiliation?"

"I didn't discuss it with anyone besides Ms. Lane if that's what you mean."

"Thank you, Mr. Stanton," Anderson said. "That's partly what I meant. As far as you know, is Ms. Lane the only person who is aware of the feelings of outrage and humiliation you mentioned previously?"

Stanton pondered the question. "I believe so. Wise Computer's spying on me was not something I wanted to broadcast."

"Move to strike the last sentence," Anderson requested.

"Denied," Judge Fielding promptly ruled.

As Anderson launched into a line of questions directed at the new business Stanton and Lane had founded, Carpenter studied the jurors. For the most part, they had appeared sympathetic to Stanton during Simon's direct examination. As Anderson's cross-examination continued, it was hard to tell whether their sympathy held. Stanton was a down-to-earth guy who came across as forthright with nothing to hide. But while his client had expressed outrage and humiliation over the GPS tracking of his whereabouts, so far Stanton had not shown anything specific as to how the tracking had caused him and Lane injury requiring compensation. The couple's chances for a major pay day likely depended on whether the jurors regarded Wise Computer's insertion of a GPS device as something underhanded that needed to be punished.

"No further questions," Anderson said, and Carpenter wondered how long his attention had drifted.

Carpenter hadn't thought of Stanton's and Lane's case as the kind of case that would turn on a defining image but with two words, Millie Lane had turned his perception on its head.

Simon had just asked Lane for her reaction when Bruce Bolton had revealed the presence of GPS in the cell phone that had been given her. Lane pivoted in the witness chair, faced the jurors, and her mild-mannered demeanor underwent an abrupt transformation to visible anger. "I was so angry I wanted to spit," Lane said, and the way she said it, Carpenter half expected flying saliva to reach the jury box. "I felt like a peeping Tom had been watching me all this time. I felt violated. I can tell you this. Now that Herbert and I are running our own company, we would never, ever do such a thing to anyone we employed."

"Peeping Tom," Simon repeated, and Carpenter was pleased that he was attuned to Lane's image. "Thank you, Ms. Lane."

Bruce Bolton stared balefully at the instruction book that had accompanied the cell phones given to his employees, an exhibit that Carpenter and Simon had deliberately not presented at his deposition.

"Yes," Bolton said. "This is the cell phone instruction book."

"Could you point out to me the instruction that explains the GPS device that was installed into your employees' phones?"

Bolton halfheartedly rifled the pages of the instruction book. "There's nothing in the instructions on that."

"Nothing!" Carpenter raised his voice to a volume he hoped imparted indignation. The jury was directing largely unfriendly looks in Bolton's direction. "Then if I understand the situation, Wise Computer made the deliberate decision to conceal the GPS feature from its employees. Is that correct?"

"It was a feature we added that was customized."

"Customized?" Carpenter thundered, enjoying himself. "The fact is that you deliberately concealed this added feature so your employees wouldn't know it existed, correct?"

"We didn't tell them about the added customized feature."

"Which means you concealed it, correct?"

"We just didn't tell the employees about it," Bolton said, avoiding eye contact with the jury.

"Which means the GPS was concealed from your employees, doesn't it?"

"I don't agree with the word concealed. It was just not something we mentioned when we distributed the cell phones."

"I'll bet you don't agree with the word concealed," Carpenter retorted.

"Objection," Anderson said, also raising his voice.

"Move on, Mr. Carpenter," Judge Fielding instructed.

"If Mr. Stanton and Ms. Lane had been tracked by GPS and were never found to be in the same location, would they have been fired?"

"Objection," Anderson pounced.

"Overruled."

Bolton hesitated and Carpenter wondered why. Surely Anderson had prepared his witness for this question.

"Probably not," Bolton said.

"In fact, if the GPS system hadn't shown Mr. Stanton and Ms. Lane to be in the same place, isn't it true that your company would not have tried to identify the nature of their locations revealed by the GPS?"

Again Bolton hesitated. "That's probably true."

"You wouldn't have fired either of them if either of them went to a motel alone, would you have?"

"I don't know."

"With the exception of Mr. Stanton and Ms. Lane, did your company ever look up the exact location of an employee that came up on the employee's GPS?"

"I don't know. I don't think so."

"Let me get this straight," Carpenter said, thinking he had things as straight as they were ever going to be. "When GPS reports showed two employees in the same place at the same time, your company made it its business to find out where they were, correct?"

"That situation only occurred with Mr. Stanton and Ms. Lane."

"When the situation occurred in the case of Mr. Stanton and Ms. Lane, your company decided it needed to know where they were, correct?"

"It was curious because it happened on more than one occasion, so we decided to look up the locations."

"Are you saying your company was curious as to where they were getting together?"

"I guess you could say that."

Carpenter shook his head in what he hoped was a mocking manner. "Your company has no rule against employees seeing each other socially or even dating, does it?"

"That's right."

"Besides nosiness, what was there to be curious about?"

Bolton colored. "We thought it odd and decided to check it out."

Carpenter decided to leave the matter there. Bolton had reddened and he was sure the jury had picked up on that fact.

Judge Fielding turned to address the jurors. Carpenter had been impressed with the recent appointee to the bench. The judge had run a tight ship and he couldn't think of an evidentiary ruling she had made that he disagreed with.

"We can thank counsel in this case for being prepared and presenting the evidence to you in one day. Tomorrow I will instruct you on the law and then you will hear closing arguments form the parties' attorneys. My previous instruction stands. You are not to discuss this case with anyone. You are excused for the day."

In Brighton, Philly closed her eyes, moved closer to Paul in the center of her bed and ran her fingers along his back. The November night was surprisingly mild, and moonlight came through the window, but Philly wanted to see with her hands.

"I want to spend more time with you," Paul whispered. She had been thinking the same thing, wondering how she could pull it off.

"Say something," Paul entreated.

"I want to spend more time together, too. Daisy's got a lot of stuff, but I could pack it all up and spend some nights at your place. If it was a night Jenny was spending with you, would she mind?"

"She'd tell her mother," Paul said morosely. "We might want to start out with nights Jenny's not around."

Philly considered options. There was no room in her house for both Paul and Jenny. For that matter, there was going to be precious little room for the current occupants when Raul's and Isabella's baby put in an appearance. If their baby was to have a room of her own, the bedroom next to Raul's and Isabella's bedroom—currently used by the couple as an office and storage room—was the most likely choice. It would be crowded on the second floor. What if either Raul or Isabella wanted to share her office at the other end of the hall? Paul's condo was too small to accommodate her and Daisy so moving there was not an option. Even if such a move was an option, Raul and Isabella might not be able to handle the Brighton house on their own. Besides, she owed Isabella and wanted to be around when Isabella's baby was born. God, it was complicated.

Philly opened her eyes to find Paul unselfconsciously studying her.

"What are you thinking about?"

"Logistics," Philly said.

"You mean here?"

Philly nodded.

"It would be a very tight fit here. My condo is too small. A new house makes the most sense for us."

"I owe Isabella and need to be around when she delivers, the way she was for me. Also, I couldn't have easily swung this house without Raul and Isabella and I know they couldn't have done it without me."

Recently Philly had felt settled. Having Raul and Isabella around had worked out. Her home office had worked out even though Carpenter was not happy with the arrangement. And Sarah Ferguson had been a godsend. These were parts of her life that had fallen into place and she didn't want any of them to change.

"You're the one for me," Paul said. "I think you feel the same way. We're going to have to think about this seriously in the near future."

Philly thought about procrastination and the way Carpenter joked that it was a victory any time an unpleasant decision was deferred to a later day. The problem was, a joke like that was always on the procrastinator.

"Next year," Philly said. "I'm not going to think about it until next year."

"Next year will be here before you look around."

"Don't remind me."

90

The next morning, by agreement of counsel, the judge had instructed the jurors on the law before closing arguments. Wayne Anderson had just finished his discourse to the jury about Herbert Stanton and Millie Lane being employees at will who could be fired for any reason or no reason at all. Watching the jurors listen to Anderson's argument about this aspect of employment law, Carpenter was convinced that there was no legal concept simple enough to prevent a jury from experiencing confusion at its explanation. Some jurors were regarding Anderson as if the subject of employees at will was on a par with an arcane point concerning the theory of relativity.

"The plaintiffs claim that their privacy rights were violated," Anderson continued. "Now that's an extraordinary claim given the fact that the evidence established that the GPS feature disclosed nothing whatsoever of a private and personal nature about the plaintiffs. Besides identifying where each plaintiff was at a given point in time, the GPS cell phone feature revealed nothing about what either plaintiff did at the location. Wise Computer learned no intimate detail of either plaintiff's life. In fact, the GPS readout disclosed nothing whatsoever about either plaintiff's life. The plaintiffs like to throw around the word spying. But if Wise Computer was engaged in spying, the company certainly did a lousy job of it. Outside of learning where a plaintiff might be at any point in time during a work day, the company came up with no information of any kind concerning the personal lives of the plaintiffs. That hardly qualifies as spying. Learning that the plaintiffs were together at a motel is not spying.

"When we think of privacy violations, we think of cases where someone obtained something of a personal nature about another person. Nothing like that happened in this case. Nothing of a personal nature about either plaintiff was ever made known or obtained. How can there be a violation of a person's privacy when no personal information about the person was revealed or learned let alone passed along to anyone else? The answer is that there cannot be a privacy right violation in that situation. The plaintiffs admitted that *they* never told anyone about what the GPS cell phone feature revealed."

Anderson paused, lost in thought. Simon was regarding his opponent with an amused expression.

"The judge explained to you that the burden was on the plaintiffs not only to prove that their privacy rights were violated—something they have totally failed to do—but also to prove that they were damaged as a result of the violation of their privacy. The plaintiffs weren't damaged at all. They admitted as much during their testimony. After their employment at Wise Computer came to an end, they went into business for themselves, took away clients of Wise Computer to their new business, and for the last several months have been making more money than they ever made while working for Wise Computer. They weren't damaged at all. Mr. Stanton admitted their reputations never suffered. In fact, this is one of those cases where as a result of having their employment terminated, two employees ended up profiting from the termination by improving themselves financially."

Carpenter observed several jurors writing on their notepads, a bad sign in his estimation. Simon was also writing, making notes on a five by eight note card which meant that he was going to depart from his prepared script. He had already proved that he could think on his feet. The kid had better be able to do that again.

Carpenter accepted that most trial lawyers eschewed any props, wanting a jury to conclude they had fully mastered the evidence and were in total control of the facts. Carpenter preferred to be safe than sorry. He wanted a list of the points he needed to make on five by eight note cards so he wouldn't omit a reference to a crucial matter. Simon was armed with note cards but, as he took his place in front of the jury, Carpenter had the feeling that he wouldn't refer to them.

"Nobody likes a sneak," Simon began, and thinking of the dress rehearsal they had gone through last night, Carpenter didn't remember this pronouncement as Simon's first words. "When we deal with people we like to be given relevant information. When we deal with people we don't appreciate having information concealed from us so that someone is able to spring a surprise on us later on. We want to be respected in our dealings with each other, not tricked. When you think about it as you will when you retire to deliberate, Wise Computer didn't deal fairly with Herbert Stanton and Millie Lane. Instead the company tricked them. Deliberately."

Simon paused and Carpenter's tension eased as the jurors focused on the young lawyer.

"Wise Computer gave Herbert Stanton and Millie Lane cell phones and told them they were required to use the cell phones at all times during the work day. But the company withheld crucial information, and I submit to you it withheld that information deliberately. First, Wise Computer didn't tell Mr. Stanton and Ms. Lane that the phones contained a tracking device. Second, the company provided them with a cell phone instruction book that contained no information about the secret tracking device. Thus, the tracking device was concealed from employees deliberately.

"What was the proper thing for Wise Computer to have done? We all know what that was. The proper, fair, aboveboard thing was to be honest with its employees, to tell them that the phones they were given contained a GPS tracking system that revealed their location at all times. If Wise Computer had done the fair thing and fully disclosed the tracking device, every employee would have had all the facts and, if the employee didn't want to be monitored twenty-four-seven, the employee could have elected to use a different cell phone once the work day ended, or the employee could have quit and found another job. And as we know from their testimony, that's what two employees did. Sam Reynolds and Lucille Stone were so offended by having their whereabouts secretly tracked that they quit Wise Computer."

Trial lawyers were often perceived as actors, playing to a jury instead of an audience. Although Carpenter didn't see himself in that light, he knew that he was witnessing a fine performance. Simon had stage presence.

"Mr. Anderson takes issue with the word 'spying,' but I'll stick by that word. That's how Sam Reynolds and Lucille Stone saw the concealed GPS tracking device. They saw the device as spying on their whereabouts which is why they quit the company. And Wise Computer spied upon Mr. Stanton and Ms. Lane. As Ms. Lane put it, she felt that she had been spied on by a peeping Tom."

Simon let the silence lengthen while he gathered himself. "Wise Computer wants you to believe that it was proper for the company to conceal a tracking device so that the company knew the location of its employees. But clearly that wasn't all they were interested in. If it had been, the company wouldn't have gone further. But they didn't stop there. They were "curious," and we all know exactly how malicious the company's curiosity was. The company used its stealth technology to find out the nature of the location where the two workers met, something that was none of their business. Ms. Lane was right on the money when she called Wise Computer a peeping Tom because, frankly, the company was creepy."

"Now, Wise Computer wants you to believe that when Mr. Stanton and Ms. Lane were on call, they were on company time. I don't know about you but when I'm not being paid, as far as I'm concerned, I'm on my own time and not accountable to my employer. And if my employer has no rule prohibiting me from socializing with a fellow employee—just as Wise Computer had no such rule—if I feel like it, I'll socialize and even date a fellow employee when I'm on my own time."

Carpenter was relieved to see three jurors writing on their notepads.

"So let's get to the bottom line. Wise Computer claims that Herbert Stanton and Millie Lane weren't damaged because of the company's spying. That's just wrong. The company's spying led to their being fired. Once they were fired, they suffered financial injury in this tight economy because they couldn't immediately find jobs. We know from the testimony that their financial injury totaled thirty thousand, two hundred dollars until the company they were forced to form started to prosper.

"But that's not the real damage that Herbert Stanton and Millie Lane suffered. They were spied on, their personal space secretly invaded, their free time comings and goings tracked without their knowledge. Nobody has to put up with that kind of personal intrusion. Herbert Stanton and Millie Lane felt humiliation and outrage over Wise Computer's spying. And who wouldn't in their shoes? This was a humiliating experience. Being spied on is humiliating. Being fired is humiliating. And that humiliation is damage done.

"Ladies and gentlemen, you are in a privileged position. You get to put a dollar value on the violation of Mr. Stanton's and Ms. Lane's right to privacy. You get to put a dollar value on their emotional pain, humiliation, and outrage. Put yourselves in their position and feel their pain. Don't shortchange them over the outrage they experienced. Make your award of damages a lesson to employers who think that Big Brother spying tactics are their prerogative.

"Thank you."

Herbert Stanton and Millie Lane had tired of pacing in the courthouse corridor and had gone off to find coffee. Carpenter and Simon took refuge in a small conference room adjacent to Judge Fielding's courtroom. "You did a nice job," Carpenter said, thinking that he might not have matched Simon's performance. "You were enjoying yourself, weren't you?"

Simon nodded, grinning.

"What rattles you?" Carpenter asked.

"This trial was pretty intense."

"But you showed no sign of nerves."

"Appearances can be misleading. This was my first jury trial. I was hoping this day would come but it came sooner than I thought it would. I was nervous."

"You've got a flair for trial work. I think you know that."

"Thanks."

Carpenter thought about Rachel and Simon pressing him and Philly about forming a firm. Both were talented. If he and Philly let things drift, the two would seek out greener pastures.

"What's your prediction?" Simon asked.

"I've given up predicting what juries will do a long time ago. If I had to guess, I'd say they're going to find for the plaintiffs. It's the damages that present the problem."

"I'm so nervous I feel like I'm about to pass out," Millie Lane said as she followed Simon back into the courtroom.

Carpenter checked his watch. It was three thirty. Taking into account a lunch break, the jury had probably deliberated about three hours.

Judge Fielding took the bench and when the clerk called the session to order, she addressed the jury. "Has the jury reached a verdict?"

The foreman, a wizened man with white hair, rose. "Yes, Your Honor."

The court clerk retrieved the verdict slips from the foreman and handed the papers to the judge. Judge Fielding studied the forms and directed the clerk to return them to the foreman.

"The first question asked you," the clerk said, "was did the defendant violate the privacy rights of the plaintiffs. How say the jury, Mr. Foreman."

"Yes."

"Were the plaintiffs damaged by the violation of their right to privacy?"

"Yes," the foreman said.

"What is the amount of the plaintiffs' damages."

The foreman studied the verdict slip papers. "Ninety-nine thousand dollars."

"Is your verdict unanimous?"

"It is."

"Is it necessary to poll the jury?" Judge Fielding asked counsel.

"No, Your Honor," Simon said, rising.

` Wayne Anderson remained seated regarding the jury intently. When he rose, he took a deep breath. "No," he said.

"Is there any matter I need to take up before I discharge the jury?"

Simon looked in his direction and Carpenter shook his head.

"No, Your Honor," Simon said."

Anderson took his time. Carpenter glanced to the rear of the courtroom where Bruce Bolton sat slumped over. Wise Computer's loss and legal fees were covered by its insurance, but the company had a sizable deductible that would put it out of pocket.

"No," Anderson said.

Judge Fielding thanked the jurors for their service and discharged them.

When the jury left the courtroom, the judge stood. "I want to commend counsel on being prepared and trying this case competently and swiftly. There being no further business, the court is adjourned."

Wayne Anderson proved gracious in defeat. He shook hands with Simon and Carpenter. "Was that your first jury trial?" he asked Simon.

"What gave it away?" Simon joked.

"Nothing. That's the damn problem."

"Thank you," Simon said.

In the corridor outside the courtroom, Millie Lane wanted to know when she and Stanton would get their money.

"Wise Computer could appeal," Simon explained, and Lane's expression soured.

"I don't see that happening," Carpenter said, "but it might. On the other hand, Wise Computer's insurer might opt to cut its losses and accept the outcome." With interest, the verdict would hit six figures, not an insignificant amount but probably not significant enough to throw further legal fees at the case.

"We don't know about you," Stanton said, "but we're going to celebrate. Would you care to join us?"

Carpenter figured that Simon would follow his lead. "Unfortunately, Simon and I have to turn our attention to another matter. But that's very kind of you."

"What other matter?" Simon asked after Stanton and Lane departed.

"There is no other matter," Carpenter admitted. "I just don't like socializing with clients. Keep in mind that other lawyers don't necessarily share that view."

"For a guy in a profession where you have to deal with people, you really don't like people very much, do you?"

"You catch on quick," Carpenter said.

91

Philly had thought that no matter how smart Martin Mercer might be, the kid would be intimidated by a battery of lawyers throwing questions at him in a deposition. But Mercer had not been rattled when two successive lawyers tried, at length, and—without much success in Philly's view—to get him to admit he had precipitated the fight with Gerald Hatch. Calvin Blaine, the lawyer for the Cambridgeport school officials, had let his irritation show when Mercer didn't provide the answers he was seeking. In contrast, Frank Price, representing Gerald Hatch's parents, remained detached as he sparred with Mercer.

The large conference room on the thirty-sixth floor of Calvin Blaine's International Place law firm looked out over the Rose Kennedy Greenway where the gray branches of the now bare trees blended with the steel of the harbor beyond. It was about as imposing a view as the city had to offer. Inside, Mercer's parents were seated behind their son. They appeared skittish as they sat erect on the front edges of their chairs. If Philly drew close to them and said boo, she thought the couple would take flight. She remembered the first time she met Gerald's parents and the distress in their eyes as they regarded their son without a clue as to how to deal with his attitude and behavior. There was a hint of helplessness in the Mercers' expressions that suggested they were also on uncharted ground when dealing with their son.

Before beginning her cross-examination of Mercer, Philly requested a five-minute recess. She used her cell phone to call Gerald Hatch and he picked up on the first ring. "I'm about to start questioning Mercer. Make it forty-five minutes."

"Okay," Gerald said, and Philly detected no nervousness in his reply.

Philly sat down beside Rachel. Yesterday, they had spent two hours on the phone going over questions to ask Mercer. But after listening to Mercer field questions from the other defense lawyers, Philly doubted her deposition outline was worth the paper it was written on.

Philly signaled the stenographer that she was ready to begin. Mercer regarded her with a smirk. He was of medium height and thin with sandy hair and pale gray eyes that maintained a mocking expression and showed little else. He and Gerald were a physical mismatch; his lawyer, Donald Fanning, would play that up before a jury. Yet Philly understood why Gerald had unloaded on the teen. Mercer's smirk invited physical reprisals. "Here goes nothing," she whispered to Rachel.

Philly consulted her notes from the deposition. The lawyers preceding her had covered Mercer's injuries and medical expenses. Mercer was now over his injuries. He had denied precipitating the fight with Gerald, and had claimed that prior to their fight, Gerald had bullied him. Throughout, Donald Fanning's expression remained serene and confident. The plaintiff's lawyer looked like he had just come from a barber, his sculpted white pompadour jutting forward like the prow of a ship.

"Do you have any close personal friends at the high school," Philly led off, moving her deposition outline aside and deciding to wing it.

"Sure," Mercer said.

"Name them."

Mercer had to think about his answer. "Andy Wilson and Darryl Woo."

"Would they be your best friends at the high school?"

"I guess."

"Nobody wants you to guess," Philly said. "Who might be a closer friend of yours than Wilson and Woo?"

"I can't think of anyone offhand."

"How did you meet Wilson and Woo?"

"We're on the chess team."

"Outside of participating in chess team activities, what was the most recent thing you did with either Wilson or Woo?"

Mercer again didn't answer right away. "Hang out at school together."

"Do you know where either Wilson or Woo live?"

Mercer cast a quick glance at Fanning who was writing on his notepad. "No."

"Have you ever been to either's house?"

"No."

"Has either been to your house?"

"No."

"Have you ever seen a movie with either of them?"

"No," Mercer said, shaking his head, his smirk gone.

"Have you ever had a meal with either Wilson or Woo that wasn't on high school grounds?"

"No."

"When was the last time you ate lunch with either Wilson or Woo at the high school?"

"I don't know. Why are you asking me this stuff?"

"Give me your best estimate of when you last ate lunch with either Wilson or Woo at the high school."

Mercer shot a glance at Fanning but received no acknowledgement in response.

"I don't know. Maybe three weeks ago."

"If I were to ask either Wilson or Woo whether he considered you to be a friend, what would you expect each of them to say?"

"Objection," Fanning said.

"Answer the question," Philly snapped, deciding to give Mercer her hard stare.

"I don't know," Mercer said.

"Isn't it true that Wilson and Woo are not friends of yours but are only chess team acquaintances?"

Mercer glared at her and Philly knew that she had struck a nerve.

"I think they're my friends, but I can't tell you what they think."

"Do you consider yourself popular at school?" Philly opted for a sudden subject change.

"Not particularly."

"Why do you think you're not particularly popular?"

Mercer paused. The lawyers for the other defendants were regarding her uncertainly. Philly ignored them.

"I don't know. Who said I wanted to be popular?"

This was the second time Mercer's answer contained a question, and again Philly refused to take the bait. "Do you want to be popular?"

"Not particularly."

"Then why the hell do you keep calling attention to yourself?" Philly raised her voice, deliberately throwing in the h-word to keep Fanning and the other lawyers guessing as to whom or what they were dealing with.

"Objection," Fanning said.

"Answer my question," Philly nearly shouted.

"I don't call attention to myself," Mercer protested weakly.

"Really!" Philly said, trying to throw a mixture of disbelief and sarcasm into the word. She pretended to consult her notes to let the silence lengthen. "Isn't it true that you make it a point to let the students in your homeroom know how you did on tests?"

"Yeah, but . . ."

"Isn't it true that when you've done well on tests you ask other students in your homeroom how they did?"

"Yeah, but . . ."

"Can you name any other student who announces his test results in homeroom or asks his homeroom classmates how they've done on tests?"

Mercer glared at her and Philly glared back at him, drawing on all of her self-control so that she wouldn't laugh out loud.

"I can't think of anyone," Mercer said.

"When you announce how you did on tests you're boasting, aren't you?"

"I wouldn't say that," Mercer answered tepidly.

"Then what the hell are you doing?"

Fanning started to object but checked himself.

"I don't know," Mercer said in a soft voice.

"Do you know what you're doing when you ask other students in your homeroom how they've done on tests?"

"Not really."

"Aren't you trying to embarrass the other kids in your homeroom by making them compare their test scores to your high test scores?"

"I don't know."

"Before the fight you had with Gerald Hatch, isn't it true that Gerald asked you not to talk about test scores in homeroom?"

"He might have said something like that."

"Why didn't you stop talking about test scores after Gerald might have said something like that?"

This time when Mercer looked Fanning's way, the lawyer returned his client's look with an expression of concern.

"I don't know. I just didn't."

"You couldn't stop yourself from talking about test scores, could you?" Philly persisted.

Mercer lowered his head. "I don't know."

"Have you ever seen a psychiatrist or psychologist for any emotional problems?" Philly shifted gears.

"No."

"Did either of your parents ever suggest that you see such a professional?"

Mercer colored. His parents were staring at the floor. Their body language gave her the answer to her question. Would Mercer lie about the matter?

"They brought it up awhile back."

"Did you nix the idea?"

"Yeah. I thought it was a load of crap."

"Why did your parents suggest that you see a therapist?"

"You'd have to ask them."

"I'm asking you."

Mercer emitted an audible sigh. "They thought I was unhappy."

"Were you unhappy?"

"Not really."

"Are you currently unhappy?"

"Not really."

The door to the conference room opened and Gerald Hatch entered. He took a chair behind Philly. Philly checked her watch. Gerald's timing was perfect.

"Let the record show that Gerald Hatch, a defendant in this case, has entered the room," Philly announced.

Mercer stared at Gerald open-mouthed. Gerald offered him a brief head nod and sat erect in his chair.

"Mr. Mercer," Philly said, and the teen turned toward her. "Are you prepared to apologize to Gerald Hatch for continuing to talk about test scores in homeroom after he requested that you not talk about that subject?"

Mercer laughed, his bravado returning. "I don't have to apologize to him for anything. Why would I do that?"

"You know why, Mr. Mercer. It has to do with whether you're happy or unhappy." Philly looked at her notes. "One more question. Did you permit Gerald Hatch to copy wrong answers on a chemistry test?"

"He shouldn't have been copying," Mercer said defiantly. "I decided to teach him a lesson."

"Is it true that you let him copy wrong answers and later changed the answers to correct answers?"

"Yeah. Like I said, I wanted to teach him a lesson."

"Nothing further," Philly said.

There were no follow up questions. Calvin Blaine declared the deposition to be over and the stenographer typed frantically for a moment and then began to pack up her equipment.

"Before we go," Philly said, "my client has something he would like to say to Mr. Mercer."

"That would be highly irregular," Blaine said. "This is neither the time nor the place."

"You're wrong on both counts. Gerald?"

Gerald stood and locked eyes with Mercer. "I'm sorry I hurt you the way I did. You were acting like a jerk in homeroom but that didn't excuse what happened later. When you came at me, things got out of hand. I'm sorry." Gerald paused and Philly couldn't read the expression on Mercer's face. "For your own good," Gerald continued, "you might want to put a lid on talking about tests in homeroom." Gerald resumed his seat.

"You don't know what the hell you're doing," Blaine directed at Philly.

"You're wrong again," Philly said. "I know exactly what I'm doing." She nodded at Gerald and Rachel. "Let's go," she said. Her last look at Fanning found Mercer's lawyer deep in thought.

Philly had sent Rachel back to the office; she wanted alone time with Gerald. They were seated at a Dunkin' Donuts. Philly chose a pumpkin latte. Gerald inhaled two chocolate sticks and then sipped at a coffee. "What happens now?" he asked.

"That's up to Mercer and his lawyer. Maybe there will be a trial. Maybe the case will settle. As far as you're concerned, it doesn't matter what happens next. Whatever happens, you'll do what you have to do. The case is pretty much over for you; you've moved on. I can't tell you how proud I am of you."

Gerald looked crestfallen. Philly wondered why he couldn't take a compliment.

"Does this mean I can't come over to your house anymore?"

Philly laughed. "Whatever gave you that idea? Daisy adores you. I like having you over. Raul and Isabella enjoy talking to you. You should know that Isabella is pregnant. Next summer there's going to be another little baby in the house."

"Wow!" Gerald exclaimed.

"How's school going?"

Gerald shrugged. "Spanish is going really well. I understand everything the teacher says. We spend most of each class talking with each other. Math is going better since I've been going to the teacher after school. English and history are so-so. Beginning physics is killing me."

"Ask Mercer to explain things to you in physics. See if he's as smart as he claims to be."

Gerald considered that advice. "I just might do that," he said. "Even though he's still an asshole."

92

Rachel had led Frederick Chun through his direct examination, and now Jane Quick, counsel for Crowe Investment Strategies, was conducting cross-examination. Philly's online search revealed that Quick was admitted to the bar twenty years ago and specialized in employment litigation. As was the case at the previous administrative hearing, she wore a blue suit that set off her red hair and blue eyes. Philly had been concerned that the hearing officer, Lewis Lightstone, had not taken any notes during Rachel's direct examination. So perhaps it was a good sign that he had yet to write anything down during Quick's cross-examination, either.

"Before you filed your complaint with the Massachusetts Commission Against Discrimination, what evidence did you have that your race was a factor in the termination of your employment?" Quick asked.

Chun shifted in his chair. Their client had never been convinced of the merits of his case, and Philly was concerned that his ambivalence would show through.

"I couldn't think of any other reason for my being fired," Chun said. "I never opened the link in the e-mail I received, and I promptly deleted the e-mail. I knew that non-Asian employees received and sent personal messages on their

Crowe e-mail addresses. It was clear to me that I was being singled out because of my race. Mr. Crowe was treating me differently. Not only was he singling me out based on my race for receiving a personal e-mail, he also refused to listen to my explanation as to what happened."

"Does that complete your answer?"

"Yes, except that the documents that the company provided in discovery confirmed what I just said. All kinds of dirty, offensive jokes were being sent and received by employees on their company e-mail addresses without any consequences to them. I was the only one fired."

"At the time you filed your complaint with the MCAD, you weren't aware of the content of other employees' e-mail messages, were you?"

"No, I wasn't."

"Who sent you the e-mail that resulted in your employment being terminated?"

"My friend Alan."

"How did Alan get your work e-mail address?"

"I probably sent him a message. It was probably a message about us hooking up after work. We hang out a lot together. He must have saved the e-mail or made a note of my Crowe e-mail address."

"Do you have a personal e-mail address that has nothing to do with Crowe Investments?"

"Yes."

"Why didn't you go on the Internet and access your personal e-mail address when you sent an e-mail to Alan?"

Chun favored Quick with an expression suggesting she had to be dumber than dirt if she needed to ask her last question.

"I was probably pressed for time. I'm sure I thought that it wasn't a big deal because like I said before, other employees were sending and receiving personal e-mail messages at their Crowe e-mail addresses."

"Did any of those employees who you say received and sent personal e-mails at their business e-mail addresses, ever receive a personal message with a link to a pornographic web site?"

Philly nudged Rachel. "Objection," Rachel said.

"Overruled."

"I don't know," Chun said. "I also have no idea whether the link in Alan's e-mail was to a pornographic site. Like I said, I never opened the link."

Quick consulted her notes. "Are you currently employed, Mr. Chun?"

"Yes. I'm working for another hedge fund."

Quick's next questions established that Chun was currently earning slightly more than what he was being paid by Crowe Investment Strategies at the time he was fired. Chun had received unemployment compensation during the months it took him to find his current job.

"Does your current employer have a policy with regard to using your work e-mail address for personal use?" Quick asked.

"Yes."

"Does the policy of your current employer prohibit using your work e-mail address for personal use?"

"Not entirely."

Quick paused and Philly said a silent prayer that, despite being a seasoned litigator, she would break the rule against asking a question that she didn't know the answer to.

"What do you mean by not entirely?"

Chun leaned forward. "Every new employee where I now work has to sign a paper that he's read and understands the company's e-mail policy. The policy is that generally, you can't use your company e-mail for personal use. But there's a big exception. My new company permits you to use your company e-mail address when it's convenient to arrange for a doctor's appointment, arrange a time to meet with a friend, or cancel a personal appointment—things like that. The company believes that an employee would end up wasting more work time if the employee had to go to his private e-mail account for these things. All e-mails are monitored and recorded and the company's policy is that the exceptions to not using the company's e-mail for personal use can't be abused. If the company finds that an employee is making excessive use of his business e-mail for personal use, a company executive will meet with the employee to discuss the matter."

Quick paused for a moment. For the first time since the hearing started, Lightstone was writing in his notebook.

"While you worked at Crowe Investments," Quick promptly resumed, "were you subject to any comments about your race or ethnicity?"

"No."

"Before you were discharged by Crowe Investments, did you regard the company as treating you fairly?"

"I would say so. I had no complaints."

"In fact, after you were discharged, you wanted to return to work at the company, correct?"

"That was then, this is now," Chun said with some heat.

Quick flashed Chun an irritated look, and Philly knew that she wouldn't probe further into Chun's last answer.

"No further questions," Quick said.

Philly whispered to Rachel and Rachel made a note on her testimony outline before standing. "What did you mean by your last answer?" Rachel asked.

"Objection," Quick pounced. "His answer speaks for itself."

"Overruled."

Chun turned toward Lightstone. "After I was fired, I tried to get Mr. Crowe to reconsider. I didn't think that I had done anything wrong. He wouldn't even listen to me. Where I work now, upper management is reasonable. If an employee has something to say, someone in management listens and gets back to you. Management may not agree with you, but at least they tell you why. I would never want to work for Crowe now that I've worked for someone who's really treated me and other employees fairly. That's what I meant by my last answer."

Rachel sat down and Quick declined to further cross-examine Chun. "Call your next witness," Lightstone instructed Rachel.

"William Crowe," Rachel announced, and a tall, muscular man wearing a dark blue three-piece suit strode aggressively from the back of the room to the witness chair. Crowe had a pugnacious bearing and Philly pegged him for a my-way-or-the-highway kind of boss. Rachel had wanted to let Quick be the one to call Crowe as a witness, but Philly had overruled Rachel on this point of strategy.

"Why was Mr. Chun fired?" Rachel asked after a series of background questions.

"He received a personal email that contained a link to a pornographic site," Crowe responded authoritatively. "This violated my company's policy."

"What precisely was your company's policy that was violated?" Rachel followed up.

"The policy against using your work computer for personal use."

"Isn't it true that your company routinely tolerated employees sending and receiving personal e-mails using their Crowe e-mail addresses?"

"We were probably not as strict about enforcing our policy as we should have been," Crowe said, without any indication that the question had troubled him.

Philly squirmed in her seat. She wanted to have a go at Crowe and she was concerned that Rachel might let him off the hook.

Rachel stared at Crowe, frowning. "I'm sorry, Mr. Crowe, but you need to answer my question. Isn't it true that your company routinely tolerated employees sending and receiving personal e-mails on their work computers using their Crowe-mail addresses?"

Now it was Crowe who was frowning. Philly resolved to keep in mind that Rachel's approach to cross-examining a witness was going to be different than her own.

"I'd say that we did tolerate that practice."

Rachel took her time considering Crowe's answer, and Philly began to relax. Rachel was engaged. She would proceed at her leisurely, measured pace and, as long as she pressed Crowe to answer her questions, she would do all right.

"If Mr. Chun's e-mail had not contained a link, would he have been fired?"

Crowe barely hesitated. "Probably not."

"Is it correct then that it was the link in the e-mail he received that led to his firing?"

"I would say so."

"What was it about the link that led you to fire Mr. Chun?"

"It was a link to a pornographic site."

"Pornographic in what sense?"

"It was a sex site," Crowe answered testily.

"In what way was it a sex site?"

"What do you mean in what way? You could tell from the title."

Rachel examined her copy of the e-mail that had led to Chun's firing. "The title is Sexy Russian Vixens. How did that title tell you the site was a sex site?"

"For God's sake!" Crowe exclaimed. "You have to use a little common sense. The title sounds like a link to a prostitution ring."

"Sounds like," Rachel repeated. "Did you actually go to the link?"

"No. Why would I do that?"

Rachel ignored Crowe's question. She reached for a piece paper, moved a finger down a column of print and then paused. "Would Mr. Chun have been fired if he received the following unsolicited e-mail? Quote. I am a twenty-seven-year-old Russian woman, well-educated, beautiful, interested in marriage to an American. I enjoy literature, dancing, classical music and soccer. End quote."

Crowe let loose with an exasperated sigh as Quick stood and said, "Objection."

"Overruled," Lightstone said, and Philly noted that the hearing officer was again writing in his notebook.

"I don't know," Crowe said, not bothering to hide his annoyance.

"Can you be more specific and helpful?"

"Objection," Quick repeated. "The witness has said that he doesn't know the answer to the question."

"Ask another question," Lightstone instructed Rachel.

"The quote I just read," Rachel said, "appears verbatim on the website you claimed sounded like a prostitution service. The website also provides a name for the woman—Martina—and a telephone number. What is pornographic or indicative of a prostitution service with respect to what I just read to you and told you about?"

"Objection," Quick interjected.

"Overruled."

"I'm sure when you call the listed number you're hit up for money," Crowe answered.

"Since you told us you never went to the link in the e-mail Mr. Chun received, is your last answer based on personal knowledge of links such as the one Mr. Chun was fired over?"

"Objection! This is outrageous," Quick intoned.

"Overruled."

Philly was now thoroughly enjoying herself. Rachel was all sweetness and light on the surface so when she asked a barbed, probing question, the question somehow lost its sting coming from her.

"No, I don't have personal knowledge of the kind of websites we're talking about. I made an assumption."

"Oh!" Rachel exclaimed innocently. "You mean like the assumption you made about the link in the e-mail that led you to fire Mr. Chun?"

"That's right," Crowe said belligerently. "There are some things that are just common sense. You don't need a road map to figure out where a site called Sexy Russian Vixens is headed."

Rachel paused. Lightstone looked like he was trying to suppress a smile.

"Is Crowe Investment Strategies a hedge fund?" Rachel asked.

"It is."

"What's a hedge fund?"

Crowe sighed audibly. "In simple terms, it's an investment firm that makes plays in connection with stocks, currencies and bonds. We try to predict the movement of those investment vehicles and place investments on the predictions we make."

"That is so interesting," Rachel said, and Philly wondered whether she was laying it on a bit thick. "Do you make these investment plays solely on assumptions?"

Crowe colored, angry. Lewis Lightstone covered his mouth with one hand and wrote with the other.

"We use data," Crowe said.

"Do you mean factual data?"

"Is there any other kind?"

"Please answer the question," Lightstone instructed the witness.

"Yes, factual data."

"So you use factual data in conducting your business and assumptions when firing employees. Is that accurate as to Mr. Chun?"

Crowe took some deep breaths and it appeared to Philly that they helped settle him down.

"I already said this but apparently I'm not getting through to you so I'll say it again. I made what I thought were commonsense assumptions based on the name of the link in the e-mail Frederick received. We don't use those kinds of assumptions when it comes to investing."

Rachel glanced at Lightstone and Philly was pleased to see that the hearing officer had continued to write in his notebook.

"Before you fired Mr. Chun, what consideration did you give to the facts that he promptly deleted the e-mail we've been talking about and never went to the e-mail link?"

Crowe paused. "Not very much consideration. Frankly, I was offended by the e-mail link and that's what drove my decision to discharge Frederick."

"Isn't it true that Mr. Chun apologized to you for receiving the e-mail and explained to you that he promptly deleted it because he knew it was inappropriate?"

"Yeah, he did," Crowe said grudgingly.

"Did you accept his apology?"

"I don't remember. It didn't change my decision to let him go."

"Why not?"

"Because I found the link offensive as I've already told you."

Rachel reached for a piece of paper and reviewed it unhurriedly. "Are you offended by this question and answer, Mr. Crowe? Quote. Question: How can you tell when a woman is having a bad day. Answer: When she has her tampon behind her ear and she can't find her cigarette. Unquote."

Crowe smoldered in his chair. "I don't approve of that exchange."

"Does it offend you?"

"Somewhat, yes," Crowe said with what Philly thought was a resigned air. "Unfortunately, off color jokes seem to be a part of our culture."

"What about this quote," Rachel said, selecting another piece of paper to review. "Quote. One day a girl decided to buy some crotchless panties to surprise her boyfriend. She went and bought them, got home, put them on and waited. When the boyfriend got home there she was spread eagle on the bed with only her panties and bra on. 'Come over here baby,' she says smiling. The boyfriend backs off. 'If your pussy can do that to your panties, I ain't going anywhere near it!' Unquote. Does that offend you?"

"Again, somewhat."

"Are you aware that the two passages I read to you come from e-mail exchanges involving Crowe employees on their business computers?"

"I'll take your word for it."

"What disciplinary action was taken against the employees involved in those e-mails?"

"There wasn't any."

"What was the race of the employees involved in those e-mails?"

"I would need to see the e-mail messages."

"That can be arranged."

Rachel received permission from Lightstone to present copies of the e-mail messages to Crowe. Crowe stared at the documents malevolently and Philly wasn't sure whether he was actually reading them.

"White," Crowe said. "That is Caucasian. The second one involved an African American."

"Am I correct that the first e-mail I quoted to you was sent by a Crowe employee and the second e-mail was received by a Crowe employee?"

"Yes."

"Why was no disciplinary action taken against the employees involved with those e-mails?"

Crowe glanced briefly in Quick's direction before returning his attention to Rachel. Philly knew that Quick had prepared him for this question.

"With twenty-twenty hindsight, perhaps I should have taken some action," Crowe said. "But I let it slide."

"I've showed you copies of two e-mails," Rachel said. "Isn't it true that there are numerous other employee e-mails containing off-color material?"

"Yes."

"Is it also true that you found some of these other e-mails somewhat offensive?"

"Yes."

"Is it true that no disciplinary action was taken against any employee who sent or received an email that you regard as somewhat offensive?"

"Yes."

"Was Mr. Chun the only employee fired over an email you found offensive?"

Crowe glared at Rachel. "I believe so."

"Let's see if we can sum up here," Rachel said, favoring Crowe with a broad smile. "One e-mail involving one of the two Asians in your employ resulted in Mr. Chun's being fired even though he never authored the e-mail, never went to the link in the e-mail, and promptly deleted the e-mail, while employee e-mails that had language that you find somewhat offensive and solely involved non-Asian Crowe employees resulted in no disciplinary action of any kind. Is that a correct summary?"

"Yes, but . . ."

"Thank you," Rachel cut Crowe off. "No further questions."

Quick promptly stood. "Ms. Boyle cut off your last answer. What were you going to say?"

"I was going to say that I regarded e-mails swapping off-color jokes less seriously than an e-mail containing a link to an obvious sex site. Mr. Chun's race never entered into any decision I made regarding his employment status."

"Thank you," Quick said. "Nothing further."

Rachel slowly stood. "If the words Sexy Russian Vixens appeared in an e-mail text received or sent by a Crowe employee as opposed to being the title of a link in such an e-mail, would the employee be fired?"

"Probably not," Crowe conceded.

Rachel paused to consider Crowe's answer. "I'm trying to understand the distinction you're trying to make. If a Crowe employee uses the words Sexy Russian Vixens in an e-mail the employee sends on his work computer nothing happens to the employee as far as discipline goes. But if those words appear in a link in an e-mail sent to an employee who deletes the e-mail without using the link, the employee is fired. Is that accurate?"

"We keep waltzing around the same pole," Crowe said, his impatience breaking out. "How many times do I have to say it? Yes, it was the offensive nature of the link in the e-mail Frederick received that led to his firing."

"I didn't mean to upset you," Rachel said, sending one of her winning smiles in Crowe's direction. "I apologize. It's just that each time you draw the distinction we've been going over, the more absurd it sounds. Nothing further. That concludes Mr. Chun's case."

Quirk proceeded to call Crowe as her witness. Crowe visibly relaxed as he fielded the softballs Quick lobbed in his direction. With the exception of Frederick Chun, no employee had ever claimed that Crowe Investment Strategies engaged in a discriminatory practice. The company's workforce reflected a diverse racial and ethnic mix confirming that Crowe Investment Strategies was in fact an equal opportunity employer.

"I don't think I should cross-examine him," Rachel whispered to Philly after Crowe concluded his direct testimony.

Philly couldn't think of a way to undermine Crowe's answers to his attorney's questions. "I agree."

"No cross-examination," Rachel announced.

Lightstone promptly closed the hearing when neither side had any further testimony to present. "You'll have my decision shortly," he said, before departing the hearing room.

Rachel slumped in her chair once Quirk and Crowe left the room. Philly nudged her when she saw Chun making his way toward them.

"Thanks," Chun said to Rachel, who stood to accept Chun's handshake. "Win or lose, you made that asshole squirm. I appreciate it."

"You're welcome," Rachel said, and Philly saw the effort it took her colleague to smile and make small talk.

"I think you made something out of nothing," Chun continued. "I don't know anything about the law, but we might win this thing."

"It remains a long shot," Philly said, when it became obvious Rachel was not going to respond to Chun. "You did a nice job on the stand."

When Chun departed, Rachel again plopped down on her chair.

"You okay?" Philly asked.

"I'm wiped out. This hearing only took the afternoon, but I feel like I've been through a war."

"You did great," Philly said, meaning it. "I'd stay and chat but I've got to get back to my kid." Darkness arrived mid-afternoon now, and at 4:00 cars already had their head lights on.

"You go ahead. I'm going to sit a minute and decompress."

"You really did do a good job. Congratulations."

"Thanks," Rachel said, without either enthusiasm or conviction.

"Admit it," Philly said. "You had fun."

"Fun is not the word that leaps off my page."

93

Philly was holding her baby in front of her computer screen. The kid had Philly's ghostly white coloring and black hair only the hair on the kid was straight and wispy, not thick and curly. "Say hello to Carpenter," Philly said. Carpenter felt like an idiot as he waved weakly. Down the road he would end up playing peek-a-boo with the kid and when that time came, the practice of law as he knew it would have gone to hell in a hand basket. Maxine would now be telling him to go with the flow but, Christ, there had to be some limits!

"Where do you want to start?" Philly asked as her baby disappeared from view and her face appeared.

"We need to pay out the contingency fee in the Stanton and Lane case," Carpenter said. Carpenter never liked talking about money, but Wise Computer Consultants had decided not to appeal the jury verdict and now it was necessary to decide how to carve up the contingency fee which, after accounting for interest, backing out costs, and figuring in the clients' retainer was $33,000. Their deal with Simon and Rachel was to split the sum in half so that each of the four lawyers would retain a fourth. Carpenter wanted to throw a little more money at Simon and Rachel but sensed that Philly could use the money since she wasn't putting in much billable hours.

"Good. I could use the money."

"I was thinking of giving a little more of the pot to Simon and Rachel."

Philly frowned. If this discussion had proceeded by a phone call, Carpenter couldn't have gauged her reaction. With Skype, it was easy to see.

"How much more?"

"If we split it up four ways we'd each walk away with eighty-two fifty. I was thinking we let each of them have ten thousand, and you and I split the other thirteen. We'd each take a hit of seventeen hundred fifty."

Philly's expression didn't soften, and Carpenter wondered whether he'd made a mistake. Philly now had to think of her kid. "I don't feel strongly about this," he said.

Philly's baby was now in her lap and Philly leaned down to kiss the top of the kid's head. The baby was staring at him and Carpenter felt compelled to offer another timid wave.

"I remember the first year we started to seriously work together," Philly said. "We wrote—I should say you mostly wrote—a letter on behalf of Anna Penn and it produced a contingency fee of ten thousand dollars for each of us. I remember staring at that five-figure check and thinking I'd gone to heaven. At the time, I never thought I'd see a five-figure payday."

Carpenter remembered the case. Without telling Philly, he had taken part of his share of the fee and paid a referral fee to Robert Finn, the lawyer who had sent the case his way.

"Okay," Philly said. "Let's do it. You told me that Simon did a good job at trial. And Rachel's been doing great work. But I want to be there. I want to see the expression on their faces when they get their first five-figure payoff."

Carpenter was relieved. He tended to forget how goodhearted Philly was. Over the years, she had taken on cases that were losers because she felt compelled to help people. "Great," he said.

Philly filled him in on the Gerald Hatch case and watching her describe what had gone on during the depositions, Carpenter was struck by how much Philly liked her client. He remembered the Hatch kid as a thug. Philly was talking about a kid who was anything but. Carpenter knew that his expression had turned sour but what the hell! Philly already knew his position that the practice of law didn't involve social work. He heard Daisy cry, and Philly's face disappeared and reappeared without the baby.

"I've got the Top Tier Finance case early next month," Carpenter said. "Jerome Singer is threatening not to testify. It's driving me nuts."

"You don't have much of a case if he doesn't testify."

"Tell me about it."

"Write him a letter that tells him he'd better testify," Philly suggested.

"I may have to," Carpenter said. He disliked writing cover-your-ass letters to clients, but Singer was so likely to seek a scapegoat if his case went down the tubes that it might be necessary in his case. "Simon and I will be meeting with him. What do you have?"

"The workers' compensation insurer denied Gerard Gorman's claim and has moved to dismiss Gorman's appeal," Philly said. "Rachel's doing the legal memorandum. I'll argue."

"Before the legal memorandum goes out, let me take a look at it."

"You're going to be a busy guy."

"Tell me about it." Carpenter knew that he should be feeling upbeat. He liked being busy.

"You seem down," Philly said.

Goddamn Skype, Carpenter thought; there was no place to hide. "They're all tough cases."

"I thought that's the way you liked your cases," Philly said.

"Maybe I'm smartening up."

94

Carpenter had just finished telling Jerome Singer that Top Tier's case was headed down the toilet if Singer didn't testify before the Loan Company Licensure Review Board. Carpenter had refused to meet in Singer's office so they were in Carpenter's conference room instead. He wanted Singer on unfamiliar turf. Now, watching his client, he concluded that the location of this meeting was irrelevant to whether Singer listened to sound advice.

"If you don't testify," Carpenter said, "there will be no witnesses from the company. That's not only bad, it looks bad."

"You told me that the Board has to go first at the hearing," Singer said, placidly. "Let's play it by ear and see where we are after the Board finishes its case."

Carpenter's irritation rose. "There's no need to play anything by ear. We know what the Board's case is. Norman Cassidy will say that you told him his company would have ninety days to cure a loan default. The Board attorney will play the recording of the conversation where you made the statement that Cassidy didn't have to worry about the ten-day cure period in the loan agreement. Cassidy will say that you went back on your word. *You* need to tell the Board that you weren't told that the conversation was taped. *You* need to tell the Board that you acted before the ninety days because you were suspicious Devonshire Plastic's assets would be gone if you waited the ninety days. If we're missing something here, now is the time for you to set us straight."

Singer shrugged and remained silent. For a man whose company could be shut down by a licensing board, Singer appeared unperturbed. His attitude was bizarre. Surely Singer wanted his company to remain in business, but he was unwilling to personally involve himself in the company's defense.

"Did Mr. Cassidy tell you he was going to record your call?" Simon asked.

"No."

"Did he say something that suggested he was about to turn on a recorder?" Simon followed up.

"I don't remember anything like that," Singer answered.

"Did Cassidy have you on a speaker phone?" Simon said.

"He may have."

"Was there anyone with Cassidy when you had your conversation?"

"I don't remember."

Watching Singer respond to Simon's questions, Carpenter had no read on whether his client was telling the truth.

"Mr. Jeffries and I have been discussing your situation," Carpenter said. "The only reason we can come up with for your not testifying is that Cassidy has some evidence that he did tell you he was going to record your call."

Singer again shrugged. "I can't control what Cassidy will say."

"That's right," Carpenter said. "But what you can control is making sure your lawyers have all the facts. Is there anything that you haven't told us about that could surface at this hearing?"

"Not that I can recall," Singer said, too quickly for Carpenter's liking.

Carpenter silently counted to ten. "Here's something else you can control. You can control stepping up to the plate so that your company's case is the best it can be. If you don't testify, even though the Board shouldn't hold that against you, you can count on the fact that it will."

"You've made your point," Singer said dismissively, "and I hope I've been clear as to how I wish you to proceed. We'll see where things sit after the Board concludes its case. Is there anything else that we need to discuss?"

"If you take the stand," Carpenter said, "you'll be asked about the earlier case where you mentioned a ninety-day cure period and foreclosed after ten days."

"I understand," Singer said.

"Has Top Tier continued to tell potential borrowers about a ninety-day cure period?" Simon inquired.

"No. If a borrower asks, the borrower is told that the company has a right to begin legal action within ten days after a loan default but might not do so if the parties are trying to come up with a workout plan. We caution that the ten-day cure period in the loan agreement is what controls."

Singer seemed poised to make a quick exit from this meeting. This was probably their last shot at him before the administrative hearing took place. "We've been unable to take Cassidy's deposition in the lawsuit you filed against him," Carpenter said. "In your lawsuit, Cassidy filed a motion to delay his deposition until after the regulatory hearing and, as you know, a judge allowed that motion. Therefore, we don't fully know what Cassidy will be saying when he testifies. Is there anything you can think of Cassidy testifying about that we haven't discussed?"

"No," Singer said, and his quick response decided Carpenter—he was going to write Singer the cover-your-ass letter that Philly had suggested he write.

Singer looked at his watch. "I really need to cut this short."

"Here's another thing," Carpenter pushed on. "I've gone over with you the questions that you are likely to be asked if you testify. I've also pointed out possible answers to those questions. But we haven't spent uninterrupted time where I repeat the questions and you supply your answers."

"That's not a problem. I know how to deal with the questions. Are we done?"

"Yeah, we're done," Carpenter said, thinking that his answer covered more areas than one.

95

"Two down and one to go," Philly said as Paul parked his car in front of the North Andover house of Philip's parents. They had started Thanksgiving Day with breakfast at her parents' house in Fall River. That was followed by a one o'clock spread with Paul's family in Somerville. Daisy had made the Fall River reunion more than bearable. Paul came from a large family; there seemed to be no end of little girls wanting to hold Daisy.

Staring at the Sizemore's massive house, Philly realized that that hardest part of the day was still ahead. For this leg of the journey Jenny was with them. Listening to Paul's end of the phone conversation that had freed up his daughter, Philly hoped that she'd never meet Paul's ex-wife, April.

Paul continued to clutch the steering wheel. "I don't think I can do this," he whispered softly so that Jenny wouldn't hear from the back seat.

"It'll be okay," Philly whispered back, stifling her own doubts because for Philip's parents it likely would not be okay. Pamela, Philip's sister, had urged her to bring Paul, assuring her that her parents would be okay with his joining the family dinner. But it had been only a year since Philip's death and Paul's presence would remind Philip's parents of that anniversary and of how quickly their son had been replaced.

"They're going to resent me," Paul said softly.

"That's not true," Philly said. "They're going to be sad, but it has nothing to do with you or me."

"Why are we waiting?" Jenny asked from the back seat.

"We're not, sweetheart," Paul said, releasing the steering wheel and opening the driver's side door.

Philly said a silent prayer of thanks that Pamela was the one to greet them. Philip's sister hugged Paul and Jenny, stuck her face close to Daisy's while blowing the baby a kiss, and took charge of their coats.

Philly recognized familiar faces from the last two Thanksgiving dinners she had attended. She spied Genie, Pamela's daughter, seated on the living room floor playing with dolls, adults navigating around her as if she were an off-limits island.

"Let's get the grandparent thing out of the way," Pamela said, leading them to the kitchen.

"Oh my, isn't she getting big," Philip's mother said, abandoning the stove and reaching for Daisy. She was tall and stout and Philip's father, much shorter, had to stand on tiptoe to plant a kiss on Daisy's cheek.

"Mom and dad, this is Paul and Jenny," Pamela continued to take charge. "I told you that Philly would be bringing guests."

"Thanks for inviting us," Paul said when he shook Philip's father's hand.

If the elder Sizemores were in distress over her being with another man, Philly felt that they were hiding it well. Philip's mother bent at the waist and reached out a hand to Jenny. "There are other girls here, but you may be the oldest. Come with me and I'll introduce you."

Jenny cast an imploring look at Paul, but her father responded with a curt head nod and Jenny reluctantly trailed Mrs. Sizemore back to the living room.

"What do you do, Paul?" Mr. Sizemore asked, and Pamela spirited Philly to the dining room.

"I hope you two are serious," Pamela said when they were alone. "He's gorgeous."

"I'd say we are," Philly said.

"Well, sound a little more enthusiastic."

"It's just . . ." Pamela had always been direct with her, but Philly wasn't sure she could match Pamela's forthrightness.

"What?"

"This whole thing is awkward. It's got to be rough on your parents."

"You're right," Pamela said thoughtfully. "But they are simply going to have to accept the fact you are not going to permanently worship before a shrine in honor of Philip. You have a life to live."

Philly responded with a desultory nod. So many things were easier said than done.

"I'll deal with my parents," Pamela said.

"I need to ask you about something," Philly said. "Paul has been talking to me about forgiving the kid who ran Philip down."

"What?"

"You heard me. I'd like to know what you think about that. For a while I was so full of rage at the kid I swear to God I would have killed him if given the chance."

"Why does Paul want you to forgive him?"

"Because he believes that it's the only way I'll get rid of the anger I'm keeping inside me. He thinks that anger is bad for our relationship."

"What do you know about the kid?"

"Not that much. He's a mess, doing badly in school. He's racked with guilt."

"He damn well better be racked with guilt," Pamela let loose, flushing. "I don't think I could ever forgive him. I know that's not very enlightened thinking these days, but there's a part of me that believes hatred sometimes gets a bad rap."

Philly thought of Gerald Hatch. She hadn't been lying when she told Gerald how proud she was of him for apologizing to Martin Mercer. And it was Gerald who had said that in Colin Feeney's position he would want to be forgiven.

"Don't mention this to you parents," Philly said. "I'm still thinking about it. I don't know what I'm going to do."

Pamela nodded. "To be honest, I'm not sure how they'd react."

"We should be ready to eat in about twenty more minutes," Mrs. Sizemore raised her voice above the living room noise.

Daisy rested on her shoulder and Philly was sure that her daughter was taking in the sights with her customary calm, curious expression. Philly felt the rush of cold air when the front door opened. When she turned to view the late arrival, her heart began to pound. The tall, blond man had her back to her and was giving Pamela a hug and for just a moment Philly experienced a flash of hope that Philip had returned. But then Tom Grange released Pamela and turned to survey the room. Philly quickly pivoted so that Tom would only see Daisy's face, and not hers, and moved to a seat next to where Genie and Jenny were playing, the younger girl plainly excited to find a new playmate, Jenny literally grinning and bearing Genie's bossy roleplaying with her dolls.

"Hey, Genie," Philly said. "I need to borrow Jenny to help me with Daisy."

Jenny was on her feet in an instant. Philly handed Daisy off to the girl. "You're a sweetheart," Philly said. "I know Genie can be bossy. Thanks for putting up with her. Give me five minutes. Walk Daisy around and then bring her back to me."

Philly searched out Paul who was in a discussion with Mr. Sizemore and Pamela's husband, George, in the kitchen. Another person who needs rescuing, Philly thought.

"I need to borrow Paul," Philly intervened, and before anyone could object, she led him to a corner of the dining room. "I need a hug," she said when she was sure they were alone.

Paul obliged. "Are you okay?" he asked.

"I just had a start. Tom Grange, Philip's best friend from when they were growing up, arrived and for a moment I thought it was Philip. All I could see was this tall blond guy."

"It's okay," Paul said, patting her back.

"I can't believe how easy it is for me to become unglued. I've turned into a wuss."

"You've got that right."

Philly gave a half-hearted poke to Paul's chest. "Thanks a lot. How are you holding up?"

"Pretty good. But if someone else asks me about what was my most dangerous case, I may have to make an arrest on general principles."

Jenny appeared with Daisy. "I think she did a number two."

"Hand her over," Philly directed. "I'll change her and feed her upstairs. If we're lucky she'll sleep through the meal."

"If I'm lucky *I'll* sleep through the meal," Paul said.

"Dad!"

Once upstairs, Philly sat on the bed in what used to be Philip's bedroom. There was no present sign of Philip; his boyhood memorabilia had been stored away.

The room served as a guest bedroom with a chest of drawers, a small writing desk, a straight-backed chair, and a pole reading lamp beside the desk. Philly had used the writing desk as a changing table.

Daisy's sucking became less urgent and her eyes fluttered. Philly's eyes begin to tear; Philip had never seen his daughter.

The door opened and Tom Grange entered and stopped short, quickly averting his eyes. "I'm sorry."

Philly switched breasts and covered up. "It's okay."

Tom turned and regarded her sheepishly. "Whenever I visit I stick my head in here for old time's sake."

"It's okay," Philly repeated.

"Were you crying?"

"I was just having a moment. All done."

Tom stood in the doorway, plainly still embarrassed by his intrusion. Philly remembered that he was the wild one and Philip the sensible one back when they were kids.

"What's the craziest thing you and Philip ever did as kids?" Philly asked. She needed to gather lore; it was her responsibility to make sure Daisy knew her father.

Tom shuffled his feet in the doorway, grinned. "That would be a tossup between sneaking three pigs into the high school on a Sunday night and the time we chained shut all the doors to the high school."

"I can't picture Philip doing either of those things."

"Neither could he. I was a very bad influence on him. But I think somewhere deep down he enjoyed himself whenever I'd talk him into doing something really stupid."

Philly wondered if she had represented to Philip the female counterpart to Tom, someone unpredictable, a little wild, someone outside his comfort zone.

"I *was* crying when you came in. I was thinking that Philip never got to see Daisy. It makes me so sad I could scream. Maybe you could write Daisy a letter for later delivery and tell her what her father was like."

"Let me think about it. I'm not much of a letter writer." Tom moved into the room and flipped the desk chair around so that when he sat down he was grasping its back. "I met Paul. He seems like a good guy."

"He is."

"Can I be honest with you?"

Tom was nervous, anything but impulsive. "Sure," Philly said.

"I'm not very good at this. I never know when to shut my mouth. Do you remember that baby shower at your house?"

Philly nodded. On that occasion, just as earlier this evening, Tom's entrance had led her to believe for a fleeting moment that Philip was alive.

"When push came to shove, I didn't have the guts to follow through on something I had decided to do. I had gotten it in my head to stand in for Philip and be there for you. I was going to ask you out. It was like I felt I owed it to Philip. That would have been a disaster. To be honest, I'm glad you found someone else."

Tom had colored, lowered his head.

"It's okay you bringing this up. Paul was the police officer who was first on the scene of Philip's accident. He stayed in contact with me and I knew it wasn't because of his official role. He's looked out for me and he's just been great." She glanced at Tom but couldn't read his expression. "He's not Philip," she added.

"I understand."

Daisy had stopped nursing. Her eyes were closed and her mouth was open. Philly got herself together and draped a diaper over her shoulder. She positioned Daisy over the diaper and began to rub her back.

"She looks like you," Tom said. "Nothing like Philip except for the eyes."

"Give her time."

"Can I hold her?"

Philly waited until she had induced a burp and then handed Daisy over. Tom held her daughter as if she were breakable.

"Paul wants me to forgive the kid who ran Philip down," Philly said.

"No shit!"

"The kid's messed up. He's screwing up school. His mother died some years ago and that seems to have been what got him drinking. He's full of guilt over what he did."

"How do you know all this?"

"Paul's talked to the kid's probation officer."

"What are you going to do?"

"I don't know."

"Dinner is served!" came Mrs. Sizemore's shout from downstairs.

Tom was regarding her thoughtfully. "What?" Philly said.

"I'll tell you what Philip would say to you," Tom said. "He'd tell you to forgive the kid."

"How can you be so sure?"

"He was the nice one, remember? I was the one who was not so nice."

Paul's breathing had slowed. Philly knew him well enough by now to know he was close to dropping off. "Will Jenny be okay when I'm around in the morning," she whispered.

Paul stirred. "I think so, but I'm not sure. I've told her about us. I said we cared for each other and how I hoped you would more and more be in my life. I'm not sure what's registering."

After the Thanksgiving meal, Mr. Sizemore had turned on the backyard lights and after putting on their coats, Jenny and Genie and another little girl and boy had raced around the yard like the kids they were. Not having to deal with Genie's dolls, Jenny had directed their play. "She did real well considering she was thrown into an unfamiliar environment."

Paul didn't respond.

"What about you?" Philly asked.

"Me? I thought I did real well too considering I was thrown into an unfamiliar environment."

"Are you angry?"

Paul turned to face her showing no signs of sleepiness. "Serious discussion," he said.

Philly nodded, not knowing what to expect.

"I'm not angry. There were times tonight when I was uncomfortable. A lot of that had to do with what was unsaid. Philip was like the elephant in the room no one would talk about. But the Sizemores went out of their way to be friendly and welcoming. That had to be hard on them. I know they're Daisy's grandparents and need to be in her life. I guess I'm saying that the third Thanksgiving meal was a mixed bag for me."

Philly was struck by Paul's directness, the way, like Philip, he never sugarcoated a subject so that she would hear what she wanted to hear.

"Thanks for going over there," Philly said.

"It's going to be a yearly event, isn't it?"

"I think so. I hope so."

"I can live with that."

"Right answer."

"But just so you know, I'm turkeyed out."

Philly closed her eyes, weariness all at once overwhelming her.

"What's the story with Tom Grange?" Paul asked. "I felt like he was interviewing me."

The serious discussion hadn't ended, so Philly opened her eyes and related her meeting with Tom, only leaving out the part about Tom telling her what Philip would want her to do in Colin Feeney's case.

"Are you attracted to the guy?"

"I'm attracted to you."

"Right answer."

"I thought it took some guts for him to talk to me the way he did."

"I suppose it did," Paul said.

"Are you jealous or something?"

"Maybe I am."

"Right answer," Philly said.

December

Philly's Untitled Playlist

Glitter in the Air

Pink

96

Carpenter and Simon sat at a counsel table in the hearing room of the Loan Company Licensure Review Board. Top Tier's hearing was well attended. Herbert Brown was huddled with two men in a back corner of the hearing room. Jerome Singer had brought his administrative assistant and one of his company vice-presidents to sit in. Louise Fuller, the attorney presenting the Board's case against Top Tier, was accompanied by a man and a woman whom Carpenter pegged as lawyers. A smartly dressed woman sat alone in the back of the hearing room, and Carpenter believed he knew who she was. He was surprised by Michelle Smith's attendance; she had given him a wink and a wave and Carpenter wondered whether her presence would throw Jerome Singer off his stride.

Serena Jones, all business, entered and took the chair behind the desk at the front of the hearing room. "Let's come to order so we can begin."

Carpenter's misgivings returned. Jones and Louise Fuller were two middle-aged women who had carved out legal careers in public service and who would feel simpatico with each other.

"I don't need to hear opening statements," Jones said. "The Board will be the first to present its case. Please call your first witness, Ms. Fuller."

"Norman Cassidy."

One of the men who had been conferring with Herbert Brown moved forward. Cassidy looked to be in his late fifties. He was of medium height, wiry, and thin. His thick gray eyebrows contrasted with his full head of black hair and probably made him look older than he was.

Fuller's beginning questions brought out that Devonshire Plastics made plastic molds for industrial use. Before failing, the company had been in existence for some twenty-five years. Cassidy had purchased the company eleven years ago from the family who had founded the enterprise.

"Did your company at some time obtain a loan from Top Tier?" Fuller asked.

"We did."

"Who negotiated the business terms?"

"I did for my company. Mr. Singer did the negotiating for Top Tier."

"Were the business terms negotiated with lawyers?"

"No. The lawyers took what Singer and I agreed to and put it into a loan agreement."

"Was Top Tier the only finance company you considered for a loan?"

"No. We had proposals from a number of companies."

"Why did your company elect to do business with Top Tier?"

"Top Tier's interest rate on the working capital part of the loan was slightly lower than the interest rates of the other companies we were talking to."

"Did you record any telephone conversation you had with Mr. Singer during the loan negotiation?"

"I recorded one."

"How did that come about?"

Cassidy leveled a steely glance at Singer. "We were down to a short list of business issues that needed to be resolved and we scheduled a call to go over them. At the outset of the call I told Singer that I wanted to make a record of our conversation, and when we got down to the issues I turned on a tape recorder."

Singer, Carpenter saw, appeared unruffled and untroubled.

"Did you bring the tape of the conversation with you today?"

"I did."

Carpenter objected but Jones reiterated her previous ruling that the tape was admissible. The recorded conversation was remarkably clear. Carpenter studied his transcribed copy of Singer's key words as the recording sounded in the hearing room.

> *"Don't worry about the ten days, Norman. That's what the lawyers insist upon. I pretty much give my borrowers ninety days to cure. I try to work things out."*

"Did you rely on any aspect of the telephone conversation we just heard in deciding to have your company borrow from Top Tier?" Fuller asked

"I relied on all of it."

"In connection with the discussion of a cure period in case there was a default on the loan, what specifically did you rely on?"

"The loan agreement said that if Devonshire Plastics defaulted by not complying with the agreement, Top Tier would give us ten days to cure the default before they took legal action against us. As you just heard, I told Singer that ten days was too short a time. That's when he said not to worry about what the agreement said. He said that his company allowed a borrower ninety days to cure a default. I took him at his word."

"Objection," Carpenter intervened. "Mr. Cassidy quoted Mr. Singer's words incorrectly. I move to strike the answer."

Jones pondered the objection briefly. "Overruled," she pronounced. "I'll review Mr. Cassidy's testimony against the tape before issuing a decision.

Fuller's final questions established that Top Tier took legal action against Devonshire before ninety days had run, and that the legal action had been derailed when a judge ordered that Devonshire Plastics be given a ninety-day cure period.

When Carpenter rose to cross-examine Cassidy, Herbert Brown took a seat at the counsel table at which Louise Fuller was sitting. Carpenter decided not to object to the move.

"Isn't it true, Mr. Cassidy," Carpenter led off, "that you and your company planned to use the ninety-day period to spend assets of Devonshire Plastic so that Top Tier's loss on its loan would increase?"

Cassidy smirked. "No."

With the hearing officer's permission, Carpenter had two financial statements placed before Cassidy. "Do you recognize these documents?"

Cassidy nodded. "They're interim financial statements of Devonshire Plastics."

"Is it correct that the date of the earlier financial statement is ten days prior to the time Top Tier notified your company it had defaulted on its loan?"

Cassidy studied the document. "That appears right."

"Would you agree that the date of the second financial statement is ninety days after the earlier statement?"

"That's what it says."

"What are current assets?"

"I'm not an accountant, but current assets include things like cash and investments that can be turned into cash."

"What is the difference between the current asset figures on the two statements I've asked you to look at?"

Cassidy studied the two documents. "Current assets on the first statement exceed current assets on the second statement by about two million one hundred thousand dollars."

"If Top Tier had been able to freeze your company's assets at the time of the first balance sheet statement as opposed to the time of the second statement, isn't it true that Top Tier's loss on its loan would have been approximately two million one hundred thousand dollars less than the loss turned out to be."

"I guess Singer shouldn't have spouted off about a ninety-day cure period," Cassidy said with his smirk in place.

"I move to strike the last answer and request the hearing officer to instruct the witness to answer the question he was asked."

Jones scowled at Cassidy. "Answer Mr. Carpenter's question please. I'm going to disregard your last answer."

"Yeah," Cassidy said grudgingly. "There would have been about two million one hundred thousand in additional current assets available to Top Tier."

"What happened to the two million one hundred thousand dollars?"

"Devonshire paid other bills."

"Let's look at some of those other bills."

Simon handed a set of documents to Jones and provided copies of the documents to Fuller and Cassidy. Jones took her time going through the papers. When she finished her review, she looked up and nodded at Carpenter.

"Do you recognize these documents?" Carpenter asked.

"They look like copies of bills Devonshire paid and there are copies of the front and back of the Devonshire checks that paid the bills."

"How many bills are in the documents you've been handed?"

Cassidy slowly went through the papers. "Six."

"Someone can check my math," Carpenter directed at Jones, "but the six bills total sixty-two thousand five hundred dollars."

"Thank you, Mr. Carpenter," Jones said. "We'll be sure to check your math."

Carpenter refocused his attention on Cassidy. "That's your signature on your company's checks isn't it?"

"Yeah. I don't actually sign each check. We used some kind of signature stamp."

"Did you approve the payment of the invoices I've asked you to look at?"

"Generally, but not specifically."

"What do you mean by that?" Carpenter pressed.

"I don't review each invoice. I'm usually given a batch of invoices and I skim through them and I initial a form that says the invoices can be paid."

"Is that what you did before these invoices were paid?"

"Probably. I don't remember these invoices specifically."

"Were you generally aware of your company's vendors?"

Cassidy hesitated before answering. "I would say so."

"Were you familiar with the vendors whose invoices I asked you to look at?"

"I recognize the names, if that's what you mean. I can tell you Devonshire Plastics did business with these vendors."

"Do you agree that the dates on the checks which made payments to the vendors occurred between the dates of the two financial statements I asked you to look at previously?"

Cassidy studied the checks that had been placed before him. "Yeah. That's what the dates show."

"I'm going to object," Louise Fuller said. "I've kept silent to give Mr. Carpenter leeway but none of these documents or his questions has to do with what Mr. Singer represented to Mr. Cassidy."

"What do you say to that, Mr. Carpenter?" Jones asked.

"The relevance of the documents and questions will become clear in a moment."

"Proceed," Jones said with what Carpenter took to be evident misgivings.

Simon delivered another set of documents to Jones and again provided copies of the papers to Fuller and Cassidy. Herbert Brown leaned forward to peruse the papers given to Fuller.

Carpenter watched Jones review the documents and was heartened by the fact that when the hearing officer finished her review, she turned to stare at Cassidy.

"These certified copies of corporate filings show that the companies you just testified were paid by Devonshire Plastics had dissolved years prior to your company's payments and the dates on the companies' bills. Please explain to the hearing officer why your company made payments to companies that had gone out of business before the dates on the companies' invoices?"

Carpenter was pleased to see that Cassidy was no longer smirking. Still, Devonshire's president didn't seem unsettled by the trap that Carpenter thought he had laid.

"I really can't explain it. I wasn't aware that the companies had dissolved. The bills looked legitimate and I approved them. Like I said, I recognized the vendors' names and knew that we had done business with them."

"Would you agree that the invoices describe generally the services being billed for?"

Cassidy skimmed through the invoices. "Yeah."

"Were those services actually performed?"

"I assume so."

"Do you know?"

"No."

"If the companies Devonshire paid were no longer in business, who cashed Devonshire's checks and pocketed the money?"

"How the hell should I know?" Cassidy retorted.

"Was it you?" Carpenter asked.

"Screw you! I don't have to put up with your insinuations."

Carpenter kept his eyes on Cassidy, avoided looking at Jones. He let a few beats go by but to his credit, Cassidy continued to look him in the eye.

"Actually, Mr. Cassidy, you do have to put up with my questions and insinuations if that's what they are. So, I'm going to ask you again, and this time you're going to answer me. Was it you who pocketed the money?"

Cassidy, visibly angry, sputtered, unable to get a word out.

"Answer the question," Jones directed.

"This is bullshit! The answer is no!"

"Are you sure?"

"Objection!" Fuller nearly shouted.

"Sustained. Move on, Mr. Carpenter."

"When any of these companies we've been talking about dissolved, were you told of that fact?"

Cassidy frowned. "Not that I can remember. I might have been."

"When you approved the invoices for payment, did you ask yourself why you were being billed by companies that were no longer in business?"

Cassidy was making an effort to keep his emotions under control. Herbert Brown was writing furiously on his notepad.

"I wasn't aware the companies had gone out of business and even if I had been told that had happened, I didn't remember it when I approved the invoices for payment."

"How come the payments sent to these companies at their former addresses weren't returned to your company?"

"I couldn't tell you."

"Isn't it true that the payments to these companies were never mailed?"

"Not as far as I know."

"Your company's checks were stamped on the back 'For Deposit Only.' Do you know where the checks were deposited?"

"I have no idea."

Carpenter paused. He had deliberately opted not to find out where the checks were deposited, reasoning that unanswered questions might be more helpful than answers that might blow up in his face.

"You said that you told Mr. Singer that you were going to make a record of the call you recorded. Is that your testimony?"

"Yeah."

"So, isn't it true that you never used the words recording or tape recorder?"

Cassidy paused and stared for a moment at Herbert Brown. "I don't remember using those words."

"You said that you turned a tape recorder on, correct?"

"Yeah, I did."

"Then how come, after the tape recorder was turned on, you didn't state for the recorded call that you had turned the tape recorder on?"

"I didn't think I had to. I had already said I wanted to make a record of the call."

"Isn't it true that you never mentioned that you wanted to make a record of the call?"

"No, that's not true."

"Isn't it true that you recorded the call without ever telling Mr. Singer that you were going to do so?"

"You're wrong again," Cassidy bristled.

"Was anybody with you when the call was recorded?"

"Yeah." Cassidy pointed to the rear of the hearing room in the direction of the other man Herbert Brown had been talking to. A beefy man with pendulous jowls looked up and nodded at Cassidy. "Warren Meade, my vice-president of operations, was with me."

"Did you tell Mr. Singer that Mr. Meade was with you?"

"I might have. I don't remember."

At Carpenter's request, Simon delivered another set of documents to Jones, Cassidy and Fuller. "Please take your time to review these documents," Carpenter requested Cassidy.

Cassidy slowly paged through the documents. When he finally looked up, Carpenter couldn't read his expression.

"Is it correct, Mr. Cassidy that I have asked you to review a number of vendor contracts, bills to Devonshire Plastic by the vendors, and records of payments by Devonshire Plastic of those vendor bills?"

"Yeah, I'd agree with that."

"Were the payments made between the dates on the two financial statements you previously testified about?"

Cassidy again took his time reviewing the papers before him. "Yeah," he finally answered.

"Is it true that in each case, Devonshire Plastics paid a penalty to the vendor?"

"I noticed that," Cassidy said. "That's correct."

"Isn't it true that in each of the vendor contracts there was no provision for penalty payments?"

"I'd have to go back over the contracts," Cassidy said.

"Then do so," Carpenter directed.

After ten minutes, Jones and Fuller became visibly irritated. Carpenter tuned them out.

"I didn't see any penalty payment provision in the contracts," Cassidy finally said.

"Then explain to the hearing officer why Devonshire Plastics made penalty payments to vendors when your company wasn't contractually obligated to do so?"

Cassidy frowned. "I'm not sure. There must have been a reason."

"What was the reason?"

"I just told you I'm not sure."

"Isn't it a fact that you paid these vendors penalty payments so that they could kickback part of the payments to you?"

"Objection!" Fuller shouted.

Jones started. The hearing officer regarded Cassidy for a long moment. "Overruled," she said.

"You're full of shit," Cassidy hissed. "My answer is no."

"Are you sure?"

"Objection!"

"Sustained."

"Your Honor," Carpenter addressed Jones. "You're probably going to want to check my math again, but by my count, the penalty payments in the contracts total three hundred two thousand dollars."

Jones stare turned hard and Carpenter wondered whether his last comment had come across as snippy. He met her gaze and decided he didn't care how she regarded his tone. He took his time going over his cross-examination outline and then huddled with Simon.

"I could waste some time asking marginal questions," Carpenter whispered. "But I'm thinking of leaving it where it is."

Simon glanced at Cassidy and then studied his notes. "Okay," Simon whispered. "Just reserve the right to call him as a witness in our case."

"Nothing further, Your Honor," Carpenter announced. "We've subpoenaed Mr. Cassidy and reserve the right to call him as a witness in Top Tier's case."

Jones nodded. "Any redirect examination, Ms. Fuller? No? Then call your next witness.

After being sworn in, Warren Meade calmly responded to Fuller's questions. He confirmed the major points of Cassidy's testimony. As he stood to cross-examine, Carpenter doubted he could dent Meade's testimony.

"Since Devonshire Plastics went out of business, has Mr. Cassidy or any company that Mr. Cassidy is involved with paid you any money?"

"Yes. Mr. Cassidy owns some apartment buildings and I currently help him manage them."

"That means you currently work for him, correct?"

"Right."

"What do you do for him exactly?"

"I run his business office and manage the buildings. I deal with tenant complaints, building repairs, you name it."

"Is this a full-time job?"

"Yeah."

"Did Mr. Cassidy introduce you to Mr. Singer during the call Mr. Cassidy recorded?"

"No."

"Do you agree that Mr. Cassidy never used the words tape recorder or recording before he turned on the tape recorder?"

"Yes."

"Did you say anything during the call that was recorded?"

"No."

"Did Mr. Cassidy tell you not to say anything during the call?"

Meade looked at Cassidy, remaining at ease. "Not in those words. He said that he would handle the negotiation with Singer, but he wanted me to sit in. I took it to mean I wasn't to say anything."

"Isn't it true that Mr. Cassidy never said anything about making a record of the call?"

"No, that's not true. It's like I said before. Mr. Cassidy said he wanted to make a record of the call."

"Was that a handwritten record?"

"That's not the way I took it."

"Is that because Mr. Cassidy had put a tape recorder on the table?"

Meade paused. "That may have had something to do with it."

“Mr. Singer would have had no way of knowing that a tape recorder had but put on the table, would he?”

“Not unless he had some kind of x-ray vision.”

“When you worked for Devonshire Plastics, were you the company’s director of operations?”

“Yes.”

“What were your duties?”

“Pretty much what the job title suggests. I oversaw the company’s operations. That involved production and sales.”

“Did you get involved with Devonshire Plastic’s contracts?”

Meade nodded. “I didn’t negotiate them, but to do my job I often had to get familiar with them.”

Carpenter paused. Meade didn’t seem like the kind of guy who would lie for Cassidy, so he decided to take a chance fully expecting his gambit to blow up in his face. “What’s your explanation for Devonshire Plastic’s paying bills for dissolved companies?”

Meade cast a brief glance in Cassidy’s direction. “I can’t explain it.”

Carpenter had the invoices that he had presented to Cassidy placed before Meade and asked Meade to review the documents.

“Were the services described in these invoices performed for Devonshire Plastics?” Carpenter asked when Meade finished his review.

“I’m not sure about some of the work but I’m reasonably sure that most of the services described in the bills weren’t performed.”

Carpenter began to relax. “Do you have an explanation as to why Devonshire Plastics paid vendors penalties totaling three hundred two thousand dollars when the contracts with the vendors didn’t contain penalty provisions?”

“That’s not my area,” Meade said, “so I couldn’t comment one way or the other.”

“Nothing further.”

“Let’s break for lunch,” Jones said after establishing that Fuller had no further questions for Meade. “Does the Board have any other witnesses, Ms. Fuller?”

“We have one more witness.”

“Very well. We’ll start with your last witness when we return.”

Carpenter had to make an effort to focus on Fuller’s direct examination of Eleanor Morgan, the woman he had seen earlier at the back of the hearing room. He was still fuming over his lunch with Singer. Singer had gotten it into his head that the Board's case was being shredded and that there was no need for him to take the stand. No matter how many times Carpenter had reminded Singer that he had misled Cassidy, Top Tier's president pushed that fact to the side. Singer was convinced that Cassidy had been made out to be a crook and that anything he had said or done to Cassidy was, if not justified, explainable. Even when Simon reminded Singer that he had acted before he had any idea Cassidy was a possible crook, Singer dismissed that timing with a shrug.

Morgan was a no-nonsense witness, a poised, middle-aged corporate executive who had run a company that had taken out a loan from Top Tier. When her company defaulted on its loan, Top Tier disregarded Singer's promise of a ninety-day cure period and took legal action against the company ten days after the loan default.

"What happened when you reminded Mr. Singer that he had promised your company a ninety-day cure period," Fuller inquired.

Morgan pivoted so that she faced Singer. "I'll never forget what happened. Mr. Singer laughed and said that the written agreement controlled and he was not about to let the collateral on the loan disappear."

"Did that harm your company?"

"It put us out of business," Morgan said bitterly. "The company was late on one payment and was having cash flow problems so that the company's assets didn't compare to its liabilities in the way the loan agreement required. I believe that if we had been given the ninety days Mr. Singer had promised me, we would have worked out those issues. We never got a chance to work things out when Mr. Singer went back on his word."

"Nothing further," Fuller said.

"Did Top Tier lose money on the loan to your company?" Carpenter began.

"Yes."

"Would Top Tier's loss on its loan have increased if Top Tier had waited to take legal action after ninety days?"

"I can't tell you for sure but I have an opinion," Morgan said.

Carpenter refused to take that bait.

"What was the nature of your company's cash flow difficulties that you told us about?"

"One of the companies we did business with was behind on its payments to us. They were in the process of raising capital and I learned after Top Tier sued my company that the capital was raised. My company would have become current on its obligations to Top Tier if Mr. Singer had given us the ninety days he promised to give us."

Carpenter mentally kicked himself. By asking an open-ended question, he had permitted Morgan to give the opinion she had previously mentioned.

"Is it correct that your company never took legal action against Top Tier?"

"Yes."

"Did your company file any complaint with the Board that's conducting this hearing?"

"No."

"Is it correct that your company was in default under the Top Tier loan agreement at the time Top Tier took legal action?"

"Yes."

"Isn't it true that the company you mentioned was raising capital might not have released any of that capital to your company?"

"That's possible."

"Did your company ever recover anything it was owed from the company that had raised capital?"

"No."

"Nothing further."

Fuller stood. "Did you explain to Mr. Singer about the other company raising capital?"

"I did."

"What was Mr. Singer's response to that?"

"He laughed again. He said, 'That's not my problem.' That's a direct quote."

"Nothing further," Fuller said, as she resumed her seat smiling.

"No additional cross-examination," Carpenter said.

"Call your first witness, Mr. Carpenter."

"Paul Huggins."

Huggins struck Carpenter as someone who could be pushed around on the witness stand. He was a short, thin, nervous man who regarded the world through gold, wire-rimmed glasses whose lenses were milk bottle bottom thick. Herbert Brown had stayed seated beside Fuller which told Carpenter that he would represent Huggins if the need arose.

"Is it true that you and Norman Cassidy are close personal friends?" Carpenter led off.

"I would say so."

"The two of you are neighbors, right?"

"Yes."

"Do you socialize with Mr. Cassidy?"

"Yes."

"Were you present during Mr. Cassidy's testimony?"

"Yes."

"Did your accounting firm provide services to Devonshire Plastics before that company went out of business?"

"We did."

"Was Devonshire Plastics your firm's biggest client?"

"Yes."

"What accounting services did your firm perform for Devonshire?"

Cassidy helped himself to a glass of water. "We prepared monthly financial statements. We did the company's tax returns. We provided year end audited financial statements."

Carpenter gestured to Simon and Simon delivered to Huggins the invoices and cancelled checks that had been presented to Cassidy. "Please review these documents," Carpenter instructed.

When Huggins looked up, he again reached for his water glass.

"You were present when Mr. Cassidy confirmed that these invoices were paid to companies that had previously gone out of business, weren't you?"

"Yes."

"Did your company ever raise questions about why Devonshire was paying money to companies that had previously gone out of business?"

"No, but . . ."

"Isn't it a fact that when you audited Devonshire, you deliberately overlooked these payments out of deference to Mr. Cassidy?"

"No," Huggins said, and Carpenter was pleased to see that the accountant had colored.

"As Devonshire's accountant, do you have any idea where the money went when Devonshire paid companies that had gone out of business?"

"Not really."

"Are you saying that the money simply vanished into thin air?"

"I don't know what happened to the money."

"Did your firm prepare Devonshire's final tax returns?"

"Yes."

"Were the payments Devonshire made to dissolved companies listed as Devonshire business expenses on those tax returns?"

"I would say so."

"Is it customary, when preparing a company's tax return, for an accounting firm to deduct, as legitimate expenses, payments made to companies that were not in existence when the payments were incurred?"

"No, but . . ."

"Is it customary, when preparing a company's tax return, for an accounting firm to deduct, as legitimate expenses, payments made to companies where the accounting firm doesn't know what happened to the payments?"

"No, but . . ."

"Objection," Herbert Brown intervened. "The witness is not being permitted to finish his answers."

Jones regarded Huggins for a long moment before responding to Brown. "Regardless of whether you have any right to object, the objection is overruled."

"You didn't want to call irregularities to Mr. Cassidy's attention for fear of losing your accounting firm's biggest client, correct?" Carpenter continued immediately.

"No, that's not true."

"But it is true that there have been complaints lodged against you and your accounting firm by the firm's clients, isn't it?"

"There have been some complaints. They . . ."

"Some of those complaints allege shoddy work on your firm's part, don't they?"

Huggins' hand shook as he reached for water. "That was alleged in a few cases."

"Isn't it true that your accounting firm returned fees to clients in order to settle some of the complaints against the firm?"

"We worked out financial arrangements."

"That's not what I asked you," Carpenter raised his voice. "You need to answer my questions directly. Isn't it true that in settling complaints against your firm, the firm returned accounting fees it had received?"

"That happened," Huggins said meekly.

"Were you aware that the tax returns and financial statements your accounting firm prepared for Devonshire Plastics were being provided to Top Tier?"

"Yes."

"Do you know why those documents were provided to Top Tier?"

Huggins directed a pleading look in Cassidy's direction. "I think it was required in the loan agreement."

"Did you know that Top Tier would rely on the financial statements and tax returns that your firm prepared for Devonshire Plastics?"

"I guess I knew that."

"What good to Top Tier were the tax returns and financial statements you prepared when you've admitted today that they contain expenses to companies that submitted invoices for services rendered after the companies went out of business?"

"We did the best we could with the records we were given," Huggins said weakly.

"You need to listen to my questions and answer them," Carpenter again raised his voice. "What good were the tax returns and financial statements to Top Tier when they reflect payments to companies who had long before gone out of business?"

"I can't speak for Top Tier."

"I'm not asking you to speak for Top Tier. I'm asking you to answer my question."

"I don't know the answer."

"Is today the first time you've learned that Devonshire was paying money to companies that had dissolved?"

"Yes."

"With this new information, do you regard the tax returns and financial statements you prepared for Devonshire to be misleading?"

Huggins drained his glass of water. Sweat beaded on his forehead.

"They could be misleading. I would have to look into that."

"You're not as confident today as to the accuracy of your work for Devonshire as you were yesterday, correct?"

Huggins shot another pleading look in Cassidy's direction. "I guess not."

"No further questions."

Herbert Brown was whispering to Fuller, shielding their faces with his notepad. Fuller rose to her feat tentatively, as Herbert Brown placed a sheet of notepaper in front of her. Fuller glanced at the paper and then addressed Huggins.

"When an accounting firm does an audit of a company, does the firm investigate whether the company's vendors are in business?"

"No. That's not done and we didn't do anything like that when it came to Devonshire Plastics."

Fuller again looked at the notepaper Brown had given her. "Mr. Carpenter asked you about payments to businesses who had gone out of business and I believe you said that your firm reflected those payments on the financial statements of Devonshire. Is that correct?"

"Yes," Huggins said, and Carpenter picked up on the accountant's emboldened tone.

"Did the listing of those payments as company expenses make Devonshire more or less profitable?"

Huggins sent a brief smile Cassidy's way. "Less profitable."

"Nothing further."

Carpenter rose quickly. "Isn't it true, Mr. Huggins, that given expenses paid to non-existent companies, you have less confidence today in the reliability of Devonshire's financial statements and tax returns than you had yesterday?"

Huggins squirmed in his chair. When he reached for his water glass he seemed surprised to find it empty. "I guess that's right," he said.

"Is it also true that the expenses Devonshire paid to dissolved companies reduced Devonshire's tax liability?"

"Yes."

"Isn't it true that those claimed expenses might constitute tax fraud?"

Huggins sighed audibly. "That might be the case."

"Nothing further."

"Who's next, Mr. Carpenter?" Fuller asked.

"I need five minutes, Your Honor."

Jerome Singer was seated in the witness chair. During the recess, Singer had again balked at providing testimony and Carpenter had surprised himself by not arguing with his client. "Have it your way," he had said, and that was when Singer abruptly announced that he had changed his mind causing Carpenter to wonder whether he'd been dealing with a two-year old who only responded to reverse psychology. Singer's sudden about-face wasn't the only problem Carpenter now had to deal with. Singer had also refused to be fully prepped for his hearing testimony. But compared to the risks inherent in Singer not testifying, Carpenter would do what had to be done in dealing with a witness who was not fully prepared.

Singer fielded background questions smoothly, addressing his comments to Jones as he had been instructed to do.

"Prior to Mr. Cassidy's filing a complaint with the Board has there been any complaint of any kind made against Top Tier?"

"No."

"Were you present when Ms. Morgan testified?"

"I was."

"Do you recall the conversation between you and Ms. Morgan that she testified about?"

"I do generally."

"Did you ever laugh at her during that conversation?"

"No."

"Did she bring up the subject of a ninety-day cure period?"

"She did."

"Was that something you had mentioned to her before her company signed its loan agreement with Top Tier?"

"Yes."

"What did you say about a ninety-day cure period to Ms. Morgan before her company borrowed money from Top Tier?"

"I told her that we typically provide borrowers with a ninety-day window to cure defaults while workout terms are being negotiated, but that I was not going to change the ten-day cure period set forth in the agreement."

"What did she say to that?"

"Nothing as well as I can remember."

"Let's go back to the conversation Ms. Morgan had with you when her company defaulted on the loan. She testified that she brought up the ninety-day cure period. What was your response to her?"

"I told her that Top Tier couldn't afford her the ninety days. I told her it was unreasonable for her to ask Top Tier to hold off taking legal action in the hope that some other company might obtain capital or some kind of financing. Even if the other company obtained money, there was no assurance that any of that money would end up with Ms. Morgan's company."

"How did Ms. Morgan respond to your position?"

Singer looked to the back of the hearing room where Morgan was seated. "She called me a cheat and liar."

"Were you present when Mr. Cassidy testified earlier today?"

"Yes."

So far Singer had put to the side his arrogance and superior air. "Let's start with his taping of your conversation. Did Mr. Cassidy ever tell you that he was going to make a tape or tape recording of the conversation?"

"No."

"Did he ever say that he was going to make a record of the conversation?"

"I don't remember him saying anything to that effect."

"Did Mr. Cassidy have you on a speaker phone at his end of the phone line?"

Singer took his time considering the question. "I don't remember one way or the other."

"Did Mr. Cassidy ever mention that there was anyone on his end of the conversation listening to what was being said?"

"No. At the time I believed the two of us were having a private conversation to try to hash out the business terms of a loan."

"If Mr. Cassidy had told you that he was making a recording of the telephone call, would you have participated in the call?"

Singer shrugged. "I'm not sure. Nobody has ever told me that he or she was recording one of my calls. If I went along with the recording, I would probably have insisted on making my own tape. But as I said, I don't really know what I would have done."

Carpenter believed that Singer's uncertainty had the ring of truth.

"Mr. Singer, I'm going to read you one of your statements on the recorded call. Quote. Don't worry about the ten days, Norman. That's what the lawyers insist upon. I pretty much give my borrowers ninety days to cure. I try to work things out. Unquote. Was that statement true at the time you made it?"

"Yes."

"On how many occasions did Top Tier not afford a borrower a ninety-day cure period when that length of time for a cure had been discussed with the borrower?"

"Twice. In the case of Ms. Morgan's company and in the case of Devonshire Plastics."

"Nothing further."

Fuller was instantly on her feet. For a moment she stared at Singer as if too many areas for cross-examination vied for her attention.

"Is it correct, Mr. Singer, that when asked about the ten-day cure period in Top Tier's standard loan agreement, you brought up the ninety-day cure period as a selling point to do business with you?"

Singer didn't answer straight away. Carpenter was instantly alert, but kept a neutral expression.

"I can't answer you yes or no," Singer said. "There's probably some truth to what you asked. But in my business, I try to make foreclosing on a loan a last resort. It's preferable to work things out and when I said that we *pretty much* give borrowers ninety days to cure a loan default, that is in fact the case." Singer made quotation marks in the air when he used the words *pretty much.*

Carpenter breathed a sigh of relief. Singer's answer sounded believable.

"You knew that Ms. Morgan and Mr. Cassidy were relying on a ninety-day cure period, didn't you?"

Carpenter kept silent. Any objection to the question would likely be overruled.

"They may have gotten that into their heads, but that's their business, not mine. I never said to either of them that they were guaranteed a ninety-day cure period."

"Why not tell them they were stuck with a ten-day cure period and any extension of that ten-day period was in your discretion and couldn't be counted upon?"

"I thought that's what I did."

"You told Mr. Cassidy that he could count on a ninety-day cure period, didn't you?"

"Objection," Carpenter said. "That's not what Mr. Singer said during the recorded call."

Serena Jones consulted her notes. "You told Mr. Cassidy that he could pretty much count on a ninety-day cure period, didn't you?" the hearing officer asked.

"I told him we pretty much provide ninety days, but I never said he could count on that."

"Did you expect Mr. Cassidy to rely on that statement?" Fuller asked, not put out that Jones had rephrased her previous question.

"I don't think I consciously expected him to rely on that statement."

"But it would be reasonable for him to rely on it, wouldn't it?"

Singer regarded Fuller calmly for a moment. "I suppose it would be reasonable provided he listened to what I told him and didn't put words in my mouth."

"You wanted Mr. Cassidy to think he was getting what he wanted as to the length of the cure period, didn't you?" Fuller followed up.

"I didn't want Mr. Cassidy to think anything," Singer responded with a touch of irritation. "I explained to him what was true in my business, namely that most borrowers that defaulted on loans were not held to the ten-day cure period written into the loan agreement but were given additional time to reach a work out."

"Why didn't you provide in the agreement the ninety-day cure period Mr. Cassidy asked for?"

"The ten-day cure period is standard in our loan agreements."

"But why didn't you give him ninety days to cure his company's default?"

"I didn't trust him. The man illegally recorded our conversation."

"You refused him the ninety-day cure period before he told you he recorded your prior conversation. Why did you refuse him the ninety days before he brought up the recording?"

Fuller had been clever to pick up on the timing. Singer had better watch himself, Carpenter thought.

"You're right," Singer said. "The recording of the call has made me so angry that it's the main thing I think about when it comes to Mr. Cassidy. I did say no to him as to the ninety days before he brought up the recording. His company's financial statements were so dismal I didn't see any realistic way for him to turn the situation around. I was certain Top Tier was going to take a major loss on the loan and I wanted to minimize the damage."

Carpenter figured Singer had earned a point for a nice recovery. But Jones was regarding Singer as if trying to assess whether he was too slick for his own good.

"Top Tier went to court to try to freeze Devonshire Plastics' assets, didn't it?"

"That's correct."

"How did that work out for Top Tier?"

"Badly. The judge refused to freeze the assets and ordered Top Tier to give Devonshire Plastics ninety days to cure any loan default."

"Is it true that the recorded conversation we heard today was played before the judge who held Top Tier to the ninety-day cure period?"

"Yes."

"Are these words familiar to you, Mr. Singer? Quote. Based on a recorded conversation between Mr. Singer and Mr. Cassidy, it was reasonable for Mr. Cassidy to assume that his company had ninety days to cure any loan default. Unquote."

"Yes," Singer said frowning.

"Why are those words familiar to you?"

"I believe that they come from the judge's decision you just asked me about."

"Right you are," Fuller said, before moving to introduce the judge's ruling into evidence.

Carpenter objected to the exhibit, but Jones allowed the judge's decision as a hearing exhibit.

"You've been present throughout this hearing haven't you, Mr. Singer?"

"Yes."

"At the time you refused to allow Devonshire Plastic a ninety-day cure period, were you aware that Devonshire had made payments to companies that had dissolved?"

"No"

"At the time you refused to allow Devonshire the ninety-day cure period, were you aware of the specifics as to checks that company had written, or specific invoices that company had received?"

"No."

"At the time you refused to allow Devonshire the ninety-day cure period, were you aware that Devonshire had made penalty payments to vendors?"

"No."

"Did you just tell us that Devonshire's financial statements were dismal?"

"Yes."

"Are you claiming that either Devonshire or its accountant did anything to make those financial statements rosier than they were?"

Fuller had timed her questions well, Carpenter thought. Unless Singer wanted to appear a fool, he would have to answer her last question no.

"No," Singer said.

"Nothing further," Fuller said.

Carpenter decided to keep damage control questions to a minimum. "Did Mr. Cassidy ever ask you to clarify what you meant by *pretty much* when you told him Top Tier pretty much gave borrowers ninety days to come up with a work out?"

"No."

"Did Mr. Cassidy ever ask you whether you had held any borrower to the ten-day cure period in Top Tier's standard loan agreement?"

"No."

"Did you ever state or promise to Mr. Cassidy that Devonshire Plastics would be guaranteed a ninety-day cure period?"

"No."

"Nothing further," Carpenter said, thinking that sometimes ending on a high note simply wasn't possible.

"Any other witness, Mr. Carpenter?" Jones inquired.

"No."

"Any rebuttal witness, Ms. Fuller?"

"No."

"That closes the evidence," Jones announced. She looked at her watch. "I'm going to conclude this hearing today. You may each have ten minutes to present closing argument. I will also allow each of you seven days to file a post-hearing legal memorandum that is not to exceed ten pages. Please don't burden me with arguments that you've already presented in written form. With respect to closing arguments, we'll start with you, Mr. Carpenter."

"Sometimes people hear what they want to hear," Carpenter began. "Both Ms. Morgan and Mr. Cassidy claimed that they were guaranteed a ninety-day cure period if their companies defaulted on their loans to Top Tier. Mr. Singer has made it clear that he gave no guaranty of any kind. And we know that in the case of Devonshire Plastics, Mr. Singer made no guaranty of any kind. In the illegally recorded telephone conversation, Mr. Singer told Mr. Cassidy that Top Tier *pretty much* gave defaulting borrowers ninety days to come up with a work out which cannot be translated into a guaranty of any kind."

"Does that mean that you're withdrawing your objection to the admission of the recorded telephone conversation?" Jones asked.

Carpenter knew he was on the receiving end of a "gotcha" moment. Shit. Well, perhaps he could have his cake and eat it, too. "No, Your Honor. The case was tried with the recorded conversation in evidence and an objection is necessary to protect Top Tier's rights."

Jones presented an ambiguous shrug and made a note on her legal pad.

Carpenter took a moment to regain his train of thought. "In each case that was cited by the Board, Top Tier had reasonable business grounds to adhere to the language in the loan agreements. With respect to Ms. Morgan's company, she admitted that her plan was dependent upon another company that had nothing to do with Top Tier, coming up with capital. That's not even a plan. That's a wing and a prayer that is so tenuous and problematic that Top Tier cannot be faulted for not accepting it. Top Tier wasn't required to gamble its resources on Ms. Morgan's vague hope that the tooth fairy would place some money under the pillow of a third party and that the money would somehow find its way to her company."

Carpenter paused. Jones' serious expression provided no clue as to whether he had scored a point.

"In Devonshire Plastic's case, Top Tier was confronted with financial information, provided by the company, that was, in Mr. Singer's words, dismal. Mr. Singer feared that Devonshire Plastics would dissipate its assets leaving Top Tier high and dry. His concern grew when Mr. Cassidy confessed to illegally recording their phone conversation. When a court gave Devonshire Plastics ninety days to cure its loan default, the company did dissipate its assets with a number of payments going to nonexistent companies and a number of payments going to other vendors as penalty payments to which those vendors had no contractual right. Despite Mr. Cassidy's disclaimers, the inference can be drawn that Mr. Cassidy put that money in his own pocket to defraud creditors such as Top Tier.

Mr. Singer's instincts not to trust Mr. Cassidy or his company's financial statements were spot on. His assessments of Mr. Cassidy and Devonshire's financial statements were confirmed when Mr. Cassidy admitted to breaking the law by illegally recording a telephone conversation, and by the testimony we heard at this hearing that Mr. Cassidy approved payments to companies that weren't in business.

"Mr. Singer was never told his discussion with Mr. Cassidy over business terms of the loan was being recorded. Even if Mr. Cassidy is believed that he said he was going to make a record of the call, that remark is so ambiguous it counts for nothing. Mr. Cassidy has admitted that he never told Mr. Singer he was going to make a recording of their call and Mr. Meade, his right-hand man, confirmed that fact.

"Nothing Mr. Cassidy said at this hearing can be credited. The man and his company broke the law whenever it suited them. They illegally recorded a telephone conversation. They defrauded creditors by making payments to non-existent companies and by making penalty payments they were not obligated to make. In addition, his company's tax returns were false and inaccurate. Even his close personal friend and accountant wouldn't and couldn't vouch for the accuracy of Devonshire Plastics' tax returns."

"Your time is just about up," Jones said.

Carpenter checked his watch. He didn't like to be interrupted during a closing argument but Jones' statement as to the time he had left was correct.

"In that case, let me simply conclude by saying that there is nothing that Top Tier did that warrants any action against it by the Board. The most serious allegation against Top Tier concerned Devonshire Plastics not being given a ninety-day period to cure its default under its loan from Top Tier. Devonshire was never promised or guaranteed a ninety-day cure period. The allegation is simply false and baseless, words that apply to Devonshire's president."

"Ms. Fuller?" Jones said.

"The taped conversation speaks for itself," Fuller declared authoritatively. "Mr. Singer's mention of a ninety-day cure period was plainly a substantive selling point that he used to obtain Devonshire's business. He used the same bait and switch tactic with Ms. Morgan's company. Mr. Carpenter claims that the telephone conversation was ambiguous. We know that it wasn't ambiguous. A disinterested party, a judge of the superior court, made a clear ruling that it was reasonable for Mr. Cassidy to rely on Mr. Singer's statement that Devonshire would be afforded a ninety-day cure period. By extension, the judge's reasoning equally applies to Ms. Morgan's company even though we don't have a recording of the discussion between Ms. Morgan and Mr. Singer.

"Top Tier's defense to the serious charge against it is to blame someone else. The lion's share of Top Tier's case concerned picking apart financial information relating to Devonshire. Since none of that information had anything to do with Top Tier making representations to potential borrowers about a ninety-day cure period—representations that became misrepresentations—none of that testimony is relevant or material to this case."

Having made two telling points, Fuller paused. "I won't take up more of your time. The Board will make any further points in its post-hearing legal memorandum. But I do want to remind the hearing officer why we're here. We're here because the Board licenses loan companies and its rules and regulations prohibit licensed loan companies from making misrepresentations and engaging in bait and switch tactics. Top Tier, a licensed loan company, represented to two borrowers that the borrowers would have ninety days to cure a default. Then Top Tier refused to honor its representations which means that Top Tier went back on its word. Loan companies that lie to potential borrowers to get the borrowers' business shouldn't be doing business in Massachusetts. Top Tier's license should be revoked."

Jones rose. "Thank you, counsel," she said as she made for the door. "Seven days for final legal memoranda."

Carpenter had sent Simon on ahead so that he could have a private word with Michelle Smith, who had lingered at the back of the hearing room. Singer had offered him grudging thanks before departing, but his client's heart wasn't in it. Singer was worried, as well he should be. Carpenter had no idea how Jones would rule but he had a bad feeling as to the direction she was leaning.

"Learn much?" Carpenter asked when Smith joined him at his counsel table.

"Jerome could be in trouble. I didn't like the look of the hearing officer."

That makes two of us, Carpenter thought, but kept to himself. "Are you really going to write a paper about this case?"

"No," Smith said. "The case is interesting, but I really don't want to involve myself with anything that concerns Jerome. I don't know what I was thinking before."

"How are you?"

"Good," Smith said. "My timing is perfect. I'll be getting an MBA when the economy is in the toilet and a bumper crop of MBAs are hanging from the trees."

"Are you enjoying the program?"

"I love it."

"Still flying?"

"On occasion, I fill in when my schedule allows. When I end up with my degree, I'll basically be starting from scratch. My savings will have taken a hit although the money you got for me has really helped. I'm trying not to think about the reality facing me when I graduate."

Carpenter was curious as to Smith's read on the evidence. "Any thoughts about what you heard today?"

"I thought you did a good job making that guy Cassidy look like he crawled out of a dung hill. But that may not be enough."

Carpenter nodded. Fuller's point in her closing argument would probably carry the day: when Singer spoke to Cassidy about a ninety-day cure period, he hadn't known that Cassidy was a bad actor.

"From what I heard, I don't think Top Tier should be forced permanently out of business. Maybe a month or two suspension. Perhaps a fine of some sort. Maybe Top Tier should have an outside authority monitor the company's business for a year."

Smith's lesser sanctions sounded reasonable which probably meant that Singer would be outraged by any of them. Singer, as Smith well knew, was not the kind of guy who would admit he was wrong.

"By the way," Smith said, "you get my vote for the best one liner."

"What was that?"

"The one about the tooth fairy. It cracked me up."

97

Philly returned a call from Donald Fanning while Daisy was asleep on a mat on the floor of her home office. Moments before, Carpenter's account of the Top Tier hearing had left her with a sour taste; she couldn't imagine anything that Martin Mercer's lawyer could say that would sweeten her mood.

"Thanks for getting back to me, Ms. Piper. That was quite a performance at my client's deposition."

"Should I say thanks or tell you to fuck off?"

Fanning laughed. "People say I'm a character. They don't mean the term kindly. Usually it's a euphemism for showboating, flamboyant asshole. Still, when all is said and done, I'm okay with being a character. I can live with that. I think you may be a character too."

"I just had a baby," Philly said, deciding to be candid with Fanning. "It's given me a new perspective. A year ago, I wouldn't have done what I did at the deposition. I saw two troubled young men and decided to wing it."

"I understand what you were trying to do. Your client, Mr. Hatch, may not have filled you in on this, but the other day my client apologized to their homeroom class about constantly bringing up how well he did on tests."

Philly wondered whether Fanning had played a part in Mercer providing an apology but decided not to inquire. "Good for him," she said.

"It was good for him. I hear that my client helped your client with some physics course. Was that your doing?"

"I'm not sure," Philly answered. "Gerald said he was having trouble with physics and I said something like why not ask Mercer for help if he's as smart as he claims to be? I was halfway joking."

"It seems that you've earned your client's trust," Fanning said.

"It's complicated. Gerald has done some growing up as a result of this case. May I ask why you're calling?"

"I'm going to make a demand to settle the case and I hope you'll recommend that the case be settled at the figure I have in mind."

"What's the demand?"

"One hundred fifty thousand dollars."

"Gerald is judgment proof so why do you need my support?"

"I'm aware he's judgment proof. Perhaps that made your deposition performance of little or no risk. Still, your performance is having a ripple effect that is largely to the good. I'm paying you a compliment here."

"I don't see the Hatches paying part of the demand figure."

"Neither do I."

Philly mentally kicked herself for being slow on the uptake. "You want me and the lawyer for the Hatches to gang up on the lawyer for the school officials and try to get the school officials to accept your proposal."

"That's exactly what I want. The demand figure I threw out is low. If you knew me better, you'd understand that I typically won't settle a case for a low figure because I'm fairly confident that I can persuade a jury to come back with a substantial verdict. In this instance, there is something to be said for putting the matter behind everyone and moving on."

Philly knew Fanning was buttering her up, but she decided to let it slide and considered his proposal analytically. Gerald was the only defendant plainly on the hook for damages because there was no dispute he had beaten Mercer up. But Fanning was correct that a money judgment against Gerald was worthless. It would take a lot of doing for a jury to hold the Hatches liable for Mercer's injuries, and Fanning had to know that as well. When it came to the school officials, Fanning would claim that they had ignored Mercer's complaints of being bullied. But the school officials had some immunity defenses that might carry the day. Still, if the school officials would agree to pay Fanning's demand, the case would be over and the Hatches wouldn't have the litigation hanging over them. There really was no reason not to help Fanning get what he wanted for his client.

"Okay, I'll try to get you what you want. But I don't think the lawyer representing the school officials will go for your number."

"You may be right about Calvin Blaine," Fanning acknowledged. "That's where you come in. We've established that you're a character. Time to live up to your reputation."

"You haven't exactly given me talking points to work with."

"Scare the shit out of Blaine," Fanning said. "Tell him I'm a wild man who knows how to pull at a jury's heartstrings. You won't be lying."

"I don't see Blaine agreeing to six figures," Philly said.

"See what you can do," Fanning replied. "Have a nice day. As they say on that cable TV station, 'characters welcome.'"

Philly was almost finished with washing up the evening dishes. From the living room, she heard Raul and Isabella and Gerald Hatch jabbering away in Spanish with Daisy's occasional high-pitched squeals the only interruption of the mellifluous dialogue. Gerald's accent sounded good. Philly dried her hands and moved to the kitchen doorway. Gerald was holding Daisy in his lap and, as he intently listened to Raul, he leaned forward and planted a kiss on the top of her head. The gesture was so spontaneous and natural that Philly was taken aback. This teenager loved her daughter. Somehow, holding Daisy, Gerald's size and strength were less in evidence and it was hard to imagine him as the angry, brooding, uncommunicative teenager she had first met.

"Bath time coming up in five minutes," Philly announced. Gerald gave her an absentminded wave of acknowledgement and she went back to the kitchen to run warm water in the sink. "Ready!" she called out when the sink was two-thirds full.

Gerald produced Daisy and held her under her shoulders while Philly worked her out of a fuzzy winter onesie and her diaper. Daisy wriggled, knowing what was coming. Philly took hold of Daisy and eased her into the sink, tilted her head back, and with a cupped hand spooned water over her flyaway hair. "You do the shampoo," she directed Gerald and he applied a dab and began to rub it into Daisy's hair.

"I got a call from Mercer's lawyer," Philly said. "He told me that Mercer apologized to your homeroom and helped you with physics. How did the physics go?"

"Mercer's a jerk. When I asked him to help me he said, 'You think we're going to be friends now because you apologized for kicking the shit out of me?' I told him I didn't want to be friends with him because I didn't like him. I said all I wanted was help with physics. He said that I was just trying to get him to go easy on me in the court case. I told him I didn't give a rat's ass about the court case."

Daisy began kicking and Philly absorbed the brunt of the splashes.

"Then why'd he help you?"

"I don't know. But he agreed to meet me after school. He spent an hour with me and it helped. Mercer really is smart. I thanked him, but he didn't say you're welcome or anything. I think he really didn't know what to say."

"Good for you," Philly said. "I'm proud of you for reaching out to him even if he is an asshole."

Philly began to rinse Daisy's hair. Her daughter closed her eyes and seemed at peace with the water flowing through her hair.

"Do you want to know what my Spanish teacher said?" Gerald asked, changing the subject.

"I do."

"He said that if I kept up my work, I could win the Spanish award at graduation."

"That's wonderful. Did you tell your parents?"

"Not yet."

"What are you waiting for?"

"I don't know."

"Think about telling them. Now that I'm a mother I can better appreciate how nice it is to hear good things about your kid."

Philly added several plastic cups to the water and Daisy began playing with them. "I've been meaning to ask you something," she said. "Why this tremendous interest in Spanish?"

Gerald colored. "Do you promise not to laugh?"

"I promise."

"Sophomore year we had an exchange student from Spain. She was beautiful. I loved to listen to her talk. She had this very sexy accent. I wanted to try talking to her in Spanish, but I never got up the nerve. I probably wouldn't have said anything to her even if I spoke better. After she went back to Spain, I made a promise to myself to try to learn the language. I love speaking it. When I speak it, I'm no longer a jerk-off from Cambridgeport."

"You're not a jerk-off from anywhere," Philly tried to sound reassuring without striking a false note. "Are you thinking about college?"

"I've applied to a few places. I'll probably apply to a few more."

"Good. Enough about you."

Philly quickly rinsed Daisy off, lifted her out of the sink, and swaddled her in a bath towel. She had a freshly scrubbed look and a smell that Philly savored. When Daisy was dry, Philly laid her down on the counter by the sink. "Let's see those diapering skills I taught you," she said to Gerald.

"There's something else I wanted to mention to you," Philly said as Gerald set to work arranging a diaper under Daisy. "When Mercer's lawyer called, he made a proposal to settle the lawsuit." As Philly related Fanning's offer, she noticed that Gerald slowed down on his diapering duties.

"What are you going to do?" Gerald asked.

"I'm going to try to get the case settled."

Gerald didn't say anything as he worked Daisy into rubber pants and a fresh onesie.

"Getting the case settled is a good thing," Philly said.

"I don't know," Gerald said in a soft voice. "I don't want anything to change. I'm happy right now."

"I'll repeat what I said before. It's not going to change anything here. You get to hang out here whenever you want. Let me work on the legal stuff. You take care of business at school the way you've been doing. Also, think about your parents. If this case goes away, it's a big load off their shoulders."

Gerald nodded but didn't look convinced. He stood a freshly dressed Daisy on the counter and she reached out to touch his nose. Normally that would have brought a smile from Gerald, but now he remained solemn.

"Come on," Philly said. "Let's get this kid to sleep. If you want, I'll drive you home. It's cold out there."

"That's all right. I'll take my bike. I've got a lot to think about."

98

Philly left Daisy with Sarah Ferguson early to get to her Boston office well before her scheduled meeting with Carpenter, Simon, and Rachel. She had done research on Calvin Blaine, the lawyer who represented the school officials in Martin Mercer's lawsuit. Blaine's downtown Boston law firm had a sizable litigation department that specialized in representing municipalities when they were sued for personal injuries.

A helpful feature of law firm websites was providing each lawyer's direct line. Blaine picked up on the second ring.

"This is Calvin Blaine."

"Good morning, Mr. Blaine. This is Philomena Piper. As you know, I represent Gerald Hatch in the Martin Mercer case."

There was a pause that went on a beat too long which Philly took as a bad sign.

"What can I do for you, Ms. Piper?"

"Donald Fanning called me and presented an offer to settle the Mercer case."

"Called *you*?"

"Yes."

"Why didn't he contact me directly?"

"I don't know. He asked me to convey the offer to other defense counsel. I've filled in Mr. Price, the lawyer for Mr. and Mrs. Hatch, and I'm now calling you." Philly resisted an urge to tell Blaine she had saved the worst for last.

"When did he make his proposal?"

"Some days ago."

"And you're only now reaching out to me?"

"That's right," Philly said, keeping her irritation under wraps even though Blaine was asking some appropriate questions.

"Well, you certainly took your sweet time passing on the information. What's his proposal?"

"One hundred fifty thousand dollars."

Blaine didn't immediately react to the figure. "That's not a number I would have thought Fanning would start with," he finally said.

"It surprised me as well."

"So how much are the Hatches willing to kick in if the offer is accepted?"

"Nothing."

"I take it the Hatches want Cambridgeport to foot the entire settlement. That's not going to happen if I have anything to say about it."

Philly had expected this reaction from Blaine. Still, his tone put her off.

"Fanning made clear to me that he would not go lower than the one hundred fifty thousand dollars and that he had been given authority by the Mercers to make that offer. I want to urge you and your client to consider accepting his proposal."

"I'll just bet you do since the Hatches walk away without paying anything."

"You can't seriously expect Gerald to contribute. He's a teenager with no assets. Fanning pretty much admitted that Gerald was judgment proof. That leaves the Hatches. According to their lawyer, they don't have the money to contribute to a settlement, but I don't want to speak for them. When you talk to their lawyer, he's going to tell you that even though the Hatches so far couldn't get the case dismissed, Mercer hasn't come up with any facts showing that they were on notice that Gerald would beat up Mercer. That leaves your clients."

"My clients can't be responsible for what your client did. They couldn't foresee your client's assault on the Mercer boy."

Philly had played out her response to Blaine's predictable position. "You might want to talk to Fanning directly about that point. Fanning believes that he can convince a jury that the school officials you represent ignored Mercer's complaints about being bullied and should be held liable for doing so. I don't know Mr. Fanning and I've never seen him try cases. But a senior lawyer I associate with and who has been litigating for over thirty years tells me that Fanning is terrific with juries."

Blaine didn't say anything and Philly decided to let him stew for the moment.

"I'll pass the offer on to my clients but I'm not going to recommend it."

"I understand you have your reasons," Philly said. "My suspicion is that your legal fees will end up pretty close to what Fanning is proposing."

"You have no idea what my firm's charges are."

Philly had a pretty good idea, but all she said was, "You're probably right. Perhaps it wasn't fair of me to make that comment. It's just that I've been in litigation involving good sized firms like yours and it always amazes me what the hourly charges are compared to mine. Your client might prefer to break even now instead of going to trial with a weak case and a charismatic opposing counsel. Oh, and in this case, my hourly rate is two hundred dollars."

Blaine again fell silent. Her low hourly rate had left him without a ready comeback.

"I'm not trying to hard sell you," Philly lied. "You've made clear what your position is and I hope that you'll reconsider."

"Thank you, Ms. Piper. As I said, I'll talk to the lawyer representing the parents of your client, and I may give Mr. Fanning a call. I'll get back to you."

"I appreciate that," Philly lied again. "By the way, something Fanning said might provide a clue as to why he made the offer he did."

Philly waited until Blaine gave into his curiosity.

"What was that?"

"I'm only guessing here. But Fanning told me that the Mercer kid apologized to his homeroom for always bragging about his test scores. And the Hatch kid asked Mercer for help in a physics class, and Mercer gave him the help."

"What are they, buddies now? What does any of this have to do with anything?"

"You're representing school officials," Philly said, deliberately giving her words an edge. "They're supposed to help their students. If your clients accept Fanning's offer they'll be helping two of their students. I think Fanning believes that resolving the case will be a good thing for the Mercer boy."

"You've really got a lot of nerve," Blaine said irritably.

"That's true, and you haven't seen anything yet. Wait till you see me at trial. Thanks for taking my call. I'm available if you want to talk further."

After she hung up, Philly took her time assessing the call. None of the points she raised appeared to have struck a chord with Blaine. But maybe the last one would. Blaine had a read on Fanning, knew what he was up against when it came to Mercer's lawyer. If he thought Philly would be a loose cannon at trial, then he'd have to worry about both of them at once. Fanning would be proud of her, she concluded. She had played the character card.

Philly thought that the looks on the faces of Simon and Rachel were priceless. They were sitting in the conference room and Carpenter had just handed them checks for the work they had done on the Stanton and Lane case. The two young lawyers were looking at their payments wide-eyed. Rachel's hands were shaking.

"This is too much," Simon said.

"Philly and I decided to change our deal," Carpenter replied. "Congratulations, you earned every penny."

"I could really use this," Simon said.

"Wow!" Rachel exclaimed. "This is very generous."

"And just think," Carpenter said. "We may get to do this again fairly soon although for not quite as much money."

"I still can't believe the decision in Frederick Chun's case," Rachel said. "I didn't think we had a chance of winning the case."

"You're selling yourself short," Philly said, although she too had been surprised at the decision. Lewis Lightstone, the MCAD hearing officer, had ruled that Chun's firing had been because of his race. Lightstone had regarded the dirty jokes circulated by other employees as more offensive than anything that appeared on the e-mail that Chun had received from his friend and promptly deleted. The MCAD had awarded Chun back pay and emotional distress damages totaling $60,000.

Rachel looked guilty, as if she had gotten away with something that she shouldn't have. "What's the matter?" Philly asked.

Rachel colored. "I know I shouldn't be saying this, but I really don't believe that Chun's race had anything to do with his being fired."

"You're right," Carpenter said. "You shouldn't be saying that."

"It's just . . ."

"Look," Carpenter said. "Chun got screwed here. He didn't deserve to be fired for what he did. We came up with an approach that got him vindicated. Who gives a shit if the approach we came up with had nothing behind it?"

Rachel continued to look abashed. "I guess I give a shit," she directed at Carpenter.

"Get over it," Carpenter said, and Philly knew that he wanted to move on.

"Do you think there will be an appeal?" Simon asked, raising a pragmatic question.

Carpenter shrugged. "It's hard to say. If Crowe Investment has to pay legal fees, filing an appeal isn't cost effective. But they might offer to pay less with the stipulation that they won't appeal."

"What would we do then?" Simon followed up.

"I know what I'd do," Carpenter said. "I'd tell the guy to pound sand. Chun may see things differently."

Philly agreed with Carpenter. There really was no need to compromise. "Have you heard anything from the hearing officer in the Top Tier case?" she asked.

"Nothing," Carpenter said. "Not a goddamn thing."

99

Carpenter knew that his evaluation of Serena Jones' decision in the Top Tier Finance Company case would differ markedly with Jerome Singer's assessment. Singer would never consider it a victory; Carpenter, on the other hand, viewed the decision as a win, since Top Tier still had its license. Well, no doubt he'd be called upon to explain that to Singer, so Carpenter put the hearing decision in PDF form and sent it to his client, with copies to Simon, Rachel, Philly, and Daniel Catching. He didn't comment on the decision; he simply requested that Singer call him after reviewing the document.

Carpenter confronted the hard stare of the man in the photograph facing his desk. "I don't care what you think," Carpenter declared. "I think this is a win."

Sarah Ferguson had stopped by Philly's house to deliver a small carton of strawberries which had been on sale, and Philly had invited her for lunch, rustling up two tuna melts. To her surprise, Ferguson seemed to be enjoying hers. Philly didn't want to think of the time when she stopped nursing and would have to prepare food for Daisy. That time was rapidly approaching. Whenever Philly took a bite of her sandwich, Daisy, sitting in her lap, made a grab for the food.

"I've had it with winter," Ferguson complained.

Philly reflected that so far, winter hadn't been too bad. True, she was spending a lot of time at home and not getting much exercise. But all in all, she hadn't minded the cold.

"Whenever you feel like it," Philly said, "you can stop by here if you want some company. If I'm tied up with something, I'll let you know."

"It's the cold mostly," Ferguson clarified. "I don't mind being alone."

Philly wasn't convinced by the older woman's explanation. Recently, when handing Daisy off, she had the sense that Ferguson was looking forward to watching over her daughter.

Philly's office phone sounded from upstairs. When Raul and Isabella were away, she set the ring sound on high volume.

"Why don't you get that?" Ferguson said.

"The machine will pick up."

"I don't mind," Ferguson said, reaching out for Daisy.

"Okay."

In her second-floor office Philly saw that she had missed a call from Calvin Blaine. She hadn't expected to hear from Blaine for another week.

"Thanks for getting back to me," Blaine said when her return call had been put through. "To get right to it, I've been directed to accept Fanning's offer."

Philly paused so that her first response wouldn't show surprise. "Who's going to draw up the settlement documents?" she asked.

"Work that out with Fanning and the lawyer for the Hatches."

"You don't sound too pleased," Philly stated the obvious.

"I'm not. I didn't recommend the settlement especially since the Hatches were contributing nothing to the pot."

Blaine could sulk all he wanted to. "I'll deal with Fanning," Philly said.

"I bet you will. Send me drafts of the settlement documents. Now that there's a deal, let's get this over with."

"Works for me," Philly said and ended the call.

Philly spent the next twenty minutes on the phone. She relayed the settlement news to Frank Price, the lawyer for the Hatches, and he offered to draw up the documents that would bring the case to a close. When she reached Fanning, Mercer's lawyer sounded genuinely pleased with the news.

"Do I want to know what you did to make this happen?" Fanning asked.

"Not really," Philly replied. "Blaine didn't recommend the settlement. If I had to guess, Cambridgeport officials did a cost benefit analysis and rejected his recommendation. Blaine is likely to insist that the settlement be kept confidential."

"That's fine with me," Fanning said. "I'll look forward to seeing the documents."

Philly e-mailed Carpenter, Rachel, and Simon the settlement news and went downstairs. Ferguson had taken Daisy to the living room where she was reading to her from a little kid's book about animals, saying each animal's name and mimicking the sound the animal made. Daisy was not squirming, her eyes on the book.

Philly thought about how Gerald would react to the settlement. He could have mixed emotions if he still worried that the end of the case severed his connection to her and Raul and Isabella and Daisy. Somehow, she had to preserve the relationship.

"Do you see the dog?" Ferguson asked and, when Daisy said nothing, Ferguson pointed to the page that was open and repeated the word dog.

Philly had her own mixed emotions. She liked the outcome. But the settlement meant there was one less billable hour case to support her. She and Carpenter needed more business.

"Do you see the cat?" Ferguson asked, and this time Daisy let loose with one of those full body wiggles that seemed to come from nowhere.

"Cat," Ferguson repeated as she turned the page.

Philly quietly retraced her steps to her second-floor office. Her calendar for December was empty except for the motion to dismiss Gerard Gorman's workers' compensation case. Her yearend talk with Carpenter was likely to be depressing. She didn't want economics to drive her decision about whether to keep her Boston office open. But if something didn't break favorably in short order, money—or more accurately the lack of money—would begin to call the tune.

100

The moment he saw Daniel Catching seated at the conference room table in Top Tier's Boston office suite, Carpenter knew how this meeting with Jerome Singer would play out. Catching offered a sheepish grin which Carpenter returned: they were about to undergo a role reversal and each of them knew it. The point was driven home for Carpenter by Catching's breezy self-assurance being nowhere in evidence.

Singer nodded curtly but stayed seated at the head of the table. Carpenter and Simon took seats across from Catching.

"Needless to say, I'm very disappointed with the hearing officer's decision," Singer began.

Carpenter remained silent. He was not about to make it easy for Singer.

"I particularly find the amount of the fine outrageous," Singer continued. "And where the hell does this state board get off to demand a say in how I run my company?"

Carpenter regarded Singer for a long moment. His client appeared unruffled, was immaculately dressed as always, his above-it-all air in place. "Anything else?" he asked.

"Let's start with what I've identified," Singer said. "That should keep us going for a while."

Carpenter nodded. He would have winked at Catching if he thought the gesture would have escaped Singer's notice.

"I guess I'm confused," Carpenter said, trying, successfully he believed, to keep sarcasm out of his voice. "I don't understand why you're trying to find fault with a decision that handed you a victory."

Singer's jaw dropped. "Surely, you're joking!"

"No, I'm not," Carpenter said, evenly. "Top Tier's license remains in place. Not only is there no license revocation, but there's not even a suspension. I told you before that your company keeping its license was a win."

Singer's look was now overtly hostile. But Carpenter decided to get through his prepared speech no matter how irate Singer became.

"I agree that a five-hundred-thousand-dollar fine is an unpleasant financial hit. But the hearing officer could have decided to revoke or suspend Top Tier's license *and also* levy a fine. And it's true that Top Tier has to open its doors for a year to two new board members who are disinterested persons, and to engage a compliance consultant who will monitor the company's lending practices for six months. But the new board members would be a minority on a five-person board; you and the other two directors you've handpicked would still control Top Tier. In a year, Top Tier will be governed the way it used to be and the fine will be a distant memory. The bottom line here is that Top Tier still has a license to make loans, a license you almost lost. This is a win."

Singer colored, furious. Carpenter decided to add a further zinger while Singer was tongue-tied.

"And finally, keep in mind that the hearing officer determined that you made promises to two of your borrowers that you reneged on. That is a factual finding that is never going to be overturned no matter how much you disagree with it. The decision is painful, but my recommendation is that Top Tier not appeal, take its medicine, and move on."

"If you seriously think I'm going to sit back and accept this hearing officer calling me a liar, you are sadly mistaken." Singer glanced briefly at Catching before again turning to face Carpenter and Simon. "A half-million-dollar fine will make our financials look horrible. We might have trouble getting other lenders to participate with us in making loans. This decision stinks. I can't put it more succinctly."

"I'll say it again," Carpenter said. "Throwing more money at lawyers is just going to make your company's financial situation worse than it is. I know this is hard for you, but I think you need to take a deep breath and consider carefully what I've just said."

While Singer fumed, Carpenter did some simple addition. This was the third time he was telling Singer something the man didn't want to hear. Singer hadn't followed his advice on the first two occasions and seemed prepared to go for the hat trick.

"What do you think, Daniel?" Singer directed at Catching. "You wanted to hear from Mr. Carpenter before you offered your opinion. You've now heard what he had to say."

Carpenter remembered how Catching had acted with grace when Singer took the regulatory hearing away from Catching and his firm. Now the big firm lawyer was faced with another difficult moment. Catching could back him up and incur Singer's wrath, or Catching could disagree with him in the hope of obtaining the appeal work for his firm.

"You need to understand something, Jerome," Catching began. "Carpenter is right about the hearing officer's finding that you told two companies one thing about cure periods and went back on your word to them. That finding is never going to be tipped over on any appeal you file because the hearing officer had the opportunity to assess each witness' credibility and that assessment, unless plainly wrong, is going to remain in place."

"So I have to accept that bitch calling me a liar!" Singer exploded.

"Please, Jerome. You asked for my opinion so I'm giving it to you. The way the hearing officer viewed the testimony isn't going to be reversed. For that reason, I go along with Carpenter's recommendation not to appeal. You know that if you choose to appeal, both of us will fight like hell to get the decision reversed. But I'd say the odds of that happening are long."

Singer was no longer simmering; in Carpenter's estimation, he had boiled over.

"Maybe I need someone to take a fresh look at this mess and get a new legal opinion," Singer seethed. "I knew I was dealing with one gutless wonder but now I think I've got two on my hands."

Carpenter had decided that when it came to this part of the meeting he would grin and bear it rather than tell Singer to fuck himself. Singer's judgment was so clouded by anger that it would be pointless to remind the man of the two previous instances when Singer had made the mistake of rejecting his advice.

"That's your prerogative," Catching said.

"Anything else?" Singer asked.

"I would like you to do me a favor, Jerome," Catching said. "Don't make any decision today. Call me tomorrow."

"I've made one decision that I'm not going back on," Singer said before turning to Carpenter. "You're fired. Send me a final bill."

"What about your suit against Cassidy?" Carpenter asked.

"I'll be replacing you. I'll let you know who will take that case over."

Carpenter stood without replying. He nodded to Simon and the two of them left the room.

In the lobby of the office building, Carpenter thought of telling Simon to go on ahead, but decided that the young lawyer should learn from what had transpired.

Five minutes later Catching emerged from an elevator and joined them.

"That went well," Catching said.

"Yeah," Carpenter grunted. "As soon as I saw you sitting in, I knew where we were headed. Do you think he'll use you for the appeal?"

"Who the hell knows? If I had to guess, I'd say yes. I think he's going to stick with the devil he knows rather than break in someone new. You're right about him throwing his money away but, if he's going to do that, I'd just as soon he throw it in my direction."

"I appreciate your telling him what you thought," Carpenter said.

Catching smiled sheepishly. "I haven't been around as long as you have, but I've learned one thing. Giving a client an honest opinion never comes back to bite you on your ass. Well, almost never."

Catching shook their hands and departed into the chill December air.

"Anything you want to say to me?" Carpenter asked Simon. "Ány observations?"

"Singer's an asshole."

"I meant beyond the obvious."
"I've got nothing," Simon said.

101

Philly, with Rachel by her side, studied her argument outline. The hearing on the motion to dismiss Gerard Gorman's workers' compensation claim would begin shortly. She tried to take her mind off her departure from the house. For the first time, Daisy had emitted protesting squawks when she had handed her off to Sarah Ferguson. Sarah had been taken aback by Daisy's reaction. God only knew how Daisy and Sarah were getting on. Was that something she should worry about?

Rachel had checked out the opposing counsel. For more than twenty years, Nelson Frost had been a partner in a small firm that represented workers' compensation insurers in opposing employees' injury claims. Frost was of medium height, had started to go bald in back, and sported silver-framed glasses.

The hearing officer would be Courtney Rush, blond and hazel eyed with a winning smile that somehow had not been turned into a frown from hearing tales of carnage in the workplace. Rush took her seat at the table in front of the hearing room. According to Rachel, Rush had been a hearing officer in worker's compensation cases since she graduated from law school over five years ago.

Rush called the hearing to order. "I'm giving counsel fair warning. I'm not a sports person and I know very little about hockey. Please keep that in mind as you make your arguments. We're here today on the insurer's motion to dismiss the workers' compensation appeal claim of Mr. Gerard Gorman. Mr. Gorman played hockey for the Merrimack Marauders for some ten years beginning in 1976. The insurance company argues that Mr. Gorman's claim is barred because the claim was filed too late. The insurance company also claims that Mr. Gorman's current medical difficulties were not caused by his playing hockey years ago. I've got affidavits before me from Mr. Gorman's wife, his treating physician, Dr. Nancy Corrigan, and from a physician on behalf of the insurer, Dr. Laurence Booker. I also have before me a number of affidavits from individuals who played hockey with Mr. Gorman which recount occasions when he became disoriented after being hit by an opposing player or by crashing into the boards that surround a hockey rink. I'll start with you, Mr. Frost, since it's your motion that's before me."

Frost stood without notes. "There is no medical evidence establishing that Mr. Gorman's present dementia was caused by his hockey playing days. Once he retired from playing hockey, he spent more than twenty years as a physical education teacher in a high school. He obtained a teaching certificate and his teacher performance evaluations which are in evidence show that he was an effective teacher. Mr. Gorman's twenty years of normal life, after hanging up his skates, belies the assertion that his dementia was directly caused by playing hockey. Dr. Corrigan's opinion is pure speculation."

Frost paused and Philly wondered what it was like for Gorman's wife to hear her husband's dementia talked about so openly. Joe Baird was sitting with Lila Gorman and would probably need to buck her up.

"I've been involved with workers' compensation cases for more years than I want to think about," Frost continued. "I've never seen a case in which an employee is seeking to extend the normal rule that a workers' compensation claim has to be filed within four years to more than twenty years."

"But isn't it true that the four years begin when the employee knows that there is a causal connection between his employment and disability?" Rush interrupted.

"Yes," Frost acknowledged. "The evidence before you shows that Mr. Gorman became disoriented at times during his hockey career. While there is no evidence confirming that Mr. Gorman ever suffered a concussion, at a minimum he should have raised any claim when he experienced disorientation."

"I don't think that holds together," Rush said, and Philly began to entertain hope that the hearing might go her way. That hope was promptly dashed by Rush's next question.

"Ms. Piper, what do you say to the insurer's contention that there is no medical evidence that Mr. Gorman suffered a concussion during his hockey playing days?"

"I would dispute that there is no evidence on that point," Philly said, as she stood. "The disorientation that Mr. Gorman experienced and that Mr. Frost seems to downplay, is a primary symptom of a concussion as Dr. Corrigan makes clear in her affidavit."

"I understand your point," Rush came back. "However, Mr. Frost's contention goes to the fact that in the ten years during which Mr. Gorman played hockey, there is no contemporaneous *medical* evaluation that he suffered a concussion."

"Again, I respectfully disagree. There is medical evidence. The disorientation is attested to by Mrs. Gorman and the other players. That Mr. Gorman's symptoms were not recorded by a physician does not make them less real, nor any less pertinent to reaching a sound medical diagnosis in the present. It simply reflects the fact that, in hockey culture at that time, seeking medical help was regarded as a sign of weakness. Mrs. Gorman's affidavit is supported in that regard by the affidavits of several of Mr. Gorman's former teammates. The disorientation episodes are medical evidence Mr. Gorman suffered concussions."

Rush wrote in her notebook and then looked up. "I don't see how the insurer can be penalized because Mr. Gorman didn't listen to his wife and never consulted a doctor. Also, Dr. Booker states in his affidavit that periods of disorientation do not necessarily mean that there has been a concussion. He makes the point that in Mr. Gorman's case it is not reasonable to conclude that he suffered a concussion because he never sat out a game because of disorientation. In his view, if Mr. Gorman had experienced a concussion, he wouldn't have been able to bounce back and resume playing the way he did."

"Dr. Corrigan reaches a totally different conclusion," Philly countered. "In Dr. Corrigan's opinion, the disorientation episodes experienced by Mr. Gorman, notwithstanding they didn't keep him off the ice for any extended periods, represent classic symptoms of a concussion. The conflicting opinions of the experts should not be resolved by a motion to dismiss but should be sorted out after a full trial."

"I think that Ms. Piper has a point," Rush directed at Frost. "I shouldn't dismiss a case because experts have come to differing conclusions in affidavits. Where experts disagree, the disagreement should be decided by a trial where I could assess each expert's credibility. Do you agree?"

"No," Frost said promptly. "Mr. Gorman cannot get around the fact that there is no medical evidence during his hockey playing days that supports his experiencing a concussion. The existence of a concussion is the sole basis for Dr. Corrigan's opinion that Mr. Gorman's current dementia relates to his hockey playing days. Therefore, a predicate for Dr. Corrigan's opinion is missing."

Frost resumed his seat and Rush stared straight ahead. Philly glanced briefly at the back of the hearing room. Joe Baird was holding Mrs. Gorman's hand.

"I'm ready to make my ruling," Rush said. "It's a close case but I'm going to deny the insurer's motion to dismiss because I am of the view that factual disputes need to be resolved after a full evidentiary hearing. We have two experts in disagreement and that disagreement needs to be resolved after a hearing where all witnesses are subject to cross-examination. Also, I believe that Mr. Gorman has established that he filed his claim within four years of learning from Dr.

Corrigan's diagnosis that his disability related back to his hockey playing days. The motion to dismiss is denied. Thank you very much counsel."

Mrs. Gorman hugged Philly and Rachel in turn. "Thank you," she said on the verge of tears.

"We've surmounted our first obstacle," Philly said. "Now we have to try the case."

"Don't be surprised if you get a low-ball settlement offer," Joe Baird said.

"I'm thinking the insurer will litigate this," Philly said, and Rachel nodded her agreement with that assessment. "I don't think we'll see any settlement offer, even a low one."

"If I'm Frost," Baird said, "I'd be concerned with Gorman being an appealing, sympathetic claimant."

"What would it take to settle the case?" Rachel asked, and Philly was pleased to hear the question even though she wouldn't have asked it.

"I'd have to think about that," Baird said, "and Mrs. Gorman will need to take a hard look at what it will cost to care for her husband."

Philly wanted to cut this meeting short. She was anxious to get back to Daisy and Sarah Ferguson to make sure that each had survived her absence. "The important thing is that we live to fight another day," she said.

"Fight is the operative word," Baird said.

102

For a while, Paul and Philly just watched the snow fall. Then Paul turned off the car ignition. "If you want, I can go in with you," he said.

Philly shook her head. This was something she needed to do alone. Besides, Paul had already done more than his fair share by contacting Michael Feeney and arranging a time when Colin Feeney would be home. "Wish me luck," she said as she got out of the car.

"You don't need luck, but good luck just the same."

Philly advanced along the cracked walkway to the front door. The Feeney house was a narrow, two-story dwelling that had seen better days. Chipped red bricks marked the lower part of the house. Above the brickwork, white shingles had faded to a soiled gray. For some reason, the black front door had a shine to it as if it were freshly painted. Philly let her breath out as she reached for the bell. She'd been out of the car less than a minute and already she was chilled. It was a wet snow, and the fat flakes melted to ice water on her neck and face as she waited.

When the elder Feeney opened the door, Philly didn't recognize him at first. The man facing her was older, more worn-looking than the man she remembered from court many months ago. Michael Feeney appeared frightened; he held the door for her but didn't look her in the eye.

Feeney led her into a small living room. A recliner and couch faced a TV on a stand. The wallpaper was a dreary floral design. Philly imagined father and son spending evenings in front of the tube, no words passing between them.

Philly took a seat on the couch.

"I'll get Colin," Feeney said, and he seemed relieved to be making an escape.

Philly began to second-guess the strategy of not telling Colin she was coming. Paul had talked this through with the boy's father and believed that Colin would never voluntarily attend a preplanned sit down.

Colin entered the living room with his father close behind. The teen recognized Philly immediately, blanched, and tried to backtrack. But Michael Feeney firmly gripped his son above an elbow and forced him further into the room.

Philly stood. Colin hadn't changed since his court dates. The youth had entered the room with a dispirited, haunted expression, but after seeing her, he became as frightened as his father and, like his father, didn't meet her gaze.

"Colin, I'm sorry to surprise you like this. I was afraid you wouldn't meet with me if you knew I was coming. A friend of mine reached out to your father and I learned that you'd be home this afternoon."

Colin struggled to free himself from his father's grip, but the elder Feeney held firm. "Come on, son. Please give a listen to what the lady has to say."

Philly sat back down and patted the empty space on the couch beside her. "One of the reasons I came over was to apologize to you. I'm asking you to give me a chance to do that."

Colin looked at her with incomprehension. He had to be thinking that there was nothing she needed to apologize for. If anything, he should be doing the apologizing.

"Please," Philly said. "This won't take long. It took a lot for me to come over here. This isn't easy for me. I need you to give me a chance to say what I came to say to you. Please. Why don't you sit down?"

"Come on, son," Michael Feeney urged. "She's asking you nice."

The elder Feeney released his grip and Colin rubbed the spot where his father had taken hold. Philly saw the moment as a turning point. Colin could bolt—his father had left a clear path out of the room—or he could take a seat.

Colin lowered his head and sat down on the couch, as far from Philly as space allowed.

"Thanks," Philly said. "I said some really nasty things when you were in court. I wasn't myself, and it's been bothering me. That's what I wanted to apologize about. I shouldn't have said what I said. I apologize. I hope you'll forgive me."

Colin kept his head lowered. His father seemed about to speak and Philly raised a hand to stop him.

"I know you didn't mean to hit the bicycle. I know it was an accident. I know you're probably feeling guilty about what happened. I just wanted to tell you that I forgive you. Please try to forget what I said in court that day."

Colin's right knee began to jiggle up and down and Philly realized that he wasn't going to say anything, that he was incapable of saying anything.

"Is there anything you want to say to the lady?" Michael Feeney asked.

Colin's knee began jumping more frenetically. The teen still hadn't looked at her and Philly decided to put him out of his misery.

"Thanks for listening," Philly said rising. "Thank you for your hospitality, Mr. Feeney. I'll be on my way."

"That time in court," Colin said, in a voice that was barely audible. Philly turned back. "You said you were pregnant."

"That's right. I was. I gave birth to a daughter."

Philly sat back down and rummaged in her purse. "Here's a picture of her."

Colin was going to have to scoot closer to take the picture. Philly deliberately kept her distance, guessing that Colin needed to bridge the space between them on his own. He risked a glance in her direction. "Come on, take a look," she urged.

Colin slid toward her on the couch and took the picture, then moved away from her. His father moved behind where Colin was sitting for a look of his own.

"What's her name?" Colin whispered.

"Daisy."

Colin reached out, offered back the picture, all the time looking away from her.

"Keep it," Philly said. "If you'd like to meet Daisy, that can be arranged."

Colin stared at the picture. His knee had stopped jiggling, but Philly saw a shudder pass across his shoulders."

"I didn't mean it," Colin whispered. "I'm sorry."

"I know you are," Philly said. She moved next to Colin and put an arm around his shoulder. "I know you are."

"I can't stop thinking about it."

Philly held Colin close. The teen was in tears. She hadn't thought through Colin's possible reactions and for a moment was at a loss. Then suddenly she knew what to say to him. Philly began, and the words poured out of her. Colin's sobbing stopped. He eased away so that he could look at her and, fighting back her own tears, Philly kept on talking.

103

The plan was to meet Simon and Rachel at the restaurant. Given their odd collaborative status, small offices and disparate schedules, there had been no question of a traditional office party. But an end of the year lunch out was a fine substitute. Philly had deliberately arrived in Boston early in the hope of having some alone time with Carpenter. Skype calls were so-so; the picture on the screen periodically froze or scattered so that Carpenter often looked like he was being recorded by a herky-jerky, hand held camera.

"Come in," Carpenter said peevishly when she knocked on his door. But his smile was genuine when he saw who it was. Philly cleared away files and then settled onto his visitor chair; for a moment it seemed just like old times.

"You're early," Carpenter said.

"I just wanted to shoot the shit before lunch. We haven't done that in a while."

"There's not much shit to shoot," Carpenter answered, and Philly knew that he was referring to their active cases. The cupboard was bare.

"It's going to be like the beginning of this year," Philly said, recalling their meeting a year ago when they wondered where the business would come from to see them through the year that had passed. "But it's not completely bleak," she added.

"How's that?" Carpenter asked.

"I filled you in about the offer that came in to settle the Gerard Gorman case."

"Right. Two hundred fifty thousand."

"Joe Baird called me before I left. Mrs. Gorman is going to take the offer. She's looking at it as buying her five years of care for her husband. If he lives beyond five years, Baird said that she'll worry about that then."

"Nice job," Carpenter said. "You and Rachel deserve a lot of credit. I now wish it were a contingency."

"Here's the good news," Philly responded. "Baird is sending two other hockey players our way. On these it will be a contingency if we're engaged."

"I like the sound of that," Carpenter said, and what passed for a smile on his part flashed and disappeared.

"What are we going to say to Simon and Rachel?" Philly asked. "We don't really have any work for them."

"We don't have any work for ourselves, for Christ's sake!"

"We get to give them each five thou for the Chun case," Philly noted.

"Yeah. We're lucky that one wasn't appealed."

"I say we tell them the truth," Philly picked up. "I think we need to say that they should keep their day jobs because we can't guaranty them steady work."

"They may repeat their offer to contribute to your office's rent," Carpenter said.

Philly shrugged. "I'm not comfortable with that. I'll hang in there for a while. If I have to close the office later on, I will."

Neither said anything for a time. Philly realized that she didn't want to give up her Boston office. Closing the office would be an admission of defeat in some way, a severing of a tie with Carpenter that she wanted to keep intact. Not that she'd actually say that to him.

"As long as we're on upbeat topics," Philly said, "how's your health?"

Carpenter grimaced. "My last blood test was stable whatever the hell that means. I'm going about my business in total denial and keeping my fingers crossed that I have some good years left. How's motherhood?"

Philly smiled at the thought of Daisy. Her recent fussing had to do with teething, a connection that Sarah Ferguson had made. "There are times when I can picture being a fulltime mom."

"I don't like the sound of that."

Philly remembered when she had started her association with Carpenter. At that time, her cases were her dominant concern and what happened in her personal life was of lesser importance. She had caused Raul to break up with her because she wouldn't make time for their relationship. With Daisy's birth, the dynamic had flipped so maybe Carpenter had cause for worry; Daisy was the most important thing in her life and Paul was a close second. "Don't worry about it," she said with an assurance she didn't feel. "That's not going to happen. I'm just going to keep juggling things and I hope that includes new cases."

"We're a pair," Carpenter said, and Philly took it as a compliment. "What about you and the cop?"

Philly again smiled. Carpenter's directness was something she hadn't realized she had missed. "We're good, very good. We're doing a lot of sleepovers at each other's places. I don't know how that's going to work out once Isabella's baby comes." She reached for her cell phone and pulled up a photo of herself, Daisy and Paul in front of a Christmas tree. "See?" Philly changed the subject. "Remember when I asked you to sue the kid who ran down Philip?"

"Yeah. I remember telling you to find another lawyer."

"It's a moot point." Philly recounted her visit to the Feeney house; Carpenter's expression made it clear that he hadn't expected that turn of events.

"I give you a lot of credit," Carpenter said when she finished her account. "I don't think I could be so forgiving."

"To be frank, I didn't think I had it in me. Paul was right from the start. He said it was important to forgive the kid and I do feel better having done that. It's what Philip would have wanted."

Carpenter checked his watch. "We'd better get going. But here's another blast from the past. You remember Jack Lawson?"

"The kid with the medication issues in Stonington, right?"

"Yeah. That's the kid. I got a call from Maryanne Fairmount at the Wilton Center. Jack Lawson's a student there. He's on medication at lower levels than Stonington imposed—his parents gave in on that—and the kid seems to be doing very well. He hasn't needed monitors for a while. Fairmount says he could and should go back to the Stonington schools, but she thinks his parents are too pigheaded to admit they were wrong about medication."

Philly had been at motherhood a short time, but she couldn't fathom how any parents wouldn't put their kid's interests above their own.

"Let's hit the road," Carpenter said, rising from his desk chair.

Dessert had been served and Carpenter couldn't figure out what he was missing. Simon and Rachel were more upbeat than they had any business being. True, each had been handed a check for five thousand dollars for work on the Chun case and there was nothing like putting money in your pocket to brighten your mood. But then he had delivered his bleak assessment of active cases which put a damper on the prospects for the upcoming year, and yet Simon and Rachel weren't as downcast as they should have been. They were attacking ice cream sundaes with gusto and their jovial mood started to get on Carpenter's nerves.

"You remember Wayne Anderson?" Simon asked.

Carpenter nodded. "He was the lawyer on the Stanton and Lane case."

"Yeah," Simon confirmed. "He called me last week and offered me a job."

Carpenter glanced at Philly and wondered if he looked as stunned as she did. Anderson was in a good sized, established litigation firm and was probably in a position to throw some serious money Simon's way. Carpenter hoped that he was hiding his disappointment. Faced with losing Simon, he realized that he didn't want him to go.

"Good for you," Carpenter managed to get out.

"I turned him down," Simon said.

Carpenter had no response to that statement. Given the lack of work he and Philly had in the pipeline, Simon would be a fool not to reconsider Anderson's proposal.

"Do you mind if I ask you why you turned him down?" Philly inquired, asking the question that Carpenter had been too chicken-shit to broach.

Simon glanced at Rachel. "We kind of like you guys. You reached out to us and gave us a chance. We're both grateful."

Rachel nodded, her serene, thoughtful look in place.

"That's all very nice," Carpenter said, "but you need to do what's best for you. I'm sure Anderson offered you a lot more money than we can ever send your way."

"He did," Simon confirmed.

"What am I missing here?" Carpenter followed up. "We just told you that except for some possible workers' compensation cases with hockey players, our well is pretty much dry. If you took Anderson's offer, you could give up your waiter job."

"You're right," Simon said. "But like Rachel, I want to give what we've got going more of a chance."

Carpenter noted the plural pronoun. He didn't think they had much going but kept that opinion to himself.

"By the way," Rachel said. "Our well isn't totally dry."

"I'm listening," Carpenter said, again noting the plural pronoun.

"Simon's picked up a contract case that could be headed for litigation," Rachel explained. "And I've been contacted about a discrimination case, one representing an employee. The case was referred by Frederick Chun."

"I'm impressed," Carpenter said, meaning it.

"We're going to need help on the cases," Simon said. "We also want to charge more for our time."

Philly was deep in thought. "Are you still thinking about us forming a firm?" she asked.

Rachel shrugged. "Simon and I have talked more about that but for the moment, we're okay with the way things are."

Carpenter envisioned Maxine being pleased with the news that Simon and Rachel were bringing in business. She wanted him to slow down and delegate more.

"I don't mean to be nosy," Philly said, "but are you guys a couple?"

Simon and Rachel began laughing.

"No," Simon said. "I'm gay and Rachel's not. We figured it wouldn't work."

Philly colored slightly. "I didn't see that coming," she said.

"There's one other thing I want to clear the air about," Rachel said.

Here it comes, Carpenter thought. These two bright, young lawyers were throwing curves at him and Philly, and neither of them had a clue what was coming next.

"I'm going to keep at the litigation," Rachel said. "I'm not totally comfortable with that decision but I've decided to stop questioning myself and keep at it."

"Glad to hear it," Carpenter said, and Philly nodded in accord.

"Any other surprises?" Carpenter asked.

The young lawyers shook their heads in unison as they scraped the last of their sundaes from their dessert dishes.

Carpenter recognized that Simon and Rachel were voting with their feet. Even in the continuing down economy each had gained experience over the past year and could probably land a better paying job elsewhere. Christ, he and Philly would give them glowing recommendations! Yet they had elected to link their fates with him and Philly for the moment. He had planned to keep this lunch focused on the practice of law but that was no longer possible.

"I've got a personal situation you need to know about," Carpenter said, hoping that Philly wouldn't be upset by his raising the subject without giving her a heads up. For some things there was never a good or right time. Carpenter kept his medical report factual. Simon's serious expression never wavered as he heard the news. For a moment, he thought that Rachel was going to cry, but she kept herself together. Philly, bless her, gave him a smile so he knew he was doing the right thing.

"I don't know what to say," Rachel said.

"There's nothing to say," Carpenter responded. "Just keep this to yourself."

"Will you let us know if you start getting symptoms?" Simon asked.

"Yeah," Carpenter said, nodding.

"Then let's deal with it then," Simon said. "As far as I can tell, you're not slowing down so it's a non-issue."

Rachel nodded her agreement. In the silence that followed, Carpenter wondered whether the two young lawyers were now thinking they had hitched their professional wagons to a fading star that could die out on short notice.

Carpenter thought about ordering an after-dinner drink until he remembered Philly's situation. During the meal, Philly had opted for club soda while he had ordered beer and Simon and Rachel had split a bottle of wine. Philly had seemed okay with the situation, but Carpenter hadn't liked the look on her face as she watched his beer being set before him.

"As long as we're into full disclosure," Philly said, "there's something I need to tell you both."

Carpenter studied Simon and Rachel as Philly related her drinking problem. They were regarding her with concern, nothing judgmental in their looks. There was a long moment of silence once Philly finished her account.

"Here's a toast," Carpenter said, opting to raise his water glass. "Philly and I want to thank you both. You stepped in and made this a memorable year for us. We're grateful. Let's try to do it again next year."

They clinked water glasses and Carpenter thought about the end of next year. Would the four of them still be together? It wasn't worth thinking about, he decided. For all he knew Fred would assert himself and he wouldn't be around when next year came to a close.

"Happy New Year," Rachel said, and they clinked water glasses one more time.

Philly was amazed at the turnout. The basement of Saint Sebastian's Church was packed. All the folding chairs were in use and there weren't enough. People stood two deep along the walls. She had arrived late and from her spot in the rear of the basement, she could barely hear Charlie who had already started to speak.

"I'm always overwhelmed by the turnout on New Year's Eve," Charlie was saying. "I think I understand why so many of us show up on this night. For some of us, this night marks an anniversary of staying sober. For some of us, this night marks the turn of a page in the calendar and a chance to move onto the path of sobriety. For all of us, the night offers mixed emotions what with all the attention paid to champagne toasts and the images of drunken revelry this night conjures up. I think it helps all of us to be together on this night of all nights, because in numbers we can help find the will to be strong."

Philly thought about which category she fit into. She hadn't had a drink since Mace and Rainy had dragged her to a meeting in this basement. So tonight was a cause for celebration. But thinking about how liberating it would be to tie one on while wearing a silly hat and blowing into one of those obnoxious, elongated noisemakers drove home that she was not out of the woods and never would be.

"There's no reason to depart from the way we usually do things," Charlie continued. "Perhaps some of you are here for the first time and would like to introduce yourselves."

There seemed to be no takers to Charlie's invitation, but then Philly saw movement to her left and she froze, her heart pounding when she saw who stood to be recognized.

"I'm Colin and I'm an alcoholic."

"Hi, Colin!"

Author's Note

A good friend of mine, a retired third grade teacher, once remarked that she worried about boys in her classes, boys who lacked concentration and seemed to have a reservoir of nervous energy that demanded release. Maybe these comments led to a number of the story lines in *Full Circles* that feature boys experiencing distress: a third grader, a fourth grader, and two high school teens.

The first draft of *Full Circles* was written in 2010.

I am indebted to Meredith Larson for her edits, comments, and suggestions.

I want to thank Jon Behar for proofreading the manuscript and providing helpful comments.

Any and all errors are mine.

Made in the USA
Monee, IL
04 November 2026

67385391R00282